God's Economy

Faith-Based Initiatives and the Caring State

Lew Daly

These are UNCORRECTED page proofs.
Not for sale or distribution.
No part of these page proofs may be
reproduced in any form or quoted
without the written permission of
the University of Chicago Press.

ISBN-13: 978-0-226-13483-3 (Cloth)

$37.50   £26.00

304 p. 6 x 9

Publication date: December 2009

For additional information, contact:

Megan Marz
Senior Promotions Manager
University of Chicago Press
1427 East 60th Street
Chicago, IL 60637
(773) 702-7490
fax (773) 702-9756
mm@press.uch   ᵈᵘ

D1416937

God's Economy

God's Economy

Faith-Based Initiatives and the Caring State

LEW DALY

With a Foreword by E.J. Dionne Jr.

The University of Chicago Press
Chicago and London

Author bio ...

The University of Chicago Press, Chicago 60637
The University of Chicago Press, Ltd., London
© 2009 by The University of Chicago
All rights reserved. Published 2009
Printed in the United States of America

18 17 16 15 14 13 12 11 10 09   1 2 3 4 5

ISBN-13: 978-0-226-13483-3 (cloth)
ISBN-10: 0-226-13483-0 (cloth)

CIP data to come

♾ The paper used in this publication meets the minimum requirements of the American National Standard for Information Sciences—Permanence of Paper for Printed Library Materials, ANSI Z39.48-1992.

The state is a refuge for those escaping the moral consequences of individualism.

<small>ROBERT NISBET</small> (1953)

CONTENTS

Now is the time to remember that our great religious traditions, notably Christianity, once upon a time could not even conceive of reducing religious engagement with public life to a narrow list of hot-button issues. They were too concerned with the whole person and the whole of society to limit their reach to a handful of questions. Now is the time to heed the call to social justice and social inclusion embedded deeply in the scriptures. "All of the Bible leads back to this command of protecting the least among us, which is inherent in the very fact of creation," Lew Daly writes in these pages. "God gave the earth in common to all human beings, and therefore no one should go without the things of the earth that preserve and dignify our humanity." Now is definitely the time to think anew about how religious faith might properly influence our political convictions.

Lew Daly is an important new voice in our debates over religion and politics, calling us to engage anew with the social implications of Christianity. As this volume attests, Daly brings both passion and reason to his rich and fruitful explorations. With the Bush era behind us, yet great uncertainty about what lies ahead, this is a good time to reflect on the real meaning of phrases such as "faith-based initiatives" and on the obligations of our religious communities. It is also a good time to remember that our churches (and our synagogues and mosques) have long been engaged in the lives of the poor. They were doing good long before prominent politicians began paying attention to their work. "The prominent role of religious providers is not new," Daly writes. "They have always done just what they are doing today: feeding the hungry, healing the sick, sheltering the orphan, comforting the prisoner, aiding the poor mother—in short, helping the 'least of these' cope with extreme disadvantages and problems, so that some can rise above to inherit their share of human dignity under God."

I discovered Daly's work and became an admirer while working on my own book called *Souled Out*, an argument about what I saw (and still see) as the inevitable decline of the religious right. I thought it important to emphasize that if the narrow, ideological view involved in a certain brand of Christian politics was destined to fade, that did not mean that the role of religion in politics was destined to disappear. On the contrary, I saw the religious right as a detour from the broader road of American history, a story in which religious traditions and the theologians and activists they nurtured found themselves at the heart of movements for social reform and renewal. From the abolitionists to the progressives of the early twentieth century, the New Deal, the struggles of organized labor, and the civil rights movement, powerful religious voices preached a message of—and, yes, it sounds familiar from our recent presidential campaign—change and hope. Consider the honor roll of American religious prophets: John Ryan, Reinhold Niebuhr, Abraham Heschel, and Martin Luther King Jr. All spoke to society about society. All were engaged in politics in its highest and most inclusive forms. All spoke from their traditions to those who did not share their own faith, and to those who had no religious faith at all. Their theologically rooted social criticism helped transform a nation.

Daly's work on American Catholic social thought and its influence on the New Deal has been path-breaking and has been especially important to me. Daly gave Father John Ryan the credit in our time that this prophetic priest deserved. Ryan's first book, *A Living Wage*, was published in 1906, and it sparked one of the central demands of the American labor movement. In a seminal article in the *Boston Review* highlighting "the Catholic roots of American liberalism," Daly argued that the view offered in *A Living Wage* was rooted in a simple but powerful theological concept: "the moral worth of the person as measured by his intrinsic and equally given (God-given) faculties of reason, self-improvement, and love of God." Daly summarized the argument this way:

> Ryan regarded the wage system skeptically—even despairingly—for its separation of workers from the productive resources that could best secure prosperity for themselves and their families. . . . [B]oth Ryan and Pope Pius XI, Leo's great intellectual successor, strongly supported strategies to give workers a stake in the appreciating wealth of industry. But they did not draw a line against wage labor in principle. Instead they argued, as Ryan put it, that "human needs constitute the primary ethical title or claim to material goods." This standard cannot be applied "to all possible human needs," but to those basic needs the satisfaction of which safeguards a reasonable life as

measured by the faculties of self improvement that all human beings share (making them equal in their right of basic sustenance). So defined, "the validity of needs as a partial rule of wage justice" rests ultimately on the foundational principle that "God created the earth for the sustenance of all His children; therefore, that all persons are equal in their inherent claims upon the bounty of nature." The subsistence wage of modern business theory did not meet this standard. Only a living wage met this standard, supporting the person, not just the labor; supporting the person in his faculties of self development, not just in his service to capital.*

Ryan's theories laid the basis for the Catholic bishops' "Program of Social Reconstruction" issued on February 12, 1919—appropriately, as Daly points out, Abraham Lincoln's birthday. As Daly noted, the "program contained a set of immediate reforms, including the establishment of a legal minimum wage, public housing for workers, labor participation in industrial management, and social insurance for illness, disability, unemployment, and old age, funded by a levy on industry." It also urged more "fundamental" reforms for the future, including "worker ownership of capital, universal living wages, and abolition and control of monopolies." The document closed on this powerful note about "the capitalist":

> He needs to learn the long-forgotten truth that wealth is stewardship, that profit-making is not the basic justification of business enterprise, and that there are such things as fair profits, fair interest and fair prices. Above and before all, he must cultivate and strengthen within his mind the truth which many of his class have begun to grasp for the first time during the present war [World War I]; namely, that the laborer is a human being, not merely an instrument of production; and that the laborer's right to a decent livelihood is the first moral charge upon industry. The employer has a right to get a reasonable living out of his business, but he has no right to interest on his investment until his employees have obtained at least living wages. This is the human and Christian, in contrast to the purely commercial and pagan, ethics of industry.

In many ways, those ideas are at the heart of the argument this book makes.

Perhaps Daly went a bit far in suggesting that the bishops' program be-

---

* Lew Daly, "In Search of the Common Good: The Catholic Roots of American Liberalism," Boston Review, May/June, 2007.

came the blueprint for Franklin Roosevelt's New Deal. The New Deal, in its breadth and occasional incoherence, had multiple inspirations, and the bishops themselves were clearly reflecting contemporary currents in a social justice shaped as well by Protestant, Jewish, and secular thought. Nonetheless, Daly is clearly right that the ideas developed by Ryan and the Catholic bishops were essential to New Deal liberalism, reflecting Roosevelt's broad view that capitalism could be preserved only if it were reformed with an eye toward distributive justice and the rights of labor. Roosevelt himself honored Ryan with a message to a banquet on the priest's seventieth birthday. "With voice and pen," FDR declared, "you have pleaded the cause of social justice and the right of the individual to happiness through economic security, a living wage, and an opportunity to share in the things that enrich and ennoble human life." With these words, as Daly noted in his *Boston Review* essay, Roosevelt was offering "a rough draft of the famous 'Second Bill of Rights' he would propose five years later in his State of the Union Address."

In these pages, Daly paints on a broader canvas and urges us to pay more attention to the traditions of European Christian Democracy. We often think of the European welfare state as the unique contribution of the movement for Social Democracy and democratic socialism. Yet as Daly makes clear, Christian Democratic ideas were essential to the creation of a more just social order in Europe. It is fair to see Europe's tradition of social provision as the result of a fruitful marriage of Christian and Social Democracy. (Indeed, Britain's Labor Party was inspired at least as much by R. H. Tawney and the traditions of Christian socialism as by the ideas of a secular left— thus the adage that Labor owed as much to Methodism as to Marx.) Both Christian and Social Democrats insisted that there were better alternatives to pure capitalism on the one hand and state socialism on the other. They respected the market for what it could do, but did not pretend it could do everything, and understood it could produce injustices that needed democratic remedy. These critics of capitalism helped save it—and ideas drawing from their traditions may yet be necessary to save it again.

As Daly makes clear in the case of Christian Democrats, their conception of the economy was rooted not in materialism, but in a conception of human beings—their needs and their aspirations. This conception was rooted in the simple but revolutionary idea of the dignity of every person as a creature of God. It lay at the heart of Pope John Paul II's preaching and teaching on human labor, his insistence on the priority of labor over capital, and his refrain that the economy was made for human beings, as against the notion that men and women exist to serve the economy. Such assertions have been at the root of reform movements for generations, some with explicitly Christian inspirations and others indirectly (and sometimes unconsciously) inspired by the ideas of the Christian scriptures and the Jewish prophets.

I have perhaps a few more doubts than Daly does about the applicability of the Christian Democratic tradition to the United States. Our tradition of religious pluralism and a constitutional history calling for relatively clear boundaries between church and state place (and should place) both practical and philosophical limits on the partnerships that both Daly and I welcome. Government can partner with religious groups to promote good works and to build community, but it cannot promote religion itself. Yet as Daly argues, the very pluralism that characterizes our systems of public assistance and social outreach is consonant with Christian social thought. This book is hugely helpful in inspiring new and clearer thinking about words that we recite almost reflexively – "empowerment," "community," "compassion," and, of course, "justice."

There is one politician I can think of whose ideas may have something in common with Daly's. "I still believe it's a good idea to have a partnership between the White House and grassroots groups, both faith-based and secular," this politician said during the 2008 campaign. "But it has to be a real partnership—not a photo-op. That's what it will be when I'm President."

"We know that faith and values can be a source of strength in our own lives," this politician declared. "That's what it's been to me. And that's what it is to so many Americans. But it can also be something more. It can be the foundation of a new project of American renewal. And that's the kind of effort I intend to lead as President of the United States."[†]

He also said this:

> Our failure as progressives to tap into the moral underpinnings of the nation is not just rhetorical, though. Our fear of getting "preachy" may also lead us to discount the role that values and culture play in some of our most urgent social problems.
>
> After all, the problems of poverty and racism, the uninsured and the unemployed, are not simply technical problems in search of the perfect ten-point plan. They are rooted in both societal indifference and individual callousness—in the imperfections of man.
>
> Solving these problems will require changes in government policy, but it will also require changes in hearts and a change in minds. I believe in keep-

† Barack Obama, July 1, 2008, Zanesville, Ohio.

ing guns out of our inner cities, and that our leaders must say so in the face of the gun manufacturers' lobby—but I also believe that when a gang-banger shoots indiscriminately into a crowd because he feels somebody disrespected him, we've got a moral problem. There's a hole in that young man's heart—a hole that the government alone cannot fix.[‡]

I have absolutely no evidence that Barack Obama has read Lew Daly's book. I do think he would understand what Daly is getting at and why he has offered us this inspiring exploration. "How can we not recognize Lazarus, the hungry beggar . . . in the multitude of human beings without bread, a roof or a place to stay?" How indeed?

E. J. Dionne Jr.

‡ Barack Obama, remarks at Call to Renewal conference, June 28, 2006.

PREFACE AND ACKNOWLEDGMENTS

Encouraging and enabling religious involvement in social services was the signature domestic policy of the George W. Bush presidency, and one of the few Bush policies likely to survive his time in office. Contrary to what many who opposed it might like to think, however, the "faith-based initiative," as it came to be known in shorthand, did not originate with President Bush; many larger developments—legal, philosophical, and governmental—contributed to Bush's controversial efforts in this area and will continue to evolve. That President Obama has pledged to revive the faith-based initiative, to the surprise of many of his supporters, suggests that a larger change is at work.

Needless to say, however, Bush's faith-based initiative, launched shortly after he took office in 2001, is an important legacy that will shape future developments. It is a legacy with lasting implications for the policy, law, and administration of social services and for public understanding of social assistance more broadly. Thus, understanding what changed under Bush and how these changes came about is important, and I examine the relevant political facts and legal context in the first part of this book. But my main goal here is to start a new conversation about what this policy means.

The prominent role of religious providers is not new. They have always done just what Bush repeatedly praised them for from his earliest days in political office: feeding the hungry, healing the sick, sheltering the orphan, comforting the prisoner, aiding the poor mother—in short, helping the "least of these" cope with extreme disadvantages and problems, so that some can rise above to inherit their share of human dignity under God. So too, the church-state struggle over social welfare is not new. This particular domain conflict, as it might be described, is as old as the churches' recognition of the "social question" in the nineteenth century, which means it is roughly as old as the welfare state itself.

What is new today, though by no means settled, is the cooperative and supportive role of the state in this religious work, bringing the contributions and values of religion into a legal and normative framework that did not exist before in the United States—something much closer to what in Europe is known as Christian Democracy. That is the large claim I hope to prove in this book. Secondarily, there are, in my reading, communitarian implications that I hope can revive an economic dimension in the critique of liberalism, something that was lost in the "culture wars" of recent years. The faith-based model established by President Bush derives from a restorative vision of society that does not stop at reforming government. The heart of this is what I call "social pluralism" and what earlier defenders of community in Europe defined in terms of corporate personhood, the real existence of groups giving rise to their legal subjectivity in the form of collective rights. This social pluralism, attached to corporate or communal rights, is woven into the decentralized, redistributive systems of Christian Democracy in ways that illuminate America's own faith-based turn in social-service law and also reveal its limitations.

Limiting the state is necessary for pluralism and social renewal, but no true vision of renewing society can ignore what is happening to families and communities as government retreats. Over the last eight years, as the housing bubble collapsed on top of the earlier high-tech collapse, communities and families suffered, while the banks got bailed out. The American dream was stripped bare: we are a debtor nation with declining household earnings and buying power, a weakened if not shrinking middle class, and growing poverty. The trillions in corporate welfare we handed out in 2008 and 2009 dwarf by a factor of ten or more the entirety of what we spent on cash assistance for impoverished families since 1965. The latter galvanized a vicious culture war that changed our politics forever. What changes will come of this new epidemic of welfare? A culture war against the rich, one might foolishly think.

For the Reagan- and Bush-era politics that finally collapsed in 2008, the electoral sentence is clear. But the moral verdict is not as clear. For decades it seemed that no tragic need, no moral right, no common purpose was contemplated to stop the upward flow of power and wealth. A sea-change in household living standards—adding more hours of work to stay afloat as wages, benefits, and job security declined—slowly afflicted much of America, along with persistent poverty. But to avert the collapse in buying power that was actually taking place, Washington flooded the economy with easy credit while diluting the fear of debt with wealthy feelings generated by two large asset bubbles. That only compounded the underlying weakness by piling debt on top of falling wages.

All the while, growing inequality was either ignored or explained away by individualistic theories of success that made a mockery of societal contributions, ignored the common good, and degraded common feelings such as empathy and compassion. The equality of men as moral fact and material destiny, in Catholic thought and other traditions, was supplanted by a kind of "religion of inequality," as Chesterton once put it. We had a massive bailout of creditors and investors while millions of homes went underwater or on the block. The holiday season of 2008 simmered with resentment and danger: it seemed that whatever the wealthy must do to survive, they will feed on society's death.

Where we went wrong is a question many people I know might answer by pointing to, among other things, the faith-based initiatives of the last eight years. It became common to scornfully categorize every Bush failure as a "faith-based" this or a "faith-based" that. This was not only a way of discrediting the faith-based initiative; it was also a way of rebranding our Democratic political future with a bright secular stamp. As I hope this book makes clear, I have a very different view of what the faith-based initiative represented and what it could mean going forward—based on certain powerful ideas that are not well understood and a growing sense of how our faith-based future could play out as social problems deepen.

If that message is heard, the many people who helped me in this work deserve substantial credit besides my undying gratitude. First and foremost, it is fitting that a book exploring ideas and policies about religion and community has roots in a small, faithful community of its own—my family. My wife Pam Rehm stood by me throughout the two-year gestation of this difficult project and, for weeks at a time, bore most of the responsibility for our two children and our home. In the meantime she worked on the manuscript for her seventh book of poetry and also began taking in proofreading to help our finances. Our children Nate and Cora sometimes shared my tiny study with me to do their school work and may have wondered, being book-lovers themselves, how someone with so many books had any time to eat or sleep. My parents Lew and Fran Daly set an example of extraordinary effort and sacrifice in starting their own small business when I was in high school. What an endeavor this was, and what a struggle it remains as their retirement slips away. In a country where my brand of "welfare-state conservatism" reigned (as one friend describes it), a struggling small business that supports ten local families would be considered more deserving of aid than a profitable conglomerate that ships jobs overseas. Having no policy to prevent American capitalism from wrecking communities here and underwriting low-wage tyranny over there is, to my mind, a moral black hole in our political fabric that may well end up destroying much of the nation or at least several parts of it. My wife's parents, Maryellen and Delmar Rehm, remind me, though, that a whole life spent working does not lead to regret in most cases, at least not as voting does.

My academic debts reach back to another era in history and another time in my life. Professor Jim Holstun, a brilliant scholar of capitalism's influence on early modern literature, encouraged my efforts to map the rise of agrarian capitalism onto the theological landscape of the seventeenth-century English Revolution many years ago at the University at Buffalo. This was the beginning of my long intellectual engagement with religion, law, and political development. At Union Theological Seminary, Cathlin Baker, a student colleague who went on to be an executive administrator in that fabled headquarters of the social gospel during the first Gilded Age and of liberation theology during the second, first told me about Abraham Kuyper's growing influence in welfare-policy debates. The pioneering Christian ethicist Beverly Harrison taught me to read Marx out of the tributary political economy of biblical Palestine, instead of reading Marx into the Bible's very ancient and, needless to say, highly precapitalist theology. The late church historian James Melvin Washington helped me understand that the destruction of families is at the root of all oppression, however the surplus value is ultimately extracted from the slaves and workers who remain.

Stanley Carlson-Thies and James Skillen of the Center for Public Justice, whose long-developing political and philosophical work on charitable choice law and the faith-based initiative is detailed in this book, prove better than anyone else I know that "ideas matter" in American politics. Having benefited from their encouragement and careful feedback in the early stages of my writing on these issues, I hope the publication of this book draws attention to their ongoing work and helps to create a far-reaching dialogue between economic progressives and social conservatives in the new Democratic era which now seems upon us. I am also grateful to Professor Carl Esbeck, the chief legal architect of charitable choice law, for providing me with copies of his draft legislation and related materials behind the original charitable choice provisions of 1996. Thank you as well to the staff of the Archives and Special Collections at Wheaton College in Illinois for helping me to retrieve important historical materials from their valuable collection of Hon. Daniel R. Coats's papers.

As I worked on the manuscript, I had the opportunity to present my ideas in public lectures at the Divinity School of the University of Chicago and at Union Theological Seminary in New York City. The discussions that followed helped me to refine my thinking on several critical issues. Thank you to the O'Leary family for generously hosting me during my time in Chicago. I especially want to thank Anne Hale Johnson, former chairwoman of the board of trustees of Union Theological Seminary, for hosting my lecture there and for so much else. I also want to thank Dr. Allan Carlson of the Howard Center for Family, Religion and Society for arranging a timely research grant from the Kohler Family Fund. Dr. Carlson's rich comparative scholarship on family policy, well-known in social-conservative circles, deserves a wider audience.

The argument of this book was developed in several stages that began with an article I published in the *Boston Review* in the spring of 2005, focusing on Abraham Kuyper's growing influence among welfare-reform advocates. *Boston Review* co-editor Deb Chasman's support at that early stage was extremely important for my continuing efforts on this subject. She invited me to expand the original article into a short book for a new Boston Review imprint with the MIT Press. That book, *God and the Welfare State*, generated significant feedback both from confused liberal colleagues and from friends who thought I had switched sides in the culture war, as well as, more interestingly, from conservative supporters of the faith-based initiative who shared my dismay at Bush's revival of radical libertarian policies and shared as well, perhaps, the dark thought that Bush's greatest impact on working families was sending thousands of their sons and daughters to war when he did not need to.

In too many ways, President Bush undermined the community and family ideals he repeatedly extolled in promoting the faith-based initiative. I felt there was more to this contradiction than mere hypocrisy or political opportunism, which led me to look deeper into the communitarian philosophical roots of the faith-based initiative, reaching back to the late nineteenth century and in some respects much further. The initial results of this research appeared in an article published in a special issue of the political philosophy journal *Theoria*, entitled "Politics and the Return of the Sacred" (Spring 2008). Chapter 3 of this book builds on that original article, and I would like to thank Roger Deacon, the managing editor of *Theoria*, for inviting me to submit the article, and also the political philosopher Josh Cohen, co-editor of the *Boston Review*, for referring Roger to me for their special issue. Some material in chapter 4 is adapted from another article I published in the *Boston Review* ("In Search of the Common Good," May/June 2007), which was republished in an expanded version in the September 2007 edition of the Religion and Culture Web Forum of the Martin Marty Center at the University of Chicago. The afterword to this volume is partly based on commentaries I published in the *Boston Review* online in September 2008 ("Obama's Bolt from the Blue") and in *Commonweal* magazine ("What Bush Got Right," March 13, 2009).

At the University of Chicago Press, I benefited from the careful feedback of three outside readers who wished for their identities to be made known to me: Stephen Monsma, Charles Glenn, and Eugene McCarraher. It was an honor to have the political scientist Stephen Monsma as a reader for this project. His indispensable work in the field of religion and social welfare, based in social science but well-grounded in law and philosophy as well, will be well known to many readers of this book. To my mind, there is no more important (and prescient) work on the complex law and philosophy of today's faith-based initiatives than Dr. Monsma's book *Positive Neutrality: Letting Religious Freedom Ring*, published more than fifteen years ago. Boston University's Charles Glenn, a leading education scholar and school-choice proponent who also wrote a very important book about the faith-based initiative as it took shape in the late 1990s (*The Ambiguous Embrace*), graciously reviewed my book proposal and, among other valuable things, helpfully pointed me to the parallel case of pluralistic school-reform efforts in Europe. I was not able to examine these new developments closely, but I do examine the school issue as it came into focus historically during the rise of liberal politics in the mid-nineteenth century, particularly in the Netherlands and Italy—a legacy of church-state conflict still with us today. Catholic cultural historian and social theorist Eugene McCarraher provided a thorough and interesting reading of the manuscript that challenged me to adopt a more radical embrace of alternatives to neoliberal-type capitalism. While I do not dispute the importance of studying and advocating for such alternatives, the purpose of this book is not to propose a new economic model but to demonstrate how the moral and legal heritage of today's faith-based initiatives understood liberalism as a unified project of political and economic domination, not simply as a secularizing *Kulturkampf* waged by the state. I hope that is enough for one book! And of course, while owing a great debt to all three of my learned readers, I take full responsibility for any errors or interpretive problems that remain.

For other helpful feedback, thank you also to Patrick Brennan, Robert Vischer, Jennifer Butler, Patrick Deneen, John DiIulio, and Gar Alperovitz.

John Tryneski, my editor at the University of Chicago Press, took an interest in this project when many others said of the subject, "let a sleeping dog lie." In my first conversation with him in the winter of 2007, he welcomed the idea of "rewriting the history" of the faith-based initiative and setting a new course for the policy by untangling its philosophical roots. This book is as much the fruit of his patience, confidence, and facility as of my toil and tribulation in getting it done. I also greatly appreciate the efficient and friendly help of John's assistant Rodney Powell in the acquisitions and review stage, as well as Nicholas Murray's expert copyediting of the manuscript.

Two men deserve special mention for helping me with the book in different important ways. Long before I met Bill Moyers, his journalism about politics, religion, and social issues helped to rekindle my pride in our American heritage and also my connection to the Christian faith, and having the good fortune to work with Bill for a time during the George W. Bush years, as a researcher and writer, gave me a new lease on trying to do something about it. Among the several persons I most respect for what they have done with their lives, Bill is the only one whom some would describe as man of the left. But the things Bill cares about—popular sovereignty, First Amendment freedoms, racial equality, ecological sanity, economic security—do not make much sense in terms of Marx and Engels or even of John Rawls. Rather, the stuff of Bill's convictions is in the Bible, the Declaration of Independence, the Gettysburg Address, the Populist Platform of 1892, *The History of the Standard Oil Company*, "We Stand at Armageddon," and *Silent Spring*. Although I know he'll disagree with certain aspects of this book, in every bit of my education in politics, I can hear Bill's voice and always, too, the echo of his heroes' words.

Having taken me under his wing for some special projects (as a Fellow of the Schumann Center for Media and Democracy), Bill then helped me find my way to the policy think tank Dēmos, where I finished this book along with another (*Unjust Deserts*, co-authored with Gar Alperovitz) and now hold the position of Senior Fellow and Director of the Fellows Program. Although Dēmos steers clear of religion on most days, and nothing in this book should be mistaken for a Dēmos policy position of any kind, I am grateful for the support, interest, and know-how of my colleagues there, particularly president Miles Rapoport, vice president Tamara Draut, and Senior Fellows David Callahan and James Lardner. I am thankful, too, for the efforts of Communications Director Tim Rusch and his team in improving my "media profile" and, more generally, helping me understand the key ingredients of political communication (and, more important, how to get things cooking even if some of the ingredients, like White House sources in your pocket, may be missing).

Having commented on some other work of mine in his learned and richly reflective 2008 book *Souled Out*, E. J. Dionne also took an interest in this larger project and offered to write the foreword. For America's best public analyst of religion and politics to offer any kind of foreword for a book on a subject like this is personally gratifying and also, plainly, a boost in other ways. But a foreword that engages and critically validates a younger writer's work so generously and thoughtfully is rare, so I feel doubly blessed by E. J.'s efforts on my behalf. I have no doubt that he is the busiest person ever to stop and help a rather unknown writer like me. That is a kindness I can only repay with my gratitude. But I also have the hope that something here might contribute to the cause of social justice that E. J. has always understood and always championed.

Looking Back and Thinking Ahead

Christian political ideas originating in Europe more than a century ago do not often fill the pages of American social policy analysis. But in the last fifteen years, a rich heritage of European religious ideas about government and society, forged in the late nineteenth century and institutionalized in the middle decades of the twentieth, has subtly but powerfully helped to reorient the focus and larger meaning of America's long-running quest for welfare reform and an end to poverty. The emergence of these ideas within the broader "devolutionary" framework of American welfare policy has somewhat obscured their unique orientation and the distinctive church-state model they now represent in American politics.*

This transformation may be surprising for a country often described as "exceptional" by European welfare standards. I hope what follows will persuade the reader to rethink that general rule, despite continuing dramatic divergences in material welfare trends. Indeed, the advanced world's richest economy—and its most unequal, poverty-ridden, and incarcerated

---

* Throughout this book, I use the formula *church-state* as shorthand in discussing the constitutional issues (and other issues) surrounding George W. Bush's efforts to enlist religious groups in public work. Obviously the religious groups at issue here are not "churches" in the sense connoted by this formula, which originally referred to established or semi-established churches like the Anglican Church in England or the Roman Catholic Church in Italy. Most of the "churches" involved with this policy are, at most, affiliated agencies of a national church, and many are free-standing or community-based agencies with no direct affiliation to any church. Nevertheless, the legal, political, and administrative issues pertaining to these many types of religious organizations do rise to the "church-state" level in critical ways, particularly regarding institutional autonomy. Thus, it is not merely expedient to use the term. Nevertheless, I use it advisedly throughout, as we are generally far removed here from the large-scale powers and domains at stake in previous centuries of "church-state" conflict.

society—is falling further behind Western Europe by many social indicators. What may be interesting to its critics, however, is that here in exceptional America a new model of church-state relations in social-welfare provision, drawing us closer to what is known in Europe as "Christian Democracy," is increasingly well-established in constitutional law, federal and state legislation, new rules and principles of public administration, and many government contracting regimes. This book describes the legal and political developments behind this distinctive transformation of American welfare governance, the religious and political ideas that shaped it, and, more broadly, what a new era of "faith-based initiatives"—as the model came to be known under its first White House sponsor, George W. Bush— can and should mean for impoverished communities and distressed families and children across America.

Certainly we can agree that George W. Bush, one of only two born-again Christians to occupy the White House in the modern era, invited a powerful moral awakening in his first major campaign speech in 1999, which outlined the faith-based initiative as a new public vision for winning the war on poverty:

> For many people, this other society of addiction and abandonment and stolen childhood is a distant land, another world. But it is America. And these are not strangers, they are citizens, Americans, our brothers and sisters.
>
> In their hopes, we find our duties. In their hardship, we must find our calling, to serve others, relying on the goodness of America and the boundless grace of God.[1]

From this moral mandate flowed a new kind of government responsibility, summarized in the much-quoted lines, "In every instance where my administration sees a responsibility to help people, we will look first to faith-based organizations, charities and community groups that have shown their ability to save and change lives. . . . We will rally the armies of compassion in our communities to fight a very different war against poverty and hopelessness, a daily battle waged house to house and heart by heart." In another stirring speech, delivered at the University of Notre Dame in May 2001, Bush described the faith-based initiative as, effectively, a *third stage* in the war on poverty, acknowledging the important successes of Lyndon Johnson before him and reaffirming Bill Clinton's 1996 reforms against "welfare dependency." The third stage, he argued, quoting Dorothy Day, requires deployment of "the weapons of the spirit," which spring from the vision of the "Jewish prophets and Catholic teaching." Devotion to the needs of the poor is the most "radical teaching" of such faith, he further specified, echoing the terms of liberation theology. We must do better by such teaching, Bush argued, because "when poverty is considered hopeless, America is condemned to permanent social division, becoming a nation of caste and class, divided by fences and gates and guards."

As these words sadly illuminate, when Bush entered the White House in 2001, nothing seemed further from his mind than the idea of taking the country to war in the Middle East. That his presidency will be remembered for little else reflects the extraordinary impact of September 11 on our foreign policy and political institutions, but also on our religious debates. Most obviously, Bush's accidental crusade in the Muslim world sparked, for many, a simplistic, dangerous vision of clashing civilizations and global conflict between good and evil. But an important secondary effect, no less devastating, was its crowding out of the religious debate he was actually prepared to have when he came to Washington. As his own words made clear, Bush was inspired by a biblical and moral vision of social restoration, held to a prophetic standard and given the form of a new political design for church-state cooperation in distressed communities.

Bush's limited success in implementing the new church-state design is a starting point, in this book, for considering the religious ideas that guided these mainly structural changes in the social safety net. As a matter of emphasis, the religious background is important for assessing where things stand today. Put simply, if Bush's salvationist, antipoverty idiom is perhaps distinctly American, the structural idea of coordinating public responsibility with religious approaches, as a matter of public law and administrative norms, is not. Yet that was, essentially, what his faith-based initiative tried to do.

This structural focus is important quite apart from the question of "funding what works," which was a common White House talking point. In fact, the evidence for "what works" in social services remains unclear even today and is certainly not so dramatically favorable toward faith-based approaches as to warrant a major federal initiative of the kind Bush proposed.[2] No one who lives in a poor community, not even the most orthodox believers in the power of Christian faith—speaking for myself and those I know, at least—seriously believes that poverty will disappear (or even significantly diminish) simply if welfare resources are reallocated to faith-based providers.[3] But there are more than practical reasons (correct or not) for supporting the goals of the faith-based initiative. There are legal and philosophical reasons as well, and these may be more important, finally, not only for expanding faith-based welfare, but for extending the standard they embody—what I will call "pluralistic social autonomy"—to realms less protected than religion, such as families and communities.

Religion and Politics: Background Assumptions

This book is no different than any other, academic or otherwise, in that its arguments are shaped by personal experience. I have nothing unusual to report in this respect: a large extended family of Catholic and Lutheran churchgoers, as well as numerous evangelical converts; an urban church striving on a shoestring to do something more; a period of seminary study; time pastoring prisoners; studying the Bible with my wife and daughter and son; sometime involvement in "faith-based community organizing"—these ordinary Christian experiences inform my writing in this book and keep me honest in the arguments I raise. There is also no escaping the fact that this book was produced in a predominantly Christian political culture. Readers who embrace that culture or wish to engage it or oppose it may find the somewhat apologetic character of certain passages a useful guide to where it is going.

It may also be unusual to take the stated Christian faith of elected leaders seriously as a measure of their actions. When George W. Bush reportedly told a group of evangelical political supporters in 1999 that "God wants me to be president," I doubt he was referring to the wars and tax cuts and deficits he is now remembered for; if he was referring to anything specific at all, it was the effort now known as the faith-based initiative, an idea he had embraced and tried to implement as governor of Texas. Certainly nothing was more important to him on the presidential campaign trail.

I am not alarmed by this idea: that Bush thought God wanted him to be president is really no different than hoping to God he would not win, or having a strong moral purpose in what one does. No matter what a candidate thinks God wants, we have democratic elections to decide who occupies the White House, and we have strong constitutional protections for religious liberty if a president's "calling" should threaten that ultimate value in our polity. Short of this (and short of "establishing," that is favoring, a particular religion or denomination by some official action), how our leaders' religious convictions affect law and policy is not a cognizable subject of constitutional law. Would the New Deal have been unconstitutional if Franklin Roosevelt was trying to implement Catholic social teaching, as many Catholics were convinced was the case? Having a strong moral purpose and believing God wants us to do certain things are, in principle, identical kinds of claims, and so can only be judged by their fruits. In any case, the Supreme Court clarified long ago that holding religious beliefs cannot be a bar on holding office. Constitutionally, not even active ministers or priests can be denied access to the ballot or, for that matter, the White House.[4]

If political order refers to a pure system of rational choice without moral intent or larger purpose, perhaps we could separate religion and politics. But if we admit a moral intent and larger purpose into political decision making, how is following God any different than simply doing what one thinks is right? Politics grows out of values and is inseparable from moral goals. A belief in how things *should* be, in a world that has *purpose* and *meaning* inscribed in the way it is ordered and evolves, is the source of all meaningful politics, whether that of Aristotle, Thomas Aquinas, Abraham Lincoln, or Martin Luther King Jr. Defending the values and purposes that one believes should be embodied in a political system is really no different than keeping order in one's household or one's life: it is how we gain a foothold in our destiny.

Beyond these general reflections, it is helpful to deal with three significant reference points up front because they inform the whole book—although often on the level of assumptions rather than argument or evidence. First there is the broader sweep of history behind these debates that so trouble us about the social purposes of church and state. Let us admit a healthy skepticism here, as the annals of religious history offer little to recommend the idea of "rallying the armies of compassion" to build a faith-based social safety net, as President Bush often put it. Such rhetoric has rarely been more than just that—uplifting rhetoric.

Until the last century, the majority of people throughout the Christian Era lived in poverty and rarely entered middle age. Bare nutritive survival was, for many, the highest goal they could conceive on earth. It was also true that established churches and religious bodies became the dominant institutions of society and towered above it for most of the nineteen centuries of the Christian Era, across which essentially no general progress in welfare was made. There were many great heroes of ecclesial charity, of course, and many more goats, like Raoul of Wanneville, the Bishop of Lisieux, who received this admonition in the twelfth century:

> The Lord erected you bishop to be salt of the earth; beware of becoming the insipid salt that people throw on doorsteps to be crushed underfoot. . . . The Lord has shown you the straight way to salvation. . . . Therefore open you

heart and your storehouses, so as not to risk the judgment of salvation. . . .
Already thousands of paupers are dead of hunger and misery and you have
yet to touch a single one of them with the hand of mercy.[5]

Certainly the average monk lived longer and more comfortably than the
cottagers, laborers, and vagabonds who made up the bottom two-thirds of
the feudal economy. And yet, in principle, the Church viewed its property
as the "patrimony of the poor" and in some periods was said to devote one-
fourth to charitable works.[6] The comparable government figure today in
the United States would be roughly $850 billion annually (much less than
current social spending, not including entitlements), and the comparable
private figure would be more than $3 trillion (much more than current
charitable giving for social welfare). The plethora of greedy abbots and mo-
narchic popes and bishops notwithstanding, it is doubtful that some kind
of purer institution could have done much more than the Church. Indeed,
how would even modern institutions fare if analogous plagues, famines,
wars, and invasions occurred with the same regularity today as they did in
the Middle Ages, not to mention routine Malthusian scarcity and nearly
zero productivity growth for decades at a time?

The Reformations of Luther and Calvin and the English added to these
problems by further spiritualizing social conflict and by reducing the influence of canon law and church teaching on civil and economic law.[7] Despite
sola scriptura and renewed interest in the primitive church of the Book of
Acts, poor Christians' suffering was rigidly confined to a narrative of inner
and otherworldly redemption, when it was not simply excluded by tendentious misreading—for example, when Luther described Jesus's declaration
that "the meek shall inherit the earth" as a directive addressed to spoiled
heirs, advising meekness in their fortunate disposition to avoid bitter legal
fights that might dispossess them.[8] Luther's response to the communal demands of the German peasants who revolted in the 1520s carefully plotted
this spiritual orientation in a balance of encouraging popular reformation
without promoting social revolution; his dualistic hermeneutic, imposing
spiritual meaning on the most subversive biblical texts, was transparently
employed to secure political quiescence. As he argued in his *Admonition to
Peace*, challenging the Swabian peasants' third article demanding the abolition of serfdom,

That is making Christian liberty an utterly carnal thing. Did not Abraham
and other patriarchs and prophets have slaves? . . . Therefore this article is
dead against the Gospel. It is a piece of robbery by which every man takes

from his lord the body, which has become the lord's property. For a slave can be a Christian, and have Christian liberty, in the same way that a prisoner or a sick man is a Christian, and yet not free. This article would make all men equal, and turn the spiritual kingdom of Christ into a worldly, external kingdom; and that is impossible. For a worldly kingdom cannot stand unless there is in it an inequality of persons, so that some are free, some imprisoned, some lords, some subjects, etc.

Much more involved in social policy, Philipp Melanchthon carefully noted the poverty of the "working poor" as a special problem. "Hundreds of thousands of God-fearing households are poor . . . although they work and maintain property," he worriedly pointed out. These especially, he counseled, should "wisely and rightly bear poverty, and not design evil, dishonourable things." Protestant reformers naturally focused on these "house poor," who were capable of moral conversion and strategically important against the "Anabaptists and monks," as Melanchthon put it—referring to the communal heresies of the former and the institutionalized poverty of the latter.[9]

Even accounting for war and famine and plagues, the stench of hypocrisy is strong in the history of established religion, and remains so where we sit today. That so many centuries of church establishment and reformation had so little remedial effect on the dire living conditions of the people and souls claimed to be in the care of religious bodies may be the most extraordinary feat of "moral compromise" in the history of Western institutions. After all, as the radical liberal William Godwin correctly pointed out, "The doctrine of the injustice of accumulated property has been the foundation of all religious morality." Yet there was nothing the established churches did better—first and foremost, of course, the Catholic Church—than accumulate property.[10] It is a sectarian truth but a truth nonetheless that much of what Jesus condemned in the Gospel was honored by the Church, often in obvious ways.

Karl Marx's portrayal of the bourgeoisie as ruthless destroyer of traditional institutions and norms did not conceal his hatred of the established churches, quite apart from his sympathy for the faithful.[11] The reasonable impression is that when the churches were dominant, the people constantly suffered, but when the churches diminished, in the nineteenth century, the people began to make progress, or at least began to fight for it.

But this was a turning point for the churches too, and it is where our current story of "faith-based initiatives" actually began as well. At that time, socialism and the welfare state, competing state religions with comparable bureaucratic proclivities, threatened to destroy the remaining competences by which religious orthodoxy retained the loyalty of the masses, most importantly in education and social welfare. Particularly acute in countries such as Germany and the Netherlands, where strong, confessional political parties first emerged (Catholic in Germany and both Reformed and Catholic in the Netherlands), this was the struggle that forged the church-state principles and the vision of welfare governance at work in the faith-based initiatives of today.

The churches' relative silence today (or lack of an audience in many cases) is starkly contrasted with what happened during the first Gilded Age and the age of the "social question" in Europe, when religion generally strengthened its position in modernity through the development of new social teachings and played a significant role in bringing vast concentrations of wealth under moral and popular control in subsequent decades. The "deplorable cleavage" of faith and reality, "a scandal to the weak, and . . . a pretext to discredit the Church," was arduously repaired. In the face of "poverty amid plenty"—the social offspring of doctrinaire liberalism and extraordinary greed—people could see that material progress had a moral price of its own, putting the churches of old in a more sympathetic light and rejuvenating their traditional ways of thinking with a new prophetic focus on elite collective sin.

This unfolded concurrently with the churches' battle against government education and welfare, crystallizing "liberalism," in their moral teachings, as a unified destructive essence expressed in both political and economic forms. These conflicts with both public welfare and private capitalism were interpreted as marks of a staggering cultural decline, but generally not in a way that focused on individual behavior, as is common today. Before abortion was privatized and marriage and sexuality were liberalized, provoking a more "behavioral" cultural focus, there was another, more fundamental "culture war" that threatened the very autonomy and social position of religious institutions and bodies with aggressive state expansion and regulation—what in Europe became known by the name it was given in Germany, *Kulturkampf*, and what here in America mainly took the form of "neutral" anti-Catholicism in the social programming of an undeclared Protestant state. Today's simmering conflict over faith-based initiatives is not so much a "new front in the contemporary culture war," I argue, as a *Kulturkampf* in this older sense. In distinctive legal and statutory as well as theological ways, today's emerging model of faith-based social welfare emulates the Christian Democratic systems of Europe, which are direct descendants of the nineteenth-century culture war pitting confessional churches against political and economic liberalism. Today we are closer to being a Christian Democracy than a Christian nation.

The importance of the state is another major background assumption in this study. The rising income and life expectancy that separate the last century from all that came before were often described as a triumph of free markets and absolute property rights by partisans of the Reagan Revolution. But the weight of the evidence suggests that public spending, financed by a progressive tax structure, is what set us on the path of real economic progress. A simple before-and-after comparison is certainly striking. In the United States between 1870 and the Great Depression, the poverty rate of wage earners probably ranged between 40 and 60 percent, and average life expectancy was still very low. In 1890, if you made it to ten years old, you probably lived to the age of forty-eight. In 1290, ten-year-olds died at about forty-two.

In this period, prior to 1930, the share of national income devoted to poor relief never rose above 3 percent in any country. Today the average share devoted to social spending (including social insurance) is about 30 percent in Europe and significantly lower in the United States, but even here much higher than it was a century ago (in 1850, U.S. public spending on poor relief amounted to barely one-tenth of 1 percent of gross domestic product).[12] As social spending rose in the twentieth century, the poverty rate fell to an average of about 8 percent (lower in parts of Europe and significantly higher in the United States), and newborn life expectancy essentially doubled in most countries. In the United States, to cite one striking example, the rate of elderly poverty declined from 35 percent in 1960 to 10 percent in 1995, largely due to Social Security and Medicare benefits. Overall, a generally accepted figure for poverty-rate reduction in the United States due to government programs is 9 percent.[13]

But perhaps the most compelling dimension of a public-investment view of human betterment is rising life expectancy. It is commonly heard that the last century's profound increase in life expectancy was a gift of free-market capitalism, but, in fact, this great achievement (arguably humanity's greatest achievement) was really a victory of basic public works like sewage systems, vaccination programs, and, later, antibiotics—in short, public, scientific control of infectious disease.[14] This example among others (most notably, government investment in research and education) exemplifies the strong causal links between public investment and human betterment. Advocates for a free-market theory of rising living standards are reduced to arguing, essentially, from a counterfactual position, as Milton Friedman did in decrying the government "failures" of the New Deal era in *Capitalism and*

Freedom.[15] This is not to say that efficiency concerns are negligible in the design of public investments, but in any larger project of rethinking public responsibility for the future, whether faith-based or not, it is important to understand that the so-called "big trade-off" between equity and efficiency, as Arthur Okun famously termed it in the 1970s, is not inevitable and in many respects does not exist at all.[16]

The third important thing to clarify up front is the relevant content of Jewish and Christian teaching for a book on this subject. In his Notre Dame commencement speech in 2001, President Bush was correct in pointing to the "Jewish prophets" as the starting point for understanding the problem of poverty and social welfare. In fact, the prophets gave voice to a consistent social vision. They defended God's covenant with the people of Israel, who were brought out of slavery into a land of familial abundance and shared prosperity. The covenant laws embraced justice: they gave relief to the indebted, resources to the property-less, and freedom to the enslaved. For example, the poor must have access to no-interest loans (Exod. 22:25), and after seven years even the principal is to be forgiven: "The Lord's time for canceling debts has been proclaimed" (Deut. 15:1–11). The Jubilee commands of Leviticus 25 comprised an economic institution designed to maintain an equitable distribution of land—productive resources—among God's people. Every fifty years, the land was to be restored to the control of kinship clans as originally provided, based on proportionate need, when Israel took possession of the land. "The land shall not be sold permanently" (Lev. 25: 23). Such a policy of permanent redistribution was founded on the simple theological premise that God, the Creator, was the only true "owner" of the land. All God's people are equally guests of God in his land and so subject to his covenant laws and to the social objectives they are meant to secure.

A consistent objective of the ancient covenant was to insure basic sustenance for all God's people and to prevent accumulations of land and power that would lead to deprivation and servitude among the people. Thus the laws of the covenant combined tithings earmarked for social welfare (Deut. 14:28–29) with redistributive policies such as Jubilee. Sustenance meant more than subsistence. In Hannah's prayer, God not only helps the poor, but reverses their fortunes: "He raises the poor from the dust and lifts the needy from the ash heap; in order to give them a place with nobles, and have them inherit a throne of honor" (1 Sam. 2:8).

When the prophets arose against backsliding regimes, oppression of the poor was viewed as evidence of covenant failure. Isaiah declares, "Woe to those who make unjust laws, to those who issue oppressive decrees, to deprive the poor of their rights and rob my oppressed people of justice, making widows their prey and robbing the fatherless" (10:1–2). Amos decries those who "trample on the heads of the poor as upon the dust of the ground, and deny justice to the oppressed" (2:7). Micah castigates the legalized thievery of the wealthy rulers who devise new laws to subvert God's justice: "Woe to those who plan iniquity, to those who plot evil on their beds! At morning light they carry it out because it is in their power to do it. They covet fields and seize them, and houses, and take them. They defraud a man of his home, a fellowman of his inheritance" (2:1–2).

In timeless fashion, Psalm 73 describes how the wealthy and powerful turn the nation against God with false piety and seductive rhetoric. The petitioner tells of how he "almost lost his foothold" because he envied the "prosperity of the wicked":

> They have no struggles; their bodies are healthy and strong. They are free from the burdens common to man; they are not plagued by human ills. Therefore pride is their necklace; they clothe themselves with violence. . . . Their mouths lay claim to heaven, and their tongues take possession of the earth. Therefore their people turn to them and drink up waters in abundance. They say, 'How can God Know? Does the Most High have knowledge?' This is what the wicked are like—always carefree, they increase in wealth.

The Hebrew idea of idolatry, Hans Urs von Balthasar argues, cannot be distinguished from God's care for the poor. Indeed, "If Yahweh's justice is incarnated in his people, then a very close relationship is established between idolatry and the oppression of the poor, so that these become interchangeable terms." Then "God takes zealous action . . . and his judgment extirpates the proud and haughty," because they have rejected Him by oppressing the poor, which are one and the same thing.[17]

The New Testament extends these prophetic themes. The Letter of James warns of the woes awaiting those who have "hoarded wealth in the last days." "Look! The wages you failed to pay the workmen who mowed your fields cry out against you." In the Gospel of Mark, Jesus tells crowds gathered in the Temple about a man who rented a vineyard to some farmers and then went away on a journey. At harvest time, the owner sent a servant to collect a portion of the fruit from the tenants. But they beat the servant and sent him away empty-handed. A second servant they struck on the head, and a third they killed. Finally, the owner of the vineyard sent his own son, but the tenants, seeing that he was the heir to the vineyard, killed him to make the inheritance theirs. "What then will the owner of the vineyard do?" Jesus asked. "He will come and kill those tenants and give the vineyard to others." The covenant theme of God's ownership of the land was used here, of course, to attack the economic injustices of the Jerusalem elites and portend their violent overthrow. Only the crowds at Jesus's side prevented the authorities from arresting him on the spot, the Gospel tells us.

From today's perspective, what is most striking in prophetic teaching is the richly detailed understanding of how poverty is created and perpetuated in defiance of God's justice. With a few exceptions in the wisdom literature, the Hebrew Bible is generally silent on the behavior or "deservingness" of the poor. So are the Gospels, although Matthew's claim that many social problems "come out of the heart" (15:19) is sometimes interpreted to mean that you can only change society "one heart at a time," not through broader efforts to establish justice. Clearly, however, the behavior and institutions of the rich and powerful are a major focus of prophetic authority in the Bible. While the ultimate suffering is corporate—exile and re-enslavement of the nation—Israel's covenant failure is laid again and again at the feet of the wealthy and powerful. In a contemporary light, it could be said the prophetic tradition does not "blame the victim."

Immediate human needs cannot be ignored in expectation of the mighty being toppled from their thrones. My experience working with prisoners led me to see anew what Jesus told his disciples shortly before he died. It seems Jesus wanted to help his followers avoid any confusion in the event of his death, so he gathered them together to discuss his central teachings one last time. His "final answer," appropriately, is given in a vision of the last judgment, marking it as literally inescapable. When the Son of Man comes in his glory to judge the world (Matt. 25: 31–46), he will divide humanity as a shepherd divides the sheep from the goats. There will be one simple criterion for this judgment: You that *fed and clothed me* and *quenched my thirst*, you that *welcomed me as a stranger* and *visited me in prison*, you are "the righteous," and you will inherit the "kingdom prepared for you since the creation of the world." But the people may wonder how the Lord who comes in glory with all the angels around him could have needed so much care! "I tell you the truth," He will say to them, "whatever you did for one of the least of these brothers of mine, you did for me." And just the same, "whatever you did not do for one of the least of these," you did not do for me. That clear distinction is what separates us in the end. Those who did good for the least among us will get eternal life, and those who did not "will go away to eternal punishment."

Policy developments in faith-based services are motivated by compassion and hope and often by a sense of justice rooted in biblical teachings on wealth and poverty. This still-meaningful religious framework gives moral coherence to the legal and political changes surrounding faith-based providers today, and helps to explain the momentum of "faith-based initiatives" in a way that goes deeper than politics. After all, why are we "leveling the playing field" for religious providers, as one White House document described it, if we are not ultimately thinking about, trying to understand, what religion can teach us about our failures in the past and what the future may bring if we embrace the true faith? Secular ideology, refracted through constitutional litigation, will continue to deter this work, but we cannot afford to squander the prophets' vision in arguments having nothing to do with poverty.

Let me suggest what this means to me: it means increasingly connecting today's extraordinary multidimensional debate on faith-based social services—political, legal, and social-scientific—to a divine, ordering justice that protects human beings and strengthens the bonds they most need. This restorative orientation is singularly evident throughout the Bible in the themes of justice and righteousness,[18] and it shines deeply in many facets of Christian tradition, including the Catechism of the Catholic Church. "How can we not recognize Lazarus, the hungry beggar . . . in the multitude of human beings without bread, a roof or a place to stay? How can we fail to hear Jesus: 'As you did it not to one of the least of these, you did it not to me,'"? the Church asks. We must pass judgment, then, "about economic and social matters when the fundamental rights of the person or the salvation of souls requires it." The Church is indeed "concerned with the temporal common good of men because they are ordered to the sovereign Good, their ultimate end." And it shines as well in the most fundamental principle of all: the common right of dignity and prosperity that arises from the permanent debt of all who have life, the debt incurred simply in being created by God. Thus, wealth affords its possessor no certain rights except in accordance with the common good: as the Catechism declares, "The goods of creation are destined for the entire human race. The right to private property does not abolish the universal destination of goods." Or as Saint Ambrose insisted, those who have more than enough of the goods of the earth owe a portion to those who do not, and this is not welcomed as a gift but prosecuted as a debt. Eternal life or death is no less attached to the payment of social debts than to aversion of private vice, because, as Jesus made clear in the parable of the sheep and goats and as church teaching states, "the Church does not separate a proper regard for temporal welfare from solicitude for the eternal."[19]

In day-to-day encounters with deprivation, it is tempting to view the services Jesus prescribes in Matthew's vision of the last judgment somewhat more literally than the consequences prepared for us by our actions or neglect. It is rather convenient to do so because such actions as feeding and clothing the needy, welcoming the stranger, and visiting people in prison do not seem that difficult, given the consequences. These acts occur every day in every neighborhood, town, and city. They seem rather a small price to pay for eternal life. Of course, to Jesus and his followers, they were also an eschatological shadow of God's coming kingdom, when the meek will inherit the earth, and the wealthy are toppled from their thrones. To what degree human agency was limited to these small personal acts by expectations of a final judgment is difficult to know. When Jesus casts the money-men out of the Temple, that too, scholars agree, was an eschatological symbol. Although I do not pretend to know what these acts mean now that Christian tradition has far outlasted the immediate eschatological hope of its founders, from a very young age the Lord's Prayer taught me to think of the "meek inheriting the earth" as a positive human goal—"thy will be done, *on earth*, as it is in heaven."

If the simplest aid one can give is a serious, non-negotiable charge that we must keep, on pain of eternal life or death, this is not just a message of service: it is a message of judgment based on a vision of justice. Quoting Isaiah throughout his Gospel and in his vision of the last judgment, Matthew's call to service is clearly part of the broader structure of critical thought handed down from the Hebrew prophets. Social deprivation is caused by human sin and the structures humans erect to live sinfully and oppose God's law, instead of living "righteously"—upholding God's law by protecting the poor. All of the Bible leads back to this command of protecting the least among us, which is inherent in the very fact of creation: God gave the earth in common to all human beings, and therefore no one should go without the things of the earth that preserve and dignify our humanity. This conclusion plainly follows from how we were made, and to mutually assure earthly adequacy for all is, in fact, to worship God, because our humanity is God's gift, and preserving that gift is how we honor God. Too much inequality in the things we need to maintain our God-given dignity is ignorance and defiance of God in its purest form. Clearly, an unfunded mandate accompanies the gift of life. Again, as Saint Ambrose preached: "The earth belongs to all; not to the rich. But those who possess their shares are fewer than those who do not. Therefore, you are paying a debt, not bestowing a gift."

Believe it or not, most ordinary Christians like myself do acknowledge this at some level and do wish to abide by it in some small way, and I believe our politics has retained a vital religious force because of this, one that is far from being exhausted today. For all the rancor of the culture wars of the last quarter century, America's many renascent centers of religious culture in this era are the main reason, I believe, why the problem of poverty now enjoys so much agreement about ultimate goals—much more so than in the early Goldwaterite stages of the conservative revival, when reforming government was mainly a philosophical crusade in defense of individual liberty. I certainly agreed with George W. Bush when, in his first Inaugural Address, he simply said, "Where there is suffering, there is duty. Americans in need are not strangers, they are citizens, not problems, but priorities." At the same time, bitter fights about how to achieve these goals, some, it is true, masking indifference or worse, have stymied real progress on poverty (arguably, any progress) for nearly forty years.

Tying these preliminary threads together, let me point to a final core assumption of this book and suggest what may evolve from it in the future: faith perspectives and faith-based institutions are increasingly welcome in public life as a matter of constitutional law. The Supreme Court standard for church-state relations today, evolving for two decades, is "neutrality" or "equal treatment"—essentially, that religion and religious institutions have a "right to public life" equal to other perspectives and institutions, as long as one religion is not favored over other religions, and religion in general is not favored over nonreligion. As John DiIulio argues, in embracing such neutrality over "strict separation" (or what legal scholar Carl Esbeck calls "no-aid separationism"), church-state law is merely catching up with a cultural consensus that has long existed.[20]

This constitutional trend creates a new point of departure in the larger debate on religion and politics: on the "level constitutional playing field" that has now emerged, the true political problem of faith in public life evolves dramatically from one of demanding fairness *from* the establishment to one of *maintaining integrity within it*. Statutory foundations exist for this in what is known as "charitable choice" law, established in 1996 as part of the welfare reform bill signed by President Clinton. Charitable choice requires that faith-based institutions be treated equally with secular institutions in the competition for federal social-service funds, and it provides protections to preserve the institutional and religious integrity of federally funded, faith-based providers. Most controversially, it allows faith-based contractors to retain the discretionary rights over hiring and employment policies that they enjoy under Title VII of the Civil Rights Act of 1964.

At another level that one could call normative or cultural, however, whether religious providers can stay true to the *mission* and *ethical teachings* that most were created to serve is no less a question of integrity, and so that, too, I argue, becomes a public issue if not a public responsibility under charitable choice. The fact that church-state law is increasingly accommodating of faith-based providers perhaps even gives the ethical imperative of Matthew 25 a political meaning that such teaching has not had before in American life.

The purpose of *God's Economy* is to explain precisely why this should be, and what a new era of church-state cooperation truly requires if we go forward on the model of today's faith-based initiatives. But getting this new conversation started requires salvaging the faith-based initiative from the political partisanship and the conventional "culture war" framework that hobbled it throughout Bush's presidency. I believe it can be salvaged, and should be: helping faith-based providers do their good works is a legitimate goal of American public policy and, more important, it is a good idea for our society. But it is also something more than just good policy. In giving protection to religious providers and supporting their good works, it also transforms the way we think about the government's role in society and the moral and legal standing of the structures that lie within it and give it life—most importantly, families, churches, and communities. Of course, we have heard much about the value of pluralistic "mediating structures" in recent years (indeed for decades now), particularly as they relate to the state and government power. The faith-based initiative did much to revive a pluralist vision of government and society (and, notably, it does not rely on economic rationality, as with "social capital" approaches). While the antistatist requirements of social pluralism are increasingly clear, what we have not thought about at all is the moral and legal standing of social structures as they are affected by organized *private* power. However statelike the powers that have accrued to business corporations, financial institutions, and trade regimes, we cannot legally conceptualize how to protect the natural structures of society from these powers. As Mary Ann Glendon pointed out nearly twenty years ago, "A kind of blind spot seems to float across our political vision where the communal and social, as distinct from individual or strictly economic, dimensions of a problem are concerned." And as she further explains, in a key insight that I will try to unpack in chapter 4, "Except for corporations (which the Court has recognized as "persons" and endowed with rights), groups and associations that stand between the individual and the state all too often meet with judicial incomprehension."[21] The anomaly of "corporate personhood" in legal thought is critical for understanding how social pluralism is set up to fail in America, when it is not simply ignored. Legally granting these transferable paper aggregates of wealth the status of integrated personhood is a profoundly unliberal idea, a communitarianism of wealth neatly tailored to an individualistic legal structure lacking any kind of standing for competing communal claims.

Restoring Society Out of the Church-State Divide

What came to be known as the Faith-Based and Community Initiative (FBCI) had a long evolution on several levels: intellectual, political, and constitutional. Yet today there is little understanding of how this major initiative came about and little serious discussion of what such thinking means in the broader context of welfare reform and the fight against poverty, from which it first emerged. Politically depleted by the war in Iraq (like almost everything else Bush proposed), the FBCI ended up as little more than a proxy battleground in the broader culture war between liberals and conservatives, its core ideas and unfamiliar progressive vision defined away by thoughtless biases on both sides of the argument.

The confusion I find in much liberal criticism of the faith-based initiative (which was the predominant form of criticism) rests on analytical failures that cannot be adequately addressed, as I explain in this book, without a deeper understanding of the theological roots of this policy framework. Ultimately, I aim to explain why, in contrast to what many liberals assume and what some conservatives truly want, the rise of faith-based social policy promises to *strengthen* public welfare in the United States, not dismantle it. In what way and why this should be are key questions we can address if there is a better understanding of the distinctive theological ideas about government and society that shaped these developments. Indeed, properly implemented according to its own principles, the faith-based initiative promises to "end welfare reform as we know it," I argue, turning a policy of less welfare and more poverty (for that is what we have today) into a mandate for significant new investments in poor communities and, further, new social protections for struggling families across America. This is where the theological principles of the faith-based initiative naturally lead, an argument that is borne out by comparative evidence from the Christian Democratic countries that paved the way for this model, in some cases by constitutional design.

Bush's own stated theological insights did not reveal very much beyond describing the basic impetus of helping poor communities by supporting (and scaling up) the faith-based social providers in their midst, and that was, indeed, the fundamental political goal. Bush also steadily articulated the reciprocal government standard of preserving the religious and institutional integrity of faith-based providers as they engaged with federal agencies to get support for their work. Although often portrayed as a simple matter of not "discriminating" against religious groups in the competition for federal social-welfare funds, ultimately, the faith-based initiative held a deeper understanding of the political and legal challenges related to faith-based social services.

These challenges arise from what earlier thinkers, in a European tradition of "pluralist" thought or "social pluralism," understood as the natural, self-organized reality of religious groups—the integrated beliefs and purposes that define and motivate their very existence. This natural understanding of religious groups (which extends from the existence of the family, the fundamental natural structure of society) deeply colors the constitutional, statutory, and administrative vision of America's faith-based initiatives. As an approach to social welfare, however, it originated in Europe more than a century ago, with the rise of confessional movements that resisted the onset of centralized, liberal welfare states and gave birth to what is now known as Christian Democracy.

Two concepts of political order, Catholic "subsidiarity" and Dutch Calvinist "sphere sovereignty," were crystallized in this struggle and helped to define the unique confessional character of the German and Dutch welfare systems, among others. Ultimately, these ideas and the welfare systems they inspired served as a model for America's faith-based initiatives as they emerged in the 1990s. Although well-known to the small group of legal and policy advisors who worked with Bush on these matters from his earliest days in elected office, this intellectual genealogy remained in the shadows during Bush's presidency, and likely obscure to Bush himself. Yet the legal and administrative design of the FBCI is no arbitrary thing lacking distinctive intellectual roots.

Clearly this is part of a larger political context shaped by many things, but it is hard not to see certain very specific trends involving religion. In a very general sense, it is clear that the public debate and academic output on faith-based involvement in social programs has grown significantly in the last decade and may be characterized today as defining a new policy field.[22] Drawing together inputs from religious thought, political theory, public administration, antipoverty social science, and constitutional law, the Bush-era faith-based initiative was the first major policy product to emerge from this growing field. If the substance was flawed and the politics dysfunctional, as even sympathetic critics have said, the blueprint remains and will continue hold the interest of advocates and critics alike: poverty is growing, and the state is weakening, yet new moral energies and commitments among the diverse faithful majority are beginning to emerge.[23] This suggests a much longer life for the coordinated church-state model put in place by Bush's faith-based initiative, longer than many opponents would hope and harboring radical implications that many proponents may be surprised to discover.

President Bush's extraordinary political failures notwithstanding, a new cooperative vision of community renewal and public responsibility—a vision of public community renewal—clearly emerged in the last decade, drawing poor and distressed communities out of the shadows of a welfare reform debate that basically ended in the late 1990s, with both sides declaring their respective political victories and leaving it at that.[24] The new faith-based vision of public community renewal was only the principled understanding of a few religious intellectuals and legal scholars when the welfare reform debate began to escalate in the late 1980s, but by the turn of the century it had seized and redirected that debate, pointing beyond the gray-shaded spectrum of liberal and conservative differences successfully negotiated in 1996. In general, religion and government were viewed as competing sources of welfare prior to the political story I tell in this book. Today, however, the most significant new thinking in the field is focused precisely on how to coordinate religion and government in a system that distinguishes these great powers constitutionally but unites them, all the more, in a common purpose of restoring families and communities to their proper place of dignity in a morally ordered world. Compared to the rank political expediency that gave us welfare reform in the first place—I shared Senator Daniel Patrick Moynihan's principled views on the subject at the time—this is a genuinely constructive development in American policy history. For one thing, unlike welfare reform, it actually addresses the problem of poverty.

On his way out of office, President Bush called his faith-based initiative a "quiet revolution." The term is accurate as a description of the *design* and *objectives* of this policy agenda, which are the focus of this book; admittedly, however, the disappointing *political results* over Bush's two terms (which we review in chapter 1) somewhat cloud what these structural achievements really mean. Let me briefly summarize here: at its core, the faith-based initiative was a policy of legal and administrative "redesign" of the federal procurement process in social services, the financial engine, if you will, of our increasingly decentralized social-welfare system. Resting on changes in constitutional and statutory law that gathered strength in the 1990s but were never given a unified policy expression, the explicit objective of this redesign was to transform the administration of social spending in ways that support and increase the involvement of smaller faith-based providers in the social-welfare system.

In its coherence and comprehensiveness, this new administrative design—termed "leveling the playing field" by the Bush White House—has no precedent either in presidential history or, more surprisingly, in the conservative agenda that so influenced American politics in 1980s and 1990s. Yet it stands today, certainly, as one of the defining conservative policy experiments of the last decade and one of the most challenging and surprising from certain progressive perspectives as well. At the same time, of course, it is also clear that the substantive results were only modestly successful in some ways and in other ways quite dismal. The share of social service grants going to faith-based providers did rise modestly, even as the overall share of resources devoted to social assistance declined. Moreover, this mixed record was punctuated by several "insider" exposés suggesting that, whatever moral vision lay behind it, the faith-based initiative was mostly a political pawn in the stratagems of Karl Rove.[25]

Today, now that Bush is gone, many view the poor results and the insider exposés as proof enough that the whole idea is mistaken or at least unlikely to be maintained in anything like the comprehensive form he put in place. For a number of reasons that I describe here briefly, I believe this view is wrong. America's "faith-based future," as John DiIulio termed it in 2007, did not start with President Bush and will not disappear from our politics now that he is gone.[26]

One reason is that the small but dedicated movement Bush worked with to design and implement the faith-based initiative is (now ten years later) well-established in a variety of think tanks (or think-tank programs) and in a number of advocacy networks bridging policy and social ministry at the state and federal level, as well as in the mainstream media, the publishing world, and the academy. Advocates for these ideas are more prevalent today than they were in 2001, and they will continue to promote their ideas in Congress and presidential politics. Furthermore, these advocates are unlikely to face fundamental constitutional hurdles in the future, as the Supreme Court has moved steadily in their direction since the late 1980s.

Another important reason is that the "devolutionary" welfare trends that have made this kind of church-state cooperation increasingly plausible, if not necessary, in recent years, will continue to keep the issue alive. Jay Hein, the third of four directors of the White House Office of Faith-Based and Community Initiatives, made it clear that Bush's primary goal before leaving office was to help expand the number of faith-based offices or liaisons at the state level, and that has happened. As most federal social-welfare funding is in fact allocated by state governments (through block grants), this network of state-level offices can generate a potentially much-expanded phase of the original vision, even as the spotlight may fade somewhat in Washington.

Third, the antipoverty focus that was reborn with these ideas (out of the doldrums of welfare reform, let's be clear) will lead more Democrats into sympathetic engagement with Bush's faith-based legacy, picking up where Al Gore left off on the presidential campaign trail in 1999 (when he proposed a similar plan with stricter church-state limitations).[27] The Catholic shift back toward the Democratic Party in 2006 and 2008 (a swing of 8–10 percent, it appears) may also spark renewed faith-based approaches in social policy. Catholics were the strongest supporters of Bush's faith-based initiative.

Fourth, the historical and political significance of the faith-based initiative, particularly as seen in the comparative religious context I establish here, is in fact not well understood and in some respects grossly misunderstood. Simply put, there is still a lot to learn about these issues. And whether or not we can count on a "faith-based future," it is almost certain that the legal and statutory groundwork, the restorative social vision, and what I would call the "political theology" or the "religious state-theory" at the heart of these important changes will continue to evolve and further influence political developments.

The important opportunity now is to look in two directions—backward toward a clearer understanding of how the faith-based initiative emerged and what it proposed and accomplished, and forward to what a different political future may hold for the ideas it embodied and the legal and administrative design it put in place. I have written this book by looking back and thinking ahead in this way, and the result, I hope, is the first (and hopefully not the last) in-depth study of the confessional political ideas behind the faith-based initiative, set in both the political context of Bush's evolving policy efforts beginning in 1995, as well as in a larger historical and comparative context that helps to clarify the limitations of Bush's approach while also defining what a more consistent application of his faith-based principles could mean in the United States. Three basic lines of investigation emerge: (1) the political story of the rise of the faith-based initiative; (2) the theological and historical roots of this policy agenda; and (3) a comparative analysis that draws out the far-reaching implications of this essentially European theological tradition for U.S. social policy. These analyses taken together provide historical documentation of an important recent policy development along with new insight into the ideas that gave it coherence and the continuing potential of these ideas—if and as faith-based policy approaches find new advocates with a more consistent theological understanding and better circumstances in which to advocate that understanding and act on it in political life.

Outline of the Book

Chapter 1 examines the faith-based initiative as it was put in place during President Bush's first term, largely through executive action. From the underlying design, two goals emerged: the first was to enlarge the share of federal social-welfare funding going to faith-based groups; the second was to insure the institutional autonomy and religious identity of participating faith-based providers, basically by enforcing existing church-state rules known as "charitable choice," as provided under welfare reform and other social assistance laws. Largely an administrative process—given the charitable choice groundwork already in place—the faith-based initiative was implemented by the White House with mixed results over Bush's two terms. Here I describe what happened under Bush, and, secondarily, I examine in some detail the legislative and legal developments that preceded the launching of the FBCI, reaching back to the early 1980s as part of the emerging welfare reform debate.

At the outset of any such policy analysis, however, it is important to place these recent developments in a larger historical context. In fact, the problems addressed by the faith-based initiative have been debated in the United States, along roughly similar lines, since the Great Depression, and in Europe since the mid-nineteenth century. Ultimately, the central problem of church-state "domain conflict" in social welfare has deep structural roots in a changing political economy, something barely noticed amidst the alarmist outcries that greeted the launching of the faith-based initiative in 2001. Certainly, trying to resolve this domain conflict was never simply a religious crusade for power, as some seem to believe today; if anything, the striking consistency in how these problems have been understood across many decades reveals what is essentially a structural problem common to many other areas in which government spending and authority have expanded.

Parallel to this remarkable political story, chapter 2 considers debates within the conservative movement and the religious right that intersected with the legal and legislative developments behind the FBCI but ultimately remained on the margins when it was launched in 2001. Conservative Catholics such as William Lind and William Marshner, of the Free Congress Foundation, promoted a devolutionary welfare policy that integrated faith-based providers in ways not unlike the FBCI, but with the explicit purpose of restoring a "culture of life" in poor communities, including restrictive views on abortion and no-fault divorce. Leaders of the Protestant far right, such as Marvin Olasky and George Grant, advanced a more libertarian vision of transferring antipoverty responsibilities from the government to the churches through charity tax-credits offset by reductions in welfare spending. Juxtaposed with what these and other religious conservatives wanted out of welfare reform, the faith-based initiative was a strikingly "progressive" departure, I argue, promising to strengthen public welfare by creating a new class of faith-based stakeholders with reciprocal constitutional protections and obligations. Liberal critics of the faith-based initiative failed to grasp the public expansion implicit in its design, something that becomes much clearer in considering the Christian Democratic influences that shaped it.

Chapter 3 examines the Catholic and Dutch Calvinist theories of the limited state that shaped the design and implementation of the faith-based initiative. First, I investigate the Catholic concept of subsidiarity, formulated officially in the papal encyclical *Quadragesimo anno* (1931),† but building on the powerful church-state arguments of Pope Leo XIII in the late nineteenth century. Second, I investigate the concept of sphere sovereignty, developed by the Dutch Calvinist statesman and theologian Abraham Kuyper.

Sphere sovereignty and subsidiarity both derive from older traditions of political thought on church and state and on the rights of religious bodies and communities within the state. The Catholic model reaches back across many centuries, perhaps as far back as the formulation *Duo sunt* ("two there are") of Pope Gelasius I, which he used to describe church and state as dual or parallel sovereignties, each originating from a separate divine purpose and each therefore protected from interference within its distinctive areas of competence. The early development of this idea arguably culminated in the famous Investiture Controversy (1075–1122), in which Pope Gregory VII challenged royal power in defense of the Church's right to appoint its own bishops. The Jesuit theologian John Courtney Murray's little-studied

---

† Papal encyclicals are cited in the text throughout by name, date, and, where text is quoted, section number. The best digital archive of modern papal encyclicals is at www.vatican.va/holy_father/index.htm.

writings on Leo XIII's "Gelasian" texts help us understand the modern resurgence of these ideas and, more particularly, the development of subsidiarity as a framework for preserving the autonomy of natural associations in
the modern era of religious disestablishment.

Understanding these ideas requires a careful consideration of the historical context that gave rise to their modern formulations in the late nineteenth century. The full or partial disestablishment of many European
churches in the nineteenth century diminished their political power and
their property. But as class antagonisms and poverty grew to unprecedented
modern levels toward the end of the century, an even greater eclipse of the
churches' authority loomed. The rise of socialism and the liberal welfare
state threatened the church in several of the core competences through
which it had retained its authority after disestablishment—particularly in
education, social welfare, and family law. This led Kuyper and Pope Leo
XIII (and later Pope Pius XI) to renew and clarify a religious understanding
of political order. The thrust of this thinking was to limit the state's power
in areas deemed the churches' sovereign or natural domain. Essentially, this
meant new (or renewed) legal accommodation of the public work of religious organizations, coupled with government aid to help those organizations fulfill their social purposes without interference.

The Dutch term *sovereiniteit in eigen sfeer* (literally, "sovereignty in one's
own circle") was first used by the antiliberal Calvinist politician Groen van
Prinsterer in the early 1860s. For both Groen and his disciple Abraham
Kuyper, the guiding aim of sphere sovereignty was to protect confessional
institutions and culture from the secular liberal state. At the heart of this
stood a natural law theory of associations reaching back, in the Protestant
heritage, to Johannes Althusius, a German Calvinist jurist and magistrate
who died in 1638. In his extraordinary work *Politica* (1603), Althusius defined politics as "symbiotics," the "art of associating men for the purpose
of establishing, cultivating, and conserving social life among them." In the
Althusian commonwealth, natural associations, in units of increasing scale
beginning with the family, join together in a social compact that preserves
the unique nature and purpose of each association while also meeting their
shared needs. Kuyper likewise believed that social order, and human flourishing within and through this order, is rooted in divinely ordained structures that comprise a "natural" community, theologically and morally prior
to the state, whatever its political form. The family, the church, charitable associations, and confessional schools—these intermediary structures
between the individual and the state comprise the natural community, and
they are fully as real as individual persons. Government institutions, pro-

grams, and rules form the political community, which by its offices is ordained to help coordinate and protect the structures of society but should never absorb or destroy them for its own purposes or those of some particular group within society.

Kuyper and his Catholic counterparts sought to limit the emerging welfare state out of fear of religious eclipse, as deteriorating conditions drove workers into the arms of statist movements such as communism and Social Democracy. But they also squarely faced the "social question" of industrial modernity. These religious critics of the state saw poverty as a social sin, and they did not trust employers or believe that "market laws" could solve the social question. They believed that corrective action and assistance was necessary to preserve "human dignity"—not a sound-bite but a rich social teaching in both traditions—and to keep the system from collapsing. In contrast with Social Democracy, however, their understanding of social protection gave primary interpersonal responsibility, in terms of day-to-day contact with sources of help, to the churches.

The European welfare states inspired by these ideas largely followed this path of church-state coordination, but they also established substantial social-transfer systems to supplement direct social aid with material support for struggling families—the "family" being understood as a domain of positive or "social" rights quite apart from the negative, individualistic concept of rights established as well in most traditions of constitutional law (exclusively so in the American Constitution). This redistributive dimension, resting on principles of social right, remained buried in the shadows when the Christian Democratic model began to influence religious critics of the American welfare state in the 1980s. Drawing out the implications of these European influences, I conclude chapter 3 by comparing American welfare policy and its outcomes to those of the Christian Democratic systems that inspired the faith-based initiative. It will be no surprise to those familiar with the comparative welfare state literature, which I draw on in this chapter, that the United States does not live up to Christian Democratic welfare standards. I examine the effectiveness of Christian Democratic welfare systems in Germany and the Netherlands, both of which combine highly devolved social services, vested mainly in religious groups, with extensive social transfers to cushion families against market damages and provide support for natural family functions such as dependent care. Holding these superior outcomes up to the light of the religious teachings that inspire them helps us put the relative failures of American welfare policy in a new religious light, and this comparative understanding, in turn, helps us forge a new and better path beyond the partisan divide of the last eight years.

Chapter 4 brings the theological and political threads of chapter 3 together in an effort to "reframe" the debate on faith-based social policy. Here I argue that the confessional/philosophical genealogy of the faith-based initiative, largely ignored in the polarized political environment of the last eight years, is increasingly relevant in the emerging debate on economic insecurity. The key to this is recognizing these confessional welfare models as an expression of pluralist thought, or what I would call "social pluralism." Pluralist political theory, associated in different ways with thinkers ranging from Felicité de Lamennais and Otto von Gierke to J. N Figgis and Harold Laski, was roughly contemporary with the rise of confessional challenges to liberal education and welfare, and with the earliest stages of Christian Democratic politics. Building in part on the older legal traditions of "church autonomy" and "freedom of the church" (*libertas ecclesiae*), this "social pluralism" should not be confused with the rationalistic "interest-group" pluralism familiar from American political theory, and it is not the kind of multicultural pluralism philosophers have advocated with reference to demographic changes that seem to be fraying contemporary democracies. Rather, social pluralism as I understand it here depends on older ideas of the intrinsic sovereignty of natural social structures and morally integrated groups. Essentially, it is an idea of political order in which multiple sovereign structures are acknowledged and protected within a framework of basic civil liberties and the general peace. At the heart of this framework of "distributed sovereignty" are the intermediary social structures that humans directly create and so are "natural" or "real" in contrast with the structures of the state—most importantly, families, churches, and communities. A modern, defensive reaction to political and economic liberalism, social pluralism is not mainly a descriptive analysis of how we live, although it does reflect how most people do, in fact, live—enmeshed in natural social structures by blood, obligation, and ascription. Ultimately, however, social pluralism is a legal and normative framework designed to restrict any power that abuses or absorbs the social structures that are humanly the most essential, in both historical and evolutionary fact as well as moral right.

Families, the communities they form, and the religious faiths they share are the primary battleground. Obtaining legal protection for these natural human structures was the objective of social-pluralist thought in Europe, which was galvanized in the struggle of confessional bodies against ascendant governmental and market liberalism, culminating in the liberal welfare state. The "social rights" partly won in this struggle in Europe—and later made a cornerstone of Christian Democratic welfare states—are unheard of in the United States for many reasons, primarily because our radically individualist Constitution was unavailing as a framework for social rights or even the rudiments of pluralist thought.

Yet some aspects of public law and of religious, legal, and moral thought have planted the seeds of pluralistic social rights in American soil. *Kedroff v. Saint Nicholas Cathedral* (1952),‡ we will see, is a rare but powerful example in the constitutional canon, and it was echoed in another Supreme Court case more directly relevant to today's debate on faith-based social services, *Corporation of the Presiding Bishop v. Amos* (1987), in which the decision upheld the right of social agencies affiliated with churches to make employment decisions on the basis of religion. In Justice Brennan's concurring opinion, this was justified because religious organizations depend for their survival on the shared faith of their members and representatives. Any religious community, Brennan wrote, "represents an ongoing tradition of shared beliefs, an organic entity not reducible to a mere aggregation of individuals," and so, necessarily, must have certain collective rights in preserving the things it requires to stay whole.

Of course, for decades now political commentators have given much attention to the "mediating structures" of society, "the institutions standing between the individual in his private life and the larger institutions of public life," as Peter Berger and Richard John Neuhaus described it in their groundbreaking 1977 essay "To Empower People."[28] In the America of Reagan, Clinton, and Bush, however, the concept of mediating structures was often carelessly blended with much weaker analytical categories such as "civil society" and "social capital." These have little pluralistic meaning in the sense discussed here, and in many debates they are little more than nice-sounding surrogates of the rational marketplace. And yet the remarkable truth examined here is that pluralism in the older modern sense— familial, communal, and religious—has become increasingly visible in policy developments, most obviously in the long policy struggle over welfare reform and persistent poverty. As the social safety net was "devolved" onto states and localities in a series of major reforms, faith-based service organizations became preeminent in the theory of mediating structures and also a subject of church-state developments that changed the terms of what these structures mean. Indeed, what I hope this book can show is that America's church-state "domain conflict" in social welfare, simmering for decades, has been addressed and mostly settled in a form with social-pluralist roots. As more and more it seems that no social bond or common purpose is

---

‡ Supreme Court cases are cited throughout in text by name and date. Readers are referred to www.oyez.org ("Browse cases") for texts of decisions.

contemplated to stop the wealthy and powerful from harming society, this is an important step in the right direction. Simply put, a social pluralism that upholds the freedom of the church cannot but justify stronger support and protection for the families and communities in the care of the church.

Eliminating government barriers to religious social service groups was the mandate of Bush's effort. But restoring these and other natural associations to their proper place of dignity in God's vision of humanity does not end with government retreat. Ultimately, then, this book explains how the religious ideas behind the faith-based initiative lead us beyond the narrow government directives of the last eight years toward a broader defense of families and communities within the liberal economic order. If the faith-based initiative rectifies certain deep indignities of the liberal welfare state, as I believe it does, nevertheless, the society it implicitly seeks to restore remains under siege in what this book suggests is a "Godless economy." Quite simply, a Godless economy is one that is legally and normatively void of any enforceable responsibility for protecting the least among us, and one that is openly destructive of the social bonds that give communities their strength and therefore give rise to corresponding social rights.

But, again, why continue to think about such things now that Bush is finally gone, some may ask? It is true, of course, that the faith-based initiative was an expression of George W. Bush's personal faith and religious experience, at some level. Undoubtedly, however, it also embodies a much broader movement of ideas that preceded Bush's efforts and will continue to evolve. Clearly, a new frontier of church-state relations in welfare governance is emerging, combined with changing attitudes toward poverty and poor communities in an age of growing market extremes. This combination is, potentially, a powerful force for good. I hope this book convinces you of the promise it holds if we are serious about religious ideas and more loyal now to the Christian faith so many of us share.

ONE

A New Era of Church-State Cooperation

In 1996, the United States Congress passed a set of provisions known as "charitable choice," part of the landmark welfare reform bill signed by President Clinton on August 26 of that year. At the heart of these provisions (Section 104 of Public Law 104-193), Congress gave religious social-service providers a statutory right to contract with the government without compromising their religious identity. The Bush-era Faith-Based and Community Initiative (FBCI) was an effort to do two fundamental things, in turn, based on the core legal principles of charitable choice: first, to increase the share of federal social-welfare resources going to religious groups; and second, to protect the organizational autonomy and religious identity of these groups so enlisted by the government. This fundamental "re-design" of government contracting, as one official termed it, was considered necessary to correct a bureaucratic environment that not only restricted the participation of faith-based groups, but also, in doing so, greatly hindered the struggle against poverty. As candidate Bush put it on the presidential campaign trail in 1999,

> In the past, presidents have declared wars on poverty and promised to create a great society. But these grand gestures and honorable aims were frustrated. They have become a warning, not an example. We found that government can spend money, but it can't put hope in our hearts or a sense of purpose in our lives. This is done by churches and synagogues and mosques and charities that warm the cold of life. A quiet river of goodness and kindness that cuts through stone. Real change in our culture comes from the bottom up, not the top down. It gathers the momentum of a million committed hearts. So today I want to propose a different role for government. A fresh start. A bold new approach.[1]

Drawing groups from well outside the arena of welfare policy into the fray, the extraordinary controversy surrounding Bush's efforts gave the impression that these concerns and the changes devised to address them were radically new, if not dangerous. In fact, there is a long history behind these ideas, and fully understanding Bush's efforts requires a historical perspective reaching back to the late nineteenth century. Later in the book I explore why it also requires a comparative, transatlantic perspective in this same basic timeframe.

Before World War I, the United States had a mixed economy of social welfare, drawing on local churches, missionary societies, larger relief associations such as the St. Vincent de Paul Society, and ethnic and vocational mutual-aid fellowships. In larger towns and cities, there were public institutions for the poor, funds for emergency needs, indigent hospitals, mental wards, and orphanages. Catholics also organized their own hospitals, asylums, and orphanages to protect their poor and vulnerable from Protestant bigotry and proselytization. These combined efforts—certainly a large part of the associational genius Alexis de Tocqueville perceived in *Democracy in America*—reached only a small fraction of those in need. Although public social assistance was far from negligible when he journeyed through America, in Tocqueville's eyes churches and religious associations of the Jacksonian era operated in a largely private realm devoid of political interaction or significance. He celebrated this as a necessity of self-preservation amidst the volatile factionalism and ever-changing leadership of democratic government:

> If the Americans, who have abandoned the political world to the attempts of innovators, had not placed religion beyond their reach, where it could abide in the ebb and flow of human opinions, . . . where would that respect which belongs to it be paid, amidst the struggles of faction? And what would become of its immortality, in the midst of perpetual decay? The American clergy were the first to perceive this truth, and to act in conformity with it. They saw that they must renounce their religious influence, if they were to strive for political power; and they chose to give up the support of the State, rather than to share its vicissitudes.[2]

With the consolidation of national markets, large enterprise, and the first outcroppings of the regulatory state during the Gilded Age, this concept of religion as an essentially private good was increasingly difficult to reconcile with the growing magnitude of social need and also the sheer impact of political and economic structures on social conditions and behavior. Thus, a second phase of the mixed welfare economy sought to "scale up" and rationalize aid in response to the more structured poverty of urban industrial settings. So-called "scientific charity," embodied in the proliferation of Charity Organization Societies in many larger cities beginning in the 1870s, introduced the centralized, disciplinary casework model, attaching aid to education and behavioral control. In this period, the economy of social welfare generally (and temporarily) shifted from one based on "outdoor relief" (aid given directly to households) to one based on "indoor relief" (aid attached to institutional control in workhouses and almshouses).[3] The evidence is clear that scientific charity on its own—in cities where outdoor relief was abolished or reduced—led to increased pauperism and hardship and "lost its remaining credibility" in the depression of the 1890s.[4]

H. K. Carroll, who was in charge of gathering religious data for the 1890 census, depicted the churches of the time as, effectively, a large private welfare state built from the resources of society. Although private social assistance was but a tiny fraction of national income at the time (approximately the same as government poor relief), the churches' panoply of mission efforts, leveraged by huge inputs of voluntary labor time,[5] was highly visible in the social field—almost a private mirror image of what government looks like today:

It is to be remembered that all the houses of worship have been built by voluntary contributions. They have been provided by private gifts, but are offered to the public for free use. The government has not given a dollar to provide them, nor does it appropriate a dollar for their support. And yet the church is the mightiest, most pervasive, most persistent, and most beneficent force in our civilization. It affects, directly or indirectly, all human activities and interests. It is a large property-holder, and influences the market for real estate. It is a corporation, and administers large trusts.

It is a public institution, and is therefore the subject of protective legislation. It is a capitalist, and gathers and distributes large wealth. It is an employer, and furnishes means of support to ministers, organists, singers, janitors, and others. It is a relief organization feeding the hungry, clothing the naked, and assisting the destitute. It is a university, training children and instructing old and young, by public lectures on religion, morals, industry, thrift, and the duties of citizenship. It is a reformatory influence, recovering the vicious, immoral, and dangerous elements of society and making them exemplary citizens. It is a philanthropic association, sending missionaries to the remotest countries to Christianize savage and degraded races. It is organized beneficence, founding hospitals for the sick, asylums for orphans, refuges for the homeless, and schools, colleges, and universities for the ignorant. . . . Who that considers these moral and material aspects of the church can deny that it is beneficent in its aims, unselfish in its plans, and impartial in the distribution of its blessings? It is devoted to the temporal and eternal interests of mankind. Every cornerstone it lays, it lays for humanity; every temple it opens, it opens to the world; every altar it establishes, it establishes for the salvation of souls. Its spires are fingers pointing heavenward; its ministers are messengers of good tidings, ambassadors of hope, and angels of mercy. What is there among men to compare with the church in its power to educate, elevate, and civilize mankind?[6]

Rising destitution at the doorstep of the private religious economy compelled a new deployment of the moral resources accumulated by the church. It was acknowledged that the great "social question" and the moral anarchy of "poverty amid plenty" had no answer or remedy in the churches' efforts alone in the private economy. A new generation of leaders became more receptive to the idea of legislative reforms of the capitalist system, following in the footsteps of trade unionism. Catholic Archbishop John Ireland of Minnesota helped to inspire them amid the wrenching contradictions of the Gilded Age when he asked, in 1889, "What has come over us that we shun the work which is essentially ours to do? These are days of action, days of warfare. . . . Into the arena, priest and layman! Seek out social evils, and lead in movements that tend to rectify them."[7] Such a concept of warfare against social evils is perhaps, to us, more redolent of the Great Society, with its War on Poverty; but in 1889, social evils were still considered the unique province of religion. By the turn of the century, however, the visible inadequacy of voluntary religious assistance threatened the Christian faith with popular—and sometimes populist—disaffection as never before. When Pope Leo XIII issued *Rerum novarum* in 1891, American Catholics experienced a profound political awakening in the form of "solidarist" and "social justice" teaching, as did their Protestant counterparts in the form of the Social Gospel.

In the years before and immediately after World War I, the churches formed national welfare councils to advise and better coordinate charitable missions as well as advocate for certain kinds of government intervention, such as workplace safety rules. By this time it was increasingly acknowledged that the forces of industrial capitalism had far outstripped not simply the churches' capacity for charitable assistance, but the capacity of charity itself, as a model of welfare, to give sufficient protection to the amassing workers and families of urban-industrial America. The 1908 Social Creed adopted by the Federal Council of Churches (at the time representing seventeen million Protestants) and the 1919 Catholic Bishops' Program of Social Reconstruction show that, despite a nineteenth-century reputation for excessive spiritual pietism, the churches' embrace of government ran well ahead of the government's own social spending and also, clearly, helped to generate the national will for significant increases in government spending and intervention when the economy collapsed in the 1930s (a point we return to in chapter 4). Total government spending on welfare or "poor relief" amounted to only one sixth of 1 percent of national income in the 1920s, roughly equal to the share of national income dedicated to private charitable relief. In the 1930s, however, the government's welfare spending grew significantly.[8]

The share of national income dedicated to *private* poor relief did not rise with the Great Depression; in fact, it essentially remained flat, at well under 1 percent, from the mid-nineteenth century across much of the twentieth century.[9] This surprising fact does not account for the value of voluntary labor, however, always a large fraction of the total value of charity. Nevertheless, with little discussion at the time, the rise of the New Deal, with its many aid programs and significant public spending, was a watershed in the structure of poor relief and social services, putting religious providers in a legally and politically subordinate position. This problem of the legal, fiscal, and administrative impact of the emerging welfare state—and what economists call the "crowd out" effects of these structural changes—had been a long-standing concern and a subject of systematic theological reflection in Europe over the previous fifty years. Owing in part to the earlier development of public welfare and education programs in countries such as Germany, Italy, and the Netherlands, but also in part to the strong confessional identity and cultural worldviews of the churches thus embattled by these encroachments, church-state "domain conflict" in social policy was arguably the central political problem in late nineteenth-century Europe. While today's American "culture war" focuses mainly on restricting individual behaviors such as abortion and homosexuality, it is important to recognize that the first self-declared culture war—known in German as *Kulturkampf* or, literally, "conflict of cultures"—was actually waged between liberal governments and religious bodies (not individual believers), and this created precisely the kinds of structural conflict over welfare provision (as well as education) that we now see at work in such developments as charitable choice and the faith-based initiative.

These political parallels are more than coincidental, as will become clearer in our later discussion of the theological influences that shaped our own institutional *Kulturkampf* over welfare reform during the last fifteen years. As indicated, its origins lie in the Great Depression. For the concerted effort that was needed in those times, public agencies and commissions were established to launch and manage the New Deal's many relief and employment programs. Among Roosevelt's brain trust there was a strong assumption that, especially in the delivery of federal funds or other kinds of material assistance, it was necessary for the government to do its own administration and not be dependent on private groups; in most programs the law stipulated that federal aid could only be distributed by federal agencies.[10]

In general, religious leaders, particularly Catholic clergy, were moderately to strongly supportive of New Deal efforts.[11] But one New Deal policy area in which church-state conflicts clearly emerged was education, which remains the most difficult of such constitutional domain conflicts to this day. A number of New Deal relief programs gave emergency aid to schools, including private and religious schools, and during Roosevelt's second term these universal but temporary measures helped to foster the idea of establishing permanent federal programs for education assistance on a pluralistic, religion-inclusive basis.[12] In the Supreme Court, the "child benefit" principle was established as early as 1930 (in *Cochran v. Louisiana Board of Education*) to justify public provision of materials and services (in this case textbooks) to private schools.

In 1938, Roosevelt's Advisory Committee on Education recommended the establishment of a federal education grant program in support of primary and secondary schools, for which private schools would be eligible, as well as a program providing materials, transportation, and other services directly to students, regardless of the school setting. These proposals became part of legislation introduced in 1939, with the eligibility of private schools left to the determination of the states. Catholic leaders sought a federal provision requiring equal treatment of public and private schools by the states administering these programs. This reflected a significant evolution of the Catholic position on federal education policy; previously, the push for federal education policy was generally oriented toward establishing de facto Protestant "common schools," and some states (like Oregon) had already passed or proposed laws effecting the closure of Catholic schools and forcing all children into the common schools. The pluralistic design of New Deal education proposals and related bills opened the door for Catholics to embrace a federal role. The key to understanding such a change of position is the Church's social teaching known as subsidiarity, a principle of governance requiring public support for, but opposing control or usurpation of, traditional religious functions. We will discuss this in more detail later, but it is worth noting here Pope Pius XI's most important encyclical of the 1920s, *Divini illius magistri* ("On Christian Education"). Here he argued these points as applied to the European context (particularly in Germany and Italy), declaring "unjust and unlawful" any education policy that creates a monopoly forcing families "to make use of government schools contrary to the dictates of their Christian conscience" (sec. 48).

With the New Deal education proposals of 1938 and 1939 came a barrage of Protestant protest tempered only by the view of the Federal Council of Churches, which emphasized the role of state discretion in classifying eligible schools and the fact that the aid in question was for auxiliary purposes and not core operations. Some Protestant opponents sought to strip the bill of state discretion over eligibility and establish clear federal language excluding private and parochial schools from any benefits. Baptists in particular decried it as a "dangerous violation of the principle of separation of church and state,"[13] or simply opposed any federal education policy at all. The Methodist Episcopal Church in the southern states announced official opposition on both church-state and federalist grounds. No further progress was made on these federal proposals at the time, although a number of states continued to pass measures for disbursing materials and services to both public and private schoolchildren, which later brought forth the landmark Supreme Court decision *Everson v. Board of Education of Ewing Township* in 1947, discussed in more detail in the next section.

In 1956, the National Council of Churches (NCC) sought to develop guidelines on "church-state relations in social welfare," revealing the obvious point that these issues were publicly contested long before charitable choice. It may be helpful to compare earlier discussions to today's much more heated debate. In fact there are striking theoretical consistencies. In the printed proceedings of its first conference on the churches and social welfare, the NCC stated the church-state problem in a nearly classical expression of the idea of dual or parallel sovereignties, the core tenet of confessional freedom in the European antiliberal mold, which we will later see has also been formative for today's faith-based initiatives. "From the beginning," the NCC proceedings declared (with rather surprising Catholic overtones),

> The church has stood for the dignity of the individual and the supreme worth of the human personality. Over the centuries, as democracy has followed despotism, government by the people as represented in the state has shown more and more concern for the well-being of people. Inevitably, therefore,

these two great institutions—church and state—have faced each other at times with issues bristling with doubts as to the role and authority of each, and at times have found hearty acceptance that church and state together, yet separately, are essential to the well-being of the people.[14]

What was notably missing in the more concrete discussion of church-state domain issues that followed was any expressed concern about religious content in publicly funded programs. Much more attention was paid to putting the human welfare of those receiving services before institutional self-interest, whether that of government or church. This was viewed as a "coordination" issue between public and private contributions, as reflected in questions such as these: "Do the several types of agencies adequately understand the social role of the other types?"; "Do different agencies which are working toward the same or similar objectives get into each other's way or undermine each other's effectiveness?"[15]

Where governments are involved, the NCC stipulated several core principles which, to one degree or another, are now emphasized in policy or best practices, or actually exist in federal law in this area. These included the principle that financing through grants to individuals is preferable to direct funding of agencies, and any agency should avoid becoming dependent even on indirect subsidies for its stability; that no grants should be taken if they require faith-based agencies to give up their autonomy or their "corporate witness"; that a faith-based agency with a monopoly position in a given community cannot receive government funds if their use is associated with sectarian requirements imposed on clients and staff; that is, religious liberty is especially to be accounted for where the range of available providers is limited.[16]

Significant growth in government aid programs obviously lay in the background of these church-state discussions. After World War II, with the American economy resurrected, the federal government began to subsidize state and local welfare efforts, particularly in the improvement of health care. The Hill-Burton Hospital Construction Act of 1947 (known as the Hill-Burton Program) provided federal subsidies to state and local governments for hospital construction, a significant share of which were religiously affiliated.[17] As of 1960, more than 1,600 religiously affiliated hospitals (including 889 Catholic hospitals) had received Hill-Burton funds totaling approximately $330 million.[18] In one survey of 407 religious social service agencies, 290 reported receiving tax dollars by way of subsidies or purchase-of-service contracts. On a denominational basis, including Jewish, Catholic, and Protestant agencies, all but the Southern Baptists had more agencies receiving tax dollars than not. Sixteen percent of the agencies reported receiving public funds amounting to 50 percent or more of their operating budgets.[19] A related survey of 407 agency administrators, Protestant, Catholic, Jewish, and nonsectarian, found that 44 percent saw no violation of church-state principles in the receipt of public grants by religious agencies, while 20 percent saw it as an extreme violation. Purchase-of-service contracts had substantially more constitutional approval, with 76 percent seeing no violation of church-state principles in such an arrangement. Also notable, the survey revealed that 53 percent of administrators viewed government funding as posing "some" or "considerable" danger to agency "autonomy" (defined as preservation of "principles or ideology"). It seems reasonable to conclude that many administrators felt that government aid posed dangers to autonomy that were not necessary for constitutional purposes.[20]

The involvement of religious groups under fiscal-administrative arrangements in other areas besides hospitals and children's care also expanded in the decades following World War II, including maternal health, juvenile delinquency, housing, and work-incentive programs.[21] One striking example of church-state welfare cooperation unfolded in the Department of State's food aid program, established in the Agricultural Act of 1949. Section 416 of that act authorized the Secretary of Agriculture to donate government-owned surplus farm commodities to voluntary agencies registered with the State Department. By the late 1960s, nearly 30 billion pounds of government surplus food, worth about $4 billion, was donated to more than a dozen voluntary agencies for foreign distribution. Nearly 90 percent, however, went to four large agencies—Catholic Relief Services, Lutheran World Relief, Church World Service, and CARE.[22] While most of the food distributed in this way went to Western Europe at the beginning, in the 1960s, Catholic Relief Services, led by Bishop Edward E. Swanstrom, campaigned for expanding this government partnership into the developing world, particularly Latin American and Africa.[23] The increasingly difficult church-state climate of those years was reflected in a letter Swanstrom wrote to President Kennedy urging him to recognize the distinction between helping religiously affiliated social-service agencies do their work and simply financing churches out of government coffers. Notably, it was liberal Democrats, led by Senator Hubert Humphrey, who were most supportive of expanded cooperation with faith-based providers in foreign material-aid programs.[24] In 1962, Swanstrom obtained a policy directive to this effect from the White House, noting in a letter to Cardinal Cicognani (who was then Vatican Secretary of State) that, in addition to helping Catholic efforts overseas, it "may easily have bearing on the overall Church-State discussion." Lutheran World Relief opposed this trend because it feared further government cooperation would corrupt the religious mission of overseas efforts. Southern Baptists and church-state separation groups opposed it on constitutional grounds and, more generally, because they feared and disliked the Catholic Church. Church World Service (the overseas mission arm of the predominantly mainline Protestant National Council of Churches) was internally divided but officially supportive, and later joined with the Catholics in pushing for an amendment giving voluntary agencies access to foreign currency earned by the U.S. government from surplus food sales under Title 1 of Public Law 480.[25]

It should also be remembered that the Economic Opportunity Act of 1964, part of Lyndon Johnson's War on Poverty, made churches and parochial schools eligible for participation in many of its programs, but with blanket restrictions on religious use of funds and on religious discretion in screening clients or staff. The Community Action programs under Title II of the bill included education grants for which parochial schools were considered eligible. However, these were to be administered by local public school boards, a design Catholics believed would exclude their participation. In the end direct grants to schools were excluded from the legislation, but public and parochial schools together remained eligible to provide certain services with federal support in the final version of the bill.[26]

As the U.S. welfare state expanded further in the late 1960s and early 1970s, nonprofit revenues coming from government began to rise relative to other sources.[27] The growth in government social spending in particular was accompanied by operational changes described by scholars as the rise of a "government-by-proxy" system, whereby public services are "outsourced" for implementation to private organizations, mainly nonprofits.[28] As the government-by-proxy system expanded in the 1980s and 1990s, certain larger faith-based organizations in fact received (and continue to receive) a significant fraction of federal social-welfare funds, and those funds, in turn, comprise a large or predominant share of their operating budgets. As of 1993, according to political scientist Stephen Monsma, 65 percent of Catholic Charities' revenue was drawn from government sources. For the Jewish Board of Family and Children's Agencies, it was 75 percent, and for Lutheran Social Services it was 92 percent.[29] Thus while secular nonprofits were generally more "government friendly," large religious nonprofits were no exception to the rule. Another definable sector in faith-based social services is that of congregation-based coalitions, which are often interfaith in character. A recent study of 656 such coalitions shows markedly less dependence on government funding, with an average budget-share of 16.5 percent, compared to 25 percent from congregations and denominational judicatories, 18.7 percent from individuals, and 12.5 percent from foundations.[30]

As government programs proliferated and budgets grew, extending public policy and regulation further and further into society, the secularizing effects of this government aid, perceived or real, were increasingly magnified as an issue in public life. Certainly, along with other factors such as mass culture and academic influences, government funding contributed to increasing secularization of the large religious social-welfare agencies, and these agencies, in turn, increasingly monopolized government funding. The formula stating that "shekels bring shackles" became an administrative commonplace.

An anecdote told by former Senator Rick Santorum, concerning a priest who failed his test for a psychology internship at a Catholic Charities clinic, illustrates the problem. As George Will describes it, "when presented with hypothetical counseling situations involving a depressed pregnant woman seeking an abortion, two homosexuals seeking advice on their relationship and a couple seeking a divorce," the priest "advised against abortion, would not endorse homosexual unions and encouraged the couple to persevere in marriage." Reportedly, the supervisor who failed him, said, "We get government funds, so we are not Catholic."[31] If this seems to be an extreme example, there is no doubt that, generally speaking, the culture of these large religious contractors became increasingly secular as they took more government money. In their extremely influential 1977 essay on "mediating structures," *To Empower People*, Peter Berger and Richard John Neuhaus captured the problem well:

> Where government agencies are not directly taking over areas previously serviced by religious institutions, such institutions are being turned into quasi-governmental agencies through the powers of funding, certification, licensing, and the like. The loss of religious and cultural distinctiveness is abetted also by the dynamics of professionalization within the religious institutions and by the failure of the churches either to support their agencies or to insist that public policy respect their distinctiveness.[32]

From these still-relevant insights of more than thirty years ago, we can see that the momentum behind charitable choice has been building for a long time. The basic sentiment behind charitable choice was already prevalent, in fact, prior to the establishment of strict separationism by the

Supreme Court in the 1960s and 1970s. In 1955, for example, E. Theodore Bachmann claimed to summarize the view of Protestant leaders on church-state relations in social welfare: "Within the past decades there has been growing concern on the part of many churchmen, clergy and laity alike, that the increasing secularization of the welfare services . . . has just about left religion out. Therefore there are denominational leaders . . . who feel that the time may have arrived when the church, which was the originator of most modern social work, must reassert itself, and reclaim some of the ground it has lost."[33]

Two decades later, in the aftermath of the Great Society and the War on Poverty, the share of government spending dedicated to social assistance had risen more than fourfold, from approximately 2 percent to 8.6 percent.[34] Thus, the share of money available through government was growing exponentially, while private giving remained relatively constant. By 1990, moreover, combined paid and voluntary nonprofit employment equaled nearly 13 percent of total employment in the country. As John DiIulio and others have stressed, government expansion prompted an institutional growth mentality that led to monopolistic qualities in contracting regimes. Large organizations like Catholic Charities obtained built-in advantages that denied entry to smaller and possibly more effective groups with new ways of doing things on the ground. Critical perspectives on this oligarchical trend (even somewhat "corporatist," arguably, when combined with the lobbying effects of related bodies such as the National Conference of Catholic Bishops), initially blended with bureaucratic reform efforts more generally. What galvanized active dissent, however, were the apparent secularizing effects of government expansion in sensitive areas such as schooling and welfare. As the "religious right" stood up to be counted in the 1970s, initially provoked by *Roe v. Wade*, government exclusion of religion from schools and other institutions became a major national issue. This was the moment when the definable features of a charitable choice–type reform of government systems began to emerge, particularly in moderate evangelical circles.

One prominent feature of this thinking was the idea of government "crowd out," that is, how expanding public welfare may distort or suppress charitable giving and activities. Although research in this area—a small subfield of public economics—is in its relative infancy, several studies suggest that there are significant crowd-out effects in the history of American public welfare. One complex statistical study of changes in congregational community-service spending after welfare reform (focusing on congregations of the Presbyterian Church, USA) found that for every dollar cut from federal welfare spending, congregational social spending rises by 40 cents.[35] Another study of the 1930s concludes that "higher government spending leads to lower church charitable activity": church spending fell by an estimated 30 percent in response to the New Deal.[36] It is a matter of rather elementary economic logic to recognize that the rising tax burden required by expanding public welfare potentially has had the effect of diverting control of significant resources from private charity to public agencies. One could go further: accounting for government crowd-out effects means that religious social providers, whose freedom is inseparable from their ability to serve, are essentially losing their freedom when the welfare state expands. Certainly, it is not really plausible to regard the dictum that "public shekels bring private shackles" as a matter of religious groups simply making a "choice" to pursue public funds and thus reaping the consequences. Such "choices" are likely constrained by the effects of government spending to a degree that moral philosophers, at least, would recognize as constituting a form of compulsion. As we will see below, a shift toward "equal treatment" theory in church-state law, allowing more accommodation of religious providers in programs of government aid, is subtly integrated with assumptions of government crowd-out and related compulsion. This question is arguably quite important, then, for the constitutional and political future of faith-based initiatives on the Bush model.[37]

The other core feature of the emerging critique is the question of discrimination against religious providers. John DiIulio, the most prominent academic advocate of today's faith-based initiatives, went so far as to describe conventional welfare contracting as an actual system of discrimination, and he accused the government of "funding discrimination." Putting the historical problem in a contemporary light, he cited statistical patterns that illustrate, if not conscious bias against religion in the federal bureaucracy, then at least a striking degree of bureaucratic disconnection from what is happening on the ground. The case of criminal justice programs to deter youth deviancy is a striking example. One comprehensive study of fifteen cities reveals extensive cooperation in this area between local criminal justice organizations and grassroots religious groups. Yet, in 2001, DiIulio points out, only one-third of 1 percent of U.S. Department of Justice discretionary funds was awarded to faith-based groups, and virtually no money went to the "street ministries," which are closest to the problem and arguably best positioned to do effective work.[38] The broader picture has become increasingly clear:

There is growing evidence that grassroots nonprofit social service organizations, especially small community-serving religious groups that serve primarily low-income urban Latino and African-American children, youth, and
families, are discriminated against at each and every stage of the government-
by-proxy process. While it is true that some grassroots religious groups obtain minimal funding from larger, more established religious nonprofit organizations, receive nominal support from local governments, and occasion-
ally attract foundation dollars, for the most part, grassroots organizations
receive little or no public money or corporate or philanthropic support. Even
in situations in which the grassroots organizations supply the bulk of social
services; serve the youngest, the neediest, or the most difficult-to-serve populations without regard to beneficiaries' religious orientations; have long-
standing working partnerships with local government agencies and/or secular nonprofit organizations; have been subjected to independent performance evaluations; and have achieved 501(c)3 status, faith-based organization programs receive last priority in terms of obtaining financial support.[39]

Although there is little doubt that government bureaucracies create entry
problems for smaller players, there is little evidence that government is directly "imposing" secularism in the social safety net. In fact, some evidence
shows the opposite: that government agencies have a long track record of
conspicuously avoiding constitutional review of the faith-based institutions
and programs under their contracting authority. As Stephen Monsma concludes in one study (based on survey data culled from faith-based contractors), "most of the nonprofits studied here appear to experience a surprisingly low level of problems or pressures due to the religious practices in
which they engage."[40] Under a welfare system increasingly based on devolutionary block grants, coupled with significant state and local discretion at
the levels of policy and administration, meaningful constitutional review
is not likely to be a benchmark for public management, unless required by
federal policy. This should be a concern for advocates of charitable choice
law, which, as we shall see, has always strictly prohibited using federal funds
(at least those directly disbursed to an organization) to pay for "inherently
religious" activities such as worship and prayer. One county official, speaking on a panel with charitable choice advocates at a 2002 Hudson Institute
event at the National Press Club, says that her agency does "nothing" to
monitor the religious content of the faith-based organizations they fund.
Whatever program content is described by the provider in the original procurement application and in monthly "best practices" meetings with the
county is simply assumed to be the case.[41] In a study of faith-based pro-

viders of welfare-to-work services in four metropolitan areas, Monsma reports (broadly reinforcing his own earlier findings) that "[many] directors of faith-based programs receiving government funds bore witness to the fact that they have been able to do so without compromising their religious commitments and goals."[42] A Government Accountability Office report issued in 2006 found, in a small sample, that some participating groups in the faith-based initiative seemed to be violating the law regarding separation of federal funds and religious activities.[43]

The lack of constitutional oversight in the pre–charitable choice era of large-scale welfare contracting may be surprising, given the relatively strict separationism concurrently embraced by the courts. But this does not mean that government contracting did not have secularizing effects, as any large-sample comparison between contracting and noncontracting religious providers would likely reveal. Much of this secularization, however, is "tacit"; that is, it occurs through internalization of government expectations rather than through actual government monitoring and enforcement. The argument that faith-based contractors have actually "lost their souls" in taking government money refers mainly to this kind of tacit secularization, not aggressive government enforcement of secularism.[44] According to this line of analysis, in benefiting from the government's financial support year after year, the leaders of many religious nonprofits have more or less internalized the value system of the liberal welfare state, forgetting how to promote "traditional values and God-fearing behavior" in their services, as in the past.[45] In a related argument, some conservatives are no less concerned with the deterioration of religious life within many faith-based nonprofits. One of the most careful and insightful theorists of the school-voucher movement, Charles Glenn, for example, sees institutional self-limitation, through loss of confessional focus, as a greater threat to the religious freedom and mission of faith-based providers than government regulation at this point.[46] Although Monsma found that approximately 30 percent of the heads of religious agencies receiving public funds reported being questioned or pressured by government officials "with regard to their religiously motivated practices," or reported general hostility toward religious practices, Glenn concludes that self-limitation due to cultural inhibition is a major problem as well, perhaps the bigger problem.[47]

Robert Rector of the Heritage Foundation frankly argues that many agencies are spiritually corrupt. As he put it, "Private welfare institutions not only are not immune from the permissive entitlement ethos, but on average are more corrupted than are federal programs," referring to soup kitchens and food pantries.[48] This is certainly exaggerated, but it is broadly true that a routinized, bureaucratic, professional mentality, mirroring that of the government, shapes the operation of many larger religious agencies, making them virtually indistinguishable from any other kind of agency. And it is also broadly true that the social-welfare field was increasingly secularized as social spending grew and government bureaucracies overshadowed private charitable giving.

Church and State in Society: From Separation to Cooperation

To the extent that constitutional doctrine has become more accommodating of government aid to religious organizations, the 1970s were the highwater mark of non-accommodation. It is known as the era of "strict separation," sometimes called "no-aid separationism." Historically, in fact, only two Supreme Court decisions, nearly ninety years apart, actually addressed the constitutionality of direct government funding of religiously affiliated service institutions prior to the development of charitable choice, both deciding in the affirmative against establishment clause challenges: *Bradfield v. Roberts* (1899), upholding federal financing of new construction and patient care at a Catholic hospital; and *Bowen v. Kendrick* (1988), upholding a federal law stipulating the eligibility of religious organizations for government contracts in sex education and family planning services. As we saw earlier, *Bradfield v. Roberts*–type arrangements became quite common with the advent of the New Deal and government programs focused on health and human services.[49] In the 1970s, after a series of earlier decisions barring school prayer and public financing of parochial schools, a second barrage of strict-separation decisions put a stop to nearly all forms of government aid to nonpublic primary and secondary schools. In *Lemon v. Kurtzmann* (1971), *Committee for Public Education & Religious Liberty v. Nyquist* (1973), and *Meek v. Pittenger* (1975), no-aid separationism was consolidated, erecting a self-declared Jeffersonian "wall of separation" between government and religious institutions by throwing out even modest forms of indirect aid such as maintenance and repair grants, eligibility for programs supplying instructional materials and auxiliary services, and tax benefits related to private school tuition. The most important legal principle that unified the no-aid era was the second rule of the so-called Lemon test (actually inherited from *Abington v. Schempp*, decided in 1963) — that the "primary effect" of any government aid to religious institutions must be one that "neither advances nor inhibits religion." As Laurence Tribe argues in his constitutional law textbook, when the "primary secular effect" standard was applied after Lemon, it was analytically transformed into a screening point for even remote or incidental religious effects, so that any such effects disqualified aid even when the main effect was secular. This shift is "analytically significant," Tribe wrote, because it promoted "a more searching inquiry, and comes closer to the absolutist no-aid approach to the establishment clause than the primary effect test did."[50]

Scholars have noted the irony of the fact that the decision in which the "wall of separation" formula first entered Supreme Court jurisprudence, decades earlier, actually affirmed a policy providing state aid for both public and parochial school students. In *Everson v. Board of Education of Ewing Township, New Jersey* (1947), the "controversial fountainhead" of contemporary establishment clause doctrine, as the *Harvard Law Review* later put it,[51] Justice Hugo Black authored the majority opinion (5–4) in which he formulated dicta expressing a "high and impregnable" wall-of-separation standard, invoking not only Thomas Jefferson's famous letter using the "wall" metaphor, but also the varied "turmoil, civil strife, and persecutions" of "old world" sectarian warfare. The policy at issue, however, a New Jersey program that reimbursed parents for their children's bus fare, including parochial school students, was found not to breach the high and impregnable wall of separation, because it did not benefit the schools directly and was "separate and so indisputably marked off from the religious function." Set against Black's separationist dicta,[52] this ruling actually foreshadowed, faintly, today's more nuanced understanding of what government "establishment" of religion involves—but only faintly, as Black specified that the Everson decision pressed to the "verge" of religion clause permissibility (a point duly noted in *Lemon v. Kurtzman*'s stricter reading based on more controversial facts).[53] And yet, in Black's connotation of differing religious and public "functions," we do see an outline of the kind of institutional analysis underlying current "equal treatment" doctrine, drawing a comparatively reasonable distinction between secular statutory intent and public benefits, on the one hand, and religious identity and functions, on the other. In the meantime, however, *Lemon v. Kurtzman* and its progeny had basically erased such distinctions, at least for establishment clause purposes, working instead from the assumption (more or less defined by Black in *Everson* and a subsequent decision, *McCollum v. Board of Education*, 1948) that any direct material aid to religious institutions, even if generally available and affixed to a secular statutory purpose, would have the effect of advancing the religious mission of the institutions, and therefore religion itself, thereby violating the establishment clause.[54]

The movement away from strict separationism began in the early 1980s, with the development of "equal access" principles. In *Widmar v. Vincent*

(1981), the Supreme Court decided that a university's prohibition on the use of school facilities by religious student groups during nonschool hours (when these facilities were available to nonreligious student groups) violated the free-exercise clause of the First Amendment while being unnecessary under the establishment clause (as the university argued). Congress extended the Court's "equal access" principle to cover secondary schools in the Equal Access Act of 1984 (Title VIII, Public Law 98-377), which was upheld against an establishment clause challenge in *Board of Education v. Mergens* (1990).[55]

While the Equal Access Act was a "religious liberty" bill, aimed at preventing government discrimination against religious speech in secondary schools, other legislative developments began an equally significant push to give religious social-service agencies access to government aid programs, most importantly, as contractors or grantees in the provision of government-funded services. These legislative developments eroded the secularizing ethos of federal welfare contracting in an incremental way that would culminate in positive protections afforded by charitable choice law. The Supreme Court followed the lead of legislators by significantly modifying establishment clause restrictions pertaining to government aid programs in *Bowen v. Kendrick* in 1988 (as described earlier); *Rosenberger v. Rector and Visitors* in 1995 (finding a university policy denying student-activity funds for a religious magazine to violate the religious liberty of student petitioners while not being required by the establishment clause); *Agostini v. Felton* in 1997 (overturning an earlier Supreme Court Decision prohibiting public school teachers from teaching in parochial schools); and *Mitchell v. Helms* in 2000 (upholding eligibility of religious schools for material aid under a federal education law).

The legislative impetus behind these constitutional developments first surfaced in the Adolescent Family Life Act of 1981 (AFLA), sponsored by Jeremiah Denton, a Republican Senator from Alabama. Responding to an earlier teen pregnancy bill that focused on contraception, AFLA had the goal of promoting abstinence-based services and adoption, with an emphasis on excluding abortion and also involving religious groups. Grant applicants were specifically directed to explain how they would work with religious groups.[56] According to Rebekah Saul, funding under AFLA was used to develop "fear-based" curricula such as *Sex Respect*, and one grantee used a curriculum with such themes as "The Church's Teachings on Abortion."[57] The American Civil Liberties Union and the American Jewish Congress brought a First Amendment challenge against AFLA in 1983, achieving a U.S. District Court decision declaring the statute unconstitutional on its face. In

1988, the Supreme Court reversed this decision in *Bowen v. Kendrick*, ruling that AFLA was not unconstitutional on its face simply for allowing religious providers to participate in the program. However, it remanded the case for further scrutiny to see if the act, as applied, was allowing aid to flow to "pervasively sectarian" institutions for constitutionally prohibited religious purposes such as worship, prayer, bible study, and so on. Thus emerged the "equal treatment" doctrine as applied to faith-based social services, providing for "neutral" (open to all faiths and no faith alike) accommodation of religious providers as contractors, grantees, and so forth, yet maintaining a categorical persuasion against programs not sufficiently segregated from congregations/houses of worship, as well as a strict separation of government funds from religious activities and content. Although the category of "pervasively sectarian" would later be set aside as unworkable (in *Mitchell v. Helms*, 2000), neutral eligibility of religious providers, contingent on strict separation of funds from religious activities, is now the prevailing constitutional standard for faith-based initiatives on the Bush model. Ira Lupu, a leading constitutional scholar (and advocate of the closest thing to a consensus view among charitable choice supporters) sharply summarized, in congressional testimony provided on June 7, 2001, the evolution of establishment clause law as it pertains to faith-based social providers: "Government may become a partner in the secular activities of faith-based organizations whose efforts advance secular purposes, but may not become a partner in—nor regulate—the private project of religious worship, transformation, and belief."

Yet Lupu further argued that current and proposed charitable choice provisions, which generally prohibit use of federal funds for "sectarian worship, instruction, or proselytization," do not go far enough in specifying what is prohibited under the establishment clause. Government funds cannot be used, Lupu determines, for "any materials, any counseling, or any other services that incorporate concepts of divine, ultimate, or superhuman authority," as, for example, in the case of Alcoholics Anonymous, which he notes has been denied government support in recent federal court cases.[58] Although I am not a constitutional scholar and propose no alternative theory of my own, it can be argued that Lupu pulls back too far from the logic of neutrality to maintain any semblance of the principle. A more promising approach, formulated around the idea of limiting government's impact on religious choices and pursuits, has been developed similarly by Douglas Laycock and Carl Esbeck. I return to this matter in the conclusion below, but for the moment point to a formulation of the neutrality principle Esbeck published in 1997, discussing *Bowen*: "When the dispute is over a welfare program in which faith-based social service providers desire to participate, the neutrality principle requires government to follow a rule of minimizing the impact of its actions on religion, to wit: all service providers may participate in a welfare program without regard to religion and free of eligibility criteria that require the abandonment of a provider's religious expression or character."[59] The contrast between Lupu's separationist standard, essentially prohibiting federal contact with religion, and Esbeck's more functional approach of minimizing government impact *on* religion, reflects deep conceptual differences about the purposes of the establishment clause and may ultimately portend the battle lines to be drawn should the *Bowen/Mitchell* line be pressed further in the future.

As *Bowen* was being decided, another bill, the Act for Better Child Care, was introduced by Senator Christopher Dodd of Connecticut (D-CT), known by shorthand as the ABC bill.[60] The $2.5 billion bill (the final version grew to $12.5 billion), backed by a large advocacy coalition led by the Children's Defense Fund, created the first government program of child-care subsidies for low-income families, in addition to regulatory measures designed to improve the quality of child care and create a pool of eligible providers. This legislation was a response to the growing number of mothers and young women entering the labor force. The bill did not specifically call for the inclusion of religious groups, but rather assumed this involvement (the 1980s saw a significant rise in the number of church-based child-care centers) and provided detailed guidelines in what appeared to be a very aggressive effort to separate religion from the services funded by government (in sections 19 and 20 of the original bill). There is some evidence that this separation framework was added at the urging of school-voucher opponents (particularly teachers' unions), who saw the bill as a wedge for further development of private-school subsidies at the primary and secondary levels.[61] The guidelines for faith-based child-care centers receiving federal funds under the bill included the removal or covering of religious symbols and required compliance with state and local licensing laws, even where some states themselves provided certain exemptions. Non-discrimination in religion pertaining to both beneficiaries and employees paid with public funds was strictly required, answering the constitutional question of how federal funding affects religious hiring-rights as provided under Title VII the Civil Rights Act of 1964. This question was left hanging by the Supreme Court in *Corporation of the Presiding Bishop v. Amos* in 1987, which held that the social agencies of a church or religious association retain faith-based hiring rights but did not address whether or how the receipt of federal funds by such agencies affects their employment discretion. The ABC bill was the first effort to explicitly prohibit "government-funded religious discrimination"—a commonly heard slogan in the later battle over the faith-base initiative—in the emerging field of federal contracting with religious groups. Sections 19 and 20 aroused fierce opposition from the U.S. Catholic Conference and the National Association of Evangelicals, as well as Phyllis Schlafly of the Eagle Form, who made the most far-reaching point when she described the bill as discriminatory against mothers who care for their own children at home.[62] Marian Wright Edelman of the progressive Children's Defense Fund actually agreed with conservative criticisms of the church-state provisions in the bill and even recommended removing the anti-discrimination clauses. Such restrictive measures were unprecedented in a federal statute and threatened the whole political idea of federal child-care support, some progressives believed. Some otherwise supportive groups such as the National Organization of Women, however, threatened to withdraw their support if the strict church-state language was removed.[63]

With input from the U.S. Catholic Conference (the American bishops' advocacy association) and other groups, substantial changes appeared in the ABC bill when it was considered by the Senate Labor and Human Resources Committee in the summer of 1988. These included replacing the detailed church-state guidance of the original bill with a general prohibition against using federal funds for proselytizing. The prohibition on religious hiring rights was removed, as was a prohibition on churches using federal funds for health and safety upgrades as required by the statute. The National Education Association (the country's largest teachers' union) cited church-state concerns and fear of "subsidizing discrimination" in withdrawing support for this version of the bill.[64] At the same time, religious groups had mixed reactions. The National Council of Churches, the American Jewish committee, and liberal Baptist groups sought stronger constitutional safeguards to prevent a "segregated child-care system based on religion," while conservative groups attacked the legislation as a government assault on parental rights and "traditional homes."[65] The Catholic Conference and the Orthodox Jewish group Agudath Israel, among other religious groups, led the way in pushing further for pluralistic accommodation of sectarian providers, through a voucher mechanism if necessary. They argued that *Bowen v. Kendrick* should be read as allowing such accommodation of faith-based child care on grounds of neutrality between different types, particularly if federal funds were directed to such providers by parental choice in a voucherized form.[66] This view eventually prevailed in the final version of the legislation signed by the elder President Bush in 1990. Renamed the Child Care Development Block Grant Act, this legislation resolved the interest-group conflict over church-state separation in federal child-care assistance programs by incorporating a voucher mechanism through which sectarian providers would be eligible to receive government funds. Those receiving funds directly under purchase-of-service contracts, on the other hand, were prohibited from incorporating religious activities or instruction and could not use religious criteria in hiring for positions supported with federal funds. The voucher component was retained when the legislation was reauthorized in 1996 under the Personal Responsibility and Work Opportunity Reconciliation Act. As one scholar described it in 2001, in a Washington panel discussion sponsored by the Pew Forum on Religion and Public Life, this act "represents the first significant effort to legislatively define church-state relations in the provisions of a social service program," although, as she further noted, little hard data was then available on either the extent of federal voucher use to aid in the purchase of sectarian child-care or on the level of interest and engagement in this subsidy program among different denominations and faith traditions.[67]

Although the voucher component of the Child Care Development Block Grant Act quelled the storm over child-care assistance, that battle and the earlier battle over AFLA set the stage for further efforts to expand the participation of religious service providers in federal aid programs and to codify a new general regime of protections to insure their religious integrity. With its entrance into sex education and child care, two areas of long-standing traditional concern to religious communities, the American welfare state had clearly reached a cultural tipping point in its social expansion.

As chapter 2 shows in more detail, with the build-up toward welfare reform in the early 1990s, religious conservatives took the problems that had emerged in the battles over sex education and child care in, essentially, two different directions. The most vocal religious conservatives, evangelicals aligned with the Republican Party or further to the right, increasingly argued that the solution to this problem was "rolling back" the welfare state, that is, public disengagement from social needs and a return to private charity centered on the church. The guiding assumption of this view was not simply that government welfare was wrong or bad in any form, but that, in particular, it had failed (or was failing) to reduce poverty and social dysfunction precisely because the presence of government in these areas seriously *weakened* the very institutions best positioned and most suited to help struggling people. It did so by usurping the traditional mission functions of the churches and, more generally, by replacing voluntary giving with redistributive compulsion, thereby voiding the whole system of essential human ingredients such as compassion and responsibility. Other religious conservatives, particularly Roman Catholics and Reformed Christians in the Dutch tradition, however, took a more positive, even "progressive" view of this "domain conflict," seeing it as an opportunity to reconstruct the welfare system from a very different traditional standpoint of distinct but coordinated responsibilities. As framed in the Welfare Responsibility Project of the Center for Public Justice as early as 1993 (whose input would later play a defining role in the development of the faith-based initiative), effective welfare reform required not simply a rollback of the state but a re-ordering of its purposes and operation around the goal of protecting social structures and enabling groups and communities to obtain a stake in the common welfare and a just or sufficient share of the benefits of the land:

> In contrast to current approaches to poverty, a biblical perspective suggests that in order for governments to fulfill their own moral obligation to do jus-tice, they must do more than react to the negative economic effects of social degradation. They must do more than simply redistribute material resources to those beneath the poverty line or withhold such resources in order to pro-pel unemployed individuals back into the marketplace. Rather, governments should pursue more fundamental reforms, seeking to restore effective action on the part of all who bear responsibility for poverty.[68]

In the aftermath of the battle over church-state issues in federal child-care legislation, moreover, few were satisfied with the "voucher" solution that it codified in this important area. Church-state separation groups and some liberal religious group did not see vouchers as a constitutional solution, and some argued that it was even more constitutionally problematic be-cause, whatever the mechanism of payment, it permitted federal dollars to flow into the coffers of religious organizations and, potentially, to finance religious instruction and activities. The role of parental choice did not mit-igate this potential unconstitutional effect, many argued. From the conser-vative side, some considered vouchers to be a weak alternative that would be under-utilized because of information deficits, leaving intact the over-whelmingly secular composition of the social welfare system, when it was clear that a new diversity of approaches was now needed. Sidestepping this conflict entirely, other pieces of legislation after the Child Care Develop-ment Block Grant Act simply provided blanket restrictions on "religious use" of federal funds, as many laws commonly provided before AFLA began the push for more specific (and accommodating) terms. For example, the statute that created the Corporation for National Service, which became law in 1995, categorizes religious organizations as an "ineligible service category" along with businesses, political groups, and labor unions, unless the services they provide with government assistance do not involve any kind of religious instruction or activities or maintenance/operation of facilities devoted to such activities.[69] Thus, even as the voucher compromise seemed to open new ground in this growing conflict between expanding welfare and faith-based approaches, the main channels of federal program activity and funding remained blocked to religious providers operating outside of the secular ethos of welfare contracting.

In some circles—those that would ultimately most influence political developments in this area—practical skepticism about the limited scope and feasibility of voucher programs reflected, also, a distinctive view of the role of government. Here, while the problem of restricted religious choice in social services was central—something particularly addressed by vouchers—a deeper, structural focus on the role of religious groups also grew clearer. This was partly informed by the jurisprudence of "religious autonomy": churches and religious groups have long had a kind of collective or group freedom from state interference in a limited range of internal aspects, such as clerical appointments and theological content. Now, however, there was a sense that the greatly expanded welfare services of recent decades had reached a point of fatally compromising the character of religious organizations by exacting high spiritual entry-costs for access to their own mission fields. In this analysis, however, the problem was not seen as simply inherent in any notion of public welfare or even extensive social spending, as was the view of many religious conservatives, most notably Marvin Olasky and other politically engaged evangelicals, who were looking at the same problem at the same time. Rather, the problem was seen as one of disordered structure and disordered purpose in the design of welfare spending and its goals. There was no question of the need for social spending, and significant reason, perhaps, to believe that more social spending was needed precisely to uplift the religious work and the family and neighborly bonds that create communities and protect them from destructive forces.

With President Clinton's promise to "end welfare as we know it," American welfare policy became the laboratory for Washington's largest experiment in devolutionary policy reform to date. Although it was a much bigger prize in the church-state struggle that had been simmering and boiling up in social policy debates since the Adolescent Family Life Act, welfare reform did not generate much input on these issues. Indeed they were hardly even considered as welfare reform became a reality in 1995 and 1996. The charitable choice provisions of the welfare reform bill of 1996 (Section 104), well known now as the statutory foundation of the faith-based initiative, were quietly inserted by then-Senator John Ashcroft with virtually no floor debate or public comment. In fact, these provisions were the product of fairly extensive debate and revision among a small network of religious lawyers and intellectuals working far outside the standard precincts of conservative religious influence in those revivalistic two years after the Republican revolution of 1994.

The 1996 charitable choice provisions were the brainchild of Carl Esbeck, a law professor at the University of Missouri who would later head up the task-force for faith-based initiatives in the Bush Justice Department. Esbeck began working on charitable choice with fellow Missourian John Ashcroft's Senate staff early in 1995; his former law student Annie Billings was a legislative aide to Ashcroft and a chief liaison on charitable choice. Esbeck was motivated to develop charitable choice by what he describes as "government discrimination against faith-based social service providers," and indirectly, he believes, discrimination against poor communities, where people are unnecessarily restricted in accessing services offered by religious entities.[70] He began thinking about developing provisions to remedy this problem after attending a consultation on faith-based providers and social policy held by the Center for Public Justice (CPJ) based near Washington, D.C. (and a key influence that I discuss in more detail further on). In the spring of 1995, Esbeck developed the first draft of provisions for what he termed "Institutional Independence—Religious Social Sector." Interestingly, the first point he emphasizes in these early drafts is that federal monies received for services provided by faith-based organizations are not to be considered "federal financial assistance" under civil rights laws if the organization receives no more than the "fair market value of such services as the organization in turn provides in assistance to beneficiaries." This seems to have been an effort to protect religious providers from challenges pertaining to their receipt of government funds—that is, by classifying them as contractors of third-party services rather than as beneficiaries of government assistance.

It is also interesting to note the greater force and specificity of Esbeck's original language pertaining to religious autonomy:

> Such an organization [defined as a contractor for third-party services] retains
> its independence from government, including the organization's control over
> the definition, development, expression, and transmission of its religious be-
> liefs and practices. Such an organization's polity or form of internal gover-
> nance shall not be required to be altered in order to be eligible as a provider,
> nor shall such an organization be required to remove religious art, icons,

scripture, or other symbols from buildings used to provide assistance to the ultimate beneficiaries. Such an organization may, on a religious basis, select, employ, promote, discipline, and dismiss its clerics and other ecclesiastics, directors, officers, employees, members, and volunteers. Such an organization may require that ultimate beneficiaries not disrupt its social-service program[;] accordingly the organization may deny services to beneficiaries who are disruptive.[71]

In a brief paper he put together that spring for a legal conference a De-Paul University (dated April 4, 1995), Esbeck lays out the remedial rationale for charitable choice as illustrated in lower-level case law, including the following cases: *Arneth v. Gross* (1988), in which a federally funded Catholic foster-care home for girls was forced to provide them with contraceptive prescriptions; *Wilder v. Bernstein* (1988), in which church-operated foster-care homes receiving government funding were regulated as to religious discretion used in placing children and religious symbols visible in homes, and were required to provide access to contraception and abortion services for children under care; *Dodge v. Salvation Army*, in which a member of the Wiccan religion successfully sued the Salvation Army for employment discrimination when she was fired for using office resources for religious purposes—arguing that a religious organizations' Title VII hiring rights violate the establishment clause if the positions in question are substantially financed with federal funds; *Fordham University v. Brown* (1994), in which a university radio station was denied federal funding because its programming included weekly Roman Catholic mass broadcasts.[72]

Esbeck further lays out in interesting fashion the political theory of charitable choice, as expressed (in his view) in the Supreme Court's doctrinal shift toward what he and other architects of the new regime describe as "equal treatment," "neutrality," or sometimes "substantive neutrality" toward religious groups. We will look more closely at the legal arguments in the next section, but it is important to understand how the policy design of charitable choice was influenced by developments in constitutional law. Esbeck describes two different kinds of "neutrality," one that leads to more cooperation between church and state, and one that requires further separation. What might be called "cooperative neutrality" is based on the principle that government should not act in any way that influences "religious choice" in society—whether it be the decisions of religious bodies trying to find a way to carry out their social missions, or the choices of those seeking services who may prefer a religious approach (as one option among many). The First Amendment's "Congress shall make no law respecting an establishment of religion," in Esbeck's view (which he has developed with vast scholarship over the last twenty years), does not simply restrict government support of religious organizations (as many believe); rather it embodies what he describes as a "structural principle" of minimizing the impact of government on religion. The separation of church and state does not require a complete institutional separation of all government functions and resources from any kind of contact with religious organizations or expression—that is, a public purgation of religion. Rather, separation means a minimization of impact or constraints on religion.

From this perspective, a policy design such as charitable choice necessarily begins with the problem of what I have called the welfare state's "domain conflict" with religious welfare provision. This kind of political diagnosis, the heart of the original *Kulturkampf* (long before there was an ascendant middle-class counterculture) begins with the problem of welfare-state expansion into the churches' natural mission fields. The welfare state's increasing control (through taxation and other powers) of the "resources diverted to charitable use," Esbeck argued, creates a context in which the church is more or less forced to seek government support in order to perform its essential missions with meaningful effect, which compulsion, in turn, requires greater care for religious autonomy on the part of the state. This is not "establishment" of religion precisely because it is an effort to diminish the government's impact on religion. Neutrality toward religion in a context of functional displacement of its mission must begin with a premise of cooperation. That is, promoting pluralistic cooperation not only treats religion "neutrally" or "equally" but also ameliorates its functional displacement from welfare domains increasingly dominated by the state. Furthermore, "avoiding a monolithic, state-monopolized structure to the delivery of services is desirable. Words such as *diversity, enrichment, enliven, pluralistic, innovative, creative, competitive,* and *free choice* attractively package this sought-after differentiated social order."[73] So too, the concept of subsidiarity, Esbeck specified in the same briefing paper, helps us differentiate between the church and its social agencies. According to this Catholic idea, later to become a commonplace in public commentary on the faith-based initiative, government should fund the latter—the social agencies—precisely because their natural (and only) purpose is to meet temporal needs, as so many statutes prescribe. So too, religious fear of government is "pathological" in a democracy—if you consider that government, like religious association, is a creation of society.[74]

These terms and ideas were refined in consultation with academic colleagues at the conference on church-state law at DePaul University and later with members of the Center for Public Justice, whom Esbeck had known for many years. Further draft language was added in a version faxed to Ashcroft's Senate office on April 11, 1995. Here the "Purpose" is specified first: "Participation by religious providers is essential if the continued privatization of social services is to succeed.[75] Many such organizations, however, are reluctant to participate as providers in Federal programs because the regulations that accompany Federal financial assistance are often invasive of their religious autonomy."[76] Here the language calls for religious providers under a given social service statute to retain independent control over their administration, beliefs, and practices, and it prohibits government from requiring alterations of internal governance or the removal of religious symbolism from facilities to be eligible to participate in government grant or contract programs. Here too is the idea, later discarded, of protecting religious organizations' "civil rights exemption" regarding employment by deeming that monies disbursed to religious organizations under the statute are not construed as "federal financial assistance." It also adds a provision of federal judicial recourse for religious groups denied their rights as specified under the statute.[77] Notably, the earliest drafts of charitable choice did not include provisions for protecting the religious liberty of service recipients, a gap later rectified by a religious non-discrimination clause imposed on providers as well as a notice requirement for client right-of-access to nonreligious providers.

Charitable choice made its legislative debut on May 23, 1995, as part of a welfare reform bill introduced in the Senate by John Ashcroft (The Individual Accountability Act, S 842, 104th Cong., 1st sess.). Later, on August 11, 1995, Senator Robert Dole inserted a slightly different version as a modification of the Senate Republican leadership's welfare reform bill, the Work Opportunity Act of 1995.[78] The most notable adjustment compared to Esbeck's draft language was the inclusion of a clause requiring religious nondiscrimination against beneficiaries. In terms of religious hiring rights, Esbeck's rationale of protecting religious organizations' Title VII exemptions by stipulating that receipt of federal funds by faith-based contractors/grantees shall not be considered "federal financial assistance" was replaced with a statement of general principle to the effect that faith-based hiring and employment discretion are not affected by receipt of federal funds.

Church-state separation advocates and liberal religious groups sprang into action on finding the charitable choice language in the modified Senate leadership welfare bill, forming an alliance called the Coalition Against Religious Discrimination. Proposed legislative amendments that came out of this advocacy included provisions requiring that grant recipients be fiscally structured in such a way as to strictly segregate federal welfare funds from houses of worship or any program dedicated to inherently religious activities. Other immediate controversies addressed by proposed amendments included the problem of federal preemption of state laws under charitable choice, as many states have strict "no aid to religion" standards (constitutional and statutory) attached to public funds as well as anti-discrimination laws that would prohibit religious employment discrimination as permitted under charitable choice.

The Republican bill (HR 4), still containing charitable choice, made it out of conference and was passed by both houses at the end of 1995, but President Clinton vetoed the bill. By the following summer, however, Clinton needed to sign a version of welfare reform. What amounted to waving a white flag in the home-stretch of his presidential reelection bid (more about this in the next chapter) thus became welfare reform as we know it today (The Personal Responsibility and Work Opportunity Reconciliation Act, P.L. 104-193 [1996]); and charitable choice (Section 104), carefully preserved by John Ashcroft as welfare reform evolved, became the law of the land. Few would have predicted at the time that one tiny section of the bill, which drew little attention at the time, would generate far more controversy, in the end, than any of the main provisions of welfare reform itself. Certainly no one foresaw Section 104 becoming the cornerstone of a transgovernmental reform movement and the signature domestic policy of a born-again Republican president.

The contours of charitable choice as passed into law flow from a new central principle of public administration: religious social-service providers have a statutory right to contract with the government without sacrificing their religious character. This right originally had it broadest reach under Title I of welfare reform, known as Temporary Assistance for Needy Families (TANF). TANF replaced traditional cash assistance welfare (Aid to Families with Dependent Children) with a block-grant system in which states design and administer their own welfare programs consistent with certain federal policy rules and regulations, including charitable choice. The reason why charitable choice is important under TANF is that the policy emphasis here (enforced by benefit time-limits) is on getting people off welfare and into the workforce, a process requiring more spending on services and less on cash assistance—less than 40 percent of TANF money is spent on cash assistance today. Three other programs approved by Congress since 1996 have incorporated charitable choice provisions: a reauthorization of the Community Services Block Grant Program, and addiction treatment and prevention programs under Titles V and XIX of the

Public Health Services Act. As a matter of public law, charitable choice applied to programs disseminating nearly $22 billion annually in federal funds as of 2001.

In the first phase of charitable choice implementation, from 1996 to 2002, service areas governed by its rules included job training, education, nutrition, health, and housing. Under the Personal Responsibility and Work Opportunity Reconciliation Act, charitable choice also applies to the food stamp program, Medicaid, and Supplemental Security Income (SSI) where these might be implemented by nongovernmental providers under contract with state governments or as part of a voucher program. Many other bills introduced but not enacted by Congress after 1996 incorporated charitable choice provisions into other areas, such as juvenile justice, youth drug and mental health services, fatherhood and marriage promotion, child support, homeownership, community renewal incentives, and literacy.

Charitable choice law substantially follows the direction Esbeck provided, with certain additions and adjustments.[79] Pertaining to welfare reform, as originally enacted, the most basic requirement of charitable choice is religious eligibility: if a TANF-funded program chooses to work with nongovernmental agencies to deliver services or benefits, no organization can be excluded from participating simply because it is a religious organization or affiliated with a religion. As Douglas Laycock argued before a House Judiciary Committee hearing on charitable choice and the constitution, in June 2001, the importance of non-discrimination rules pertaining to religion is generally underestimated as a matter of government administration. Decisions about who receives contracts under a given social service statute are, in most cases, lodged entirely in the executive branch, it is important to remember. As Laycock described it, "Under most of our existing and historic programs, contracting with a religious provider is discretionary with the executive. Some bureaucrats prefer to deal with religious organizations; some prefer to avoid them. Some bureaucrats may prefer certain religions and avoid others."[80] Statutory rules for contracting with religious providers, as provided by charitable choice, effectively void executive discretion in this area of discriminatory potential, and this is a "step forward for religious liberty," Laycock explained.

Beyond the basic principle of religious nonexclusion, the primary goal of charitable choice, formulated in the earliest stages of its development, is to protect the religious autonomy and character of faith-based organizations that deliver public services. States are required to deal with religious organizations "on the same basis as any other nongovernmental provider" and "without impairing [their] religious character." Reciprocally, faith-based providers cannot discriminate against beneficiaries, and beneficiaries must have access to a nonreligious provider if they so desire or if no preferred religious provider is available. Both providers and beneficiaries may bring claims against infringements of these rights in a federal court.

Charitable choice provides for protection of religious autonomy regarding corporate structure, governance, trusteeship, and so on, as well as control of mission—"control over the definition, development, practice, and expression of its religious beliefs." Also permitted is the maintenance of a religious environment: there can be no requirement to remove "religious art, icons, scripture, or other symbols" from a participating religious facility. Another protection that charitable choice law affords faith-based providers is control over employment policy—which for many is the most important assurance from government. Much more clearly than in the earlier drafts, charitable choice law (in every ratified version) explicitly affirms that faith-based contractors retain their Title VII right of religious discretion in hiring and employment policy. Decried as "government-funded discrimination," this was the biggest source of controversy as Ashcroft and, later, Bush and congressional Republicans sought to expand charitable choice across the whole social safety net.[81] Charitable choice law also explicitly states that faith-based contractors are subject to all other non-discrimination laws (covering race, sex, age, national origin, etc.), but it also stipulates federal preemption of any state laws (including constitutional provisions) that might restrict or exclude religious participation in public programs financed with federal dollars, including laws prohibiting religious employment discrimination in publicly funded programs. If states mingle federal and state funds in their TANF programs, charitable choice preempts state law as generally provided. States are given the option, however, of segregating federal and state funds, thereby limiting the reach of charitable choice only to those programs or contracts financed with segregated federal funds.

Requirements attached to federal funding differ according to the type of funding arrangements. Most commonly, a state TANF program will use federal funds to make purchase-of-service contracts for the delivery of services. Under these contracts, no federal funds can be spent on religious activities, instruction, or materials (a strong common thread with earlier church-state provisions in social-welfare laws). The other basic arrangement states are permitted to use is a voucher system, whereby individuals receive certificates directly from the government that they can redeem for specified services from eligible providers. In this form, charitable choice law does not explicitly prohibit religious activities, instruction, and so on as part of a social service purchased with federal funds.

Although charitable choice is clearly the cornerstone of the whole edifice of faith-based initiatives constructed during the Bush years, Bush himself developed a template for the faith-based initiative long before coming to Washington, and he did so in consultation with the same religious experts who first devised charitable choice and, later, would play an important role in organizing and implementing the White House effort. We return to this in chapter 2, but here I simply note how unusual a process this was, rare not only in the consistency of ideas and goals, as a unique state experiment was transformed into a signature national policy, but also, I argue, in the transformative content of the ideas as they defied categorization in the conventional terms of either welfare reform or the culture war of those times. That result was not simply innovation for the sake of change, but rather a new application of certain very old ideas.

Shortly after he took office in January 2001, President Bush issued two executive orders to launch his Faith-Based and Community Initiative (FBCI). The first (Executive Order 13198) created the White House Office of Faith-Based and Community Initiatives, and the second (Executive Order 13199) created satellite offices in each of the five major cabinet agencies—Health and Human Services, Housing and Urban Development, Labor, Education, and Justice. He also released a legislative prospectus for the FBCI called *Rallying the Armies of Compassion*, in which he described the new White House office as "the engine that drives the Administration's goal of reorienting Federal social policy across the board."[82] This reorientation of federal social policy had three dimensions: (1) to promote and help devise legislative action in Congress on behalf of faith-based social services; (2) to systematically identify and dismantle executive-branch programmatic barriers to federal support for religious institutions in the provision of social services; and (3) to increase public support for both federal action on behalf of faith-based social services as well as increased private giving to religious charities and service providers.[83] Translated from the campaign trail and his earlier Texas effort, the faith-based initiative was clearly set out as Bush's signature domestic policy agenda for the nation. It was also a major innovation in presidential history: never before had a dedicated infrastructure been established for the purpose of helping religious groups participate in government aid programs. This was immediately set in motion as Bush ordered the satellite offices to conduct in-depth internal audits of rules, regulations, procurement practices, and outreach methods in their agencies, with the aim of removing barriers to faith-based providers. Additional satellite offices were later established in the Departments of Agriculture, Commerce, and

Veterans Affairs, as well as the Small Business Administration and the U.S. Agency for International Development.

A coalition of liberal clergy, civil rights advocates, civil libertarians, and church-state separationists sprang into action as the FBCI put a national spotlight on charitable choice law for the first time, something they had only fought in a piecemeal way up to that point. Yet there was also a fair amount of conservative resistance as well, largely from the Protestant far-right, including Pat Robertson and Marvin Olasky. The latter's more friendly criticism was nonetheless surprising to many, as he was considered at the time to be the chief inspiration behind Bush's embrace of "compassionate conservatism." In fact, Olasky's break (more or less) with Bush occurred along preexisting fault lines that reveal an important political story about charitable choice and the public church-state model it reflects—as we will see in the next chapter. But aside from these more principled disputes, perhaps the loudest criticism came from fundamentalists decrying government "meddling" in religion and the possibility that cults and fringe religions might benefit from Bush's plan, which stressed "equal treatment."[84] At the same time, moderate evangelicals were put on guard and sometimes angered by official comments of the OFBCI's first director, John DiIulio. DiIulio repeatedly stressed that the faith-based initiative had nothing to do with "funding religion," and in a major speech before the National Association of Evangelicals, he essentially took Bush's evangelical critics to task as denizens of white, ex-urban enclaves with little experience in "community-serving missions" compared to the urban black and Latino pastors who had rallied to Bush's side.[85]

With a push from religious conservatives, Representatives J. C. Watts (R-OK) and Tony Hall (D-OH) introduced HR 7, the Community Solutions Act of 2001, two months after Bush's launching of the FBCI. This bill was the House Republicans' major legislation in support of the faith-based initiative. Primarily, it was a vehicle to expand charitable choice into new program areas, including juvenile crime, domestic violence, housing, and GED assistance. HR 7's charitable choice provisions were more aggressive than existing law in several sensitive areas. It introduced more specific language permitting federal preemption of state anti-discrimination laws under charitable choice, and it weakened beneficiary protections against proselytization.[86] Another change introduced later, of critical interest to religious conservatives, was a provision permitting the executive branch to "voucherize" grant programs without congressional approval, thereby removing constitutional barriers to government funding of otherwise prohibited religious activities and content, on the principle of "beneficiary choice."[87] As discussed earlier, the Child Care Development Block Grant established the first such religion-oriented voucher program in the early 1990s, which was never challenged in the courts; in 2002, however, the Supreme Court (in *Zelman v. Simmons-Harris*) upheld a Cleveland school voucher program that included religious schools, giving constitutional approval to religious receipt of indirect, "voucherized" aid for the first time.

HR 7, however, never became law and so was not affected by this Supreme Court decision. On July 19, 2001, over opposition mainly centered on the question of faith-based hiring rights and federal preemption of state anti-discrimination laws, the bill passed in the House of Representatives by a vote of 233 to 198. But in the Senate, which had come under Democratic control the previous spring after Vermont Senator Jim Jeffords left the Republican Party, there was no chance of passing even a compromise version of this bill. Instead, Connecticut Democrat Joseph Lieberman worked with Pennsylvania Republican Rick Santorum to introduce a bill packaging charitable-giving incentives (which both had been supporting in different forms even prior to Bush's arrival in Washington) with technical support provisions for smaller, community-based providers. In February 2002, the Charity, Aid, Recovery, and Empowerment Act (CARE) was introduced with support from the White House, centered on charitable tax deductions at a cost of about $11 billion, "compassion capital" funds for technical assistance, and an increase in the Social Service Block Grant. While the bill provided for no expansion of charitable choice, Title III restated charitable choice rules in compromise language denying federal preemption of state and local anti-discrimination laws while remaining silent on faith-based hiring rights more generally. Social-service advocacy groups supported the bill for the tax provisions, but Republican support dwindled without charitable choice expansion, and some Democratic Senators withheld their support over the bill's silence on faith-based hiring rights. With left and right pulling against the broader consensus supporting the bill's tax provisions, the bill did not make it to the floor of the Senate and finally died in the fall of 2002 over controversies regarding proposed Democratic amendments.[88]

Even as charitable choice legislation had begun to falter in the summer of 2001, however, the White House was laying the groundwork for an administrative strategy to achieve similar goals. In August 2001, the White House released *Unlevel Playing Field*, the administrative audit of federal agencies ordered by the president when he took office. This is an important document for understanding what the faith-based initiative was about. Although framed in the language of group rights and anti-discrimination — creating a "level playing field" for religious groups — the motivation was not only about securing religious rights; it was also about transforming the role of government and restoring a proper order of public responsibility and religious life. Key people involved in the effort have publicly acknowledged this, but more broadly, the contours are plain to see in light of how church-state relations have evolved in this important policy area over twenty years. More than superficial resemblances with Christian Democratic welfare systems, at least as pertaining to social services, are revealing, as I clarify later. Yet even in its own stated terms of "non-discrimination," the faith-based initiative reordered welfare governance as no other reform and no other executive mandate in the modern era had done.

This was summarized well in a statement by law professor Robert Tuttle, a leading expert on the faith-based initiative:

> I think we have seen about the most dramatic administrative change that is possible for those inside the Beltway to conceive. . . . The idea that you go from a government that was in form as well as practice quite hostile to many kinds of religious organizations participating in government funding programs to one that has now institutionalized an expectation—it's not always practiced, but an expectation of equal treatment. I mean, that's a remarkable change, and that's a change that didn't happen because of Charitable Choice, although the groundwork was there. It's happened because of the Faith-Based and Community Initiative.[89]

A report from the nonpartisan Roundtable on Religion and Social Welfare Policy documented how the faith-based initiative penetrated ten government agencies in what can only be described as a systemwide effort at regime change. "In the absence of new legislative authority," the report asserts, "the President has aggressively advanced the Faith-Based Initiative through executive orders, rule changes, managerial realignment in federal agencies, and other innovative uses of the prerogatives of his office."[90] The report argues that other presidents, from Franklin D. Roosevelt to Ronald Reagan, have used executive powers in similar ways, but these efforts "typically lack *local cells* that provide the *feet and hands* needed to organize and implement presidential initiatives."[91] What Bush did differently was to endow his initiative with a dedicated, transgovernmental infrastructure, with a White House hub and satellite offices "empowered to articulate, advance and oversee *coordinated* efforts to win more financial support for faith-based groups as publicly aided providers of domestic public services."[92]

Following the recommendations of *Unlevel Playing Field*, White House agencies overhauled internal procedures to encourage and assist smaller religious providers to apply for and win federal discretionary grants as well as an increasing share of block-grant funds available through states and localities. This overhaul included numerous regulatory changes, either proposed or finalized, which "together mark a major shift in the constitutional separation of church and state," the Roundtable asserted. Federal job-training vouchers can now be used to obtain educational credentials for religious employment. Government-forfeited properties can now be converted into houses of worship, and government funds can be used for repairs or preservation of religious buildings. A government grantee's right to discriminate in employment decisions based on religion is now enshrined in the new rules, although still prohibited where statutory restrictions exist (for example in the Workforce Investment Act of 1998) or where preempted by state or local anti-discrimination laws. All together, sixteen new regulations, remedying agency barriers to charitable choice implementation, were proposed and put into effect between 2003 and 2006.

These administrative changes applied to $65 billion in discretionary grants made by federal agencies, according to the White House. In May 2004, an official tally of faith-based grants at the departments of Health and Human Services, Housing and Urban Development, Labor, Education, and Justice totaled $1.17 billion—8 percent out of a total of $14.5 billion. In 2005, about $2.1 billion was give to religious groups, nearly 11 percent of the total pool of $20 billion. In 2006, according to the White House, faith-based organizations received more than three thousand social-service grants, a 16 percent share, worth nearly $2.2 billion. Between 2003 and 2006, the number of grants awarded to faith-based organizations by the five main cabinet agencies of the FBCI rose 41 percent.[93] In addition, the FBCI's Compassion Capital Fund distributed approximately $264 million for small-organization capacity-building as well as grassroots subcontracting through intermediary organizations.

The FCBI also moved aggressively to promote state-level dedicated action. While only eight states enacted legislation incorporating charitable choice provisions between 1996 and 2003, by 2005, twenty-seven states had passed legislation that included provisions regarding involvement with faith-based organizations. Twenty-eight states launched significant administrative initiatives to encourage faith-based involvement in their social programs.[94] As of 2008, thirty-five states and more than one hundred cities had designated an office or individual to serve as a liaison with faith-based groups.[95] Some of the actions resulting from these changes include modifying contract processes, encouraging contractors to subcontract with religious groups, and providing capacity-building grants and technical assistance. [96] Between 2002 and 2004, sixteen states increased both the amount of funding and the number of awards that went to faith-based organizations.

A New Church-State Order

In his final State of the Union Address, President Bush called on Congress to "permanently extend Charitable Choice," returning to the primary theme of his first presidential campaign:

> In communities across our land, we must trust in the good heart of the American people and empower them to serve their neighbors in need. Over the past seven years, more of our fellow citizens have discovered that the pursuit of happiness leads to the path of service. Americans have volunteered in record numbers. Charitable donations are higher than ever. Faith-based groups are bringing hope to pockets of despair, with newfound support from the federal government. And to help guarantee equal treatment of faith-based organizations when they compete for federal funds, I ask you to permanently extend Charitable Choice.

Needless to say, because it is a structural component of the executive branch, there is no public consensus on the faith-based initiative, and its political future remains highly uncertain. In contrast to the presidential campaign of 2000, when Al Gore actually preempted Bush (momentarily) with his own version of a faith-based initiative, the 2008 presidential campaign saw very little discussion of these issues on either side. Barack Obama was the only candidate with a chance of winning who explicitly stated that he would continue the faith-based initiative if elected. These were his exact words at a Democratic "Compassion Forum" on April 13, 2008: "I want to keep the Office of Faith-Based Initiatives open, but I want to make sure that its mission is clear. It's not to—it's not to simply build a particular faith community; the faith-based initiatives should be targeted specifically at the issue of poverty and how to lift people up." Upon winning the presidency, of course, he followed through on that pledge, to the surprise of many (I address this development in the afterword). Clearly, therefore, much is still at stake in how we, the public, assess Bush's legacy of "rallying the armies of compassion."

From its beginnings, however, charitable choice was a project of legal and political ideas, not normal politics. There was little public demand or

Christian Democratic theory of the state and moves us closer to the actual welfare systems of European countries generally categorized as Christian Democratic, particularly Germany and the Netherlands. While I develop this political argument in more detail in the next chapter and look more closely at the Dutch and German systems later in the book, it is important to grasp here the basic structural and qualitative similarities that are now evident, while keeping in mind the vastly greater social spending (and anti-poverty success) of our European counterparts.

On one level, it is mainly from Dutch and German (or German-influenced) thinkers that American welfare reformers assimilated the theories of subsidiarity and sphere sovereignty, establishing an important philosophical genealogy for pluralist reforms, from equal access law to charitable choice and the faith-based initiative. More directly (and not coincidentally), the Dutch and German welfare systems share many of the features, proposed or implemented, that defined the faith-based initiative as a new design for serving social needs.

Three similar objectives are evident in this transatlantic comparison: (1) devolving service provision to religious groups; (2) recognizing and protecting the autonomy of religious groups in their public service work; and (3) enabling the public work of religious groups with public funds. Thus, in all three cases, Dutch, German, and American, the basic model is a publicly funded, privately operated social safety net. Of course, the American welfare state has been transforming itself into a "government-by-proxy" system for several decades now, but what is especially notable, comparatively, are the demands and rights of autonomy that particularly arise from public reliance on religious groups, turning welfare policy into an enabling force for social pluralism and the freedom of the church.

Religious autonomy is not something new in American governance: like the Christian Democracies and the rest of Europe (to one degree or another), the United States has long embraced religious autonomy in a narrow sense, as "the right of religious communities (hierarchical, connectional, and congregational) to decide upon and administer their own internal religious affairs without interference by the institutions of government."[98] Internal religious autonomy is fairly robustly protected in the United States, certainly in matters of ecclesiastical structure and finances, church teachings and disputes related to these, the use of religious criteria in employment decisions, and protection from most clergy/employee tort and contract claims (under the "ministry exception" principle).[99] More controversially, religious bodies are also exempt from most forms of taxation, including federal payroll taxes and unemployment taxes.[100]

When it comes to the educational and charitable works of religious bodies, however, the United States differs markedly from countries such as Germany and the Netherlands, which "extend" religious autonomy principles much further. In part this reflects an essentially communal understanding of religion as compared to a more individualistic view in the United States, something I discuss further in chapters 3 and 4. Essentially, "church autonomy" means that the church as an entity, in all the things which define it as an entity, has a right of self-determination. European church autonomy law, which is constitutionally grounded in Germany as well as in a few other countries, grows out of a much older Roman Catholic heritage known as *libertas ecclesiae*, "freedom of the church." Freedom of the church is an idea of the sovereignty of the church as something distinct and separate from the sovereign authority of the state, a distinction rooted in the fundamental theological categories of nature (the state) and grace (the church). Just as nature and grace are interdependent in human existence (and in human progress toward salvation), however, church and state are not unworkably distinguished as absolute sovereignties one over the other; rather, each has sovereignty within the limits set by its own purposes and competence. Thus there are "civil" and "spiritual" jurisdictions shielded one from the other in essentials but also called to cooperate where their responsibilities overlap in society—for example, in providing assistance to the poor, which is a legitimate responsibility of both the state (charged with securing the common welfare) and the church (charged with serving the least among us because they are children of God).

Any such cooperation must preserve the sovereignty of the church, but only within the limits of the laws applicable to all for the general peace, the proper jurisdiction of the state. In the late middle ages, John of Paris (in *De potestate regia et papali*) and others greatly strengthened the freedom of the church by repudiating the idea of the temporal power of the Papacy, or as Abraham Kuyper later confirmed in the program for the confessional political party he founded in 1879, "We absolutely deny the church the right to establish political principles that would bind the state. The church is, of course, free to influence its members in the direction it deems desirable, but it may not establish rules that would bind the state."[101]

In the Dutch Constitution, the famous Article 23 (installed in 1917) provides for the right of development of private schools, religious and nonreligious, with the support of public funds, a model basically replicated in social services but not by constitutional provision.[102] This example is more "pluralistic" than the faith-based initiative in that the state's "neutrality" in providing public funds to religious schools is not restricted to "public purposes" defined as something inherently secular. It is restricted simply by the general educational and operational standards applied to all schools, religious or secular. In the United States, our continuing efforts to constitutionally distinguish "public purpose" from "religion" or "religious methods" bespeaks a shallower pluralism compared to that of the Netherlands.

Building on Weimar precedents, the German Basic Law enshrines church autonomy majestically in several articles set apart from other provisions for the protection of individual religious freedom. The basic principle of these church autonomy provisions is self-determination in "own matters," extending from the internal order and administration of ecclesial bodies to church-related service entities. Self-determination extends to the charitable functions of a church, including, the Federal Constitutional Court has determined, "all measures, which have to be made in pursuit of charitable tasks determined by the fundamental mission of the church, e.g., specifications of structural type, the choice of personnel and the precautions to guarantee the 'religious dimensions' of the operation in the sense of the ecclesiastical understanding, which are inseparably connected to these decisions."[103] Government funding does not shrink this expansive requirement of self-determination into mere allowances for "religious identity," as it does under charitable choice. Thus, here too is a much deeper pluralism, at least as regarding the proper roles of church and state. Yet in other respects, such as tax collection for those churches incorporated under public law, the German model veers toward semi-establishment.

Comparatively, it is an open question for us whether the Supreme Court's neutrality reasoning will continue to evolve in a more "cooperationist" direction resembling the Dutch or German model. Minimally, it seems clear that constitutional challenges are unlikely to reach to the essence of charitable choice or the faith-based initiative as an executive-branch policy. Most dramatically, in *Hein v. Freedom from Religion Foundation* (2007), the Supreme Court threw out a lawsuit charging the White House with violating the establishment clause by organizing informational conferences on the faith-based initiative (thereby manifesting government favoritism toward religion). In the absence of evident harms, the Court ruled, a plaintiff has no standing simply as a taxpayer to sue the executive branch in this way. In limiting taxpayer standing on these issues, the *Hein* decision drew a line against future lawsuits by ideological groups or individuals who have not been constitutionally harmed but simply do not like what is happening under charitable choice.[104]

Early in 2002, however, an actual charitable choice program was tested in federal court for the first time, and it was found to be unconstitutional in practice. The case is important for the lines it draws between impermissible practices and charitable choice law. Between 1999 and 2000, the Faith Works substance abuse rehabilitation program in Milwaukee, Wisconsin, received $600,000 from the state's TANF block grant. The funds were drawn from then Governor Tommy Thompson's discretionary portion (15 percent) of the block grant. In *Freedom from Religion Foundation v. McCallum* (2002), Federal District Court Judge Barbara B. Crabb issued a partial summary judgment upholding an establishment clause complaint against the program. Based on the undisputed facts in the case, the court upheld the plaintiffs' charge that, because religious and social service activities were not sufficiently separated in the program, and because state funding was not sufficiently restricted in the accounting structure of the Faith Works organization, state funding of Faith Works had the effect of advancing religion and was therefore unconstitutional. The court denied the defendants' claim that the lawsuit challenges the constitutionality of charitable choice itself. In fact, the plaintiffs argued that public funding of the Faith Works program actually *violates* charitable choice law, which explicitly prohibits direct federal funding of religious activities. In partial judgment, the court simply ordered the State of Wisconsin to cease providing funds to Faith Works.

Faith Works also receives state funds, through contracts with the Wisconsin Department of Corrections, for a halfway-house program serving offenders on probationary release, and this funding was the target of a second establishment clause complaint in the case before Judge Crabb. Faith Works is one of a group of providers preselected by the state for this program, in full knowledge of its religious approach, the facts show. The defendants' argued that, because the offender is not formally restricted to attending Faith Works—there are other options—and because state funding only follows from enrollment in the program on a bed-by-bed basis, through reimbursement, the funding withstands constitutional scrutiny: as with the constitutionality of private school vouchers, the mediating choice of the individual releases the state from establishment clause restrictions on its funding. Judge Crabb did not find sufficient factual grounds to accept the plaintiffs' argument that no real choice exists in the program because probation officers exercise control over the decision of the offender and because no other program in Milwaukee offers long-term, residential treatment. Denying summary judgment, the court nevertheless ordered a trial to review the complaint upon fuller discovery of the facts.

As I have stressed, the most controversial aspect of charitable choice is that it allows religious groups to discriminate on the basis of religion in hiring and setting employment rules for positions in federally funded

and clothing but also, increasingly, in day care, after-school programs, and senior citizen centers. As of 1998, about 15 percent of Salvation Army revenues nationwide came from government agencies, Glenn reports; most of the rest still comes from private donations.[107] Although other major providers, such as Catholic Charities, are more dependent on government funding, nevertheless, over recent decades there is evidence of significant "mission drift" in the social services the Army provides, as well as no church growth to speak of in a period when other evangelical churches saw significant growth.[108] One might interpret these trends as caused by external pressures associated with the lure of more government contracting, but there has been little direct conflict with governments in this regard.[109] Instead, as Glenn argues,

> More insidious than governmental infringement have been the internal pressures within the Army itself associated with balancing its dual identities as both a social service agency and a church. Many within the Salvation Army have simply accepted the terms on which they receive government funding. They do not have sufficient distance to recognize the subtle and unconscious shifts that have occurred in the character of their programs as a result of the lure of doing more good through government funding.[110]

One internal pattern of mission drift may come from efforts to professionalize staff according to social-work norms commonly required or favored by government agencies in charge of allocating social-program funds. Another source of mission drift may come from a more secular clientele that is less receptive to hearing religious messages when seeking services, thereby dulling the sense of religious purpose experienced by service staff. From the early 1980s in fact, the Salvation Army implemented a series of directives and guidelines aimed at preventing further mission drift and inculcating a new sense of religious purpose among social service staff.[111] The *Lown* complaint, with its unusual facts reflecting what seems to be a particularly intensive local effort to reintegrate mission and service (on the One Army principle), may be evidence that charitable choice has emboldened some groups to take intentional steps to de-secularize their operations. If this is true in the case of the Salvation Army, it suggests that the Army's many previous efforts to do so in the past may have been hampered, internally, by the fear of public reprisal or even litigation. With a legal framework in place to protect themselves against negative and potentially costly government responses, it is now easier to organize and mobilize internal de-secularization efforts.

One key point that we can take away from the controversy surrounding faith-based hiring rights (and charitable choice more generally) is the intervening factor of social need as church-state thinking has evolved. As we can see with educational aid and school vouchers, the Supreme Court appears to be more willing to accommodate religion when government is addressing real social needs; the idea of a statute's social purpose (and the representative will behind it) is given a high value in the Court's establishment clause reasoning: compare *Mitchell's* confirmation of federal aid to religious schools to the strong refusal of official public-school prayer in *Santa Fe Independent School District v. Doe,* 2000.

At bottom, however, it seems that the still-controlling standard of "no direct aid to religion," maintained even as the eligibility of religious institutions in government aid programs is no longer in question, may be further weakened in the future. Carl Esbeck, a careful scholar who held in check the worst excesses of HR 7 in his capacity as faith-based liaison in the Department of Justice (especially regarding rules against proselytization), has argued as much. If the Supreme Court continues to expand its application of the "equal-treatment" theory, he suggests, this is likely to take the form of "permitting direct funding of what now would be considered pervasively sectarian social-service organizations, as well as permitting individuals to elect to 'spend' government-issued vouchers at both religious and secular schools."[112] Of course, we know that the latter prediction was affirmed by the Supreme Court in *Zelman,* four years later. But this was in many ways a much easier decision than one the Court might face in the future concerning direct government funding of religious activities under charitable choice.

I am not a constitutional lawyer and do not propose a complete technical answer as to why the Court will move in this direction or why it should do so, but in conclusion here I wish to note Esbeck's view of expanding the "application" of equal-treatment theory. His own work on equal treatment of religion, closely aligned with the more recent work of Douglas Laycock, suggests that further movement away from "no aid" rules will involve something more like extending the *logic* of equal treatment, not simply the application. Here is what I mean: on the now defunct *Lemon* standard of barring aid to "pervasively sectarian" groups, this standard applied to what the group *is*, its *characteristics* or *nature* as judged by the government. The more nuanced "equal-treatment" approach does not bar aid to any group (including highly religious ones) because of what it *is*, but it does make aid contingent on what it *does*—as measured not by effectiveness, but by religiosity. Thus, you can *be* a highly religious group and receive federal funds, but you cannot *act* like one in using those funds. To my mind, this seems incongruous in a way that is similar to Jim Crow segregation, where the government gave African Americans the right to vote but took it away by other means. Equal treatment of religious groups in government aid programs, offered on the condition that you cannot practice your religion when using government funds (as other groups practice their own understandings with government funds), imposes unequal terms of eligibility and so is not equal treatment. What, exactly, is being treated "equally" except a shell of religion, like a Jim Crow right? The terms of religious eligibility render religion *unequal to itself* by segregating belief and practice. The integrity of belief and practice is essential to religious autonomy by any reasonable definition of the term.

The implications of this become clearer in the structural view of the establishment clause advanced in similar terms by both Laycock and Esbeck. This view was formulated effectively by Laycock in the House Judiciary subcommittee meeting on charitable choice in June 2001. As he explained in his submitted testimony,

> With respect to government money, I long accepted the widespread fallacy that the ultimate goal is to separate religion from government *money*. But I have gradually come to realize that that is a means, not an end. The goal is to separate private religious choices and commitments from government *influence*, including the powerfully distorting influence that government can buy with its money. Government should minimize its influence over the religious choices and commitments of both the providers and the beneficiaries of government-funded social services. That goal is difficult to achieve, but charitable choice is a step in the right direction [emphasis in original].

Although Laycock does not endorse allowing religious activities in charitable choice programs, by the standard of nonconstraint or noncompulsion, the implication should be clear. By restricting the use of federal funds to nonreligious methods of social service (assuming their equal effectiveness), the government is not acting neutrally toward religion but actively constraining it: a religious beneficiary cannot receive religious help he may want or need (unless he has a voucher in a voucher-based program), and a faith-based provider is forced to constrain its religious mission in a nonprofit market already highly distorted by government largesse. Serving no compelling purpose for government, the net result is less religious freedom all around. By the standard of neutrality as noncompulsion—that is, minimizing government's impact on religious choices and commitments—

current charitable choice rules obviously fall short insofar as they prohibit religious activities in federally funded service programs. This view goes deeper than Justice Thomas's much-decried opinion in *Mitchell*, where he argued that neutral provision of government aid (as between all religions and between religion and nonreligion) implicitly insulates government from having any effect of advancing religion: that is, if the government's intent is secular (according to the social purpose ordered by Congress), and if its funding for this purpose is neutrally provided to all types of providers, no effects except those intended by the statute can be attributed to government. In this view, nonestablishment is assured by the nonattribution of religious effects to government, not simply by a lack of religious effects. Laycock, however, actually recovers some of the substantive ground that is lost in Thomas's purely logical understanding of neutrality. He does so by reading separation as a metaphor for minimizing the government's influence on religion: separation does not mean no contact between government and religion; separation means minimizing the impact of government *on* religion, so as to maximize religious freedom.

Stephen Monsma has been the most forceful proponent of the "substantive neutrality" theory, or what he calls "positive neutrality." While he may technically agree with Laycock and Esbeck on the meaning of nonestablishment—separation as minimizing government impact on religion—Monsma, who is a political scientist, views this from a social-pluralist standpoint that is not really contemplated in the analysis of the constitutional lawyers. The goal of minimizing the government's impact on "private religious choices," as Laycock termed it in his congressional testimony (cited above), frames the issue in a way that implicitly defines religious freedom as a freedom of individuals and does not contemplate any unique or important value of religious groups as societal structures.

It is interesting to note that separation defined as noncompulsion over religious choices was a view that had already crystallized among church leaders (if not among scholars) prior to the strict separationist wave of the 1970s. For example, in 1960, Methodist church leaders pronounced as mistaken the view that separation of church and state means the institutional separation of religion and government (this was then, as now, the predominant view of their own "free-church" Methodist brethren and most varieties of Baptists). Instead, church-state separation is a "political principle under which whatever pertains to a man's religious choice and convictions and observance must be preserved absolutely free as possible of any external pressure, force or coercion by the State." In the context of government aid programs, this meant that "'cooperation' between church and state" is sometimes "absolutely necessary in order to protect the positive free exercise of the rights of the church."[113] More than four decades ago, the legal scholar Paul Kauper argued that government contracting with religious providers is not only constitutional but follows a constitutional principle of "strict" neutrality. "By extending aid to all institutions that serve the secular purpose of the government's program, whether public or private, church-related or not, the government is being neutral." Excluding religious providers from government programs dedicated to a social purpose is itself an unconstitutional "establishment" of the ideology of secularism, he concluded.[114]

Noncompulsion in terms of the "rights of the church" was later memorably given expression in Justice Brennan's theory of communal identity and needs in his concurring opinion in *Corporation of the Presiding Bishop v. Amos* (ruling in favor of faith-based hiring rights in affiliated agencies of religious institutions). From a social-pluralist perspective, however, this is not just a question limited to institutional control over employment, important as that is for religious organizations or almost any organization. As Monsma wrote in 1993, challenging the (still-controlling) idea that a religious organization can be funded by government only if the services it renders are severed from religious activities and content, "To put such requirements on religiously based groups and programs would force them to become (or to pretend they have become) something they are not. This would be a violation of their sovereignty in their role as providers of services, which, in turn, means that their full freedom of religious belief and practice would be violated."[115]

The important qualitative difference in Monsma's view is that it does not restrict the definition of freedom to something that only individuals possess, in terms of choice, action, and so forth, as is seemingly implied in Laycock's testimony as well as Esbeck's work. Monsma's variety of substantive neutrality assumes that religious groups have a kind of sovereignty related to their preservation, just as individuals are viewed as sovereign (within general limits) in the tradition of civil liberties, religious liberty first among them. The integrity of belief and action being a pivotal dimension of any religious organization's survival, it is only from a pluralist perspective (according preservative sovereignty to social groups) that we can fully grasp the radical implications of church-state neutrality in social welfare, extending beyond the organizational eligibility of religious groups to their very beliefs and practices as servants of God.

A final point leads us back into the political story that I address in the next chapter. In 2005, the legal scholar Noah Feldman proposed a much-discussed "settlement" of the church-state conflict in his book *Divided by God*. He argued for a new church-state compromise allowing more room for government religious speech (school graduation prayers, public religious displays, etc.) in exchange for reining-in government aid to faith-based organizations. He bases this on a historical reading of interpretations of the religion clauses of the First Amendment, finding that "institutional separation," most importantly in the form of severing religion from government money, was a more or less consensual view in the past. Yet he ignores precisely the question of why there is less of a consensus against government aid to religious groups today.[116]

The Supreme Court itself is moving in the opposite direction from Feldman's church-state compromise, allowing more funding for religious groups while maintaining clear and reasonably strong restrictions on government religious speech. The reason should be obvious: the Court is simply keeping pace with the devolutionary trend in welfare policy and operation, which is forcing the issue of faith-based aid and contracting on a much larger scale than in the past, given the growth in social spending. The Court has become more accommodating of religious providers, in keeping with the needs of government, while holding a firmer constitutional line on the more controversial (because more visible and symbolic; less "structural") issue of government promotion of religious speech.[117]

Feldman's historical defense of his theory is valid as far as it goes, but he fatally ignores the very different political context that is driving the renewal of church-state cooperation today. There is an obvious structural reason for the seeming divergence in church-state law that we see today. Faith-based services and education are, increasingly, filling a real social need, while conflicts over public symbolism are increasingly linked to political polarization, and so are much more controversial. Welfare reform and other devolutionary trends have created more demand for partnerships with community organizations, a significant percentage of which are faith-based. The Supreme Court's innovative *Bowen* trajectory is partly motivated, in other words, by the highly experimental political environment that gave rise to welfare reform and the faith-based initiative, and now these legal and political trends are converging.

To put it another way, restricting government funding of religious social-service providers, as James Madison may have wanted it, is historically obsolete today. And more than that, if the effectiveness of faith-based methods proves out in any significant measure, church-state restrictions may be genuinely counterproductive (and convincingly portrayed as such by politicians). In any case, the reality should be clear: welfare restructuring and retrenchment is creating the space and demand for constitutional accommodation of faith-based providers. A new universal welfare state could stop these changes, as the structural need for religious providers would diminish, but the more likely scenario is further operational devolution of social services, leading to further legal accommodation of faith-based providers.

The Supreme Court's trajectory in material aid cases strongly suggests that "faith-based initiatives" will survive fundamental constitutional challenges. The major question, then, is whether the current standard of strict separation of religious content from government-funded services will hold, as it does in both charitable choice law today and in the regulatory framework put in place by the faith-based initiative. If it becomes increasingly clear that faith-based helping methods are more effective—as John Dilulio and others have devoted themselves to proving—it is highly unlikely that the current boundary separating religious activities or messages from public services will stand. If people are persuaded that religion is truly making a difference in troubled lives, abstract constitutional doctrines barring government support for effective religious solutions simply because they are religious will only seem more discriminatory for being counterproductive as well.

TWO

Religion and Welfare Reform:
Old Battles and New Directions

One common misperception about the policy innovations described in this book is that they are part of larger conservative effort to weaken and dismantle the American welfare state. Protecting religious autonomy in the social safety net—certainly the key motivation behind charitable choice—is necessarily something that, like other forms of "devolution" away from government control, weakens the welfare system by conceding more and more power and resources to the directives of private organizations, in this case churches and their social agencies. Some believe the goal is to withdraw the state from society and concede the war on poverty to private forces with authoritarian dreams.

Liberal critics of charitable choice focused mainly on civil rights and church-state concerns—this is where their advocacy strength lies. But some critics (and many more in private) also express fear of what might be called "theocratic privatization"—religious organizations using the resources of the state to gain more and more control until, effectively, religious bodies "take over" public welfare and govern social assistance by religious directive—perhaps not unlike how it was in Puritan New England or sixteenth-century Geneva. As the liberal-left's bestselling author Barbara Ehrenreich put it after Bush's reelection in 2004,

Of course, Bush's faith-based social welfare strategy only accelerates the downward spiral toward theocracy. Not only do the right-leaning evangelical churches offer their own, shamelessly proselytizing social services; not only do they attack candidates who favor expanded public services—but they stand to gain public money by doing so. It is this dangerous positive feedback loop, and not any new spiritual or moral dimension of American life, that the

Democrats have failed to comprehend: The evangelical church-based welfare system is being fed by the deliberate destruction of the secular welfare state.[1]

In their classic work *Nonprofits for Hire*, Steven Smith and Michael Lipsky long ago considered the democratic vulnerabilities associated with government contracting of services from private and nonprofit providers, starkly pointing out that "contracting gives away responsibility for important authoritative decisions about vulnerable people."[2] The concern about giving away "authority" must be particularly ominous if one sees the church-state innovations of charitable choice as a strategy of privatization.

This view is not simply exaggerated. In fact it reads the politics and normative thrust of the faith-based initiative exactly backward. Charitable choice is not a mechanism of privatization at all; its focus is precisely on the responsibility *of* government, with the assumption that public welfare is here to stay and will continue to control a significant portion of national resources devoted to social assistance. As a legal structure designed to protect the autonomy of religious providers, charitable choice has no purpose outside of the public welfare system. It does not dismantle public welfare or any part of it; to the contrary, it welcomes religious providers *into* public welfare systems by offering protections for their religious identity—thereby "bringing religion back into American welfare," as Stanley Carlson-Thies put it in 2001.[3] If charitable choice shifts the government in Washington further away from program design and execution, giving more discretion to states and providers, the vital function of allocating resources to what works becomes all the more forceful, defined as the central government's responsibility and natural role. The counterintuitive implication of this— as some libertarian critics have rightly perceived—is that charitable choice will actually *strengthen* public welfare by creating a new class of religious stakeholders, thereby creating more demand, and more effective demand, for social spending in poor and distressed communities. In this sense, charitable choice should be welcomed by the growing minority of liberals who put cooperation in the fight against poverty above cultural politics.

Ironically, the far-right critique of the FBCI came much closer to the truth of what is likely to happen in our "faith-based future," although its fears are also exaggerated in a different way. Marvin Olasky, who played an influential role in Bush's faith-based efforts in Texas and in his first presidential campaign, is an instructive critic. In voluminous commentary, mainly oriented to conservative audiences, Olasky repeatedly emphasized tax-based strategies for the FBCI, with the goal of "shrinking the government" by restructuring the whole system of social assistance around incentivized individual giving. While he pressed for further religious autonomy and religion-centered methods under charitable choice, viewing it as something generally useful in the struggle against government secularism, this was not the preferred method of faith-based devolution for Olasky and other movement conservatives.

Shortly after the faith-based initiative was launched in January 2001, Olasky joined with veteran religious freedom advocate Michael Horowitz in issuing a public "statement of principles," bringing tax-based strategies to the forefront in a debate they saw as worrisomely predicated on the idea of government contracting rather than charitable incentives:

> We believe that Tax Code–based reforms are the clearly preferable means of providing needed additional support for faith-based outreach programs, and applaud President Bush for his commitment to such reforms. With them, individuals rather than government officials evaluate and reward the work of faith-based groups. Further, the government's role under such reforms is limited to certifying the eligibility of groups to receive contributions—a role that governments now play and have long played. For these reasons, tax-based reforms will not alter the present relationship between church and state. We thus strongly endorse the Bush proposals to extend tax deductibility for charitable contributions and to establish a poverty-fighting tax credit, provided that its benefits are restricted to organizations providing direct charitable services.[4]

To operate the FBCI as an executive expansion plan for charitable choice—actually a good shorthand description for how it was designed and run—would only strengthen government and thwart privatization in the end, Olasky later warned.[5] Joseph Loconte of the Heritage Foundation simply argued that "making federal grants available to religious charities is the least important part of the president's initiative. . . . What's at stake is something much larger: the false assumption that religious belief carries no advantage over unbelief in tackling social problems."[6]

Washington Post columnist E. J. Dionne posed the question succinctly: "It is worth debating to what extent faith-based organizations replace government activities, and to what extent they supplement them."[7] For Olasky and other critics on the right, it was clear that a tax-based approach was required for the former (particularly if charity tax credits are paid for with corresponding offsets from federal program budgets), and a grant-based approach would result in the latter. But neither the far right nor the far left clearly grasped the governmental logic at the core of the faith-based initiative—embodied in charitable choice. Olasky's view that privatization should be the goal of the faith-based initiative posed the issue as one of protecting churches from the state, but since that is precisely what charitable choice was designed to do, it was fairly obvious that his preferred faith-based vision was one of simply reducing the state as much as possible—a libertarian outlook quite common among intellectuals affiliated with his Calvinist splinter church, the Presbyterian Church in America. Thus, if liberal critics mistake charitable choice for a "holy war against welfare," conservative religious critics underestimate both the protections afforded by charitable choice (and these are likely to be further extended by the Supreme Court, as discussed in chapter 1) and, more revealingly, the destructive implications of government withdrawal for the people and communities most likely to be served by religious providers.

This goes to the core mandate of public responsibility as conceived in the confessional tradition that influenced Bush's faith-based reforms. The whole thrust of this mandate—"to enlist, equip, enable, empower and expand the heroic works of faith-based and community groups," as the White House described it—rests on an assumption of divided responsibility between public resources and the natural powers of communities. As an approach to government reforms, however, the pluralistic, restorative philosophy of the faith-based initiative did not conform to the standard culture-war narrative of liberal versus conservative and big government versus private charity—a narrative that is structured in a way that obscures the public purposes of intermediate social structures and, by polarizing "public" and "private," makes it difficult to conceive of any legal framework we might dedicate to their preservation *as* social structures, not as mere aggregates of individuals with attendant individual rights. Later, in hope of reframing the larger question of faith-based social policy, we will circle back to the philosophical-juridical substratum of the faith-based model—what Gierke and other pluralists conceived as the realm of "social law," law conformed to the nature and needs of communities. But before we do that, it is important to stress here the political shift that actually did occur over the last fifteen years.

In the politics of conservative welfare reform and the corresponding politics of Olaskian "compassionate conservatism"—ascendant in the period from roughly 1984 to the late 1990s—charitable choice was an anomaly, and no one imagined the kind of transgovernmental contracting "regime change" that was eventually set in motion from the Oval Office. Although mainly the fruit of an intensive political engagement by a small network of likeminded religious advocates, these developments were no minor tangent in the politics of welfare reform. In fact, the entire debate about welfare was transformed in a significant way, not simply by injecting church-state issues (a fact striking in itself) but by reconfiguring the conventional, polarized framework of "public" versus "private" into a pluralist framework putting both in their proper place.

The contradictory fears that assailed the FBCI from the right and left (religion-destroying statism versus theocratic privatization) revealed little except a general state of confusion, something symptomatic of a shifting paradigm. Olasky and the right saw little value in the administrative reforms at the center of the FBCI or the kind of support provided by the Compassion Capital Fund, which was decried by one House negotiator on HR 7 (the Community Solutions Act) as just another "new social welfare program." But they did not succeed in their efforts to tailor the policy to narrow religious agendas, even as the left, equally extreme in its civil rights and separationist demands, was ultimately reduced to combing through grants for evidence of political corruption. Sorting through the politics and the oddly parallel confusions of the left and right reveals the key to the whole story—the power of ideas in uprooting restrictive assumptions and changing the way we can think about government and society. Although obviously shaped by other diverse influences, agendas, and contingencies—as with any major political process—the net result of charitable choice and the faith-based initiative is a rather astonishing thing: the United States has moved a considerable distance toward embracing a Christian Democratic approach in social welfare, if not anything close to the levels of social spending associated with this model in Europe.

So we turn to an important question of policy history, the question of how charitable choice and the faith-based initiative departed from conventional conservative thinking on welfare reform and the role of the state. And in excavating this significant missing piece of recent intellectual history, we reveal certain radical implications of the central ideas. It is an important and interesting story in itself, but as we enter the second decade of welfare reform, with poverty rising and the middle class shrinking, what was once a seemingly narrow debate about religious social services begins to resonate in broader ways.

The Faith-Based Turn in Civil Society

We should first remember the remarkable intellectual ferment surrounding religion in the 1990s, particularly in relation to social problems. Certainly one of the most distinctive features of American politics as we entered the twenty-first century was a sweeping turn toward "faith-based" approaches, or the idea, simply put, that government and other institutions involved in society should draw on the vital resources of religion to better meet human needs. Although George W. Bush's faith-based initiative seemed to give this general idea a new and possibly threatening form, it is important to situate his policy against the larger backdrop of growing religious influence in many policy fields and professions.

There was the launch of "faith factor" research in the social sciences, now a legitimate subfield.[8] Theistic "intelligent design" emerged in the physical sciences, to cite another example.[9] Civic professions that experienced deep secularization in the twentieth century, such as law and medicine, started revisiting and reintegrating religious teachings and norms, generally through the medium of professional ethics.[10] Cutting across confessional lines, the effect of this renewed emphasis on religion in public policy and the professions has been to fundamentally reopen a debate about transcendent origins, natural ordering principles, and moral design in societies and the larger world.

This intellectual turn has served as a catalyst for "conservative" developments in law and public policy, at least as measured by secular liberal standards. In a statement on conservative prospects in 2002, Heritage Foundation president Ed Feulner placed religion at the top of the list of "forces that add a rightward momentum to policy issues."[11] If by "rightward" one means culturally conservative, this may be true; but culturally conservative, in the sense of protecting the family and preserving natural structures of community, is not, unfortunately, what the "rightward momentum to policy issues" in recent decades has delivered at all. Much more representative of conservative influence in today's United States are the war in Iraq, the financial meltdown of 2008–2009, and record levels of inequality and private debt. At the same time, the notable decline of proudly progressive voices (until very recently) clearly tells us something about the rightward momentum. The once authoritative progressive voice of mainline Protestantism—to cite one example—has not gone silent on social problems, but no one is listening to it any more. This does not reflect popular approval of the "rightward momentum" Feulner celebrates. And it does not reflect popular rejection of progressive domestic policy positions: to the contrary, most Americans have long been, and remain, moderately "left-leaning" on the spectrum of domestic policy ranging from abolishing the welfare state, on the right, to abolishing private property, on the left.[12] The crippling of the mainline churches' moral authority is caused by a different conservative backlash—one that rejects the kind of confused moral reasoning that links the fight against poverty to secular values like reproductive choice.[13] The same kind of confusion of values is exhibited in the declared opposition to charitable choice among some (but not all) of these once mighty churches dedicated to economic justice. Their loyalty to the poor of Christ is often noted, but it has been watered down by affluent liberalism in the most visible parts of the church. Membership losses as high as 40 percent over the last three decades—although mainly demographic and not the antiliberal exodus conservatives have portrayed it to be—have obviously weakened their authority as well.[14]

Notwithstanding rather mixed sociological trends that suggest, if anything, a net national decline in religious participation in recent decades (despite significant growth in certain areas, such as Pentecostalism and non-denominational megachurches), the intellectual ascendancy of conservative religious challenges to public secularism—strict separation of church and state combined with elite cultural antagonism toward religion—has certainly been surprising and impressive, particularly in comparison with what is happening in other advanced countries. Beginning with Stephen Carter's *The Culture of Disbelief* in the early 1990s (a favorite of President Clinton), prominent intellectuals, many enjoying foundation funding and other forms of institutional support for research and public dialogue on religion, have made and remade major careers by focusing on the growing influence of religion in public life.[15] By the late 1990s, University of Chicago economist Robert Fogel was completely convinced of a religious resurgence in American politics, something comparable to other "great awakenings" in our past. "In years to come," Fogel wrote in *The Fourth Great Awakening and the Future of Egalitarianism*, "it will be impossible to understand political and ethical trends or economic developments without understanding the movement centered on enthusiastic religions."[16]

The Nobel Prize–winner's embrace of postmaterial egalitarianism contrasts sharply with the kind of prophetic social critique now emerging only ten years later as economic conditions have deteriorated.[17] Fogel constructed a grand historical narrative of the turn toward religion in the 1990s, arguing that "spiritual equity" has displaced material need as the driving force of a new age of social reform. We are in the midst of a "fourth great awakening," he claimed, one in a series of reformist revivals that have recharged the American experiment periodically since the early eighteenth century. The Fourth Great Awakening, with its emphasis on spiritual assets, should not be resisted by disciples of the materialistic "Third Great Awakening," comprising the New Deal and the Great Society, because economic and political barriers to opportunity and fulfillment have been lowered, while the nation's spiritual deficit has increased. Fogel shared with Christian Coalition leader Ralph Reed and other leaders of the religious right a fascination with the social-reformist legacy of religious revivals in American history, but he did not address the Republican Party's destructive economic distortions of this legacy that began with Ronald Reagan's massive supply-side tax cuts and his assault on trade unions.[18] Caught up in the speculative boom mentality of the time, Fogel simply assumed the fact of spiritual reawakening, claiming that its effect will "continue to be widespread and massive," leading us into a new age of "postmodern" egalitarianism based on the "struggle for self-realization."[19] Fogel's non-denominational concept of spiritual need seemed to converge with the Bush presidential campaign's "compassionate conservatism" and its bid to "rally the armies of compassion" against poverty and deprivation. At the same time, however, Fogel suggested a broad symmetry of spiritual deficits across class and income lines, merging the struggles of the poor with the therapeutic self-fulfillment quests that have increasingly replaced organized religion among professionals and cultural elites. The Fourth Great Awakening, he argued, unites rich and poor in pursuing the higher things in life, whether one is overcoming economic deprivation, white-collar hyper-productivity, or luxurious gluttony. Spiritual poverty affects us all.[20]

Princeton legal philosopher Robert George took the spiritual critique of materialistic reform in a very different direction, seeking to tear out the secular roots of modern social disease. Arguing, with James Kurth, that Samuel Huntington's much-debated "clash of civilizations" thesis overshoots the mark,[21] George advances the idea of a precipitous "clash of orthodoxies": the real problem facing Western civilization is not the non-Christian East, as Huntington claims, but rather a growing "worldview" conflict between Judeo-Christian tradition and "orthodox secularism" within the West. John DiIulio, whom President Bush appointed to direct his faith-based initiative upon taking office in 2001, wrote an admiring preface to George's major public statement on this subject, *The Clash of Orthodoxies: Law, Religion, and Morality in Crisis* (2001).[22] Not too subtly, the book is festooned with a dust jacket picture of St. Paul's Cathedral standing amid clouds of billowing black smoke during a Nazi air attack on London, suggesting that liberal secularism is somehow comparable to Nazism.[23] Tendentious and extreme, this comparison nevertheless reflects the painful experience of many conservatives faced with a secular culture they believe has been imposed by government, media, and academia.

This feeling, moreover, is not limited to fringe elements of the religious right and the anti-abortion movement. George is a successor to Woodrow Wilson and Edward S. Corwin in holding Princeton's prestigious Cyrus Hall McCormick chair of Jurisprudence, and in an issue of the centrist *Brookings Review*, Greg Easterbrook, analyzing the new "ecumenicalism" among faith traditions in America, agrees that "in America's contemporary spiritual landscape, the dividing line is not between Christians and non-Christians . . . [but] between believers and nonbelievers."[24] If the Republican collapse during Bush's second term has created new fault lines within the ranks of the "believers," it remains unclear where these new divisions, mainly generational and idealistic, will lead in terms of party politics. Certainly in its upper echelons, the values of cultural secularism remain deeply embedded within the Democratic Party. Pro-life candidates (as one measure of the party's religious attitudes) continue to have little or no access to the rich national funding sources of the party except in a small number of strategic districts and swing states.

But the political and academic currents forcing secularism into retreat are here to stay in one form or another, certainly when it comes to serving the poor. Congressman Tom Delay was not grabbing at straws when he registered his support for legislation related to the faith-based initiative (the failed HR 7) on the floor of the House of Representatives in July 2001, declaring (in characteristically extreme and divisive terms) that "this is the beginning of a very real debate in this country over two very distinctly different worldviews," a debate pitting religious believers against those who "have spent 40 to 50 years getting God out of our institutions."[25] As a resource for Democratic opposition, Delay's portentous theocratic rhetoric was ultimately quite damaging to HR 7. At a luncheon sponsored by D. James Kennedy's Center for Christian Statesmanship, drawing more than four hundred congressional staffers and interns together a week before the House vote on HR 7, Delay rebuffed religious critics of the faith-based initiative, describing it as "a great opportunity to bring God back into the public institutions of the country . . . [a way of] standing up and rebuking this notion of separation of church and state that has been imposed upon us over the last 40 or 50 years. You see, I don't believe there is a separation of church and state."[26] Of course, Carl Esbeck and other legal advocates for the faith-based initiative also challenged a separationist philosophy of church and state, but they viewed this as matter of establishing neutrality between religious and secular approaches, not as an effort to re-establish "God" at the center of government, whatever that might mean.

It is important to understand how such demagogic challenges to public secularism originally emerged against a backdrop of swelling welfare enrollments. The battle over welfare reform became infused with religious perspective pulling in both conservative and progressive directions. While most religious conservatives—certainly the most influential ones—saw welfare reform as an opportunity to shrink or dismantle public programs and revitalize private religious charity, a small network of mainly Calvinist and Catholic scholars and advocates quietly developed a model for a new (yet very old) governmental approach that elevates religion within public welfare, transforming the purposes of both. To a significant extent, charitable choice and the faith-based initiative grew out of this intellectual movement, at the heart of which stands a confessional view of the limited state quite different from the libertarian, free-market theories more commonly promoted by opponents of the welfare state.

The "devolutionary" political trends that pushed charitable choice along in policy history after 1996—in a process many conservatives hoped would lead to complete privatization—were somewhat arrested as charitable choice increasingly came to set the agenda for antipoverty policy. The conventional devolution agenda of taking power away from the federal government and finally replacing the public sector with market solutions was diverted into a very different kind of debate about the design and governance of public welfare, one that was focused on creating new public rights for religious providers in areas of competence and concern that overlap with government programs. A debate essentially pitting public provision against private responsibility had now become a debate about the public rights of religious social providers, one based, implicitly, on the idea of public, not private, responsibility for the health of social structures and the needs of embattled communities.

As we noted in the introduction, two religious ideas of political order, closely related, are crucial to understanding this distinctive approach to public responsibility: the Dutch Calvinist concept of "sphere sovereignty," particularly as developed by Abraham Kuyper, and the Catholic concept of "subsidiarity," one of the core principles of Catholic social teaching as developed by Pope Leo XIII and Pope Pius XI. Although some media discussions of the FBCI mentioned subsidiarity and even sphere sovereignty, these ideas did not arise from the main religious strongholds of that ascendant Republican era and so drew little serious attention at the time. Nevertheless, it is clear that extensive engagement with these ideas helped to generate the political and legal theory and the administrative design of the FBCI, and this intellectual core is what gave the effort its striking coherence and, in my view, gives it continuing relevance today. Certainly no domestic policy of the Bush presidency was as carefully conceived and administered, at least at the beginning. Some may ask "compared to what?"—given the administration's extraordinary failings in other areas—but such an attitude disregards a long process of intellectual, legal, and political development that preceded Bush's efforts in Washington.

Before we look more closely at these religious ideas about political order, in chapter 3, the political story of how such ideas and the policies they inspired became part of American welfare politics needs to be told. It is, in fact, a very remarkable political story whose implications, even today, are little understood. The rather monolithic, liberal narrative of the "religious right" provided no insight into what was going on, leaving critics—at least those willing to acknowledge (with the courts) the basic constitutionality of charitable choice—with little to focus on except the possibility (and some minor evidence) of political corruption in Bush's faith-based efforts.[27] More surprisingly, few critics seemed to care about the social objectives of this new welfare design or to recognize how the categories of welfare reform were being scrambled in a new and challenging way. For the most part, worsening poverty and social distress after 2001 was ignored by the critics of Bush's faith-based initiative. Most seemed much more concerned with settling old scores against religion, particularly on the issue of faith-based hiring rights or what its Democratic opponents called "government-funded discrimination."[28]

Much of the serious intellectual work behind the faith-based initiative was done in the early to mid-1990s, leading to the significant breakthrough of charitable choice and Governor Bush's embrace of the central ideas. At least one reporter took note of what has happening. In 1996, the *Washington Times* published an article called "One-Hundred-Year-Old Idea Inspires Proposals to Revamp Welfare," referring to contemporary followers of Abraham Kuyper.[29] Michael Gerson, then a speechwriter and policy director for Senator Dan Coats of Indiana, was quoted as saying that the Kuyperian influence has "the makings of a movement." Coats himself described an emerging faith-based reform movement that was "consistent with a great and noble tradition of Catholic and Protestant social thought originating before the turn of the century with Pope Leo XIII and Abraham Kuyper."[30] By the time Coats retired from the Senate in 1999, a new, more powerful champion of these ideas was on his way to the White House, executive blueprint in hand.

Beginning with work they did with George W. Bush in Texas, a small, Washington-area think tank called the Center for Public Justice (CPJ) set in motion the policy developments that would culminate in President Bush's faith-based initiative. As one political study described it, CPJ was "deeply involved" in a movement of "sympathetic constitutional scholars and lawyers" who, in the wake of the conservative takeover of congress in 1994, "helped the politicians fashion legal arguments to support greater cooperation between the government and religious providers of social services."[31]

CPJ is shaped by a transatlantic Calvinist heritage. Both James Skillen, the center's president, and Stanley Carlson-Thies, its chief policy scholar, are Reformed Christians with close ties to the Netherlands and particularly to the orthodox "worldview" teachings of Abraham Kuyper.[32] Carlson-Thies, who was a senior official in the White House Office of Faith-Based and Community Initiatives during Bush's first term, has directly stated that "Kuyper's idea is embodied in the faith-based initiative."[33] By this he meant Kuyper's theory of sphere sovereignty, and there is a long track record of CPJ initiative behind this claim, discussed briefly below. Other CPJ affiliates who did (and continue to do) influential work related to the FBCI include Amy Sherman, a well-known advocate for faith-based social services, now with the Sagamore Institute; Stephen Monsma, a Pepperdine political scientist and leading expert on government contracting with religious groups;[34] and Charles Glenn, a Boston University education professor and author of *The Ambiguous Embrace: Government and Faith-Based Schools and Social Agencies*—an important study that devotes significant comparative attention to European examples. Other leading evangelical supporters of the faith-based initiative were also self-declared Kuyperians.[35]

Catholic interest and influence began to coalesce somewhat later in the process, particularly after Bush publicly unveiled the faith-based initiative in July 1999, during his first major campaign speech, "The Duty of Hope." It is interesting to note, regarding Catholic involvement, that the very day charitable choice was introduced as part of the Senate Republican leadership's welfare reform proposal, on August 11, 1995, a coalition of religious groups, led by the National Conference of Catholic Bishops, requested that a set of guidelines for welfare reform, announced that week, be introduced into the *Congressional Record*. Notably absent from their stinging critique of the emerging welfare reform consensus in Congress was any mention of the religious-autonomy concerns addressed by charitable choice. The only concern the Catholic bishops and their liberal Protestant and Jewish allies registered from the standpoint of religious social-service agencies was that proposed budget cuts would make their already difficult situation even harder.[36] Unlike welfare reform, charitable choice was not a product of popular demand or political positioning. It was product of ideas, and the seemingly divergent purposes revealed in the *Congressional Record* of August 11, 1995, suggest a very important political point about the faith-based vision resting on charitable choice—namely, that it originated in a set of concerns and a way of thinking about the state that stood outside the conventional boundaries of welfare reform as it had evolved to this point.

Catholic support for Bush's faith-based plan blossomed rapidly during the presidential campaign, but they were merely catching up to something that had been in the works for several years, having evolved from a few small provisions of welfare reform that, originally, drew almost no attention from religious groups. Nevertheless, the ground was shifting under the complacent welfare consensus of the late 1990s, and when Bush put forward his outline of the faith-based initiative in 1999, it seemed that the whole earlier conflict (and compromise) over welfare rules was swallowed up in a new kind of debate.

The conservative commentator George Will put subsidiarity front and center in a column published shortly after Bush launched the faith-based initiative in January 2001.[37] Influential Catholic advisors to the Bush Administration, such as Deal Hudson of *Crisis* magazine and Paul Weyrich of the Free Congress Foundation, became vocal proponents of the faith-based initiative after Bush took office, both arguing that government must adhere to the doctrine of subsidiarity to be effective. In a remarkable commentary issued on March 13, 2001, Weyrich (who died in 2008) describes a phone call with Bush's top political advisor Karl Rove. Weyrich told Rove that Bush has "mastered the art of Catholic governance," to which Rove added that Bush "understands the Catholic principle of subsidiarity." John DiIulio, the first director of the White House Office of Faith-Based and Community Initiatives, and a self-proclaimed "born again" Catholic, frequently referred to subsidiarity in speeches and articles. He characterized the "Duty of Hope" speech as a "blueprint for applied subsidiarity."[38] It was soon clear that Bush's strongest support on this issue would come from Catholic leaders. Although it is notable, again, that they had not pressed for anything like charitable choice in their previous fifteen years of advocacy on welfare reform, they quickly embraced the renewed focus on church autonomy as the outlines of Bush's plans became clear during the 2000 presidential campaign.[39] As Jo Renee Formicola and Mary Segers argue, Catholic leaders saw the faith-based initiative as a new opening for church-state cooperation, a traditional political good in their eyes:

Catholic bishops hope to maintain and enlarge the freedom of the church to carry out its salvific and social responsibility by altering the relationship between church and state, thereby possibly bringing about a partnership with the government on educational, social, and charitable services. President Bush's faith-based initiative has been instrumental in cementing ties between the Bush administration and the Catholic hierarchy. While the Bush administration anticipates winning Catholic votes in future elections, the bishops look forward to the institutionalization of major change with regard to a more favorable church-state relationship in American society. Indeed, both groups seek to get the best part of the faith-based bargain, and on their own terms.[40]

"Freedom of the church" is a long and storied component of Catholic tradition, as we noted in the introduction and will discuss in more detail in chapter 3. And while this concept applies with great force in all areas where church and state have overlapping social responsibilities, freedom of the church has a unique urgency related to the religious priority of serving the poor. Most conservative commentators showed no serious understanding of these principles, but a few at least recognized that they had something to do with fighting poverty. The reaction of liberal critics, in contrast, focused largely on church-state issues and framed the antipoverty objectives in purely political terms—often cynically assuming that Bush was simply trying to "de-fund the welfare state" and channel taxpayer money to his "religious base." While there is no evidence that such a political agenda was implemented or even existed, a more challenging progressive critique might have emerged if the antipoverty goals of Bush's effort were taken seriously. Once Bush passed his first round of tax cuts tilted toward the wealthy in the spring of 2001, however, this undermined any good will he might have received from progressive antipoverty advocates—the Children's Defense Fund, for one, had long been favorable toward accommodating religious providers in social-service programs. Bush's shameless coddling of the rich sparked a polarization leaving little room for compromise on other things.

At bottom, however, the faith-based initiative grows out of an antipoverty vision substantially more generous and effective than anything we have ever had in the United States, before or after welfare reform. This surprising truth is illuminated by the confessional ideas that influenced its design. Focused on political order and the nature of the state, these ideas, as we pointed out earlier, gained influence and political power in the late nineteenth century, when the Catholic Church, orthodox Calvinists, and other European confessions sought to strengthen the churches' position in a time when socialism and centralized welfare systems threatened to marginalize their power and authority. The resulting "Christian Democratic" welfare model—dominant particularly in Germany and the Netherlands—reduced inequality and poverty to levels comparable to those of the Nordic Social Democracies, while elevating the role of religion. The United States, by contrast, with its secular, liberal, market-based welfare system, was and remains the most unequal and poverty-ridden among advanced countries. While the FBCI clearly drew on certain core principles of Christian Democratic welfare governance, it did so in a limited way that prevented most critics (and many proponents) from understanding the full social meaning of pluralistic religious autonomy, which was, historically, not only the cornerstone of social freedoms more generally, but also a formative influence on the development of social protections for working families and the indigent.

At a minimum, it is important to understand the distinctive political nature of the faith-based initiative as compared with more conventional religious policy goals. Many people became increasingly concerned with organized religious influence on social policy during the Bush presidency, of course. President Bush's ban on federal funding of stem-cell research and congressional Republicans' attempted intervention in the Terry Schiavo case were the leading examples. But when the architects of President Bush's faith-based initiative claimed to be concerned with the "nature of government," as one advocate put it, they were talking about the structural balance of power between secular and religious approaches to social problems.

This notable shift in the welfare debate toward a focus on church-state governance issues in the social field was a logical outgrowth of the constitutional trends discussed in chapter 1. As the statutory and legal environment has become increasingly accommodating of religious involvement in public services, governance issues are increasingly sensitive and important. For the architects of the faith-based initiative, governance essentially meant the way newly "faith-friendly" systems are managed according to certain principles of political order. Here, the theological focus is not on "abortion" or "homosexuality," or any other isolated issue, but on how church and state are structurally coordinated to properly accommodate the perspectives and activities that God ordains the church to provide.

Although the "culture war" continues on an issue-by-issue basis, there is an increasing focus on changing how the state distributes and manages resources in areas where religious perspectives or mandates may apply, for example, in helping people find work or stay out of jail. Welfare being the most natural religious domain where the state also operates, the faith-based initiative could also be interpreted as a kind of policy template for a broader structural settlement of church and state across a range of overlapping domains, from social services to education, family policy, and health care. This might appear to give further leverage to the crusades of the religious right, but nothing in existing charitable choice law or Supreme Court reasoning on the establishment clause points in that direction. It may also appear to reinforce conservative efforts to strengthen private power in economic life. Ironically, however, the distinctly *religious* theories of the limited state embodied by the faith-based initiative explicitly reject privatization in favor of a socially protective form of public responsibility—aiming not to dismantle public welfare but to transform how it is governed and the purposes it serves.

Accounting for Charitable Choice: Factions, Policies, and Ideas

The fascinating intellectual story behind the faith-based initiative provides a unique window onto the role of ideas in policymaking. Although partly driven by devolutionary policy trends that have forced a rethinking of church-state relations in areas of social need, the surprising emergence of the faith-based initiative is also, in fact, a remarkable example of intellectual influence on policymaking. To understand this, we need to set the faith-based story against the larger backdrop of welfare reform as it has developed since the mid-1980s.

The self-described welfare-reform "consensus" that began to emerge by the late 1980s engaged religion, but in a very different way than the faith-based initiative would later succeed in implementing. For example, the influential 1987 report of the American Enterprise Institute's Working Seminar on Family and American Welfare Policy, *The New Consensus on Family and Welfare*, led by Michael Novak, recommended only that "religious social agencies should help to focus the resources of society upon the moral dimensions of dependency"—clearly a privatized view of religion's role in welfare reform.[41] These "inside the beltway" welfare reformers did not concern themselves with church-state barriers at the time. Most, including Marvin Olasky, who became the "guru of compassionate conservatism," did not see welfare reform as an opening for renegotiating church-state relations and increasing church-state contracting; the guiding directive of conservative welfare reform, as with much of the Reagan agenda, was government withdrawal leading to privatization. Yet by 2001, with the launching of the faith-based initiative, welfare programs had become the most prominent battleground in church-state law.

Let us step back further to get a better understanding of these divergent paths. In his 1986 State of the Union address, President Reagan charged his Domestic Policy Council with the task of researching and producing a major strategic blueprint for welfare reform by the end of that year. The resulting report, issued by the Council's Low Income Opportunity Working Group, was called *Up from Dependency: A New National Public Assistance Strategy*. The Low Income Opportunity Working Group was one of three key (and more or less interlocking) subunits of Reagan's Domestic Policy Council, which was led by Ed Meese. Spearheaded by the working group on federalism, headed by OMB general counsel Michael Horowitz (who would later team with Marvin Olasky, notably, to push for charity tax credits instead of contracting reforms in the FBCI), the working groups were the main operating platform for conservative ideologues in the Reagan administration and a key in-house laboratory for radical antigovernment agendas.[42]

Among the key White House members of the working group that produced *Up from Dependency* were Gary Bauer, then undersecretary of education, and Federalist Society leader Charles Cooper, who was deputy attorney general for civil rights under Ed Meese. Bauer himself, who during the Clinton years would go on to build the most potent Washington think tank of the religious right, the Family Research Council, led another Domestic Policy Council subunit called the Working Group on the Family from 1987 to1988, during which time he became director of the White House Office of Policy Development.[43]

The central thrust of *Up from Dependency* was radically federalist, recommending a freeze on new federal initiatives and appropriations, and focusing on administrative devolution designed to promote state-level and local demonstration projects aimed at replacing federal programs and policies. The report did not promote devolutionary block grants on the model of the 1996 welfare reform bill—Reagan's earlier bid for block grants had been defeated—but instead sought to detach federal financing from federal policy through vastly expanded waiver powers. Excepting civil rights and due process standards, it recommended a complete transfer of rule-making authority, with regard to benefit levels, eligibility, and work requirements, from the federal government to the states. Acting on this recommendation, Reagan established the Low Income Opportunity Advisory Board to expedite waiver requests for state and local initiatives, guided by *Up from Dependency's* main policy goals of promoting work and family responsibility in poor communities.[44]

Notably, however, the report did not specifically promote religion as an antidote to welfare dependency, let alone propose systemwide legislation to directly challenge constitutional and political barriers to government financing and other forms of support for religious social-service providers. In fact, none of the hallmarks of charitable choice—its constitutional theory, its philosophical critique of "neutral" secularism as a form of discrimination, the restorative social vision at its core—are visible in this primary document of Reagan-era welfare reform.

The American Enterprise Institute's *New Consensus* report was closely related in its politics. Produced by a working seminar chaired by Michael Novak, then the institute's director of political and social studies, *New Con-*

sensus was devoted mainly to summarizing and interpreting statistical data on poverty and the welfare system, after the fashion of Charles Murray, who was a member of the working seminar. In its concluding policy recommendations, however, the report focuses on the role of religious institutions within a broader devolutionary outlook on state and local initiatives. This focus likely reflected the input of several important religious conservatives who contributed to the report, including Michael Novak, Richard John Neuhaus, and the family-policy scholar Allan Carlson.

A section on the "voluntary sector," referencing the ubiquitous Alexis de Tocqueville on America's gift for associations, illustrates a burgeoning strain of faith-based communitarian influence within the federalist reform movement that propelled welfare politics in this period, later to be developed in the New Citizenship program of the Bradley Foundation (discussed in more detail below). The report's focus on churches as agents of welfare reform does not prefigure charitable choice, however. In fact, it is notable precisely for its contrasting assumption that religious activities should be understood independently from public policy. While recommending that churches enhance their involvement with the poor by helping "to focus the resources of society upon the moral dimensions of dependency," the government's role in welfare reform, according to the report, is simply to restructure public policy to encourage and ultimately coerce people off welfare and into the labor market (through benefit time-limits).[45] Churches and religious groups have an important role to play in this process, according to the *New Consensus*, but their work should draw on the resources of society, not government. Legal and administrative reforms of the kind later mandated by charitable choice and implemented by the faith-based initiative were not mentioned.

Even after welfare reform was passed in 1996, the leading congressional proposal for faith-based antipoverty efforts, Senator Dan Coats's Project for American Renewal, still emphasized private religious provision, in this case through a charity tax credits. Though he and his staff were familiar with the confessional ideas behind charitable choice and supported expanding those provisions in further legislation, the inherent bias of most welfare reformers, the very religious Senator Coats included, was toward private solutions unencumbered by the rules and regulations accompanying federal grants and contracts. In September 1995, with charitable choice now in place in the major welfare reform proposals, Stanley Carlson-Thies wrote to Michael Gerson on Capitol Hill to applaud Senator Coats's recently introduced Project for American Renewal (in which Gerson had a major hand), while emphasizing an alternative line of thought. Carlson-Thies was quite indifferent to the central idea of the project, a new charity tax credit of the type favored by the most radical opponents of traditional welfare. "Whether or not a charity tax credit is also promoted," he assayed, a "major structural/legal reform . . . should be adopted" in order to remove government bias against religious social providers and schools and thereby enable their work with public resources. There needs to be a "clearer articulation" that "government's positive responsibility" to assist the helping institutions of society requires it to "get right the structuring role it plays in society—the laws and regulations it promulgates that direct the actions and interactions of persons and social institutions."[46] Here the notion of a government's positive structural responsibility for protecting human dignity, enabling social goods, and ordering society toward the common good is unmistakably a Christian Democratic ideal and somewhat removed from even the more "communitarian" welfare reformers in Congress led by Coats. Coats did not conceive of renewed public responsibility as an essential structural component of social recovery so much as a remedy for past government excesses that had weakened society. The latent anti-statism that restricts the idea of public responsibility for communal structures, and correspondingly denies the moral fact that public responsibility can arise from community needs, is emblematic of how the polarized market-state dichotomy of American politics has weakened the philosophical and legal position of "community" as a bearer of rights or beneficiary of obligations. As I discuss further in chapter 4, this deficiency of communal standing in our law and politics effectively means that left and right in America are really two versions of political liberalism, one state-centered and based on the expansion and enforcement of civil liberties and government welfare provision, and the other market-centered and based on individualistic freedom of contract—but both essentially wedded to an individualistic worldview that leaves social structures in the dark.

Although as a senior speech-writer and policy advisor in the Bush White House, Michael Gerson would later become a forceful advocate for the faith-based initiative and much-quoted apologist for its limited achievements, Carlson-Thies's focus on public responsibility and the ordering role of the state in society was quite foreign to most religious conservatives, particularly to the Southern Baptists who were dominant then (as now) in the Republican Party. These fissures among religious conservatives, present in the years prior to charitable choice ratification and in the years that followed it, point to the question of how a *governmental* approach, based on certain distinctive theological assumptions about religion and the state, gained so much influence politically by the late 1990s, essentially derailing the privatization of welfare that many religious conservatives had previously sought.

Since the networks pushing for a governmental approach were small, poorly funded, and politically marginal at the time, the only reasonable explanation for this change of direction is the deep personal influence of ideas on key politicians and advisors, most importantly George W. Bush. One important lesson is that serious ideas and small networks of dedicated advocates can and do influence large-scale policy change in our political system. Thus, this book's emphasis on the intellectual genealogy of the faith-based initiative is no mere theoretical exercise.

Constitutional change was certainly a catalyst to a more Christian Democratic approach in social services. The early days of radical welfare reform, in the midst of the Reagan Revolution, witnessed developments in church-state relations that prefigured, in critical ways, the later interaction of these two fields in charitable choice law and the faith-based initiative. The watershed in church-state relations in this period was the emergence of "equal access" law in the early 1980s, as noted earlier. This marked the first step away from the strict "no-aid" separationism of the previous two decades, staked out in numerous court decisions restricting religious speech in schools and the eligibility of religious institutions in government aid programs. If equal access law provided for accommodation of private religious speech in public facilities on equal terms with other forms of private speech, the next logical step pertained to the eligibility of religious groups for inclusion in government aid programs. The weight of the question shifted from free-exercise rights to establishment clause dangers because of the active financial role of government. Nevertheless, the Court followed the logic of equal treatment, deciding in *Bowen v. Kendrick* that a federal sex-education statute did not violate the establishment clause simply for stipulating the eligibility of religious providers.

It is not coincidental that Abraham Kuyper's influence in American welfare politics had quiet beginnings in this seminal period of church-state reordering: an analogous (but stronger) pluralistic approach to "equal treatment" was constitutionally embedded in the Dutch polity after World War I—as I discuss in more detail in the next chapter. This comparative model must have seemed particularly relevant to American confessional thinkers in a time of major Supreme Court decisions pertaining to religious involvement in government social programs.[47] While the loudest voice of religious conservatism at the time, the Moral Majority, was pushing for a constitutional amendment sanctioning organized prayer in the public schools, scholars and advocates working intently from a Kuyperian church-state perspective were better attuned to Supreme Court reasoning and perhaps already understood equal treatment as an opening for faith-based social services and schooling.[48] Thus, a small network of Reformed scholars and legal theorists began to formulate the concepts now enshrined in the faith-based initiative.

In 1981, Bernard Zylstra, a Dutch Calvinist philosopher and the first president of the Institute for Christian Studies in Toronto (and notably a mentor to Stanley Carlson-Thies), published an essay that made a prescient case for government funding of religious social services. Based on a speech first delivered before the Christian Legal Society (later a key player in the development of equal access law), the essay drew on the concept of "mediating structures" popularized by Peter Berger and Richard John Neuhaus's 1977 book *To Empower People*. Zylstra posed the problem of religious welfare providers in essentially the same terms ratified fifteen years later by charitable choice.[49] He stressed that the concerns of religious "caring institutions" overlap with those of the state and asked, "Does this overlap mean that the religious character of these mediating structures must be eradicated as soon as the state becomes involved, especially when public funds are used?" His answer is striking: "The solution I am advocating," he wrote, "is the disestablishment of secularism in the mediating structures on the part of every level of government and the equal protection of the free exercise of religion in these structures." Going beyond the Supreme Court's now-reigning "equal-treatment" logic in direct-aid cases, Zylstra argued that faith-based providers' free exercise of religion must be fully protected within federal contracting regimes.*

Welfare reform also became a major focus for the school of far-right

---

* To slightly modify an argument I made in chapter 1, I believe, in line with Zylstra's point of thirty years ago, that the internal logic of equal treatment necessarily weakens the "secular purpose" prong of current establishment clause reasoning on government aid. This dichotomous, "secular" versus "religious," way of constructing legislative "purpose" founders on the philosophical entanglement involved in distinguishing "secular" statutory purposes from "religious" methodologies of service. The problem can be corrected by replacing the idea of "secular" purpose (as derived from what can only be described as arbitrary assumptions about "secular" versus "religious" motivation for addressing some particular social need) with the idea "social purpose," as measured by generally accepted objectives of human betterment and regardless of the role of faith. Just as people conceptualize and execute effective social services in different ways, some more religious than others and some not religious at all, one can have a social purpose that is not strictly defined as secular or religious, and it is this quality of a statute—its social purpose—that nonestablishment requires. Whether the social purpose is "secular" or "religious" is a question of motivation that legislatures and courts have neither the capability nor the need to determine. In this I agree with the argument of Stephen V. Monsma in his ahead-of-the-curve book *Positive Neutrality: Letting Religious Freedom Ring* (Grand Rapids: Baker Books 1993), 191; esp. chap. 5.

evangelicals loosely described by scholars as "dominionists"—a largely Reformed, splinter-church movement with explicitly theocratic goals, sometimes including the direct implementation of biblical law. Their emerging views reveal further contrasts that are instructive for understanding charitable choice. George Grant's *Bringing in the Sheaves* was the trendsetting work in the field of dominionist welfare reform.[50] Grant's radical approach, like many others at the time, began with Charles Murray's seminal antiwelfare tract *Losing Ground*, which provided an empirical opening (it seemed) for considering new religious approaches to welfare. As Herbert Schlossberg put it in the foreword to *Bringing in the Sheaves*, Grant developed a blueprint for serving the poor "through the communal actors and activities that the Biblical commands place at the center of our loyalties: family and church."[51] Abraham Kuyper and Leo XIII would have agreed with this view to a point. Certainly they would agree that family and church are the most natural social forms and therefore the starting point of all social goods. The Kuyperian and Catholic promoters of faith-based initiatives today would agree with this as well. But in important ways, as we will see in chapter 3, the latter's communal vision of welfare, in contrast with that of Grant and others on the far right, gives the state significant responsibilities of protection and assistance, properly ordered to sustain communal autonomy but backed by extensive fiscal resources and policy development. Also essential, both the Kuyperian tradition and, more passively, Catholic social teaching, promoted religious pluralism as a basic requirement of political order. For Grant, on the other hand, the explicit goal is to inaugurate Christian dominion by dismantling the state: "God has called the Church to serve. And through service He grants us favor with the people. This is a fundamental principle of dominion in the Bible: *dominion through service*."[52]

Grant envisioned welfare reform as a process of dismantling public programs by "re-mantling" private charity. As Marvin Olasky and Senator Coats would later propose, Grant saw charity tax credits as the most effective tool of faith-based welfare, even proposing the establishment of church-appointed certification boards—an innovation Bush would briefly adopt in Texas—to insure the legitimacy of participating institutions. Unlike Bush, however, Grant openly conceived of charity tax credits as an endgame strategy of "public-to-private transfer." This "temporary" infusion or "re-mantling" of the private sector is the political precondition, he believed, for "abolishing" the welfare state. As he put it, "Government cannot get *out* of the way if the church does not get *in* the way."[53]

It is little known in political circles that Marvin Olasky, once consid-

ered the "guru" behind Bush's "compassionate conservatism," was men-
tored by George Grant, and that his views of welfare and poverty were
largely formed in dominionist circles prior to his arrival on the Washington
scene as a Bradley Resident Scholar at the Heritage Foundation, where he
wrote his best-known book *The Tragedy of American Compassion*. Although
this publication famously launched Olasky's national career, his later repudiation (more or less) of the faith-based initiative was symptomatic of
the far-right libertarian views he absorbed from dominionist circles in the
1980s.[54] We examine this particular "divergent path" more closely in the
next section, because it helps us clarify the political moment we reached in
2001 and why it confounded so many observers trapped in the categories
of liberalism, seeing the state as either heroic uplifter or villainous usurper
but never as restorative social facilitator—the servant of community and
human dignity. Before turning to Olasky, however, it is important to discuss certain early formulations of faith-based welfare among conservative
Catholics, who shared with the Kuyperians an approach that predicated
social-assistance strategy on a proper ordering of church and state.

One Catholic voice that prefigured charitable choice in the early days
of welfare reform was heard in the manifesto *Cultural Conservatism: Toward
a New National Agenda*, a work associated with Paul Weyrich's Free Congress Foundation.[55] This document presaged the next decade's remarkable
rebirth of Catholic intellectual life centered around the periodicals *First
Things* and *Crisis*, and the revival of natural law theory by scholars such as
Robert George. *Cultural Conservatism* was written by William S. Lind, a military systems analyst and former legislative aide to Senator Robert Taft Jr.
Lind's coauthor for *Cultural Conservatism* was William Marshner, professor
of theology at Christendom College in Front Royal, Virginia, a former
speechwriter for Senator Trent Lott, and the husband of conservative activ-
ist Connie Marshner, who would later put together an advocacy coalition in
support of legislation expanding the faith-based initiative in 2001.

In *Cultural Conservatism*, Lind and Marshner outlined a new principled
framework for policies that would strengthen traditional religious culture.
Their main antagonists came from within conservatism itself as well as
from social liberalism and the economic left. Supply-side economics and,
alongside it, libertarianism, were censured for not understanding the foundational nature of culture and religion in establishing social order and
political liberty.

It is rather stunning to read Lind and Marshner's prescriptions for welfare policy in 1987. What they called "cultural welfare" is essentially the

same model, using the same language, as what is now called charitable choice: "Government should find ways to contract out the delivery of welfare services to churches that take on the task of reviving traditional values in underclass communities. The contracts should be written so as to safeguard the freedom and integrity of the churches' internal discipline and doctrine."[56]

This view, almost to the word a prefiguring of charitable choice, follows the subsidiarity principle in Catholic teaching about the state. But in contrast to the free-market iterations of this idea common among the more prominent Catholic "neoconservatives" of the time, such as Michael Novak and the business-oriented Catholic Lay Commission (set up to oppose the American Bishops' "Economic Justice for All"), the *Cultural Conservatism* approach proposed a substantial increase in public investments. A welfare system designed to save poor communities with work, savings, and strong families, they argued, should be a "top priority in the competition for Federal funds, equal in our view to defense."[57]

Lind and Marshner also recognized that enabling and protecting religious social-service providers depended significantly on administrative reforms of the government contracting system. This emphasis converged with the White House's various federalism initiatives and many other "government reinvention" ideas of the time, but it specifically focused on reviving faith-based service methodologies as a primary instrument of social welfare, calling for a liberalization of "the rules governing the credentials of service providers . . . to permit volunteer groups and community organizations, including churches, to qualify as distributors of the services, ending the monopoly of the professional welfare bureaucracies."[58] Just as Lind and Marshner's welfare design proposals seem to prefigure the Bush initiative, so too does their social philosophy in some respects. They emphasize the Catholic doctrine of subsidiarity as well as the importance of restoring "mediating structures," in contrast to the government, as the true sources of social welfare.[59] The accompanying moral values agenda of the *Cultural Conservatism* project, such as opposition to abortion and ending no-fault divorce—this was a work of Catholic traditionalism through and through—may seem troubling to liberal advocates who might, at the same time, be more sympathetic today to Catholic ideas about subsidiary welfare provision. But these are really two different areas of law: they may be philosophically linked, but legislating traditional values, wherever that might be possible today, faces constitutional hurdles in terms of individual rights, and certainly has no possibility of application through anything resembling the legal and political structure of faith-based social services.[60]

The Civil Society Movement

If the particular legal and administrative reforms of the faith-based initiative were influenced by certain distinctive confessional understandings of the state and its role in society, it is also clear that these developments drew on and, for many, were an expression of the broader "civil-society" movement that swept over American political thought in the 1990s. This is not the place to investigate the civil-society movement in general, which would be a vast undertaking touching on virtually every domestic policy development of the last twenty years. But if the initial thrust of civil-society thinking in the United States was profoundly shaped by the fall of Communism and was market-oriented, I think we can also recognize how religious influences somewhat complicated the simplistic picture of bad governments and good markets painted by some American interpreters inspired by what happened in Eastern Europe. It is also important to recognize how religious perspectives on civil society naturally gravitated toward welfare reform as a policy laboratory—as one would expect, given the emphasis on poverty relief in Scripture and church teaching.

The most important and sophisticated platform for civil-society renewal from a "religion and poverty" standpoint was the New Citizenship Agenda, a program initiative of the Lynde and Harry Bradley Foundation, developed by Michael Joyce and William Schambra in the 1990s. As one of the most influential long-range strategists in conservative philanthropy over the last quarter century, Michael Joyce (who died in 2006) played an important role in pushing the broader civil-society discussion toward a focus on religion and poverty. At least initially, as noted earlier, the intellectual momentum in this direction was generated by Charles Murray's *Losing Ground* (1984), which Joyce helped finance from his pre-Bradley perch at the John M. Olin Foundation.[61] *Losing Ground*, with its impressive (and soon partly discredited) statistical display of the failings of the Great Society, basically kicked down the door for those urging a national repudiation of welfare entitlement in favor of community reliance and market solutions, a view that was credibly reinforced within the research community by another Bradley project we have already mentioned, *The New Consensus on Family and Welfare* (1987). The *New Consensus*, it is worth restating, was arguably the most influential of the post–*Losing Ground* policy projects; the working group that produced it was headed by Catholic neoconservative Michael Novak and included Murray himself and other representatives of the far right, along with mainstream analysts, including Richard Nathan and Alice Rivlin.[62] As discussed above, the strong civil-society thrust of the *New*

Consensus modulated Murray's politically unrealistic agenda of abolishing all welfare programs, pushing against radical libertarian assumptions toward the more moderate "carrot and stick" approach of the Family Support Act of 1988. David Ellwood's *Poor Support: Poverty in the American Family* (1988) was, in at least two key respects—workfare and cash benefit time-limits—effectively the liberal white flag that conceded the terrain of welfare policy to the new conservative establishment in Washington.[63]

Michael Joyce's influence in pushing key institutions of the conservative movement in the direction of faith-based social-welfare policy had a significant impact both on the legislative debate surrounding welfare reform, culminating in the 1996 bill, and in the "post-entitlement" environment of Clinton's second term. First and foremost, Joyce influenced the Heritage Foundation. According to Lee Edwards, Joyce effectively convinced Heritage to "join the culture war" by appointing William Bennett as its Distinguished Fellow in Cultural Policy Studies in 1991.[64] Extending Heritage beyond its traditional focus on economic policy and foreign relations, this move began to pay major dividends beginning in 1993, with the joint release (by Heritage, Empower America, and the Free Congress Foundation) of Bennett's public affairs blockbuster, the *Index of Leading Cultural Indicators*, which in turn launched Bennett and the cultural conservative agenda on their way to mainstream media stardom, culminating with *The Book of Virtues*.[65]

More important on the policy side, however, was the establishment of the Bradley Resident Scholars program at Heritage, launched in 1987 with a grant of $510,000. This program was the first of its kind for Heritage and an important launching pad for religious conservatives and leaders of the faith-based wing of the antiwelfare movement, especially Marvin Olasky, who was a Bradley Fellow at Heritage in 1989 and 1990. Conservative movement historian Lee Edwards, in fact, singles out Olasky's growing influence in the 1990s as the most important accomplishment of the Bradley program at Heritage in terms of impact on national politics.[66]

Soon after Olasky's *The Tragedy of American Compassion* was published, Michael Joyce delivered an address to the Heritage Foundation's board of trustees in December 1992, essentially demanding that conservative think tanks stop operating on the assumption that Bradley Foundation funding for their policy research was a permanent entitlement without any obligation to innovate and move toward finding concrete solutions for social problems. He told the Heritage trustees that they had to start focusing their attention on the restoration of civil society and the development of a "new citizenship."[67] The Bradley Foundation then held a closed-door strategy summit for conservative leaders in February 1993 to further develop the funding and think-tank strategy behind the new citizenship.

Named the Bradley Project on the 90s, the new citizenship initiative was initially directed by William Kristol, working out of the American Enterprise Institute. Kristol had been chief of staff to vice president Dan Quayle during the Bush Sr. administration. As he put it in an interview with Adam Meyerson, published in the Heritage Foundation's *Policy Review*, "The new citizenship looks to strengthening civil society against government. . . . Conservatives want to liberate civil society from the therapeutic welfare state."[68] The theme of liberating society from the tyrannical powers of liberal government, with its abstract ideals of equality and social right and its elevation of public policy over private initiative, was the defining concept of the new citizenship. In the realm of social welfare in particular, the public/private dichotomy of the new citizenship went beyond the market assumptions that define libertarian and business-oriented conservative attacks on the welfare state, however, shifting the policy focus onto religious institutions, especially onto the forms of authority and the methodologies of recovery that characterize their social outreach. This conservative social critique of the public sector was forcefully articulated by Michael Joyce in a series of policy-strategy statements beginning in 1994, the best known of which is "On Self-Government," an address delivered in the Heritage Foundation's Twenty-fifth Anniversary lecture series in 1998 and subsequently reproduced in *Policy Review* and other venues.[69] The development of the new citizenship agenda cut across the Democratic administrations of the 1990s and represented a strong current of internal "out-of-power" critique within conservatism; but it was only with the stalling of the Contract with America in 1995 and, a year later, the reelection of Bill Clinton, that the new citizenship was widely embraced by Washington conservatives.[70]

The Heritage Foundation assumed the mantle of the new citizenship following Clinton's reelection. After months of internal debate with Ed Feulner and conservatives across the country, Heritage significantly revamped its flagship publication, *Policy Review*, to make it a semi-official organ of the new citizenship, even going so far as to add the subtitle, *The Journal of American Citizenship*. *Policy Review* editor (and Heritage Foundation vice president) Adam Meyerson publicly acknowledged Joyce's "major influence" and, in his letter explaining the new editorial focus of the periodical upon its relaunching in January 1996, he drew heavily on the rhetoric and analysis of Joyce and his chief deputy at the Bradley Foundation, William Schambra, in particular Schambra's 1994 *Policy Review* article "By the People: The Old Values of the New Citizenship."[71]

"Out of the ashes of George Bush's defeat in 1992 has come a bold new strategy for American conservatism," the article begins. In a strident jeremiad against public policy and the public sector, Schambra outlines a two-pronged "resistance" and "restoration" strategy for the conservative movement. The resistance strategy entails a "rolling back of the incursions of the therapeutic state into the everyday lives of Americans by challenging the political hegemony of the 'helping' and 'caring' professions and bureaucracies," and also a major challenge to "the cultural hegemony of expert knowledge on behalf of the common sense, everyday wisdom of the average American." Accompanying and building off of this rollback, the "restoration" strategy entails a revitalization of local forms of association and authority, the fabric of which, according to Schambra, has been unraveled by the "acids of modernity" and the "liberal state's" bid to "eradicate civil society."[72] As Joyce later put it, the "efflorescence of these natural groupings"—family, church, neighborhood, and voluntary association— "is the key to the perpetuity of our free and democratic political and social institutions." This is the case because the natural groupings "take into their bosom the unformed child and, through tireless repetition and reinforcement of the same moral lessons over a lifetime, slowly forge a morally responsible human being."[73]

The growing national influence of this movement was marked in 1996 when the Heritage Foundation brought Michael Joyce in to personally brief freshman members of the 104th Congress in January 1996, coinciding with its relaunching of *Policy Review*. Joyce's speech in this setting is considered by many to be an important touchstone for the ascendancy of "compassionate conservatism" out of the ashes of the Contract with America and the disastrous Dole campaign the following year. *Policy Review* editor Adam Meyerson, for one, cites the speech in his introduction to April Lassiter's "compassionate conservative" handbook, *Congress and Civil Society*, written while she was a Bradley Fellow at Heritage in 1997.[74]

Taken up and promoted by Heritage, a significant group of smaller think tanks turned increasingly to the subject of religion and welfare reform in the mid-1990s, with financial support from the Bradley Foundation and a broad adherence to the principles of the new citizenship developed by Joyce. Upon relaunching *Policy Review* in 1996, Meyerson defined the contours of a new locus of conservative innovation and influence led by a distinct set of think tanks and think-tank programs: he cited the Capital Research Center, the Manhattan Institute, the Acton Institute, Philanthropy Roundtable, the Hudson Institute, *World Magazine*, the New Citizenship Project, the Civil Society Project, and the National Center for Neighborhood Enterprise. Increased funding from Bradley for all of these projects fostered a distinctive intellectual infrastructure for reframing welfare reform from a religious perspective.

The most important intellectual influence on the new citizenship model was the conservative sociologist Robert Nisbet. According to Christopher Beem, a movement insider, Nisbet was the "spiritual godfather" of the civil-society movement of the 1990s.[75] In 1990, the Bradley-funded Institute for Contemporary Studies republished Nisbet's masterwork, *The Quest for Community*, with an introduction by Schambra. While flying well below the radar compared to the many conservative blockbusters produced during the Clinton years, *The Quest for Community* reissue was arguably more influential in terms of policy development and legislation. The liberal policy critic and historian Nicholas Lemann (now Dean of the Columbia School of Journalism) took measure of what was happening before anyone else in the progressive press. He wrote a major piece for the *Washington Monthly* on the rise of "Nisbetism" in Washington politics, calling Nisbet's work the "mother lode of anti-big-government conservatism in America." This important piece of intellectual sleuthing opened the door to a major debate on the philosophical underpinnings and social implications of conservative antiwelfare politics, but as Lemann himself suggested at the time, "it looks as if Nisbetism is well on its way to becoming, finally, consensual," referring to its growing seduction of "liberal followers."[76] One could interpret welfare reform as confirmation of Lemann's prediction, but, like many of his conservative counterparts, he did not foresee the church-state difficulties of "Nisbetism" in areas such as education and welfare, nor could he have predicted, therefore, the renewed emphasis on governance reforms and public responsibility that would arise in the form of charitable choice and the faith-based initiative.

In 1994, Michael Joyce described *The Quest for Community* as a "magnificent classic" that tells the story of how civil society, "caught in a pincers movement between individual rights and the central state," has essentially "collapsed."[77] The European origins of such a formulation were detailed in Nisbet's work in his primary field, nineteenth-century French counter-revolutionary thought. In chapter 3, we return to this in considering the similar nineteenth-century roots of charitable choice and the faith-based initiative.

Berger and Neuhaus's *To Empower People* also continued to be influential, offering a still-relevant policy blueprint for the more radical Nisbetian perspective on the new citizenship. Among other things, *To Empower People* had actually influenced certain developments within the executive branch that pointed in the right direction: according to William Schambra, the White House Office of the Public Liaison was launched under Ford in 1977 as a mechanism for reaching out to the "mediating structures" depicted by Berger and Neuhaus.[78] Later administrative developments, such as Jimmy Carter's National Commission on Neighborhoods, Reagan's Presidential Office of Private Sector Initiatives, George H. W. Bush's Thousand Points of Light program and his Empowerment Task Force (led by Jack Kemp), are part of a sequence going back to the initial conceptual impetus of Berger and Neuhaus's *To Empower People*.[79] Introducing the second edition of the book in 1995, Michael Novak argued that this "new approach"—meaning "newly prominent," surely—would do more to determine the shape of domestic politics over the next half-century than anything else—not a wildly inaccurate prediction, as it turned out:

> Those of us involved in this project think that this new approach to social policy is as potent and, in its way, as socially promising as the ideas in possession of Franklin D. Roosevelt and his closest circle in 1932, when the New Deal began its fifty-year unfolding. We think that the political party that best makes mediating structures the North Star of a new bipartisan agenda will dominate practical politics for the next fifty years.[80]

The new citizenship tried revive the Berger-Neuhaus analysis, essentially with rich dosages of nineteenth-century antiliberal thought (or what was called Anti-Revolutionary thought in Kuyper's Dutch confessional tradition). Unfortunately, their understanding of nineteenth-century thought was so anachronistically pro-market that they ended up simply replicating the most significant limitation of the Berger-Neuhaus understanding of mediating structures: both models remained trapped in an essentially neoliberal framework that excluded economic power from the analysis of social decay. In contrast with Nisbet's own quasi-Marxian critique of economic liberalism and concentrated wealth—as with many other communitarian "anti-revolutionaries" who were influenced by Marx—the new citizenship of the 1990s was decidedly unconcerned with the effects of business and financial power on, say, the structure of the family and the stability of communities. In contrast, the faith-based initiative's intellectual lineage in nineteenth-century confessional struggles saw political and economic liberalism as a philosophical unity, a coordinated worldview uniting wealth and power, market and state, against the natural structures of society. Of course, despite these influences and even the simpler charitable ideas of "compassionate conservatism," the Bush Administration fell perfectly in line with standard neoliberalism in virtually every aspect of domestic policy relevant to working families, leaving most of us worse off. Bush inherited these limitations from the new citizenship paradigm and did not probe deeply enough to recognize that the restoration of communities does not begin and end with reforming or reducing government.

The new citizenship's neoliberal problem can be traced in part to its selective and uncritical embrace of Alexis de Tocqueville's famous analysis of American society in *Democracy in America.* New citizenship writings teemed with fanciful Tocquevillian observations about citizenly associations of old, but these observations had no grounding in comparative analysis of social conditions before the rise of the welfare state. Any such analysis of antebellum America as compared to, say, the decades after WWII, would have greatly inconvenienced the new citizenship's efforts to cast itself as a vanguard in the struggle for democratic ideals. For the new citizenship's formulaic return to Tocqueville's America was hardly the "democratic" thrust against public "tyranny" that it claimed to be. *Democracy in America* is far more accurate as an implicit commentary on European hereditarianism and status hierarchy than as a measure of substantive democracy and egalitarianism in nineteenth-century America. The Jacksonian Age Tocqueville celebrated fell far short of even extending basic political rights, let alone broader social rights, to the majority of the American population—comprised of women, menial laborers, African Americans, and Native Americans. These contradictions did not escape the attention of John Stuart Mill in his famous introduction to the first English edition of *Democracy in America* (1835), where he searingly noted that "[in] the American democracy, the aristocracy of skin, and the aristocracy of sex, retain their privileges."[81] In fact, where democracy did generate demands for broader social rights, as it did in the hands of French workers in the spring of 1848, Tocqueville stepped firmly back into his public role as a leading French aristocrat and lawmaker, casting his support in the National Assembly for police suppression of workers' agitation in the streets of Paris. The contrast with his celebration of the democratic capacities of American citizens is quite striking.[82] For Tocqueville, it appears, everything depended on what the citizenly associations were organized for and, more to the point, on the extent to which they generated political activity and political power for the people involved; in this respect, the new citizenship was indeed devoutly Tocquevillian in its assumptions of the essentially private rather than public nature of the basic social structures and the associational forms they celebrate. Even more problematically, the "neo-Tocquevillians" simply ignored the fact that Tocqueville's celebration of democratic society in America assumed (and partly witnessed, to be sure) a political economy based on small, freehold farms and the implied social good of widespread ownership of productive resources. A Tocquevillian critique of the welfare state could not really make any sense in the radically different economic environment of the 1990s, and those who tried to compare Tocqueville's views to their own took vast liberties in doing so. In fact, Tocqueville himself suggested quite the opposite, arguing at the end of volume two of *Democracy in America* that the biggest threat to democracy would emerge in the form of concentrated economic power. While "the territorial aristocracy of former ages was either bound by law, or thought itself bound by usage, to come to the relief of its serving-men, and to succour [their] distress,"

> the manufacturing aristocracy of our age first impoverishes and debases the men who serve it, and then abandons them to be supported by the charity of the public. . . . I am of the opinion, upon the whole, that the manufacturing aristocracy which is growing up under our eyes, is one of the harshest which ever existed in the world; but at the same time it is one of the most confined and least dangerous. Nevertheless the friends of democracy should keep their eyes anxiously fixed in this direction; for if ever a permanent inequality of conditions and aristocracy again penetrate into the world, it may be predicted that this is the channel by which they will enter.[83]

In his introduction to the 1990 edition of *The Quest for Community*, Schambra tellingly summarizes the policy framework that the new citizenship conservatives had begun to formulate based on Nisbet's social critique of the welfare state: "If the total political state flourished as a consequence of the erosion of traditional intermediate associations, then, Nisbet suggested, friends of liberty should fight for the preservation and propagation of these institutions. If function and authority could be restored to family, neighborhood, church, and local association, individuals might once again find the sense of status and belonging they sought, without appeal to the central state."[84]

Nisbet's influence on civil-society thinking in the 1990s was selectively molded in a similar way. The conservative sociological tradition he sought to revitalize in the 1950s was largely Catholic in origin, rooted in the French counter-Enlightenment thinking of Bonald, Maistre, and Lamennais, although Nisbet's approach remained sociological rather than confessional or theological. Paul Weyrich, for one, picked up on these older themes in lending his support to the faith-based initiative for its rejection of "libertarianism" in favor of "cultural conservatism."[85] Yet this was never an easy separation in the new citizenship model through which many religious conservatives became engaged in welfare reform as a new variety of the old "social question." The dominant Catholic influence in new citizenship thinking was not Nisbetian; it was of a more recent "neoconservative" vintage epitomized by Michael Novak's efforts to re-read Catholic social teaching as an apology for free-market capitalism and even economic liberalism as a moral worldview.[86] Novak's revisionism was the leading edge of a larger movement that coalesced, as mentioned earlier, in the formation of the Lay Commission on Catholic Social Teaching. Spearheaded by former Secretary of the Treasury William E. Simon, assisted by Michael Joyce, and intellectually centered around Michael Novak's work, the Lay Commission was formed in the spring of 1984 as a pro-market counterweight to the National Conference of Catholic Bishops, which was about to release its 120-page pastoral letter "Economic Justice for All," under the direction of Milwaukee Archbishop Rembert Weakland.[87] The Lay Commission's statement, *Toward the Future*, was essentially an effort to read Catholic social teaching into the free-market ideas of Milton Friedman and Friedrich von Hayek, an effort that would greatly expand over the next fifteen years as Catholicism was increasingly appropriated as a moral basis for pro-market attacks against the welfare state. In particular, the concept of "subsidiarity" was erroneously remodeled as a principle requiring maximum freedom for markets as the basic ordering structure of society, whereas traditional Catholic teaching subordinates markets no less than government to the common good, a concept that *Toward the Future* does not even mention.[88]

Michael Joyce lectured audiences at Yale and other institutions about the Catholic Bishops' "bad economics" as a leader of the Lay Commission on Catholic Social Teaching. In a recollection of that effort published in *Crisis* magazine in 1996, Joyce emphasized subsidiarity, opining that the Bishops' "Economic Justice for All" had applied the doctrine incorrectly by insufficiently reducing the role of state. Rather than mandating public policies that improve social conditions, subsidiarity, understood correctly, according to Joyce, requires a complete dismantling of public programs. Government must retreat, Joyce argued, because "no national or international economic policy, or power of government has even a fraction of the capacity to dignify the human person that is possessed by the den mothers and Little League coaches of our communities."[89] More ominously, "a 'scientific' theory of economics," he says, referring to the Bishops' somewhat Keynesian policy recommendations, "undergirded the totalitarianism of this century." Essentially, Joyce viewed the American welfare state as species of totalitarianism on a political continuum with the that of the Soviet Union and Nazi Germany. According to this logic, whether or not a government is a democracy or is effective at reducing poverty means nothing as long as the "den mothers and Little League coaches of our communities" do not enjoy their rightful monopoly on meeting social needs.[90]

The Compassionate Conservative Breakthrough

Weaving together the threads of neoliberal anti-statism and cultural conservatism, Marvin Olasky's work in the new citizenship movement of the 1990s deserves special attention. An obscure journalism professor on the evangelical fringe in the 1980s, everything changed for Olasky when he sent a two-page proposal to the Heritage Foundation in 1989. Heritage responded by bringing him to Washington as a Bradley Resident Scholar, where he researched and wrote *The Tragedy of American Compassion*, on leave from his teaching job at the University of Texas.

Ostensibly a work of history, *Tragedy* establishes little more than the fact that, prior to the consolidation of the modern welfare state, religious organizations dominated the social-service arena with their charitable works. Like many books in this era of think-tank-driven policy, *Tragedy* is really an ideological manifesto that selectively marshals history to illustrate a political argument. Indeed, it filled a major ideological gap in the right's "antigovernment" crusade against welfare by resurrecting nineteenth-century charity as an alternative. Though tipping its hat to "early colonial" models of social service, *Tragedy* is centered on the institutionalized religious charity of the late nineteenth century. In particular, Olasky highlights certain ministries' efforts to "categorize" the needy, especially in relation to their labor value. He approvingly cites Jacob Riis's plea that charities be diligent in "enforcing Paul's plan of starving the drones into the paths of self-support: no work, nothing to eat."[91]

For many on the right, the charitable ideal has potential insofar as charity is a really a form of privatization; for Olasky and other cultural conservatives, the religious revival and conversion effect that accompanies charitable works is just as important. Remarkably, Olasky's views on charity gained authority in policymaking circles and eventually Congress itself, despite their utter lack of grounding in statistical and social-scientific analysis as to the amount and degree of poverty and social dysfunction under the pre–welfare state charitable regime that he espouses. In fact, not only was poverty more widespread and extreme prior to federal intervention, but the poverty of an entire segment of the population, African Americans, was in fact institutionalized through enslavement or, later, segregation and disenfranchisement throughout the golden age of charity—not to mention the difficult plight of many of the elderly prior to Social Security and Medicare.[92]

Furthermore, Olasky correlates today's persistent poverty with the secularization of social services, with the rise of professional certification and government programs, and so forth, on the assumption that this compromises effectiveness. Encapsulating this view, he argues that the "war on poverty" was lost because it was really a "war on God." While this question of secularization/professionalization is a very important one (as discussed in chapter 1), even today there is no hard evidence to prove that more informal, faith-based services are more effective than professional services funded by governments. Olasky's particular thesis that the punitive, stigma-based methods of nineteenth-century charity in particular are more effective is simply unprovable for obvious historical reasons.[93]

Olasky was seen as a religious counterpart for Charles Murray's arguments, and in fact Murray (who was also a major client of the Bradley Foundation in the new citizenship period) contributed a preface to the second edition of The Tragedy of American Compassion while he was writing The Bell Curve with coauthor Richard Herrnstein. Both Olasky and Murray enjoyed spotlights on Capitol Hill during the welfare reform debate. Murray stoically consoled the Senate Finance Committee for having to engage "in a necessarily brutal calculation, trying to estimate what strategy will result in the least net suffering."[94] The Bell Curve's attempt to revive IQ measurement (psychometrics) as the primary basis for understanding social inequality outflanked on the far right even Murray's own earlier assessment of the failure of Great Society welfare programs in Losing Ground (1985).[95]

Like The Bell Curve, Olasky's theories had an important ideological effect in the buildup toward welfare reform. The main political effect of The Tragedy of American Compassion was to establish welfare policy (and poverty on the ground) as a primary battleground for cultural conservatism. In his first speech as Speaker of the House, Newt Gingrich commended The Tragedy of American Compassion, and in countless speeches thereafter Gingrich plied the Olasky line on charity and poverty prior to the destructive onslaught of the welfare state. Olasky took a leave of absence from the University of Texas to push for welfare reform on Capitol Hill, during which time he met with some fifty members of Congress as well as "numerous governors, state legislators, and mayors."[96] His views were widely aired on national and local television and radio, as well as on the right-wing talk-show circuit.[97] In January 1995, Olasky gave congressional testimony on the history of American charity and its basis in biblical or "covenantal" principles.

According to the covenantal model, Olasky told members of the House of Representatives, "The goal of all suffering was personal change. Those who refused to change did not deserve to be the beneficiaries of others' suffering; they might have to be left to themselves until their own suffering become [*sic*] so great that they gave up their false pride."[98] Notions of the "undeserving" poor easily blurred with Murray's concept of an immutable racial underclass. Murray himself characterized *Tragedy*, in his preface, as a book offering "hope" to the poor. The hope lay in Olasky's showing us how people before the welfare state were sometimes saved from the worst effects of poverty by religious authority and their personal faith; but this "hope" necessarily had no bearing, in either Murray's preface or Olasky's research, on the poor and their social position as a class or even as a part of society: poverty was an individual condition with an individual cure. The hereditarian subtext of replacing the welfare state with personal salvation was unmistakable: just as social stratification is an outcome of the natural distribution of individuals' innate intelligence, so too any influence on a person's social conditions, as with intelligence, must come from within. The only way for the poor to avoid being destroyed by their social status, which is fixed, is to grow in their faith.

After the victory of welfare reform, Olasky's influence helped to define a movement within Congress that sought capitalize on the new devolutionary momentum in social policy with a full program of "civil society" reforms. Led by Indiana Senator Dan Coats, this movement, launched as a thirty-member, bicameral legislative planning group in 1997, was called the Renewal Alliance. Its platform was Coats's own Project for American Renewal, introduced in September 1995.[99] Coauthored by William Bennett, the Project for American Renewal was inspired by Marvin Olasky, according to Coats.[100] School vouchers, abstinence education, divorce prevention, citizen crime patrols, crime victim restitution, and maternity shelters were among the strong civil society planks in the Coats-Bennett platform.[101]

The centerpiece of the Renewal Alliance's efforts, however, was a new charity tax credit, as noted in chapter 1. This idea did not survive the budget stalemate of 1996 or in any later congressional incarnations, and it was not incorporated into the general framework of Bush's faith-based initiative as laid out in *Rallying the Armies of Compassion*. Against the wishes of Olasky and other religious conservatives, such as Richard Land of the Southern Baptists' Ethics and Religious Liberty Commission, tax-based strategies languished amid intensive efforts to build a new, faith-based contracting capacity within the executive branch, operating under existing charitable choice laws. As we mentioned earlier, for these conservatives, tax-based charitable incentives are the best way to transfer social services to the churches, because this approach reduces the role of government and, ideally, the need for government. At an event sponsored by the Pew Forum on Religion and Public life in 2001, Michael Horowitz characterized his preference for tax credits over direct grants as follows: "What I want to do is far more radical. I want a wholesale substitution, particularly for the faith-based groups, of the charitable choice discretionary grants with a tax credit system . . . of the sort that Dan Coats has supported." This is needed, he said, primarily to eliminate "secularizing pressures" from the charitable choice policy design.[102] When Paul Weyrich's Free Congress Foundation weighed in on charitable choice in the spring of 2001, with its thirty-member Coalition on Compassion, they issued a statement of principles prioritizing religious freedom as well. In their view, "[the] only fair criterion for assessing the right of any provider to participate in the delivery of government financed social services is its effectiveness in meeting the needs of the beneficiaries." It is a mistake, however, to view these two positions as arguing for the same thing. A charity tax credit aims to provide an incentive for private spending on social needs, and in some versions this is paid for by corresponding reductions in federal program budgets, so that the result is effectively a privatization of welfare; Weyrich's emphasis, in contrast, was not on reducing the role of the state, but on restructuring that role to provide more protection for religious providers that are financed by the state.[103] What this means, in essence, is a framework that divides responsibility according to the natural purposes of its major components: the government can allocate resources, but it has no natural purpose in the delivery of social assistance; religious providers are naturally good at delivering services to those in need, but from their position in society they do not have the power to allocate sufficient resources to achieve this goal.

The charity tax-credit plank favored by Olasky, Horowitz, Land, and other key leaders was based in part on a template developed by the Commonwealth Foundation for Public Policy Alternatives in Harrisburg, Pennsylvania, one of a new crop of state-level think tanks that emerged in the 1990s to capitalize on federalist trends in national law and policy. Don Eberly, who later worked in the Bush Administration on international issues, had founded the Commonwealth Foundation in 1987 and was its first president. A few months before Bush's election, he published an article advocating charity tax credits as the next presidency's best option for establishing an alternative to the welfare state.[104] Other conservative think tanks that pushed charity tax credits include the Beacon Institute for Public Policy Research and the National Center for Policy Analysis, led by Pete

Society.[112] Carlson-Thies later worked closely with the Bush-Cheney transition team to establish the White House Office of Faith-Based and Community Initiatives, and was soon appointed assistant director for law and policy in the White House office.[113]

Between CPJ's early, foundational work on charitable choice and the launching of the faith-based initiative, these ideas took a major detour out of the Washington spotlight, thereby avoiding the factional politics in Congress that hamstrung the Project for American Renewal, even as charitable choice was languishing in the states. Texas was the exception, and, in fact, Governor Bush was already getting involved in promoting faith-based initiatives, of a sort, before charitable choice had even become law. It all began in the summer of 1995, when the San Antonio branch of Teen Challenge, an evangelical addiction-recovery program for youth, was notified by the Texas Commission for Alcohol and Drug Abuse that to continue operations, it would have to obtain a state license, requiring professionally trained counselors and other necessary safeguards. Teen Challenge refused to comply, and by the end of the summer it had attracted national attention as a martyr for the cause of dismantling the welfare state.[114] The National Center for Neighborhood Enterprise, a longtime Washington advocate for community-based economic and social development, sponsored a demonstration in support of Teen Challenge at the Alamo in July 1995. Marvin Olasky published a now famous op-ed in the *Wall Street Journal* attacking the Texas Commission for Alcohol and Drug Abuse.[115] Clint Bolick's Institute for Justice, better known for its litigation and legal advocacy for private school voucher programs and against affirmative action, mounted a legal case on behalf of Teen Challenge, and managed to orchestrate sympathetic national news coverage by NBC.[116] Governor Bush ordered a waiver of the compliance order and a review of the situation, and in the fall of 1995, the Institute for Justice negotiated a victory for Teen Challenge out of court, in the form of a consent order allowing it to practice without a license.

The most important step came next, when Bush issued an executive order establishing an Advisory Task Force on Faith-Based Community Service Groups in the spring of 1996, followed by a second executive order in December 1996 mandating implementation of the new federal charitable choice law by Texas government agencies. The task force, comprised mainly of Texas social-service ministry leaders, drew on the Teen Challenge case to devise systemwide changes in support of faith-based social-service providers. Enlisting Marvin Olasky, Stanley Carlson-Thies, Carl Esbeck, and Stephen Monsma as expert advisors, the task force released a report, *Faith in Action: A New Vision for Church-State Cooperation in Texas*, in December

1996.[117] It began with an overview of first principles derived from the publications of the Center for Public Justice.

In 1997, the Texas legislature carried out the task force's recommendations by passing three bills to ease or eliminate legal and regulatory barriers to religious social-service providers. As noted above, Bush also issued an executive order requiring state agencies to implement charitable choice by taking "affirmative steps prescribed by the [Personal Responsibility and Work Opportunity Reconciliation] Act to protect the religious integrity and the functional autonomy of participating faith-based providers."[118] Also following the recommendations of *Faith in Action*, legislation to create an "alternative" accreditation system for faith-based youth homes was proposed and ultimately passed in the Texas legislature in 1997. Accompanying this legislation was a Senate Concurrent Resolution promoting faith-based prison ministries. Following this, Charles Colson launched his InnerChange Freedom Initiative in the Texas prison system with Bush's support.[119]

Also established at this time was an alternative accreditation system for faith-based child-care organizations, the Texas Association of Christian Child Care Agencies. One important political subtext to this particular development was the state's long-running battle with the Roloff Homes, as recounted in a 2001 *Texas Monthly* piece by Pamela Colloff.[120] Although the point of the article was to use this admittedly troubling example to discredit Bush's White House efforts, the facts of the case did seem to reveal serious problems of insufficient oversight invited by the alternative accreditation system set up in Texas. The Texas Freedom Network, a progressive advocacy group, compiled a report detailing these and other related problems.[121] In light of this evidence (which has been posted without emendation for several years and was a basis for congressional testimony, and so is presumably accurate), it is fair to say that the Texas experiment was problematic in many ways, and the kinds of issues it raises about the relative advantages and disadvantages of aggressive deregulation of welfare contracting/licensing, and so on, did not get enough attention in the devising of Bush's Washington effort. However, it should be understood that, whatever poor oversight was possible under the highly experimental conditions in Texas in the late 1990s, federal programs governed by charitable choice are also governed by contracting and evaluation procedures that, while far from foolproof, are more stringent than those of many if not most states, certainly including Texas.

On top of the controversy surrounding the Roloff Homes, it also appeared that Bush's faith-based initiatives in Texas were not widely utilized, in part, certainly, because they had only just gotten off the ground as Bush began his White House run. In January 2001, with Bush entering the White House, the Texas Workforce Commission reported only fifteen state-level contracts with faith-based organizations, and later that spring the Texas legislature decided against reauthorizing the alternative accreditation program.

But by that point the White House effort was well underway, and considering the extraordinary pressures surrounding any new White House agenda—daily public scrutiny, reams of contradictory expert advice, competing agendas in Congress, and, in this case, generally hostile media coverage—it is fair to say that the faith-based initiative matured dramatically on its path from Austin to Washington.

The most important continuity between the Texas and Washington faith-based initiatives was a core commitment to redesigning the government's role in social assistance, not reducing it. Thus, when Bush entered the White House, the first order of business was to create a structure and a process whereby the dual goals that had been central all along—encouraging and enabling new religious involvement in social services, and protecting the religious freedom of publicly financed faith-based providers—could be realized on a national scale. The White House faith-based initiative was almost entirely focused on reforming social spending governance, not on reducing social spending or diminishing the role of government in addressing social needs. This reflects a continuity with the Texas approach as well as the unique concern of the Center for Public Justice over many years, with its emphasis on "public justice." In that respect, the Texas report *Faith in Action* should be seen as a pivotal document in the progression from charitable choice to the faith-based initiative. Although in many ways uniquely reflecting the Texas social-service landscape, and in the same regard also uniquely (and overly) aggressive on questions of accreditation, licensure, and so forth, *Faith in Action* is imbued with the background work on law, policy, and administration that the Center for Public Justice had been developing to that point. So too, Marvin Olasky's theories about moral stigma and religious uplift and Dan Coats's vision of restoring civil society resonated very strongly here. But neither of these related contributions could have predicted the strong governmental approach the White House took, nor the commitment to build it essentially from scratch.

Conclusion

In a 2003 interview, a former senior official in the White House Office of FBCI, David Kuo, offered his thoughts on the meaning of "compassionate conservatism." Clearly referencing the faith-based initiative, he described the governmental logic of this policy and where it stood on the political spectrum:

> Compassionate conservatism is distinguished from traditional conservatism because it has never drawn the line that there is no government responsibility. Traditional conservatism was stipulated on the idea that the private sector would take over for the government. Compassionate conservatism says that government funds can be leveraged with private sector funds, and private sector funds can be leveraged with government funds. This is not about shifting the burden. . . . There have been some Republicans who have suggested that the burden be shifted to private organizations, but the President rejects this idea of handing off to [the] private sector that which government has a vested interest in pursuing.[122]

Kuo's emphasis on the role of government is not just an expression of some traditional progressive view of the need for more social spending. The state's obligation, Carlson-Thies writes, is "to safeguard the autonomy and scope of action of other institutions within society. . . . to uphold, not substitute for, the fulfillment of responsibility by social institutions."[123] This obligation of the state is viewed as a religious obligation, because the social institutions that fulfill human needs undoubtedly precede the state in origin, design, and purpose, and so can only be from God. So too, the state is obliged to clothe the social contributions of the faithful in a public garment of freedom, lest society suffer for lack of a healthy faith.

This approach of state responsibility for the structures of society, Coats later summarized, "is consistent with a great and noble tradition of Catholic and Protestant social thought originating before the turn of the century with Pope Leo XIII and Abraham Kuyper." Indeed, "the parallel teachings of subsidiarity and sphere sovereignty have enriched our political debates with some basic principles."[124] If this is true, as I believe it is, it signals a radical departure from the core mission of conservative politics in this era, which was to reduce the role of the government and promote private gain, no matter what the social costs. The faith-based initiative, in contrast, requires government to enable and protect society in its essential, God-given functions. As I stated at the outset and explain in more detail in the next two chapters, by its own moral logic, the faith-based initiative does not stop at reforming government; as Carlson-Thies explains, religious autonomy depends on a pluralist vision of society, and pluralism is ultimately a vision of "social justice," a rightful ordering of government and society, and of resources and power within society. Ultimately, the precious resources of society must be protected from all the gathered powers, public and private, that exploit our human wealth for material gain. "Market individualism" no less than "intrusive government" gathers power in this way.

I have argued that the legal and administrative innovations of the faith-based initiative embodied two fundamental goals: to encourage religious involvement in a system of publicly financed social assistance, and to protect religious freedom in the delivery (and receipt) of public social services. If I am correct in this essential view, then we must recognize a further political truth: the faith-based initiative created a new and significant detour from "welfare reform as we know it"—from the liberal and conservative paths of reform that seemed the limit of things, fairly closely aligned, in the mid-1990s. More strikingly, we should also recognize how the policy design put in place in 2001, with the essential goal of expanding and implement charitable choice law, moved us closer to the Christian Democratic systems of Western Europe, particularly those of Germany and the Netherlands. Thus it is surely no coincidence that so much of the intellectual, legal, and policy work lying behind the faith-based initiative was carried out by people of religious convictions sympathetic to Christian Democratic approaches or directly informed by this example.

Stanley Carlson-Thies succinctly captured the philosophical essence of the faith-based initiative when he described it as a model of "pluralism . . . overcom[ing] extreme separationism in government social services," a "powerful and just idea."[125] This question of pluralism may seem rather bland in the American context, where it often simply refers to interest-group politics or questions of cultural diversity in the aggregated, large-bloc form of "identity politics." Important as these questions are, pluralism in this context goes deeper: it concerns the very structure of power and authority in the modern liberal state. What I call "social pluralism" is therefore a much older idea, but one whose relevance grows (or recedes) precisely as states evolve in their capacity to help or destroy society. Ultimately, pluralism, here, as it has come to define a new era of religious autonomy in our social safety net, concerns the sovereignty and attendant rights of communities and other social structures within the liberal state—not simply cultural identities or even the celebrated civic associations of the "social capital" debate, but the deeper structures of family, church, and community that literally originate a person's life and have the capacity to renew it if the person goes astray. The deeper pluralism that recognizes and protects these structures according to the intrinsic authority of their own natural functions and purposes in people's lives, which Christian Democracy and other conservative traditions define as God-given, grows out of a long evolution within Western legal and political thought, the cornerstone of which is the freedom of church. Most interestingly and most vexingly, it is pluralism within the liberal state that has proven most difficult to conceive juridically or in social thought, particularly in the United States. It was also embattled in Europe across much of the nineteenth century, but in that context the resources of confessional thought as well as communal law helped pluralism prevail in certain fundamental ways under Christian Democracy, particularly in welfare and schooling. As I have shown in this chapter, these influences and this model have become more and more influential in our own welfare politics. If that is a reasonable conclusion from the facts examined thus far, the historical and philosophical lineage of Christian Democracy should be of great interest to readers at this point, and so we turn to that subject in the next chapter.

THREE

Religious Autonomy and the Limited State

Against an abstract and unreal theory of State omnipotence on the one hand, and an atomistic and artificial view of individual independence on the other, the facts of the world with its innumerable bonds of association and the naturalness of social authority should be generally recognized and become the basis of our laws, as it is of our life.

—John Neville Figgis (1907)

The intellectual genealogy of the faith-based initiative was poorly understood in a public debate dominated by ideological interest groups that thrive on creating fear about religion, whether for or against it. In much of the debate, poverty was little more than a stage prop for the culture war. Yet it is precisely in terms of its religious ideas that the faith-based initiative holds the key to a new debate on poverty, one that neither side of the culture war is prepared to have.

To understand why requires a careful exploration of the Catholic and Dutch Calvinist theories of the limited state that shaped the design and implementation of the faith-based initiative. In addition, I discuss the historical development of the welfare states that arose on these foundations, offering a comparative viewpoint for our future efforts in the United States. This "transatlantic" analysis is a critical remedial step in our understanding if we want to go forward in building a broader consensus on faith-based social services. It is also essential for waging a war on poverty newly motivated by religious ideas, something I believe is possible and, potentially, far more "progressive," even radical, than either opponents or proponents of Bush's efforts have realized.

First I investigate the Catholic concept of subsidiarity, formulated officially in the papal encyclical *Quadragesimo anno* (1931), but originating in the powerful church-state arguments of Pope Leo XIII in the late nineteenth century, themselves arguably a modern permutation of much older ideas about church and state reaching back to the middle ages. Essentially, subsidiarity is a principle of political order embodying a "bottom-up" view of how the parts and the whole are related in Catholicism's organic idea of the state. Let me stress at the outset the most basic point in my consideration: subsidiarity is often carelessly cited as a kind of theological corollary of privatization or of a market-based view of society, but we will see that it is nothing of the kind and, in fact, may require *far more* state involvement in society than we currently have.

Second, I examine the concept of sphere sovereignty as developed by the Dutch Calvinist statesman and theologian Abraham Kuyper. With roots in a broader revival of orthodox Calvinist culture against the spread of anticlerical and liberal-statist ideas associated with the French Revolution, the Kuyperian theory of sphere sovereignty (*souvereiniteit in eigen kring;* literally, "sovereignty in one's own circle") emerged in Dutch party politics and was widely debated in the latter decades of the nineteenth century. Kuyper's immediate goal was to protect confessional schools from secularizing forces in Dutch education politics, but ultimately the Dutch people embraced sphere sovereignty as an organizing principle for the whole political and social order, creating the "pillarization" much studied by social scientists and historians today. More distinctively pluralistic and anti-statist than its Catholic counterpart of the same era—in part owing to the polyglot culture and federal heritage of the early modern Dutch Republic—sphere sovereignty nevertheless captures a similar confessional outlook on the liberal state, rooted in a common antagonism toward individualistic views of society and the seeming alliance of individual rights and the power of the state against religious autonomy and authority in society.

Protective of the churches' internal life and social influence, sphere sovereignty and subsidiarity are both, essentially, *religious theories of the limited state.* I use this formulation in contrast with the more commonly understood laissez-faire vision of the limited state, which is inspired by market ideas of efficiency and entrepreneurialism. Charles Glenn describes the difference this way:

> There is a fundamental difference between *decentralization* within the institutional structures of the welfare state, and true *subsidiarity* that places primary responsibility for "the human care of human beings" upon civil society institutions. . . . Either decentralization or subsidiarity could be characterized as

measures promoting "autonomy," but the advantages of the first are limited to the greater efficiency that decentralization may bring, while promoting subsidiarity is intended to change the *nature* of the services provided.[1]

Glenn's reference to "autonomy" is important for situating sphere sovereignty and subsidiarity as part of a much longer history of church-state conflict and theory, predating the American concept of church-state separation embodied in the religion clauses of the First Amendment to the United States Constitution. Ultimately, the seminal design principles of charitable choice derive from an older church-state lineage known as *libertas ecclesiae*, or "freedom of the church," reaching back to the New Testament and to the early formulations of Pope Gelasius I in the late fifth century. The central idea is that believers united by a transcendent idea of the world's creation are directly sovereign in the offices and practices of their faith, because these are given by God, not by the state. Understanding the freedom of the church is essential in considering how Kuyper, Leo XIII, and, later, Christian Democratic welfare systems sought to protect religious autonomy within the liberal welfare state, and how and why this modernized "Christian constitutionalism," as Leo XIII called it, has become a part of U.S. welfare politics.

We should not ignore the fact, however, that among Catholic populations in particular, authoritarian, "corporatist" tendencies emerged from the Leonine church-state tradition between the two World Wars, particularly in Germany, Austria, Italy, Portugal, and Spain. These were encouraged by the 1931 encyclical *Quadragesimo anno*, which promoted a corporatist restructuring of labor-capital relations. In the encyclical, however, Pope Pius XI specifically warned against authoritarian statism (referring particularly to Italian fascism), admonishing that "the state is substituting itself in the place of private initiative, instead of limiting [itself] to necessary and sufficient help and assistance, . . . which risks serving particular political aims rather than contributing to the initiation of a better social order" (sec. 95).

At the end of the chapter I discuss the German case in particular, in which confessional critics of the Weimar Republic's social-democratic welfare system helped pave the way for the Nazi seizure of power. After Word War II, the subsidiary welfare model developed by the confessional critics of Weimar liberalism, shorn of authoritarian tendencies, was essentially reborn in the Federal Republic of Germany and established in its Constitution, known as the Grundgesetz, or Basic Law. This transformation, the institutional birth of modern Christian Democracy, is one of the most important political legacies of Leonine church-state ideas, and it sheds important comparative light, in turn, on the faith-based redesign of American welfare governance today. At the very least, the European heritage enriches our understanding of the constitutional and civil rights challenges emphasized by critics of Bush's efforts: these are essentially legal by-products, one can see, of a broader political effort to transform welfare governance under new religious principles of state action.

There is substantial truth in Virgil Nemoianu's observation that "compassionate conservatism," and particularly the faith-based initiative, "represents the arrival of Christian Democracy in American political life."[2] Nevertheless, the "subsidiary welfare state" conceived by Glenn and other advocates influenced by European Christian Democracy only partly fulfills the requirements of religious and social autonomy. Simply put, in critiquing the "destructive tenets" of liberalism, Kuyperian and Catholic social teaching saw private economic power, no less than public power, as a threat to social autonomy and to the natural sustaining order of family, church, and community. Neither saw the freedom of the church simply in terms of limiting the state, because they could also see how laissez-faire anti-statism promoted society's enslavement to capitalism. Simply limiting the state to preserve social autonomy while leaving the worker and his family defenseless against destructive economic power was not enough by any Christian standard of order, let alone justice, and this realization led to the characteristic "third way" model of Christian Democracy, combining faith-based, even confessional, social services and education with extensive social transfers to assure a minimum level of welfare outside of the market. I conclude this chapter by examining the Christian Democratic model at work and considering the limitations it exposes in American welfare policy today.

A Catholic Theory of the Limited State

Subsidiarity is best known today in the secular, federalist version enshrined in the Maastricht Treaty of the European Union, which says that "the Community shall take action, in accordance with the principle of subsidiarity, only if and in so far as the objectives of the proposed action cannot be sufficiently achieved by the Member States and can therefore, by reason of the scale or effects of the proposed action, be better achieved by the Community." Subsidiarity, here, is assimilated as a federalist idea of uniting several autonomous states in a common order. Like sphere sovereignty, however, this was originally a theological concept of governance and political order within a single state.[3]

The central document in this tradition is Pius XI's 1931 encyclical

Quadragesimo anno. "The Fortieth Year" of the title refers back to *Rerum novarum,* issued by Leo XIII in 1891. Considered the flagship of Catholic social teaching, *Rerum novarum* played an important role in salvaging the church from antimodernist currents that advantaged socialism in the competition for working-class loyalty. It promoted workplace reforms, capital-labor reconciliation, and Catholic worker organizations. In this respect, *Rerum novarum* was a product of its times. But there was a deeper historical undercurrent. Against the statism of socialist and social-democratic movements of the time—the fear that the state would "absorb paternal authority" and destroy the family featured prominently—*Rerum novarum* gave religion and the church a renewed structural priority in addressing the needs of society. This was later developed more systematically and termed the "subsidiary function" in *Quadragesimo anno.*

It is important to recognize the deeper theoretical bedrock on which subsidiarity was built. In a series of articles published in the 1950s, the American Jesuit theologian John Courtney Murray did exactly this. He investigated the so-called Gelasian texts of Leo XIII, which emerge as a brilliant reconstruction of the patristic and medieval tradition that Pope Gelasius I first inspired in the late fifth century—a tradition known as *libertas ecclesiae,* or "freedom of the church." At the root of this *libertas ecclesiae* was Gelasius's concise formulation *Duo sunt,* "two there are," a theory of dual sovereignty. Murray called Leo XIII's Gelasian challenge to liberal statism a revival of "Christian constitutionalism." In Murray's hands, this tradition took on further new life as a revival of collective religious freedom within the liberal state; and this kind of communal or group-based freedom, I argue, is really the implicit radical substance of the faith-based initiative.[4]

It should be clear that *libertas ecclesiae* is distinct from, and much older than, what we in the United States call "religious liberty." In our constitutional tradition, religious liberty protects individual freedom of worship and belief and was a concept evolving mainly from the experience of dissenting or nonconformist believers in countries with established churches. Drawing on the broader Enlightenment principle of freedom of conscience, religious liberty was enshrined in the "free exercise" clause of the First Amendment of the U.S. Constitution, which stamps it, obviously, as a freedom of the individual in relation to government. The Puritan theologian Elisha Williams defined religious freedom as the "unalienable [and divine] right of private judgment in matters of religion."[5] Thomas Jefferson described the "wall of separation between church and state," formulated in his famous 1802 letter to the Danbury Baptist Association, as an "expression of the supreme will of the nation *in behalf of rights of conscience.*"

Freedom of the church, in contrast, is a doctrine of corporate or communal religious autonomy, protecting the institutional integrity and self-governance of religious groups within the political order or state. As legal scholar Richard Garnett argues, freedom of the church, in this corporate sense, is indeed recognized in many ways in American law. This occurs under what is broadly known as the law of church autonomy. For example, government cannot interfere in the internal affairs of churches, such as worship, membership rules, ecclesial polity, or ministerial employment. Government is also restrained in litigating church conflicts that hinge on theological differences, especially in matters of personnel and property. More controversially, churches and their missions are exempt from federal income taxation and from all or most forms of property taxation in every state. Like that of other nonprofit institutions, the tax-exempt status of churches is generally conceived as a matter of "associational freedom." Yet, as Garnett stresses, the corporate, associational nature of religious freedom is not the philosophical starting point of such policies in the United States. Rather, the "independence and autonomy of churches . . . are framed as deriving from, or existing in the service of, the free-exercise or conscience rights of individual persons," not as "the basis or foundation" for those individual rights.[6]

Contrast the American emphasis on individual conscience with Murray's description of the context that drove Leo XIII to undertake a new defense of the freedom of the church:

> Leo XIII developed the theory and practice of Church-State relationships amid the conditions created by the peculiar nineteenth-century plight of the so-called Catholic nations of Europe and Latin America. The major feature of the situation consisted in the efforts of an activist ideological sect to effect, through the control and use of governmental power, the politico-social change known as "separation of Church and State." This current phrase was pregnant both of an ideology and of a political and social program. It meant, first, the alteration of the Christian structure of politics, which had been characterized by the traditional duality of Church and state, in the direction of a juridical and social monism. It meant, secondly, the evacuation of the Christian substance of society through the establishment of a surrogate political religion which went by the name of "laicism."[7]

Leo XIII became Pope in 1878, toward the end of the Prussian *Kulturkampf* against the Catholic Church in the German Empire. In Harold Laski's fascinating study of nineteenth-century church-state conflicts, Bismarck and the *Kulturkampf* epitomized the spreading collapse, under liberal regimes, of pluralistic sovereignty in the Gelasian mold of coexisting powers. Bismarck, Laski wrote, "admitted the Church's right to absolute freedom in her own domain," but he also held that the church's domain "must be defined by the state." Alluding to the medieval struggles, Bismarck himself wrote that the *Kulturkampf* was a revival of the "primeval fight for supremacy between royalty and priesthood. . . . What we aim at is the protection of the State, the establishment of a distinct boundary-line between priestly dominion and Royal rule, defined in such sort that the State may be enabled to abide by it."[8] The Jesuit order was banished, and its members were expelled in the early 1870s. The anticlerical Falk Laws (named after Adalbert Falk, Bismarck's minister of culture) ordered that clerical education and appointments be regulated by the government and that "reasons of State" were sufficient to deny any appointment.[9] Directly and indirectly, moreover, the church was being "crowded out" of its traditional mission domains by emerging liberal welfare, education, and family policies. Extreme aggressions in France, such as the confiscation of church property and the proscription of religious associations, simply carried out the logic of a new kind of absolutism, confessional advocates argued. This entailed a new kind of a "separation of church and state" that Leo XIII described as "monistic"—separation, that is, on the terms of the state and according to a logic that assumed the state to be the only truly sovereign, unencroachable authority in the life of a people, "unified, indivisible, and omnicompetent."[10] This "new regalism," Leo XIII argued, was simply an inverted form of the old divine-right regalism of the middle ages, which absorbed the church into the state under the same unifying logic that, in modern times, was now being used to proscribe the church.

Leo XIII painstakingly dissected the new monistic statism of the liberal revolution in Europe, arguing that the church's true sovereignty was violated by state-controlled separation no less than by religious control of the state.[11] In each case, a monistic view of power violated the classical Christian tradition of the "two powers," sacred and civil, handed down from the New Testament itself: "Render therefore to Caesar the things that are Caesar's; and to God the things that are God's" (Luke 20:25). In church history, it was Pope Gelasius I who, in the late fifth century, revitalized the tradition of dual sovereignty, or what Leo XIII later termed the "Christian constitution" of states in his great political encyclical *Immortale Dei* (1885).

As Brian Tierney points out, when Emperor Constantine I embraced

Christianity (granting toleration in the Edict of Milan in 313 CE), there was no legal precedent, in Roman law, for delineating the boundaries between the Christian church and the Roman state, the former having developed independently of (indeed under the censure of) the latter for more than two centuries prior to Constantine. The thinly disguised tension of Jesus's concept of dual sovereignty—one should never forget that this was an idea born of a schismatic movement within a politically subordinated minority religion—did not disappear with the legalization of the Church. Indeed, the question Jesus carefully avoided—what happens when loyalty to God and loyalty to emperor conflict—only became more pressing when Church and Empire were legally reconciled. In the late fourth century, Saint Ambrose, the bishop of Milan, rejected the idea that the Church, like everything else, was subject to the power of the emperor. "Palaces belong to the emperor, churches to the priesthood." Indeed, "The emperor is within the Church, not above the Church."[12] Ambrose's pupil Saint Augustine constructed his famous metaphor of the City of God around this same dualistic tension with worldly power, theologically identifying the latter as a consequence of, and necessary restraint on, human sin. But it was Gelasius I who directly addressed the problem in his letter to the Byzantine Emperor Anastasius (494 CE), using the memorably compact formulation *Duo sunt*: "Two there are, august emperor, by which this world is chiefly ruled, the sacred authority of the priesthood and the royal power."[13] In his treatise entitled *On the Bond of Anathema* (496 CE), Gelasius further crystallized the idea of dual powers that would ground Leo XIII's later defense of the freedom of the church. In Leo XIII's Gelasian texts, the basic idea of two distinct sovereignties gave rise to a coordinative view of church and state: the separate spheres of church and state must be coordinated by a rule of mutual nonencroachment, preserving the essential purposes and means that each is given, fully and distinctly, by God. As Gelasius I had written,

> For Christ, mindful of human frailty, regulated with an excellent disposition what pertained to the salvation of his people. Thus he distinguished between the offices of both powers according to their own proper activities and separate dignities. . . . In this fashion spiritual activity would be set apart from worldly encroachments and the "soldier of God" (2 Timothy 2:4) would not be involved in secular affairs, while on the other hand he who was involved in secular affairs would not seem to preside over divine matters. Thus the humility of each order would be preserved, neither would be exalted by the subservience of the other, and each profession would be especially fitted for its appropriate functions.[14]

Quoting Alois Dempf, Murray explained that the Gelasian theory of dual sovereignty was the "Magna Charta of the whole 'freedom of the church' in medieval times." It was "the charter of a new freedom, such as the world had never known," he added.[15] Of course, the great historical watershed for this new freedom was the investiture controversy of the late eleventh century, waged by Pope Gregory VII against King Henry IV of Germany. The pivotal issue was "lay investiture"—whether the king had the right to appoint bishops of the Church. Henry IV claimed that he did, because he held power directly "by the pious ordination of God," and thus ruled over the sacred and civil domains under a single authority above all others except God.

It is important to understand the growing breadth of the royal prerogative that sparked the investiture controversy. As Robert Wilken explains, "The capital fact of ecclesiastical life in the early Middle Ages was that the affairs of the Church were managed by kings and princes."[16] Interfering in the church's governance was not a simply a matter of practical domination for the sake of power; it was encoded in the very definition of kingship as something anointed by God and accountable only to God. At their coronation, medieval kings were invested with both spiritual and temporal authority over their realms. "These new Christian kings," Wilken writes, "became the Church's defenders and bankers and overseers as they donated their own resources to build churches, endow monasteries, and in other ways lay the foundations for a Christian society."[17] Royal patronage of the church bolstered the king's prerogative to appoint bishops and exert control over liturgical matters and church governance. As patrons of the church, Kings viewed the bishops as their servants. All down the territorial hierarchy of a given kingdom or fiefdom, the church was segmented by patronage—land donations, funds for building churches and monasteries, artistic and musical commissions, and so forth. When a nobleman constructed a church on his land using his own funds, Wilken explains, "he considered the church his own property and reserved the right to nominate a priest to serve the people living on his land."[18] The issue of lay investiture was symbolic of this general pattern of religious subordination to kings and lords:

This term originally referred to the ceremony in which a lord handed over land to a vassal in exchange for an oath of fealty. As a symbol of the transfer the lord would give the new vassal a staff or a sword or a spear. In time a similar practice developed at the installation of a bishop. At the time of consecration the king or his representative handed over the symbols of the office to the bishop (or abbot), usually a staff or crozier and a ring, and the king said:

"Receive the church." The bishop was then consecrated in an ecclesiastical rite by other bishops, but the symbols of authority had been transmitted by the king, not the bishops. It was obvious that this system encouraged greater loyalty to the local lord than to the pope or to the Church as a universal communion.[19]

Gregory VII excommunicated Henry IV for refusing to accept papal control over the appointment of bishops. As a result of this, Henry's territorial position was weakened by political defections among the nobility and bishops, forcing him to recant his position (he did so, famously, by standing barefoot in the snow for three days outside a castle at Canossa in Northern Italy, where the pope was staying on route to a council in Augsburg that was to resolve the conflict). Aside from the legendary drama of the affair, Henry's defeat in the investiture contest, Harold Berman argued, inaugurated a "total transformation" in the legal and political order of Western Europe, one in which a new legal concept of the church "almost demanded the invention of the concept of the State."[20] Some further argue that, by establishing a clear boundary between political power and the authority of the church in its own realm, the investiture contest made possible the theoretical development of the "limited state" of modern democracy. By limiting the reach of the state in religious matters, the freedom of the church established a template for the larger body of civil freedoms we enjoy today. As George Weigel explains, now the state would not be "all in all":

> The state would not occupy every inch of social space. Indeed, the state had to acknowledge that there were some things it couldn't do because it was simply incompetent to do them—and that acknowledgement of limited competence created the social and cultural conditions for the possibility of what a later generation of constitutions and democrats called the limited state. The Western ideal—a limited state in a free society—was made possible in no small part by the investiture controversy.[21]

For Leo XIII, the liberal welfare state was no less destructive of the freedom of the church than divine-right monarchy. "In either event, whether the Church be included within the political order or excluded from it, the result is the same: a profanation of the sacred takes place," Murray explained.[22] A liberal constitutionalism that did not recognize the church's authority to order its own affairs and maintain its mission in society was just another form of absolutism—not only in terms of the church, but in terms of all human loyalties that do not originate with the state. An absolutism that absorbs the church is no different than one which excludes it, because in both cases the "inviolable distinction between the sacred and the secular is subverted." The resulting "unity" actually creates disorder:

> The result may indeed be a unification; it is ordinarily in the name of the "integrity" of the political order that the process of politicization of the sacred goes forward. But the unity created is a false unity, achieved at the expense of right order. What happens is a reduction of Gelasius' "two" to "one," not an organization of the two, under respect for their distinction, into a true unity of order.[23]

Murray drew a compelling connection between the corporate freedom of the church and human freedom more generally, echoing Leo XIII's characteristic linkage of worldly oppression and spiritual death. "It is a primal mission of the Church to preserve her own being in all its sacredness against any profanation by enclosure within the state," Murray wrote. Corporate religious freedom, however, was but a means to the further end of preserving "the original sacrednesses inherent in human social life from complete politicization by the secular power."[24]

The encyclical *Immortale Dei*, issued in 1885, defined the basic problem of religious autonomy in a manner strikingly similar to Kuyper's articulation of sphere sovereignty, as we will see below. What is most important here is the recognition of the particular problems arising when church and state *both* have legitimate jurisdiction in a given social domain—education and welfare being the most obvious examples. As Leo explained in *Immortale Dei*:

> The Almighty, therefore, has given the charge of the human race to two powers, the ecclesiastical and the civil, the one being set over divine, and the other over human, things. Each in its kind is supreme, each has fixed limits within which it is contained, limits which are defined by the nature and special object of the province of each, so that there is, we may say, an orbit traced out within which the action of each is brought into play by its own native right. But, inasmuch as each of these two powers has authority over the same subjects, and as it might come to pass that one and the same thing—related differently, but still remaining one and the same thing—might belong to the jurisdiction and determination of both, therefore God, who foresees all things, and who is the author of these two powers, has marked out the course of each in right correlation to the other. "For the powers that are, are ordained of God."[25]

To preserve the church's legitimate claims in social areas increasingly addressed by the state, the "right correlation," on the dual sovereignty model, came to be called the "subsidiary function," or subsidiarity. In the encyclical *Arcanum* (1880), Leo XIII outlines the modern subsidiary function in a description of how the two distinct powers of church and state should be coordinated in areas where they both have a divinely appointed purpose or authority. Reaffirming the Gelasian position, he writes "There is no doubt that Jesus Christ . . . willed that the sacred power should be distinct from the civil power and that each should be free and untrammeled in the conduct of its own affairs."[26] But the state must not only recognize the church's role in areas of overlapping authority and purpose. "The power to which the affairs of men are entrusted should at the proper juncture wait upon the word of the power which has in its charge the affairs of heaven." Embedded in the qualification "at the proper juncture" is a strong notion of church autonomy, but one that is circumscribed by the domain—the purpose and means—God has given to the church. This "harmonious arrangement," governed by a rule of mutual non-encroachment, but bound together by the ultimate objective of human thriving on Earth and unto Eternity, secures the "best interests of both powers."[27] Looking in the direction of France and looking back at Bismarck's *Kulturkampf,* Leo XIII emphasized the freedom of the church even as he stressed a coordination of civil and sacred sovereignties where they share jurisdiction. Thus, "those who hold the high power of government ought not to perpetrate the wrong involved in forcing the Church to serve them or be subordinate to them, in allowing her less than her proper freedom to conduct her own affairs, or in taking away any part of the other rights conferred upon her by Jesus Christ." Or as he wrote in the encyclical *Sapientiae Christianae* (1890):

> The Church alike and the State, doubtless, both possess individual sovereignty; hence, in the carrying out of public affairs, neither obeys the other within the limits to which each is restricted by its constitution. . . . On this very account, the Church cannot stand by, indifferent as to the import and significance of laws enacted by the State; not insofar, indeed, as they refer to the State, but in so far as, passing beyond their due limits, they trench upon the rights of the Church. (sec. 30)

The unique modern problem that Leo XIII delineated was that of a welfare state whose growing competences in a needful society—education systems, social services, public health, family law—necessarily overlapped with the mission of the church, each having its own legitimate authority and obligations in these realms. The whole church-state struggle of the late nineteenth century revolved around this growing tension.

The most important "applied" statement of religious autonomy in the Leonine tradition was Pope Pius XI's 1929 encyclical *Divini illius magistri* ("On Christian Education"). This was the political culmination of the Church's long struggle to protect its traditional role in youth education against the rising tide of liberal public schooling in the governments of Europe. This trend was in fact epitomized by the conflict that emerged in unified Italy, where the liberal constitutional monarchy (known as the Kingdom of Italy) formed in 1861 systematically deprived the Church of its temporal powers by dismantling the Papal States (culminating in the removal of Pius IX as ruler of Rome in 1870). Accompanying this political dispossession (known generally as the Roman Question), unified Italy's liberal government worked to establish national education policies, first by extending the Piedmontese Casati Law of 1859 across the unified kingdom. This law created a central ministry of education to supervise all schools, including religious schools, throughout the new kingdom. With the dramatic reduction of the Church's temporal powers and its diminished cultural position after unification, Catholics were deterred and eventually forbidden from voting in parliamentary elections under the papal *Non Expedit* policy ("It is not expedient"), which remained Church policy until 1905 and even then was only partially lifted. In Pius IX's *Syllabus of Errors*, issued in 1864, the emerging secular education system was condemned in Errors 45 and 47.[28]

The theory of church-state relations that guided these policies was formulated by Count Cavour, the Piedmontese architect of Italian unification. He famously called for "a free church in a free state," reinscribing the classical two-powers theory as a compromise framework of preserving church autonomy (noninterference by the state in its institutional procedures and activities) while dismantling the church's temporal powers (powers of government applicable to all).[29] Although Cavour's idea of freedom of the church permitted the legal existence and autonomy of church-controlled schools, the government's efforts to create a national system of compulsory youth education, with only limited forms of religious instruction and limited supervision by the Church, effectively diminished the Church's educational domain and cultural influence in favor of a secular national culture divorced from the Church's teachings and personnel. One important turning point in this effort was a national regulation, issued in 1871, amending the Casati Law to make religious education optional in public schools; then, with a shift in power from the right wing of the Liberal Party (the *Destra*) to the left wing (the *Sinistra*), the educational "laicization" process culminated with the passage of the Coppino Law of 1877, establishing compulsory state education (for children ages 6–9) with no curricular requirements of religious instruction.[30] In the era of Giovanni Giolitti (he was installed as Prime Minister five times between 1892 and 1921) the compromise position of voluntary religious instruction in the public schools (with public financing if approved by provincial councils) became settled law.

With the fascist accession to power in 1922, Mussolini's extreme anticlericalism did not prevent him from seeking political reconciliation with the Church. This was one powerful means of dividing the opposition in his bid to establish a totalitarian state—most importantly, by driving a wedge between the Vatican and the Partito Popolare Italiano (Italian Popular Party), formed after World War I as a Catholic mass party to compete with the Italian Socialist Party (the Popular Party was dissolved in 1926 after Pius XI, installed in 1922, publicly forbade it from forming a coalition with the socialists that would have overthrown Mussolini). Mussolini's theory of the "ethical" state was simple to understand: "All within the state, nothing outside the state, and nothing against the state." The Cavourian liberal ideal of religious autonomy within a secular state, which the Church basically came to accept in key areas such as education and welfare, was viewed as subversive from the fascist perspective of national unity. Yet certain continuities between Italian fascism and liberal church-state policy are also evident. Not least of all, Mussolini basically shared the view, institutionalized by the long liberal hegemony reaching back to Cavour, that youth education administered by the state was the most important mechanism for generating adequate civic consciousness for the maintenance of a unified state.

With the Riforma Gentile of 1924 (named after Mussolini's education minister and fascist court philosopher Giovanni Gentile), the Vatican enjoyed a restoration exceeding anything the Church had ever been able to extract from the liberals. Crosses were returned to classroom walls; religious instruction was encouraged in public schools and extended to secondary schools; religious schools gained parity with public schools in qualifying students for state exams; and public funds were made available to repair war-damaged Church buildings.[31] All of this pointed toward a final resolution of the Roman Question, the great prize that lay in the background of Vatican negotiations with Mussolini from 1922 forward. The extraordinary Lateran Treaties of 1929 restored Vatican City as a neutral and sovereign territory under papal control. A Concordat on church-state relations was also secured, recognizing Catholicism as the official religion of the state; making religious instruction compulsory in primary and secondary schools; declaring marriage a sacrament and not simply a civil contract; professing the need for greater harmony between public policies and Church doctrines and teachings; and assuring freedom of association for the Church's primary lay movement, Catholic Action.

Pius XI declared of the Lateran Agreement that God had been restored to Italy and Italy to God.[32] Yet Mussolini soon delivered a four-hour speech in Parliament to "spin" the agreement as uncompromising in every respect on the ultimate sovereignty of the fascist state, noting urgently that state control in the long-contested domain of education remained "intractable." Over the next two years, Mussolini moved aggressively against Catholic Action and other youth associations, considered the most dangerous and potentially disloyal precincts of the Church. Against this and other media-fueled anti-Catholic aggressions, escalating dramatically in 1930 and 1931, Pius XI issued the encyclical *Non abbiamo bisogno* (subtitled "On Catholic Action in Italy"); here, too, the principle of divided sovereignty in education was foregrounded:

> A conception of the State which makes the rising generations belong to it entirely, without any exception, from the tenderest years up to adult life, cannot be reconciled by a Catholic either with Catholic doctrine or with the natural rights of the family. It is not possible for a Catholic to accept the claim that the Church and the Pope must limit themselves to the external practices of religion (such as Mass and the Sacraments), and that all the rest of education belongs to the State. (sec. 52)

Society Against the State

Across the battle lines drawn by liberalism and fascism, Leo XIII's framework of "Christian constitutionalism" came to be concentrated in an expression that was at once more technical and more generous. This was the rule of *subsidiarity*, a term that was broadly applied and took the freedom of the church as a template for the freedom of society. In the subsidiary state, community institutions, particularly the family and the church, are the more proximate, and therefore more natural, institutions of social support. Thus, the state must leave many social tasks to these institutions, and, at the same time, must insure their autonomy in carrying out these tasks under their own unique authority, which comes directly from God. As an ordering principle, subsidiarity assumed a pluralistic understanding of society, one that was antiliberal, prioritizing community needs and norms over individual rights and ultimately anchored in the idea that there are natural human structures originating outside the state that must be strengthened and protected if humanity is to thrive. It is no coincidence that Leo's fastidious reconstruction of a modern "subsidiary state" out of the early Christian framework of dual sovereignty was exactly contemporary with the pluralistic, legal-historical work on Germanic fellowship theory and social law undertaken by Otto von Gierke (and other "Germanist" legal scholars) as well as Gierke's British disciples, F. W. Maitland, J. N. Figgis, and Harold Laski. In *Rerum novarum*, Leo XIII formulated the social-pluralist basis of religious autonomy in strong terms. Referring to confraternities, religious orders, and trade unions, Leo explained that

> private societies, then, although they exist within the body politic, and are severally part of the commonwealth, cannot nevertheless be absolutely, and as such, prohibited by public authority. For, to enter into a "society" of this kind is the natural right of man; and the State has for its office to protect natural rights, not to destroy them; and, if it forbid its citizens to form associations, it contradicts the very principle of its own existence, for both they and it exist in virtue of the like principle, namely, the natural tendency of man to dwell in society.(sec. 51)

The immediate reference point for defining social pluralism in this way was of course the liberal "spoilation" of Church properties and the *Kulturkampf* directed against the Church's orders and social ministries in many countries, particularly Germany, Italy, and France.[33] Obviously, Leo's first concern in defining social pluralism as part of natural law was to defend religious autonomy, comparing freedom of this kind to the ruinous record of laissez-faire individualism:

> In many places the State authorities have laid violent hands on these [religious] communities, and committed manifold injustice against them; it has placed them under control of the civil law, taken away their rights as corporate bodies, and despoiled them of their property, in such property the Church had her rights, each member of the body had his or her rights, and there were also the rights of those who had founded or endowed these communities for a definite purpose, and, furthermore, of those for whose benefit and assistance they had their being. Therefore We cannot refrain from complaining of such spoilation as unjust and fraught with evil results; and with all the more reason do We complain because, at the very time when the law proclaims that association is free to all, We see that Catholic societies, however peaceful and useful, are hampered in every way, whereas the utmost liberty is conceded to individuals whose purposes are at once hurtful to religion and dangerous to the commonwealth. (sec. 53)

One could argue from this that the freedom of church is the essential foundation of social pluralism and the origin of pluralistic legal thought; certainly Leo derived his well-known (and very influential) defense of trade unions in *Rerum novarum* from the same natural law foundations as those of the freedom of the church, and this could be read as a broader affirmation of social pluralism. One important thread in such an understanding leads back to the Jesuit philosopher Luigi Taparelli, who spearheaded a revival of Thomistic natural-law reasoning in nineteenth-century Catholic thought and was an important intellectual force behind Leo XIII's transformative papal legacy in politics, law, and social thought. There is renewed interest in Taparelli today, as Catholic legal theorists and historians seek to rebuild the philosophical foundations of the freedom of the church after decades of liberal-statist overreach.[34] At the same time, this growing interest in the intellectual origins of *Rerum novarum*—focusing on Taparelli and his disciples—reaches to a broader historical issue that needs further study: the role of neo-Thomistic political theory in the nineteenth-century confessional struggle against ascendant liberalism, and more specifically, how this laid the groundwork for a social-pluralist defense of the Church in contrast to the reactionary monarchism of "official" Counter-Enlightenment thinkers such as Maistre and Bonald.[35] Leo and his mentors were primarily grappling with the problem of reconciling pluralistic social forms arising from the basic needs of human nature—family, guild, fellowship, parish—with the ordering purpose (and necessity, too) of law and political power. "The problem," as Russell Hittinger explains so well,

> lay in what the Jesuit neo-Thomists discerned to be a distinctively modern premise, namely, that unity is achieved only extrinsically by contracts, by the serendipitous outcomes of a market, or, more ominously, by the external application of law as the superior force of the state. Thomists argued that pluralities stem from intrinsic unities, beginning with human nature itself, and including matrimony, family, church, and body politic. The question was not whether there is social pluralism with distinctive modes of authority and freedom, but whether there is an ontological landscape internal to social forms. By nature and supernature, are there norms anterior to, and higher than, the laws imposed by civil law and contract? Indeed, from the nineteenth century to the present day, Catholic social thought has orbited around the issue. The great question of post-1789 Catholicism was whether the modern crisis is to be ameliorated by more or by less public freedom. Neo-Thomists reformulated this problem. It was first necessary, they argued, to understand the anthropological and social grounds of liberty and obligation.[36]

In his major work, *Saggio teoretico di dritto naturale appogiato sul fatto* (Theoretical treatise on natural right based on fact), published in the 1840s, Taparelli devised the basic terminology and conceptualization of "subsidiarity" as later developed in Catholic social teaching. The term he used drew on the lexicon of grammar, *dritto ipotattico,* or "hypotactical law," referring to the structure of subordinate clauses in a complex sentence (the Latin root of "subsidiarity," *sub sedeo,* is a literal translation of the Greek roots *hypo* and *taxis*). The smaller groups and societies in which men naturally seek company and help (*sussidio*) partake of an authority born of that very fact of their formation, an authority by which, in their unity of purpose, each "smaller society" is guided and must be respected, to the level of an inalienable natural right of development.[37] Yet precisely in order to protect the smaller societies, they must be oriented toward a common good and partly coordinated in that by external (political) rules. As perhaps the first truly modern neo-Thomist, Jacques Maritain, wrote in his most important work, *Integral Humanism,* "the conception here is of a pluralist body politic bringing together in its organic unity a diversity of social groupings and structures, each of them embodying positive liberties."[38]

Ironically, of course, the contradiction of rejecting confessional pluralism for other religions, while defending the Church's autonomy on a natural law theory of *social* pluralism, was prevalent in Catholic history for many decades after *Rerum novarum,* as the Church retained (or regained) favored legal status in many countries through treaties and concordats.[39] Nevertheless, in important ways the pluralist assumptions of the freedom of the church were increasingly refined in Catholic social thought and came to be distilled in distinctive theory of political order and state action, called the "subsidiary function" in a famous passage from *Quadragesimo anno.* Note the strong "devolutionary" thrust of this controlling formulation, which many American commentators have cited in promoting welfare reform and the privatization of other federal entitlement programs:

> Just as it is gravely wrong to take from individuals what they can accomplish by their own initiative and industry and give it to the community, so also it is an injustice and at the same time a grave evil and disturbance of right order to assign to a greater and higher association what lesser and subordinate organizations can do. For every social activity ought of its very nature to furnish help to the members of the body social, and never destroy and absorb them. (sec. 79)

Free-market advocates see in this a template for American-style devolution or even privatization, but this view is mistaken. Rather, subsidiarity is a rule of relinquishing public authority to associations with an internal life and purpose that qualifies them for freedom as the church has corporate freedom. Building on Leo XIII's "Christian constitutionalism"—reconciling church and state as two distinct but coexisting sovereignties—subsidiarity further clarifies the precise limitations of the state once the authority of other natural structures and communities is acknowledged. In a more comprehensive and radical sense than Leo XIII had expressed—spurred, surely, by the staggering growth of modern welfare states and the rise of fascism—the "subsidiary function" of *Quadragesimo anno* was a defense of corporate freedom against the centralizing power of the state (whether fascist or liberal) and, more fundamentally, against an individualistic concept of rights that the Church saw as eroding the entire natural basis of society—not only the church, but the schooling and charitable works, the occupational groups, and the patriarchal families that were in the church's care. In *Divini illius magistri*, it is clear that the *libertas ecclesiae* had become something more like the template or archetype of a fuller spectrum of corporate freedoms within society, starting with the divine rights of the family. "The family holds directly from the creator the mission and hence the right to educate the offspring." This was a an "inalienable" right, "a right anterior to any right whatever of civil society and of the state, and therefore inviolable on the part of any power on earth" (sec. 79).

As the state grew in power and breadth, subsidiarity took the form of a devolutionary principle of public assistance, putting the government (within the bounds of general public order) at the disposal of the smaller, natural structures of society that it would otherwise tend to destroy. This was not a withdrawal of the state but a reordering of its purposes and responsibility, with an emphasis on protecting and supporting natural structures instead of functionally replacing them. Skillen and McCarthy provide a clear description of how this was to work: "The concept of 'subsidiarity' combines two principles in Catholic social thought: autonomy and hierarchy. The latter concept emphasizes the *duty* of the higher societal entities towards lower ones and the lower to the higher. The former concept stresses the right of every person and institution to its own integrity as regards the fulfillment of its own *telos* and functions in society."[40] What this ultimately means, they argue, citing the Thomist scholar John Cox, is that "individuals and social groups have a right to achieve, undisturbed, their nature-given tasks." But these tasks are interdependent and mutually supportive according to the universal ordering objective of the *bonum commune* or the "common good." In contrast with American laissez-faire anti-statism, a properly subsidiary social order, Cox argues, is one in which every social function by its nature and concept is supportive of the whole.[41] The Latin root of the concept, *sub sedeo*, "sitting below," was common to many related terms but especially *subsidiarius*, meaning "of or belonging to a reserve," in the military sense of "reserves": auxiliary corps positioned to support the front lines as conditions demand. Taparelli himself used the example of the Roman legion with twenty centuries, each with its own particular function but each also oriented toward (subordinate to) the good of all.[42] This connotes a "bottom-up" approach, but it was understood to require higher-order interventions to protect and assist social structures when they are unable to function properly according to their natural purposes and responsibility. Most often such intervention was conceived out of concern to protect the family from overpowering economic forces.

Subsidiarity and the Welfare State

Proponents of the faith-based initiative who see only a need to shrink or withdraw the state do not understand subsidiarity at all. Subsidiarity restricts the state only to the extent that the natural communities of the social order are able to fulfill their tasks on their own. Indeed it requires the state to support the natural communities (especially the family and the church) in fulfilling their tasks. But if the natural communities falter, God's transcendent care for the person requires the state—with its command of resources and greater competences—to intervene.

The German theologian Oswald von Nell-Breuning, who might be considered the leading authority on this subject, as he was the primary author of *Quadragesimo anno*, defined subsidiarity as the principle of "competence" that structures the order of social assistance in a system oriented to the *bonum commune*, the common good.* Writing later, during the Cold War, Nell-Breuning noted the common view of subsidiarity as an antidote to totalitarianism, affirming that, indeed, it is a principle that "defends the rights of the small social group." The "positive substance" of subsidiarity, on the other hand, requires intervention to help the small social group achieve its

---

* In chapter 4 I investigate the particular Thomistic vision of political economy known "solidarity" or "solidarism," which developed particularly in the Germanic tradition of Catholic social teaching and significantly influenced the development of European politics, as well as American welfare policy, in the early decades of the twentieth century. The economic philosophy of solidarism, including French and German contributions, integrated an essentially Gierkean pluralist concept of communal sovereignty within a capitalist economic framework regulated by social laws and highly structured arbitration. It had important effects on American collective bargaining law, and this, I argue later, gives us a certain "indigenous" way to think about social pluralism as an avenue for social law.

ends when restricted by other private forces or when otherwise unable to function properly.43 Perhaps the most profound articulation of this idea was offered by Johannes Messner, a German "solidarist" like Nell-Breuning, who described subsidiarity in terms of "freedom and social order," beginning with the claim that "the reality underlying human nature . . . clearly points to social pluralism," as "the "social good is diversified in kind and pluralistic in structure." There are as many social goods as there are human ends pursued in different kinds of groups, and "since each of these ends is the root of responsibility it is the root of a right":

> Thus there is a plurality of equally original and elementary rights throughout the whole of individual and social human existence. The right of authority in the great society [the state], though it is comprehensive, is only one right among the equally elementary rights of the individuals and communities. Its function is subsidiary in the sense that it is restricted to providing help for the individuals and the lesser communities so that they are enabled to fulfill their essential tasks in life in self-responsibility and self-determination.44

When Pius XI gave subsidiarity its canonical formulation in *Quadragesimo anno*, it had come to be generally accepted in Catholic intellectual circles, even by the most culturally conservative social Catholics, that government assistance was a religious obligation second only to the salvation of souls. In this respect, *Rerum novarum* was the great catalyst. Looming socialist "enemies" notwithstanding, Leo XIII strongly defended state intervention, much to the dismay of laissez-faire conservatives in the United States and Great Britain. As Murray explained in his article on Leo's "Two Concepts of Government,"

> Leo XIII boldly took from the Enemy the truth that he had—the principle that government, under the conditions of modern society, must take an active role in economic life. . . . Industrialism had wrought a progressive depersonalization of economic life. And the impersonality of the employer-employee relationship had, in turn, bred moral irresponsibility. A new "master" had appeared—the corporation. And, as the American aphorism had it, "Corporations have neither bodies to be kicked nor souls to be damned." They were seemingly immune from the restraints that conscience had imposed on the old "master," the individual, in an age where economic relationships were generally personal. The private conscience had ceased to be an effective means of social control. Therefore, the only alternative to the tyranny of socialism or the anarchy of economic liberalism was the growth of the public

conscience and its expression through the medium of law and governmental act—a medium whose impersonality matched the impersonality of the economic life into which it was thrust as a principle of order. On these grounds Leo took his stand for interventionism.[45]

We can safely conclude that Leo XIII's project of Christian constitutionalism spoke to the needs of the church, and of confessional life, within the emerging liberal (and fascist) welfare states of Europe. Further refined in the concept of subsidiarity, the Leonine church-state framework had a profound effect on the development of European welfare systems, laying important groundwork for the Christian Democratic approach. Politically and theoretically, the United States was, at first, far removed from the environment that gave rise to the coordinated church-state welfare model of Christian Democracy, epitomized by the Dutch and German systems. When Leo XIII first outlined this model in the late nineteenth century, the United States was governed by plutocratic trusts and laissez-faire ideology, and the churches had little political power. Trade unions were not even fully legalized until the 1930s, and even when something resembling a welfare state emerged, with the New Deal and the Great Society after World War II, it commanded less than half the share of national resources commanded by Christian Democratic systems. This raises interesting questions about our social safety net today, under charitable choice: arguably, the net result is a welfare state somewhat less prone to privatization and somewhat closer to Christian Democracy in certain significant ways. But one thing should be clear no matter how much philosophy and history we read into these developments: even if it was "delayed" in America until the welfare state reached a certain fiscal and administrative tipping point (as one might speculate), the church-state question now raging in social policy is here to stay.

Dutch Calvinism and Sphere Sovereignty

The concept of sphere sovereignty is a unique contribution of Dutch Calvinist political thought—one notably shaped in a pluralistic direction by interconfessional commonalities, Catholic and Calvinist, in the struggle against liberalism. As a theoretical basis for confessional pluralism, sphere sovereignty grew out of a radical diagnosis of liberalism, which in Europe meant a radical diagnosis of the ideas of the French Revolution and the policies affecting religion (and other traditional structures) that spread from France to other countries as the "revolutionary spirit" took hold in the West. On this question of the revolutionary spirit, it was Abraham Kuyper's political mentor, Guillaume Groen van Prinsterer, who made the decisive contribution in a series of lectures given in the mid-1840s and published soon after under the title *Ongeloof en Revolutie* (*Unbelief and Revolution*). Later to enter Parliament as leader of an orthodox Calvinist movement, Groen (as he was called) described the French Revolution not, primarily, as an event in the history of Europe but as a system of ideas and a new radical concept of society. As Robert Nisbet has likewise stressed, as with Communism and Nazism, the French Revolution generated a significant intellectual counter-movement, as "the seizure of power, the expropriation of rulers, and the impact of new patterns of authority and freedom upon old institutions and moral certainties led to a re-examination of ideas on the nature of society."[46] Thus, for Groen, it was the "*Revolution ideas*" that needed combating: "I mean the basic maxims of liberty and equality, popular sovereignty, social contract, the artificial reconstruction of society—notions which today are venerated as the cornerstones of constitutional law."[47] As with other confessional reactions, the rejection of liberty and of a contractual view of society were not simple arguments for denying human rights or restoring an *ancien régime* of divine-right servitude. In Groen's "anti-revolutionary" thought, the issue was the removal of God as the ultimate source of authority and judgment in human institutions. "Liberty and Equality" based solely on human reason and consent does not bring freedom into the world by itself, Groen understood. Freedom comes into the world through the conformity of human law to a higher moral order, God's order of justice. "The law," wrote Groen's German contemporary Friedrich Julius Stahl (the great Lutheran jurist to whom Groen was often compared), "is to be the free human manifestation of God's order, thus at the same time the revelation of the human community's own ethically reasonable spirit and the subordination of its entire external condition to that order."[48] Disorder, Groen was certain, can be the only result if social relations originate in human choice and consent alone, severed from "the law and the ordinances of God" as revealed in the Gospel and interpreted through Christian tradition and the historic, customary rules of Christian communities. Quoting the ultramontane and theocratic Lamennais of *Essai sur l'indifférence en matière de religion*, Groen urged that "all true legislation emanates from God, Who is the eternal principle of order and the universal power ruling the society of intelligent beings. Depart from this, and I see only arbitrariness and the degrading rule of force; I see only people insolently lording it over other people; I see only slaves and tyrants."[49] As Hans Daalder later pointed out, in holding their ground against nineteenth-century liberalism, Dutch Christians insisted that "politics is not something separate and purely temporal but something to be subordinated to eternal values."[50] To modern eyes such an outlook might seem to harbor a reactionary elitism, but in the politics of the time the confessional viewpoint was considered dangerous precisely because of its "bottom-up" character as a cultural struggle of the "*kleine luyden*," the "little people," against elite liberal dominance in government and public life.

The key insight of Groen's anti-revolutionary philosophy, something also recognized by Tocqueville and Lamennais and then systematically developed by the German and English pluralists of the late nineteenth and early twentieth centuries, was to grasp the paradoxical connections between liberal individualism and the power of the state. Under liberalism, the sovereignty of God is replaced by individual self-interest and choice as the ultimate grounding of law and social relations. Individuals delegate their power to the state, which codifies and enforces their collective capacity, *as* individuals, to dissolve social bonds under protection of the state. Referring specifically to Rousseau's difficult concept of the "general will," Groen wrote, "The good pleasure of the individual citizens is channeled from the bottom up, by means of the vote, to a central point, from which point the sovereign state, embodying the sovereignty of the people in legislative power as well as executive government, imposes its omnipotent authority, in the name of the people, upon the people, while crushing every opposition."[51]

In a world ordered by individual rights but governed by a collective state, "everything is allowed, with one fatal proviso: everything insofar as the state, the collective despot, is pleased to grant." Instead of being ordered by the "unchangeable laws and ordinances of God," the person's rights "are now made to depend on the good pleasure of the State, that is to say, on the will of changeable men, and for that reason must, by definition, perish. . . . Perfect liberty there is, with one restriction—one only, but one which revokes everything just granted: perfect liberty, subject to perfect slavery."[52]

More than Tocqueville, Groen emphasized the destruction of social estates and corporate bodies as the main objective of liberal individualism's alliance with the power of the state. In the name of protecting individual rights and its own needed prerogatives of law and order, the state sets itself up to "oppose on principle any self-government of private persons or corporations and thus, under the guise of maintaining law and order, to destroy all self-determination and all genuine liberties."[53] Tocqueville alludes to communal destruction in the introduction to *Democracy in America*, declaring that "we have destroyed the independent beings which were able to cope with tyranny single-handed, but it is Government that has inherited the privileges of which families, corporations and individuals have been deprived" (xxvii). Yet Tocqueville's emphasis in his famous passage on democracy's potential "despotism" in *Democracy in America* is quite different from Groen's description of the French Revolution as an "antisocial" revolution. The fundamental danger, in Tocqueville's eyes, lies in what the state does to the individual once democracy delegates his will to the "immense and tutelary power" of the state. Tocqueville remains a theorist of individual freedom here, simply warning against the disempowering effects of representative democracy, whereas Groen is concerned with how, by conferring rights, the state allies with individuals to destroy any structures of society that might otherwise claim their loyalty—by nature, ascription, and ethical bonds.

As the instrument of the collective will of self-interested individuals, the state becomes "indivisible," Groen argued, meaning that social structures dissolve into mere aggregates of individual choices: "The differences of its component parts are dissolved and melted into the whole. There is no independent status over against the state." And further,

> There is no subject-matter which does not fall within the province of the general will, no concern which is not also a government concern. The state wields its scepter even over matters of conscience. Church and school are state institutions. The citizen belongs to the state with body and soul and cannot lay claim to any independence whatsoever except insofar as this is granted to him temporarily and conditionally by the state.[54]

The Dutch School Struggle

This decidedly pluralistic critique of liberalism crystallized around the "school question," which erupted in the middle decades of the nineteenth century as Groen, then an aging and lonely confessional voice in the lower house of Parliament, recruited Abraham Kuyper, a young pastor and budding public intellectual, into the center of a new political movement. The intensity of the school struggle was also part of a spiritual revival in Dutch Protestantism known as the *Réveil*, or Awakening. This mainly intellectual movement grew over several decades after the founding of the Kingdom of the Netherlands in 1815 (following liberation from the French Empire) and captured Groen's imagination through his mentor, the Romantic-nationalist poet and philosopher Willem Bilderdijk.[55] The so-called Groninger School of liberal theology, led by University of Groningen theologian Petrus Hofst-ede de Groot, was a special target in *Réveil* circles, as historical method and a retreat from dogma into ethics were increasingly embraced in the pastor-ate of the Dutch Reformed Church (*Hervormde Kerk*) by the middle of the nineteenth century.[56]

Addressed by Groen as early as 1840, the famous "school struggle" was, essentially, a struggle to defend confessional schools in the face of govern-ment efforts to create a secular public school system, a core objective of lib-eral politics in the Netherlands and elsewhere in Europe.† The Primary Edu-cation Act of 1857 was the first major turning point in the school struggle. The bill provided for the establishment of public schools open to students of all faiths, with a religious dimension comprised of nondogmatic civic "virtues" and what the confessionals termed a merely rational or "deistic" God. Religious instruction could be supplied by church educators on a vol-untary basis after school. Resigning his parliamentary seat over the vote, Groen interpreted the bill as an effort to purge orthodox Christianity from state education, leading him to conceptualize a new strategy of reviving confessional schools and securing their legal accommodation outside of state control. Returning to Parliament in 1862, Groen offered amendments to the 1864 reauthorization of the education bill, with the intention of fur-ther secularizing the public schools to build demand for a new parallel structure of confessional schools. When all his proposals were defeated, he retired from parliamentary politics for good.

A new liberal education bill, dubbed *decretum horribile* by Kuyper, was brought forward in the Elementary Education Act of 1878, introduced by the liberal premier, Kappeyne van de Coppello, in March of that year. The bill imposed new regulatory standards on all schools, but provided fund-ing only for public schools, a policy of "burdens without benefits" for reli-gious schools. Kuyper and his followers viewed this as discriminatory if not tyrannical, an anticonfessional end-game perpetrated by the "aristocracy of unbelief."[57] Reformed and Catholic groups together solicited 460,000 sig-natures in opposition—nearly four times the size of the entire Dutch elec-torate at the time. As Kuyper described the movement at the time, in his typically combative yet pithy style, "In the year of our Lord 1878 about half the Protestant population of The Netherlands voted for Scripture and

---

† Although not organized as a party until 1885, Dutch liberals gained control of Parliament after 1848 under the leadership of Johan Rudolf Thorbecke. Divided between social liberals and free-market liberals, the liberal coalition managed to hold an uninterrupted majority position in Parliament until 1888, often allied with the conservatives.

against Voltaire."[58] Previously, Catholics had allied with the liberals in exchange for reestablishment of the Catholic hierarchy under the new constitution of 1848. But their parochial schools remained in a disadvantaged position. The papal encyclical *Quanta cura*, a rallying cry for Catholic education issued in 1864, drove a wedge into the liberal-Catholic coalition and sparked a new, fairly durable alliance with the anti-revolutionaries on the school question and other church-state issues.[59]

As the school struggle escalated in the 1870s, Kuyper transformed the anti-revolutionary movement into the Anti-Revolutionary Party (ARP)—the Netherlands' first mass political party and also one of the earliest and most effective political formations of conservative populism in Europe. Kuyper's editorial in the ARP newspaper *De Standaard*, on June 8, 1877, provides a lucid summary of the new party's tenets.[60]

1. The idea that people decide what is normative in life (called popular sovereignty) is opposed to the Word of God, which teaches that God is sovereign as the final lawgiver.
2. Christians confess the relevance of God's Word even for politics, rejecting a vague concept of natural law or human reason.
3. The office of the state has been ordained to be God's minister for justice through the conscience of public officials who believe in his ordinances.
4. Educational responsibility rests with parents and not with the state. The idea that, for financial reasons, Christian people have only a secularist public school open to them must be rejected.
5. A Christian political movement such as the Anti-Revolutionary Party must maintain its independence (from all forms of humanism and nonbiblical political views), based on the Bible.

Although the education bill passed into law over their protests, the ARP increasingly collaborated with its Catholic counterparts, working to expand the then-limited franchise. This *Unio Mystica*, as Kuyper termed it, was called a "monstrous alliance" by the liberals.[61] In 1888, the ARP-Catholic coalition won its first majority in the lower house of Parliament. During this period Kuyper also founded the Free University of Amsterdam, at whose opening in 1880 he gave a famous speech putting sphere sovereignty at the center of confessional politics. By the turn of the century, Kuyper was installed as prime minister, serving from 1901 to 1905. After further struggle and a series of incremental gains, a decisive constitutional victory for public funding of religious schools was won in 1917, in the famous Article 23. While this became the cornerstone of the Netherlands' uniquely pluralist ("pillarized") polity, it was also a vivid policy blueprint of the type of coordinated church-state model that came to characterize Christian Democratic welfare systems more generally after World War II.

Sphere Sovereignty and Political Order

Although Kuyper gave these concepts a distinctive Reformed theological imprint based on divine sovereignty and creation order, the system of pillarization and, behind it, the concept of sphere sovereignty both also derive, in part, from a broader "federalist" legacy rooted in the historical experience of minority religious communities in Catholic and Lutheran states. The foundation for this was laid by the German legal philosopher Johannes Althusius (1557–1638), who served as magistrate of Emden, one of the first German cities to embrace the Reformed faith. In his extraordinary work *Politica Methodice Digesta* (1603), Althusius suggestively defined politics as "symbiotics," the "art of associating men for the purpose of establishing, cultivating, and conserving social life among them."[62] In the Althusian commonwealth, natural associations, in units of increasing scale beginning with the family, join together in a social compact that preserves the unique nature and purpose of each association while also meeting their shared needs. Herman Dooyeweerd, the anti-revolutionaries' greatest philosophical descendant and also a renowned legal theorist, described Althusius as the author of the "first modern formulation of the principle of internal sphere-sovereignty in the societal relationship."[63] On the Althusian model, every commonwealth or polity is formed by a compact among smaller social structures, each governed by its own natural laws of membership, purpose, and development.[64] Kuyper's concept of sphere sovereignty maintains the Althusian idea of common purpose among the self-governing, natural units of society, but one of his more interesting innovations concerns the family. Of course, Althusius considered the family the primary unit of society:

> The private and natural symbiotic association is one in which married persons, blood relatives, and in-laws, in response to natural affection and necessity, agree to a definite communication among themselves. Whence this individual, natural, necessary, economic, and domestic society is said to be contracted permanently among these symbiotic allies of life, with the same boundaries of life itself. There it is rightly called the most intense society, friendship, relationship, and union, the seedbed for every other symbiotic association.[65]

The latter point on the family as the "seedbed for every other symbiotic association" is notable for the way Althusius further specifies that the family should not only be assigned to the "economic field," defined by what it does materially to preserve itself, but also to the "political" field, the subject of which is "pious and just symbiosis . . . the governing and preserving of association and symbiotic life." In other words, while the family clearly functions as an economic unit in its own self-preservation, it also has political significance as the "seedbed" of every other form of community, placing custodial demands on the larger governing bodies:

> Certain political writers eliminate, wrongly in my judgment, the doctrine of the conjugal and kinship private associations from the field of politics and assign it to economics. . . . [Economics] and politics differ greatly as to subject and end. The subject of the former is the goods of the family; its end is the acquisition of whatever is necessary for food and clothing. The subject of the latter, namely politics, is pious and just symbiosis; its end is the governing and preserving of association and symbiotic life.[66]

The Althusian idea that the family has a certain kind of political significance for the very maintenance of associational life is echoed in later efforts to develop "social law" for the preservation of community life, an enforceable, normative protection of societal functions, as Gierke attempted to do in the late nineteenth-century struggle over the German Civil Code (see below). Concurrently with Gierke, Abraham Kuyper gave voice to a theological rationale for protecting and enabling community life in a pluralist form. In his dedication speech at the opening of the Free University in 1880, Kuyper presented what amounted to an official statement of the theory of sphere sovereignty. To understand sphere sovereignty, he began, the crisis of the times must be understood precisely as a crisis of sovereignty. And the question of sovereignty at the heart of the crisis is precisely this, he declared: "The King of the Jews is either the saving truth to which all nations must say Amen or the principal lie which all nations must oppose. This issue, once encountered in the blood of the Nazarene, has now once again torn a rift through the entire world of our spiritual, human, and national existence."[67] To acknowledge the saving truth of Jesus is to remember God's sovereignty over the world, because there is no truth in the son if the father's sovereignty does not make it so.

At the same time that God is sovereign over all created things, God's rule is manifested in a creation order designed to provision human beings by giving them power in the world: "We must acknowledge that this supreme

Sovereign has delegated and still delegates His authority to human persons," indeed that "His sovereign authority is administered in human offices." In more conservative pietistic theology, the political realm arises with the "fall into sin" and is viewed negatively, as a deterrent to violence and destruction in the post-lapsarian world of fleshly human pride. Closely following Calvin, Kuyper saw politics as an institution of sin as well, but he embraced a more constructive view of public offices as the guarantor of a limited but provident justice. As he explained in his third Stone Lecture, "Calvinism and Politics," delivered at Princeton Theological Seminary in 1898,

> Thus the word of Scripture stands: "By Me kings reign," or as the apostle has elsewhere declared: "The powers, that be, are ordained of God. Therefore he that resisteth the power, withstandeth the ordinance of God." The magistrate is an instrument of "common grace," to thwart all license and outrage and to shield the good against the evil. But he is more. Besides all this he is instituted by God as His Servant, in order that he may preserve the glorious work of God, in the creation of humanity, from total destruction. Sin attacks God's handiwork, God's plan, God's justice, God's honor, as the supreme Artificer and Builder. Thus God, ordaining the powers that be, in order that, through their instrumentality, He might maintain His justice against the strivings of sin, has given to the magistrate the terrible right of life and death. Therefore all the powers that be, whether in empires or in republics, in cities or in states, rule "by the grace of God." For the same reason justice bears a holy character. And from the same motive every citizen is bound to obey, not only from dread of punishment, but for the sake of conscience.[68]

Or, as he put it in his Free University dedication speech, citing Proverbs 29:4, the state "gives stability to the land by justice."[69] But this "public justice" is only a coordinating power, with no legitimacy except in accordance with the more natural spheres of community that truly give hope of salvation to a sinful people. Apart from shared needs, such as national defense and infrastructure, the doctrinal watchword for the state is, "sovereignty in one's own circle" (*souvereiniteit in eigen kring*).

The crisis of sovereignty, in Kuyper's view, was fundamentally a crisis in the human offices of God's rule, namely, their violation of God's will in the form of establishing man's dominion over man: "This embodiment of God's sovereignty in human office raises the very important question: how does this delegation occur? Is this all-encompassing sovereignty of God delegated to a single person undivided? Or does an earthly sovereign possess the power to compel obedience only in a limited sphere, a sphere limited by other spheres in which someone else is sovereign, and not he?"[70] The crisis of sovereignty arises when the political offices God delegates to order human society attempt to bring all of society under their control as God has control of the entire world. Against this we must set the "glorious principle of liberty," whereby God's total sovereignty "implies at the same time the forthright denial and contradiction of all absolute sovereignty among sinful men on earth. It does so by dividing life into unique spheres, each with its own sovereignty."[71] And, most important for Kuyper, we know this is God's will because it is written in the very order of creation: "There is accordingly a realm of nature in which its sovereign works formatively on matter according to fixed laws. Similarly, there is also a realm of the personal, or the family, of science, of social and ecclesiastical life—each of which obeys its own laws, and each of which stands under its own supreme authority."[72]

In Kuyper's *Ons Program* ("Our Program"), drafted at the founding of the Anti-Revolutionary Party in 1879 and one of the most extraordinary documents of nineteenth-century confessional politics, the idea of divided sovereignty or multiple sovereign structures was strikingly formulated to convey an almost anarchic image of self-determining communities: "God established the institutions of various kinds, and to each of these He awarded a certain measure of power. He thus *divided* the power He had available for distribution. He did not give all his power to one single institution but gave to every one of these institutions the power that coincided with its nature and calling."[73]

In his Stone Lecture "Calvinism and Politics," Kuyper expanded on his original formulations of sphere sovereignty to explain more fully the theological ordering of a divided sovereignty that protects the structures of society and ordains the state to give aid for their preservation without any prerogative above them except to maintain the general peace:

In a Calvinistic sense we understand hereby, that the family, the business, science, art and so forth are all social spheres, which do not owe their existence to the state, and which do not derive the law of their life from the superiority of the state, but obey a high authority within their own bosom; an authority which rules, by the grace of God, just as the sovereignty of the State does. This involves the antithesis between State and Society, but upon this condition, that we do not conceive this society as a conglomerate but as analyzed in its organic parts, to honor, in each of these parts, the independent character, which appertains to them. In this independent character a special higher authority is of necessity involved and this highest authority we intentionally call sovereignty in the individual social spheres, in order that it may be sharply and decidedly expressed that these different developments of social life have nothing above themselves but God, and that the State cannot intrude here, and has nothing to command in their domain. As you feel at once, this is the deeply interesting question of our civil liberties.[74]

That state, then, rather than obliterating the spheres under the ordering power it is given by God, has but one strict purpose: to "make it possible for the various [social] spheres, insofar as they manifest themselves externally, to interact appropriately, and to keep each sphere within its proper limits," while also, notably, protecting the individual "from the tyranny of the group." A proper ordering of society that insures the flourishing of its many self-governing spheres was what Kuyper deemed "justice." Only the state that "gives stability to the land by justice" has an authority that is of God.

Families, churches, and other natural structures must submit to justice—as enforced by the state—in respecting each other's boundaries and fulfilling obligations to their members (fulfilling, that is, their social purposes). But, as Kuyper explained in his Free University speech, each is nevertheless "ruled by another authority that descends directly from God, apart from the state." And further, "This authority is not conferred, but merely recognized by the state. And even in defining laws for the mutual relationships among these spheres the state may not adopt its own will or choice as the standard, but is bound by the decision of a higher will, as expressed in the nature and purpose of these spheres."[75]

Like Groen, Kuyper opposed the secularism and individualism of the French Revolution as the most dangerous threat to a just social order. These modes of thought threatened to destroy the natural community by elevating individuals and allying them, through individual rights, with the secular state—thus the "anti-revolutionary" response in Dutch politics. Public education was part of the disintegrative revolutionary spirit epitomized, in France, by the Chapelier ordinance of 1791 that banned trade guilds, the anticlerical doctrine of *laïcisme*, and the state annexation of Catholic schools. In 1792, the French National Assembly decreed that "a State that is truly free ought not to suffer within its bosom any corporation." The template for this "pulverizing" of corporate life—of "all that intervenes between Man and State," as Maitland later wrote—was applied in a national expropriation of the powers and property of the Catholic Church. In 1789 the French National Assembly decreed that church lands be confiscated for the utility of the nation, and control of religious offices was transferred to the state under an act establishing the Civil Constitution of the Clergy in 1790. It was also decreed that all papal communications to the

French people had to be vetted by the National Assembly before being published and distributed—this very much in contrast, as O'Melinn points out, with the freedom of expression given to individuals in the *Declaration of the Rights of Man.*[76] Talleyrand described the state as having a "very extended empire over all corporate bodies existing within its confines," and in numerous laws restricting associative activity the goal was quite literally to eradicate corporate life—any "so-called common interests" that might intervene between the individual and the state.[77] As the revolutionary Jacques Guillame Thouret declared concerning the confiscation of church properties, "The suppression of a corporation is not murder . . . the revocation of a corporation's rights to possess the funds of the land is not a theft."[78] Thus, the theory that justified communal destruction depended on stripping away any notion of a corporate right of existence joined to the "natural" right of individual self-preservation—the culmination (and *reductio ad absurdum*) of a long evolution of legal individualism out of the bosom of natural law, something that Otto von Gierke would dedicate his life to documenting in his great works on German fellowship law.

To the confessional anti-revolutionaries, French liberalism stood at the opposite pole of a world created by God, because no earthly authority, Kuyper wrote in *De Standaard*, "can ever assert itself contrary to the obedience we owe God . . . or nullify the authority with which others are clothed in their own spheres." To Groen and Kuyper, the liberal objective of eradicating community—"it is essential that there be no subsidiary groups within the State," Rousseau wrote in the *Social Contract*—seemed to promise individual freedom but only resulted in self-enslavement to the basest interests, unmoored from any responsibility except to oneself and the state. As Kuyper asserted in his keynote speech at the Christian Social Congress in 1891,

> The Christian religion speaks of a lost paradise, a state of purity from which we fell, and for that reason calls us to humility and conversion. The French Revolution saw in the state of nature the criterion of what is normally human, incited us to pride, and substituted the liberalizing of man's spirit for the need of conversion. Springing from God's love, the Christian religion brings loving compassion into the world. Over against that compassion, the French Revolution placed the egoism of a passionate struggle for possessions. And finally, to touch on the real point that lies at the heart of the social problem, the Christian religion seeks personal human dignity in the social relationships of an organically integrated society. The French Revolution disturbed that organic tissue, broke those social bonds, and left nothing but the monotonous, self-seeking individual asserting his own self-sufficiency.[79]

To "pulverize" the social bonds was to deprive the individual of precisely the social nature God created him to express, a fact incontrovertibly
borne out across all previous human history in the plenitude of groups and
associations that existed with or without a unified state.

Family and religion, schools, arts, and trades, and so on—each has its
own proper role and sovereign order as instilled by the laws of creation. The
role of the state is to provide the "justice"—the ordering power—that protects the distinct social spheres but has no authority within them. Sphere
sovereignty, then, is both a descriptive theory of social structure and a pre-
scriptive principle of political order. As an applied principle of law and
policy, sphere sovereignty restores society in the image of God's creation
order—the order of the world as God created it to be, a life-giving order.[80]
The state is ordained to do certain things but not others, and must carry out
even its ordained functions in a proper way. Governance—how the state
fulfills its ordained tasks—is especially important when it comes to religion. There must be "justice," or proper order, between government and
religion, because religion is the sphere that brings us closest to God. This
binds the state, not only in protecting freedom of belief and worship, but
in assisting religion wherever it is deemed to have a social purpose, such as
bringing good news to the poor. A church's "sovereignty in its own circle" is
not a narrow doctrine of institutional rights, however. It is the cornerstone
of a flourishing political order in which the natural structures of society are
able to freely fulfill their God-given purposes.

The state always falters by intruding on society where God has already
spoken, thus violating sphere sovereignty. When it fails to respect the separate associational spheres, the state violates its limited but essential purpose of maintaining public justice—proper order between the autonomous spheres of the natural community. As James Skillen put it in his
2000 Kuyper Lecture entitled "American Statecraft in the Twenty-First Century," "The state's distinguishable purpose is to interweave citizens and all
spheres of society in a public order of justice. And public justice means
that everything interwoven in the public order should retain rather than
lose its unique identity and responsibility before God. . . . The 'fabricated'
political community can exist properly (normatively, obediently) only by
doing justice to each of the nongovernmental spheres of responsibility."[81]
We should also recognize that Kuyper's pluralism was not simply about dividing sovereignty between the church and the state. It was about dividing
sovereignty between different churches and religions as well. Kuyper opposed the idea of religious establishment. He did not want Calvinist Christianity to be a state religion, and he opposed religious requirements for cit-

izenship. In a memorandum to Groen on the Anti-Revolutionary program, Kuyper wrote,

> Our basic principle may not be an attempt to impose Christianity by force, open or indirect, but rather should be the belief that if Christianity is to regain its free and unhampered place in society it is only in and through the nation's and the individuals' *conscience* that it shall rule and thereby liberate state and society. For this reason, no demanding any privileges; no ignoring the new phase political life has entered in part due to the Revolution; no attempts at subverting our civil liberties; but an effort to make them good and to graft them onto a better root [emphasis in original].[82]

This would require revisions of the Netherlands' constitution (in place since 1848) that Kuyper conceded might even be considered an expression of "Christian liberalism." It would be a liberalism that did not purge religion from public life, as in case of the school laws. It would be a liberalism that did not reject the past but was the fruit of the past—in place of the current "strait- jacket" offering, a "garment in which the nation can breathe and grow freely." Christian liberalism prevents the state from establishing its own religion of no-religion and from obstructing "the free development of the organic life of the people."[83]

Confessionally and ideologically pluralistic, the free development of the organic life of the people resulted in the system of "pillarization" (*verzuiling*) established in the Dutch polity over several decades after World War I, as mentioned earlier. Catholic, Calvinist, and socialist (and also liberal, some argue), the individual Dutch "pillars" are made of interlocking organizations that provide services from childhood to old age—each pillar with its own unique cultural perspective. The pillars, sociologist Göran Therborn notes, are "bent on defending a separate social world against the state, not least against the liberal state." Successful pillarization, he adds, "presupposes a weak central state and involves a political perspective of a marginal or subsidiary state."[84]

Social Pluralism and Private Power

Kuyper's contemporary followers regard him as part of the broader pluralist movement in political thought, which emerged in the late nineteenth century and early decades of the twentieth as an alternative to both individualism and the collective state. Pluralism, here, refers to the idea that self-regulating associations are essential to the health of communities and democracy, both as sources of social cohesion for individuals and as "a bulwark of liberty" against encroachments of the central state.

In the concluding chapter we return with much interest to the broader question of pluralism, specifically what I call "social pluralism," in America today. In important ways that remain obscure in today's emerging faith-based pluralism, the confessional and legal pluralists of the nineteenth century understood more clearly what preserving community required. This social purpose could not be achieved solely by limiting the state and engaging in charity as the state withdraws, as some "faith-based" advocates might be accused of proposing today. It is helpful now, however, to provide an overview of pluralist thought as it was expressed by younger contemporaries of Kuyper and Leo who were similarly influenced by German associational thought.

Two leading English theorists of social pluralism were John Neville Figgis and Harold Laski; both were heavily influenced, in turn, by F. W. Maitland's English translation of sections of Otto von Gierke's *Das deutsche Genossenschaftsrecht*, his magisterial history of German fellowship law.[85] In numerous important essays and books, both Figgis, an Anglican churchman and historian, and Laski, a legally oriented political theorist who later served as chairman of the Labour Party, focused on the question of religious association within the liberal state. Drawing on Gierke as well as other associational thinkers such as Lamennais, the English pluralists cast the church-state conflict under liberal governments in the mold of the *libertas ecclesiae* of the middle ages, what Pope Leo XIII had called "Christian constitutionalism" a generation before them. It is important to recognize here how central the religious question was to the English pluralists, which gives them an important place in any deeper investigation of the lineage of faith-based initiatives in American politics today.

J. N. Figgis often quoted Cavour's famous motto *Libera Chiesa in Libera Stato*—"a free church in a free state." As James Skillen explains, this formulation arose from a growing concern with the "constitutional and social-structural consequences of the unlimited state."[86] It was also a motto of the Anti-Revolutionary Party in the Netherlands, emblazoned on the masthead of its weekly newspaper *De Heraut*. For Figgis, the issue was not the general unity of the state, but the monistic logic of an absolutist state that denied the existence of autonomous, separate communities with their own internal purpose and authority. For Figgis as for Kuyper, the epitome of this was France. Figgis often cited the French statesman Èmile Combes, the architect of France's 1905 Law Concerning the Separation of Church and State, which put all church property under the control of local governments and famously declared that "The Republic neither recognizes, nor salaries, nor subsidizes any religion." Combes proclaimed that "There are, there can be no rights except the right of the State, and there are, and there can be no other authority than the authority of the Republic."[87] Under the 1901 Law of Associations, nearly three-quarters of the Catholic schools in France were closed by the state within a few years.

Under Gierke's influence (through Maitland's singular efforts), Figgis reinterpreted nineteenth-century church-state struggles through the lens of *Genossenschaftstheorie*—in particular Gierke's analysis of two Roman pillars of medieval law: (1) the "fiction" theory of associations, whereby only the individual is considered to have real personhood, and associations can only have an artificial or fictitious personality, being merely a collection of the several real wills of its members but not something intrinsically real like an individual person; and, closely related, (2) the "concession" theory pertaining especially to the legality of associations, whereby the right of existence and operation of any association depends solely on its recognition by the state, so that associations live or die depending on what the state needs, or wants, or wishes to create or destroy. Figgis applied the Gierkean analysis to a case he returned to many times in his writings, the infamous Free Church of Scotland case. In Figgis's repeated consideration of this case in his lectures and essays, one can see how social pluralism, as a political and legal school of thought, grew out of the domain of church-state conflict, so that the freedom of churches served as template for the freedom of society. It is important to understand this evolution from "religious" to "social" freedom in considering how today's church-state domain conflict in social services may serve as an entry point for considering socially destructive power more generally, even going beyond the problem of the state (as Figgis did not). The Free Church of Scotland case thus holds intrinsic theoretical as well as historical interest for us.

The case unfolded over several years, beginning in 1900 when the Assembly of the Free Church voted 643 against 27 to enter into a union with the more liberal United Presbyterians, forming the United Free Church of Scotland. The minority (known as the Wee Frees) brought a case in the civil courts declaring the union to be *ultra vires*—that is, beyond the legitimate power of the assembly because it altered the terms of the original constitution of the Free Church, formulated in 1843 in evangelical secession from the established Church of Scotland.[88] These terms included strict adherence to orthodox Calvinist tenets as well as support for a limited form of establishment, both of which the United Presbyterians rejected. The case was ultimately decided in the House of Lords, which, delving into obscure theological issues, decided in favor of the Wee Frees, transferring the name and all the property of the Free Church to their control.

The shocking decision—one of the United Free Church's defense lawyers said that the Lords' decision "hurl[ed] itself through the land like a tornado"—was mitigated by a parliamentary act that empowered a commission to redistribute the property of the church proportionally among the two factions. But as Figgis stressed, the Free Church case demonstrated that disestablishment was not enough to protect religious bodies from government control, as evangelicals tended to think. The deeper problem, Figgis argued, was the one Gierke had pinpointed in his work on German fellowship law: whether groups and associations that are not formed by the state have a real existence independent of the state, that is, a free existence sovereign within its own domain just as the state is sovereign within its domain of serving general needs. Although not enabled by the government prerogatives associated with religious establishment, the Lords nevertheless found themselves unable to legally conceive of the Free Church as having any existence apart from the terms of the original deed of trust that constituted it in 1843. That is, the church's existence was limited to what the state could recognize in its own legal terms—the original deed of trust. In enlisting itself on behalf of the minority complaint that union with the United Presbyterians violated the original constitution of the Free Church, the state arrogated to itself a faculty of theological and ecclesiological interpretation that the church itself contained in its own structure and had already effectively exercised in the assembly vote for union. As Figgis put it,

> What really concerns us is not so much whether or no a religious body be in the technical sense established, but whether or no it be conceived as possessing any living power of self-development, or whether it is conceived either as a creature of the State, or if allowed a private title is to be held rigidly under the trust-deeds of her foundation, thereby enslaved to the dead. . . . In other words, is the life of the society to be conceived as inherent or derived? Does the Church exist by some inward living force, with powers of self-development like a person; or is she a mere aggregate, a fortuitous concourse of ecclesiastical atoms, treated it may be as one for purposes of convenience, but with no real claim to a mind or will of her own, except so far as the civil power sees good to invest her for the nonce with a fiction of unity?[89]

For Figgis, as for Gierke, the case of one fellowship or another was merely emblematic of the broader problem of monistic legal sovereignty in the modern state. The question concerns "not only ecclesiastical privilege," Figgis stressed, "but the whole complex structure of civil society and the nature of political union."[90] As David Runciman notes in an interesting discussion of Figgis's embrace of Gierkean pluralism, the fundamental problem of "concessionary personality"—the idea that social groups have no existence (and therefore no legal rights) except by concession of the state, was in fact already addressed implicitly in the Free Church of Scotland case. By its very founding, the Free Church of Scotland was created on an authority generated by its own members and not by grant of the state. Yet the constitutional form this new authority took gave the state a residual foothold for controlling the development of the church, in Figgis's view, a way of holding the church captive against its own will. "For Figgis, no system of rules, however liberal [liberal in the sense of recognizing autonomy], could suffice on its own, because any system of rules bound the group of individuals that used it to the terms under which they used it, and thereby denied that group the capacity, as a single group, to develop, or grow."[91] As Figgis acknowledged, the Free Church case did not exemplify the problem of political absolutism in a classic sense of simply imposing external control in the name of unitary sovereignty. The problem in question was the indirect power of the civil courts in resolving a factional dispute *within* the church, effectively vesting ultimate decision-making power in the legal form of the church and not in the living will of its members. For Figgis, this was a problem not only for religious freedom but for the whole social fabric. He noted how religious conflict, once centered on doctrinal and liturgical minutiae, had begun to take the form of what was really a "social" conflict, concerning "the deepest facts of social life." The Free Church of Scotland case exemplified, he argued, a much broader assault on social life informed by "the doctrine of State omnipotence," and in "fighting their own battles religious bodies are fighting the battle of a healthy national life and alone providing the framework under which the perennial social instincts of men can develop," thus giving rise to a genuine social pluralism:[92]

> Instead of a scientific monstrosity (that of the omnipotent State facing an equally unreal aggregate of unrelated individuals) we may look for a land covered with every kind of social life, functioning not only in matters religious, intellectual, artistic, but also in the most necessary form of industrial and manufacturing and even agricultural activity, and each receiving its due place as a living member of the body politic, recognized as a real self-developing unity.[93]

In the next chapter I discuss the unique constitutional convolutions of corporation theory in the United States as this relates to current issues of social pluralism, but the point here is to recognize that the English pluralists, through Gierke's influence, sought to excavate the anti-associational legal substructure of the church-state struggle quite apart from immediate policy aggressions such as the Dutch school laws or the *Kulturkampf*. This led to a broader and more diverse view of pluralistic sovereignty, going well beyond the demands of the church. In that sense, pluralism can be said to have evolved out of church-state conflict toward a broader vision of communal autonomy. Although Figgis and others among his English followers did not go as far, for Gierke this required a comprehensive legal program of protective "social law," of which church autonomy, as traditionally understood, was only one small part. The broader Gierkean approach is important, in turn, for deepening our own search for social pluralism in the groundwork of church-state cooperation that now exists in social welfare.

Gierke's most relevant insights grew out of his understanding of the emergence of the modern state as a juristic entity. He shared with Groen and Kuyper the same basic analysis of liberalism as a destroyer of community, but where the Dutch thinkers blamed the French Revolution (no doubt partly for having been annexed for a time by Napoleon!), Gierke, working primarily in the field of German legal history, set the timeline of antisocial liberalism back at least another century to the natural rights philosophy of Grotius, Pufendorf, and Thomasius, in whose views, he argued, "we can really see how a logical individualism is inevitably impelled to annihilate any idea of the independent existence of the group"[94]—a tendency correlated with the anticommunal fiction and concession theories inherited from Roman corporation law, he also believed. There seems to be no evidence that Kuyper was directly familiar with Gierke's work (or with Althusius's, for that matter, whereas Gierke himself published a seminal book on Althusius in 1880); nevertheless, the parallels are striking, as when Gierke described the late-medieval emergence of natural rights and a contractual theory of the absolutist state:

> The fundamental fact which chiefly concerns us when we contemplate this process of evolution is that in medieval theory itself we may see a drift which makes for a theoretical concentration of right and power in the highest and widest group on the one hand and the individual man on the other, at the cost of all intermediate groups. The Sovereignty of the State and the Sovereignty of the Individual were steadily on their way towards becoming the two

central axioms from which all theories of social structure would proceed, and whose relationship to each other would be the focus of all theoretical controversy."[95]

The central jural typology in Gierke's historical analysis was the conflict between fellowship structures (*Genossenschaften*) and lordship structures (*Herrschaften*), that is, between communal self-determination and rule from above, which in the broadest sense he defined as a conflict between freedom and domination.[96]

In the Dutch school struggle, similarly, Groen and Kuyper sought legal recognition, in policy and constitutional law, for a community of faith. Although Kuyper's main focus beyond the church-state question was on social policy and not juridical like Gierke's, his call for "a different arrangement of the social order" (discussed further below) echoes with Gierke's efforts to develop a framework for establishing what he called "social law." Standing between the private law governing individual exchange (such as contracts and torts) and the public (constitutional) law, the "social law" encompassed both the law internal to groups—varied and independent bodies of rules and customs that communities and fellowships create internally according to their own nature and purposes—and certain orders of policy needed to regulate the interaction these distinct and sometimes conflicting groups (such as labor associations and business enterprise, or landlords and tenants). Always in Gierke's view of the evolving state there is the Roman *Herrschaft* tendency that can only be thwarted by fellowship creation and the free operation of the social law. In depriving workers of free access to productive property, Gierke considered capitalist enterprise to be a lordship structure parallel to the state, not a natural fellowship. His disciples Hugo Preuss and Hugo Siznheimer later made important contributions to labor law in part derived from these social-pluralist legal ideas.[97]

Gierke's legal pluralism was an answer to what he viewed as a kind of liberal absolutism, an alliance of individual rights and centralized power against community life, and one paradoxically strengthened by economic liberalization because communities had no legal defenses or even simple moral validity in the increasingly deregulated marketplace. Gierke's theory and defense of German fellowship law became quite well known in the extensive debates leading up to the creation of the Bürgerliches Gesetzbuch (Civil Code) of 1896, the great monument of German liberalism's quest for the Rechsstaat, or "rule of law" (literally, having a "state of laws"). Gierke's critique of the Civil Code is important not only as an expression of legal pluralist thought but because it sheds light on similar limitations in

American legal thought during the same period.[98] We will circle back to the latter in the final chapter, but here Gierke's particular involvement is illustrative of the broader social analysis that shaped his and others' passionate concern for the legal rights of communities and communal forms.

Basic norms of civil liberty were long widely accepted among the German peoples of the Vormärz. After 1848 and the political retrenchment in Prussia and other states, attention turned to the need for legal codification and eventually a unified code of German civil law. The founding of the German Confederation and the establishment of the Reichstag in 1867 gave momentum to codification, which became closely associated with the National Liberals, who were dominant in the Reichstag in these years. In 1888, a Reichstag commission published a draft code for public response, which led to significant revisions in the final code. Gierke took the lead among the "social" critics of the draft code, who saw in it a bourgeoisified German liberalism seeking to void the Rechsstaat of teleological social purpose (from natural law) as well as communal norms. Instead, a formalistic rule-structure aimed at securing individual autonomy and private property had taken over the social spirit of German law. As historian Michael John describes it, social critics saw a new emphasis on "the private, 'unpolitical' sphere of property rights," which signified a retreat from the reformist ideals that animated earlier efforts to expand civil liberties and connect democratization with social reform.[99] Gierke's efforts to reform the Civil Code naturally prioritized the agrarian sector and the need to retain communal-law protections for small family farms. He was very concerned with the problem of small farmers' indebtedness and, more generally, the supplanting of cooperative credit by capitalist finance. These views, which Michael John describes as upholding an idea of social right—"the right of society as a higher unity to restrain individual freedoms"—found embodiment in a proposed framework of "homestead" laws that would, among other things, protect small family farms from foreclosure and ensure undivided inheritance in cases of intestate succession. As Gierke wrote in a letter to homestead advocacy leader Baron von Riepenhausen-Crangen, "The restoration of harmony in our entire economy depends in the first place on not imposing the law of movable capital on landed property but rather on securing for it the law which it was born with."[100] Amoral positivism and formalistic separation of public and private law effectively "desocialized" the law, giving free reign to the propertied and capitalized, and little protection for everyone else. A formal expression of this, John points out, was the adoption (in part from the towering Friedrich Carl von Savigny, a founder of legal historicism and outspoken detractor of natural law) of the *Abstrak-*

tionsprinzip, the "principle of abstraction," which, as might be guessed, removed consideration of circumstances from legal judgments regarding the validity of transactions. For example, on the principle of abstraction, a signature on a note of debt would be binding whether or not the credit was thereafter transferred to the signatory. As John stresses, however, the main impact of the abstraction principle was in the arena of land-law reforms, which, particularly in Prussia, were aimed at creating free markets in land by removing transfer and credit restrictions that limited capitalist entry.[101]

One aspect of the Civil Code that Gierke shaped in a communal direction was the law of associations, which became a dominant concern in German legal thought after 1848. Two competing approaches crystallized after 1848, the Romanist concessionary-fiction approach, developed particularly by Savigny and the German historical school, and the Germanic real entity theory or, as Gierke termed it, "real collective person" theory (*realer Gesammtperson*). These two theories (also sometime discussed in terms of the "artificial" vs. the "natural" existence of associations) had different ramifications in each of the two basic arenas of law, public law (pertaining to an association's very right to exist), and private law (pertaining to its status in holding property, contracts, etc.); but the most controversial problem, in the wake of 1848, was the *Konzessionssystem* that remained in place in many states.[102] This was (or came to be) essentially a bureaucratic blacklist power whereby associations were accorded or denied the right to exist by government decision—often, of course, for political or ideological reasons. Communitarian critics, led by Gierke, interpreted this policy through the legal lens of fiction and concession theory, giving the whole question of associations a distinctive anti-statist cast. In Gierke's work especially, the concession theory, which he traced to Pope Boniface III (and, more generally, to papal-royalist absorption of Roman law),[103] was among the chief weapons in Germany's later victimization by Roman law—Savigny's great project, in Gierke's view, which in this doctrinal respect, combined with Romanist (individualist) property theory, was transforming Germany, he felt, into a homogeneous commercial society ballasted by an emerging autocratic state.

Consistent with Gierke's legal attack on the same basic forces, confessional antiliberals like Kuyper and Leo XIII did not hesitate to hold private power, no less than public power, accountable to the demands of pluralistic social freedom. Gierke had already shown how the space of liberty created by individual natural rights within a framework of unified state sovereignty had the effect of reducing or eliminating individual obligations to the community. "State and Individual" placed "in immediate contact" by the structure of political authority and private rights, he explained, together create a strong tendency "to emancipate the Individual from all bonds that are not of the State's making."[104] If Gierke saw this as a matter of legal corruption of authentic German *Genossenschaftsrecht*, the confessional antiliberals viewed the same problem of communal disintegration as a consequence of God's expulsion from positive law. Stahl's uncompromising formulations of this view clearly influenced Groen and Kuyper (and many others in the Germanic anti-revolutionary tradition), although nothing as rich as a *Genossenschaftstheorie*, or a creation theory of communal sovereignty, emerged from Stahl's jural works. Nevertheless, communal assumptions clearly structure Stahl's thought. Addressing the rise of individual natural right in the work of Grotius and his Erastian liberal follower Christian Thomasius, Stahl argued that a life in common, not a life apart, is the "grounding of the law":

> Philosophy did not . . . close itself off to that other truth, that the requirements of common life, the common order of the human race, termed in an appropriate expression "sociability" [*Socialität*], form the ground of the law. This truth is accessible even in abstraction from God. . . . However, apart from Aristotle the basis was conceived to be the mere empirical datum of the need for society rather than ethical common requirements, and likewise mutual necessity rather than original unity; this tendency was realized fully by Grotius, who conceived of sociability simply as the instinct of the individual. When, however, Thomasius replaced the drive toward sociability with the *drive toward happiness*, by which the individual of necessity becomes isolated, the last remnant of an objective legal principle was eliminated [emphasis in original].[105]

The proper relationship between morality and law is impossible to know if it is conditioned on the individual's natural right, Stahl argues, because law's moral purpose derives not only from the nature of the individual but "from the equally original existence and task of the community."[106] The ultimate consequence of ignoring that moral fact, he wrote, was exemplified in Kant's definition of freedom, the "sharply expressed heresy of restricting the legal sphere to the *external freedom of individual men* and the *coexistence of this freedom*," when in truth, "the life of human commonality . . . is not mere coexistence; . . . rather, it is the common unified fulfillment of a higher order, the ethical world plan; the freedom of the individual man is not the sphere of law, but only a part of it."[107]

Citing John Paul II's reaffirmation of the traditional Church teaching that subordinates private ownership of property to common use, the contemporary Catholic ethicist Lisa Sowle Cahill captures the idea of a social dimension of freedom in way that is quite consistent with the antiliberal critique of two centuries ago: "Individuals do have a right to acquire freely those material conditions essential to the fulfillment of obligations to the self, family, and society. Nonetheless, the freedom of each to do so is limited not only by the parallel freedom of others, but by the obligation to respect and contribute to a common life supportive of the conditions necessary to make everyone's respective rights and duties effective."[108] Such expressions all reach back to a nineteenth-century antiliberalism that formulated the idea of a freedom or body or rights that stands apart from the mere coexistence of free individuals. This was an essential first step in the development of social laws in the late nineteenth century, as advocated both by Gierkean communitarians as well as radical labor theorists such as Anton Menger (a fellow critic with Gierke of the *Bürgerliches Gesetzbuch*). But it was also a part of anti-revolutionary thought in its lineage of confessional pluralism. Although sharing certain common roots with Gierkean legal communitarianism (particularly Stahl's critique of individualistic law), the anti-revolutionaries might seem fairly disengaged from the social question. But one of the least-studied dimensions of confessional pluralism, and least as applied today, is its prophetic social witness against oppressive wealth.

Confessional Pluralism and the Social Question

In Kuyper's view of the state as a coordinating power among the social spheres, the implication that one social sphere might encroach on another, absorbing or destroying it just as an unlimited state tends to do, is often noted but rarely probed further. Yet in his political writings as well as major speeches, Kuyper's prophetic witness is consistent and clear, following in the footsteps of his mentor Groen van Prinsterer. As James Bratt has argued, Kuyper's "passion for the poor" was pervasive in virtually all of his many types of writing, from biblical commentary to ecclesiology and social policy.[109] His best-known statement of solidarity with the poor was given in his keynote address before the first Christian Social Congress of the Netherlands in 1891 (an event that was inspired by the example of *Rerum novarum*, issued earlier that year).[110] "You do not honor God's word if you ever forget how the Christ (just as his prophets before him and his apostles after him) invariably took sides *against* those who were powerful and living in luxury, and *for* the suffering and oppressed." These are not the kind of words one usually heard from conservative party leaders of the late nineteenth century, but the ARP was not really a conservative party so much as a grassroots social movement of the type we would call "populist" today, a movement of the *kleine luyden*, or "little people," as Kuyper often stated. A top political priority was expanding the franchise by eliminating property requirements for the right to vote. In fact, the ARP was arguably the first populist political party in Europe or America, defined by the powerful combination of religious conservatism and anti-elitist economic criticism. This was not just a product of the sharp economic upheavals of the late nineteenth century either. Decades earlier Groen himself had written, "Our worst ailment is pauperism," and, like secularization, this too was a product of the liberal revolution, he argued:

> It came from "Liberty and Equality" as understood by the Revolution. Just one detail. When that slogan was first raised, guilds and corporations too had to go. The desire was for free competition; no restraints on skills and industry; no hateful monopoly exercised by individuals or societies; then the development of private initiative and commerce would guarantee a better future. The future that was envisioned has arrived. Can it be called better? *I am of one voice here with the leading spokesmen of the present-day revolution.* It is this liberty, this unrestricted competition, this removal, as much as possible, of the natural relationship of employer and employee, which tears the social bonds, ends in the dominance of the rich and the rule of the banking house, robs artisans of regular sustenance, splits society into two hostile camps, gives rise to a countless host of paupers, prepares for the attack by the have-nots on the well-to-do and would in many people's eyes render such a deed excusable and almost lawful. It has brought Europe to a state so dreary and somber as to cause many to tremble and cry out. Is there no way to revive, in some altered form, the associations that were so recklessly crushed under the revolutionary ruins?[111]

As Bratt emphasizes, anti-revolutionary thought was not singularly aimed at liberal statism. It was also a platform for social criticism linking the state's dissolution of community with the evils of laissez-faire capitalism — particularly its attacks on the family embodied in loss of land, child labor, unregulated working conditions, and oppressive indoor poor relief. In a view quite consistent with Marxism, the anti-revolutionaries saw that the net result of liberal revolution was not new freedoms but simply a new kind of ruling-class tyranny, operating through the market instead of the state. As Kuyper explicitly understood, the "one-dimensional individualism of the French Revolution" correlated directly with the "economic school of laissez faire." Liberalism was not simply an alliance of the individual and the state against community (as it was often described); rather, liberalism was really a unified, antisocial worldview with both political and economic dimensions. This definition gets much closer to the reality of how communities live or die, as Marx's (and Karl Polanyi's) still relevant work on early capitalist development confirms. Indeed as Robert Nisbet argued, following Marx and Polanyi, there is a profound structural causality linking economic liberalism (what Nisbet called the "old laissez faire") to the rise of the omnicompetent liberal state. "Far from proving a check upon the growth of the omnicompetent State, the old *laissez faire* accelerated this growth. Its indifference to every form of community and association left the State as the sole area of reform and security."[112]

This was certainly the view of Wilhelm Emmanuel von Ketteler, the great Bishop of Mainz whom Leo XIII publicly credited as the inspiration behind *Rerum novarum*. In an analysis of Physiocratic laissez-faire that echoed Tocqueville's predictions of a despotic liberal statism, Ketteler drove at the question of economic oppression as Groen had done and as Leo would later put it to the world, focusing like Gierke on the loss of communal forms. The laissez-faire economists (the true authors of the French Revolution, in Ketteler's view) "annihilated the grand constitution of labor handed on to them by the Middle Ages, instead of reforming it and incorporating with it all those portions of the toiling masses that were still excluded from it." This unraveling of organized labor they deemed "a restoration of *le gouvernement de la nature*": "They applied their so-called system of nature with such fanaticism that the French National Convention forbade the artisans to discuss their interests in common, because they looked upon such a proceeding as an obstacle to freedom of trade and of intercourse between man and man." What they called the natural order was really new kind of despotism fed by market freedom, "the powers of the State vested in a bureaucratic officialdom on the one side, and on the other, unbridled competition amongst the people dissolved into isolated individuals under the sole Control of an absolute monarch or an equally absolute National Assembly. Such too is the spirit of Liberalism, not merely the spirit of its economic teachings but also of its politics and of its social theories."[113]

Ketteler, it should be stressed, was by birth a conservative aristocrat, and his profound engagement in the formation of Catholic social teaching reflected an older tradition of aristocratic communitarian populism, certain aspects of which persisted through the 1930s. Aristocratic populism in Ketteler's bold style arose in the Vormärz in response to widespread pauperization and social upheaval fueled by rising prices (so-called *Teuerungskrisen*). Across most of the states of the German Confederation, but particularly in the Prussian east, the working population experienced wage declines and loss of land, punctuated by hunger crises in the 1840s. A rural proletariat emerged as liberal agrarian reforms weakened the customary bonds of the feudal *Herrschaft* and dissolved the common lands (*Allmende*). Likewise, the artisanal system crumbled with the advance of "industrial freedom"—wage and price marketization coupled with trade liberalization and the rise of factory production.[114]

While Ketteler and Pope Leo XIII would later adopt a more moderate position of philosophical neutrality (spiked with a heavy dose of *real politick*) toward political liberalization and democracy, the conservative critique of economic liberalism, truly the cornerstone of Catholic social teaching, was particularly antidemocratic in mid-nineteenth-century Germany, less so in Italy. In part this reflected a theological orientation in German thought that viewed politics as an instrumental good subject to natural law: the structure of any political system was less important than the common welfare it secured.[115] Yet, at the same time, religious thought was nowhere more anticapitalist than in Germany, a fact owing much, it is clear, to the influence of Catholicism and the communal heritage of German law. The Prussian statesman Josef Maria von Radowitz exemplified this in his theory of a *Sociales Königtum* (social kingdom), essentially, a monarchical welfare state uniting aristocrats and commoners against the commercial classes. In his best-known work, *Gespräche aus der Gegenwart über Kirk und Staat*, he argued that it is the duty of the state to terminate the "heathen unrestrictedness of property . . . and replace it with the inveterate principle that all possessions are but borrowed, each proprietor but a steward of his property, for the use of which he shall be held accountable not only toward the eternal judge but [also] toward his fellow humans."[116] Such a view of property was of course completely orthodox within Catholic thought and was precisely Ketteler's view as well.

Liberal government, of course, had its own intrinsic antagonisms against religious bodies, leaving aside their restrictive teachings on bourgeois property. Like his Dutch anti-revolutionary counterparts, Ketteler was intimately concerned with maintaining confessional autonomy amidst the enlarging competences of the liberal state. In his proposed Catholic Political Program of 1873 (devised in the midst of the *Kulturkampf*), he demanded the restoration of "corporative freedom" as provided in the now-deleted paragraphs of the Prussian Constitution regarding confessional autonomy: approved Christian bodies should be left alone to regulate and administer their own affairs independently, and public education should not exclude religion but conform to the "real religious, intellectual, and moral condition of the people."

Yet it cannot be emphasized enough that confessional autonomy, for Ketteler and Leo as for Groen and Kuyper, was not strictly a political idea; it was also a social template for reintegrating faith-based communities against the market strife. Political suppression of the church was not a separate order of domination but one closely allied with individual domination in the marketplace: dissolving the economic basis of community went hand in hand with political absorption of the functions of the church. There was no doubt in Ketteler's mind that, for the vast majority, liberalism was a system of domination, not freedom, the ultimate goal of liberal government being the removal of communal barriers to market exchange, as Marx and later Polanyi would document under the rubric of "primitive accumulation." As Ketteler stated, "No class has suffered more from the dissolution of all natural organizations than the laboring class," and, in a famous speech at the Twenty-First Catholic Congress in Mainz, September 11, 1871, he declared that "All that socialism says is true as against liberalism":

> All men are born equal and must become equal again. The abolition of class distinctions is of no avail so long as property remains in the hands of only a few; thus making equality an idle phrase. Property destroys social equality; it destroys educational equality; . . . it destroys political equality, because the very right of franchise is controlled by money; . . . it destroys equality before the law of which you speak so much, because the rich man has far other means at his disposal for obtaining the protection of the law than the poor man.[117]

Among the policies Ketteler advocated were a stock exchange tax (first enacted in 1885 and further extended in the 1890s and early 1900s); a corporate income tax (first passed in 1885); state management of railways; reductions in the war budget; exemption of basic household goods from taxation; employee ownership; legal protection of wives and children of workmen against the exploitation of capital; labor-hours regulation and Sunday rest; health and safety regulation in the mines, factories, and workshops.

In these and other policies, Catholic social teaching demanded economic conformity to religious ideals. In this respect the state was reinvested with a social purpose. Shorn of its monistic designs against communal structures, by the subsidiary function, the state was empowered to protect the weak from the strong within society and to prevent the market from completely dissolving social structures.

Christian Democracy versus Christian America

A startling irony puts all of this in perspective. Simply compare the United States to those European countries where Bush's faith-based principles have actually governed. These also happen to be among the least impoverished and most equal countries in the world, and the contrast is telling. Germany and the Netherlands are good examples, as Kees van Kersbergen documents in his important book *Social Capitalism: A Study of Christian Democracy and the Welfare State*.[118] As he notes in his introduction, the Christian Democratic model is not well understood and little studied, even within Europe. Yet it ruled significant portions of Europe for substantial periods after World War II, with particular strength in Germany, the Netherlands, Belgium, and Italy. The German and Dutch systems in particular—very different from Nordic social democracies—were carefully constructed on the principles of subsidiarity and sphere sovereignty. Much of the thinking behind these welfare systems was inherited from earlier religious struggles against liberalism and fascism, led by Kuyper, Leo XIII, and other confessional theorists of the limited state.

In 1917, sphere sovereignty was enshrined in the Dutch constitution in the form of public support for religious schools. The famous Article 23 says, first "All persons shall be free to provide education"—to found schools and direct education based on varying philosophies. Second, "Private primary schools . . . shall be financed from public funds according to the same standards as public-authority schools." Today approximately 69 percent of Dutch primary students and 73 percent of secondary students attend private schools financed by the government; an estimated one-third of all primary school students attend religious schools. As noted earlier, public support for religious education was replicated in other areas to form the Dutch system of cultural pillarization—predominant in health care, social services, and even broadcasting through the 1960s. In short, the Dutch welfare system was structured by a pluralistic social order in which "establishing religion" or having "religious effects"—the whole hairsplitting corpus of modern American establishment clause adjudication—are quite meaningless ideas. A pluralistic view of the state already divides its power so that it does not really exist in the way that constitutional law in America views the state—as a power unto itself, distinct and separate from society and not simply one kind of power coordinated among many.

Although many Dutch social agencies maintain a religious identity today, pillarization began to unravel in the 1970s, in part due to the strong countercultural currents that swept through Europe in this period. Being served from cradle to grave along a single confessional pillar is rare today, as people tend to "shop around" based on factors other than religion, such as quality and location. Ironically, de-pillarization is confirmed by the merger, in the late 1970s, of the ARP and the Catholic People's Party, to form the Christian Democratic Appeal. But confessional alignments remain an important force. The CDA or its constituent parties were part of every government from 1918 to 1994.

The Rooms Katholieke Staatspartij was formed in 1926, controlling approximately 30 percent of the seats in Parliament in the 1930s. Dutch Catholics supported the growth of a comprehensive welfare state after World War II, often in alignment with the Dutch Labor Party. The ARP, however, struggled internally over the rise of the Dutch *verzorgingsstaat*, or "caring state," with some leaders (and many members) fearing a depletion of Calvinist identity. Under ARP control in the 1930s, laissez-faire policies led to disaster, shattering the Reformed-Catholic coalition dating back to the 1880s and putting ARP delegates in the minority for decades thereafter. In the 1960s, however progressive ARP leaders, claiming the mantle of the "young" Kuyper, adopted a more prophetic stance of "social solidarity" with the oppressed, pushing for increased welfare spending and more aid for international development.

Like the Netherlands, Germany has a strong legal tradition of protecting church autonomy and supporting the social mission of religious groups, and it also has a well-funded, comprehensive welfare system. This system, absorbing 25 percent of GDP on average since 1980, is the historical product, essentially, of Christian Democratic rule combined with pressures from the Social Democratic left. The extensive role of religious service providers in Germany is largely a Catholic story of subsidiarity, resulting in a neo-corporatist system dominated by six large umbrella organizations, the *freie Wohlfahrtsverbände*, or "free welfare associations." The two largest of these are religious—Catholic and Protestant.

Germany's subsidiary welfare state grew out of a remarkable struggle that began in the 1920s, when the Weimar Republic sought to create a new public welfare system.[119] Between 1919 and the Nazi seizure of power, Catholic and Protestant charities struggled to maintain their influence and their religious self-governance within the emerging Republican welfare system. They fought bitterly against both liberal and fascist constructions of centralized welfare. A closer look at the churches' *"kulturkampf"* against public welfare reveals certain philosophical similarities with America's faith-based initiatives eight decades later.

The Weimar welfare system was based on a concept of social citizenship and attendant individual rights to basic welfare. It was also marked by an approach to poverty known as *soziale Fürsorge,* or "social relief." In contrast with charity, social relief emphasized external conditions, preventative measures, and, increasingly, social insurance against market forces. The "social evolution" of poor relief was furthered by Marxist ideas of the state as a site of struggle between workers and the ruling class. This "politicization" of welfare, as critics termed it, was marked by state expansion into domains of social need previously left to self-governing religious charities.

In 1919, the Social Democratic Party established Arbeiterwohlfahrt (Worker's Welfare), a national welfare organization. This provoked the two main religious welfare organizations, the Catholics' Caritasverband and the Protestant Inner Mission, to coordinate in defense of the rights and powers they had enjoyed under the voluntary welfare system of previous decades. The cleavages between Social Democratic welfare and religious charity were heightened in a series of legislative battles, beginning with the National Youth Welfare Law of 1922. By establishing a network of regional and municipal welfare offices to coordinate services, this law incited competition for funds and clients among secular and religious providers. The conflict was defined by confessional leaders as a *Weltanschauungskampf,* or "battle of worldviews." As one confessional leader wrote in 1931, "Social work has become the great, decisive area of a cultural conflict, a violent struggle for hegemony and dominance between the Christian confessions and the irreligious, anti-ecclesiastical worldviews. . . . The time when everyone believed that welfare could confidently be left to the state is at an end." Welfare, he added, "cannot be made the object of administration." Instead it has a "personal, confessional, *Weltanschaulich* ['ideological'], cultural-political nature whose preconditions, methods, and strategies are rooted in ultimate beliefs."[120] The best way to manifest this religious approach, on a scale that matched the problems caused by industrial society, was to "corporatize" confessional welfare by giving faith-based providers substantial public funds and, at the same time, substantial autonomy over policy and implementation at the local level. The 1923 Public Finance Law introduced regulations that recognized seven *Spitzenverbände* (umbrella organizations) as "peak associations"—essentially, intermediaries between the public welfare bureaucracy and the private religious providers. Individual states and municipalities allowed varying degrees of religious involvement and autonomy, however, which led the peak associations to form a national league that could speak with one voice and establish uniform subsidiary governance throughout all levels of the welfare system. The members of this new, interconfessional league saw themselves, Young-Sun Hong argues, "as a corporatist body which would remove the welfare sector from the sphere of parliamentary control at both the national and district levels."[121]

They did not succeed in this effort, however, and the bitter divisions that persisted between public welfare and religious providers helped to feed Nazi influence in the early 1930s. Religious exclusion from public welfare became an essential feature of the Nazi critique of Weimar liberalism, and the Nazi seizure of power was welcomed by many of the leading confessional antagonists of liberal welfare. The Nazis and the confessionals generally agreed that the root of the problem with liberal welfare was its inflation of individual rights at the expense of reciprocal obligations and a supra-individual purpose. In a haunting prefiguration of the American welfare-reform debate of the early 1990s, some confessional leaders saw the collapse of Weimar liberalism as vindication of a religious worldview emphasizing "duties" and "work" over "rights" and "economic justice"—in what Hermann Althaus characterized as a triumph of "achievement socialism" (*Leistungssozialismus*) over Weimar's redistributive socialism.[122] In Hellmuth Reichert's description of the Nazi "reorganization" of social-welfare work, the root of the problem was the "transformation of a subsidiary right to public assistance into a de facto actionable right of the individual against the state."[123] In 1933, the Nazis declared Christianity the "unshakeable foundation of the ethical and moral life of our people," denouncing the expansion of public welfare during the Republic as an attempt to exclude the churches and dispense with Christian charity. The Nazis, however, did not overthrow the Republic in order to restore the Church. Their goal was not the de-secularization of public welfare, but the total mobilization of society in an authoritarian racial state. The churches retained some autonomy in education, but they were rapidly pushed out of welfare as the Nazis redefined it along eugenic lines and ultimately reorganized the confessional welfare associations as the National-Socialist People's Welfare.[124] From the standpoint of legal history, the Nazi policy of *Gleichschaltung*, or "mandatory conformity" of political and social groups is best understood as an effort to obliterate social pluralism in the Nazi state. As Oliver Lepsius writes, "The ending of intermediary associations meant removal of social pluralism, and the one-party system in practice suspended the separation of State and society."[125]

Nevertheless, after World War II, something very close to the corporatist welfare system envisioned by confessional leaders of the 1920s was finally realized in Germany. Now revived in a pluralist form that excluded authoritarian tendencies, subsidiarity was enshrined in three separate laws after World War II: the Youth Welfare Act of 1952, the Federal Social Assistance

Act of 1961, and the Social Code of 1976. These laws require "public bodies responsible for social assistance" to enlist churches, religious communities, and the free welfare associations while acknowledging "their independence in the targeting and execution of their functions."[126] The charitable choice law undergirding Bush's faith-based initiative is essentially the same thing. In fact, the German and American systems are superficially quite similar. Both systems rely extensively on nongovernmental providers. Responsibilities are divided between the public and nonprofit sectors: the public responsibility is to authorize and finance social programs, whereas private responsibility governs the delivery of services and benefits. Germany has enshrined religious autonomy in the latter domain. The faith-based initiative clearly emulates this and seeks to institutionalize it as a key dimension of welfare governance here.

But Germany's subsidiary welfare state is different from the United States in almost every other respect. The American system is fragmented and pragmatic, a "polyarchic" patchwork of compromises and interests. The German social laws, in contrast, are more corporatist, requiring government consultation with the free welfare associations. The result is a centralized, consultative apparatus for policy development, bearing little resemblance to Washington's fragmented, partisan advocacy environment.

In a comparative light Bush's faith-based initiative appears to be a weak version of Christian Democracy, one that elevates certain communal rights against the state but fails to protect the natural structures of society from other forces no less threatening from a religious point of view. The faith-based initiative is Christian Democratic in that it maintains the state's financial role while reducing its operational reach and power to a "subsidiary" level where religion must be supported as the "prior" ground for social problems. But Bush deviated from the religious roots of the faith-based initiative by his unquestioning fealty to economic liberalism. Most obviously, he failed to recognize the theological necessity of protecting poor families and communities from destructive market forces. This is something that requires a public commitment much greater, in fact, than that of the Great Society welfare programs Bush rejected when he called his faith-based initiative the next phase in the War on Poverty in 2001. Bush's failure notwithstanding, many critics underestimate the faith-based initiative because they do not understand the confessional critique of liberalism at its heart.

Germany and the Netherlands uphold social pluralism in the design of their social welfare systems, based on the principles of subsidiarity and sphere sovereignty. They are also key examples of what Kees van Kersbergen calls the Christian Democratic model of "social capitalism." This approach, he argues, recognizes the autonomy and self-governance of social groups and organizations in a pluralistic society, yet strives toward harmony between groups—the "common good" in Catholic thought—as an object of public responsibility and direction.[127] The original political impetus for Christian Democracy was to forestall class struggle by promoting cooperation between capital and labor. But the cornerstone ideal is the prospering family, with its natural capacities and obligations. Public services are troubling, then, because they substitute abstract dependency for family duty. The proper role of a "caring" state is to modify the wage system to guarantee a living family wage. Family allowances, a minimum social income, and unemployment and pension benefits with high replacement rates are hallmarks of this system. The role of the state is to assist families where they cannot help themselves, rather than displace their natural functions where they *can* help themselves, or blame them when things go badly.

In both Germany and the Netherlands, Catholic influence was certainly a major cultural force in the rise of their respective subsidiary welfare states. Kersbergen states the theory that explains such an alliance quite well when he describes Christian Democracy as viewing the state and society as functionally distinct but part of an organic unity:

> The state furthers this unity and maintains the legal framework of social action. The political and legal framework sets the conditions under which the parts of the organic unity can best perform their functions. Direct state intervention in social and economic relations is permitted only to the extent that the organic and natural order or society is restored by providing relief for poverty or by recreating solidarity . . . between various social groups.[128]

The state is subsidiary in that it is a source of help for social structures and natural assignments, not a replacement for them. Thus, economic controls and government-run programs are severely disfavored, while cash assistance and social insurance are generously provided. Indeed, the fundamental mechanism of Christian Democracy is the social transfer of income, seeking to "moderate the outcome of the logic of the imperfect market by transferring considerable sums of money to families and other social institutions in need," as van Kersbergen states. Full employment policy is not ideal, because it reaches too far in adjusting social structures. Where markets fail, social transfers rehabilitate families and communities to the material level proper to their needs and dignity. Where social services are necessary for emergencies or temporary needs, the "subsidiary function," approximating as much as possible a family approach, is the standard. "Privately governed, but publicly financed welfare arrangements are the ideal."[129]

Sphere sovereignty and subsidiarity require independent service providers and neutral funding of even the most religious. But these principles do not operate in a social vacuum, where the primary goal is simply to increase religious involvement in social services. To the contrary, subsidiarity in social services is a means to an end—a "principled" means, but nonetheless in the service of a broader goal, the common good. Thus, the sovereignty of social structures, upheld in principle by the design of social services, is coordinated with a comprehensive system of social transfers, guaranteeing a living family wage in good times and bad. Quite simply, Christian Democracy repudiates charity in favor of the public transfer of resources, yet embraces religion in the design of social services and other social domains. The responsibility of the state is limited by the sovereignty of other social structures, but it does not stop short of adjusting market outcomes, as if they, too, are something sacred. Finding this balance of social sovereignty and market adjustment is what the "social question" was finally about in 1891, and the comparative results are striking.

The U.S. poverty rate in the 1990s, using the standard international poverty threshold of 50 percent of national median income, was around 17 percent, the highest among nineteen OECD nations comparably measured, and more than twice the level in Christian Democratic countries and the Nordic states. In the ten-year period after 1984, the United States had less "pre-government" or "market" poverty than Germany, and only slightly more that the Netherlands. Yet "post-government" poverty in the United States—poverty after transfers and taxes—was much higher. Over ten years, the percentage reduction in overall poverty in the United States—pre- to post-government—was only around 20 percent, while in the Netherlands it was more than 90 percent and in Germany nearly 70 percent.[130] The reason for such success is obvious: both countries devote significantly more of their national product to social spending, or, as one recent study put it, "social transfers matter." Further comparisons with Germany are instructive. In the lowest quartile of the income scale, German social transfers for four-person households with two children equal, on average, 23 percent of mean pre-tax income; while American social transfers to the same kind of family amount to only 11 percent of average pre-tax income. For all households in the bottom quartile the respective shares are 50 percent and 24 percent.[131] Whether public commitments strengthen or weaken traditional community is a question of benefit types and the structure of services—

who provides them—not their finances. Without adequate finances, on the other hand, social needs are denied and so too is "social justice" in a religious sense.

Critics of secularism who care about poverty often fail to see the underlying unity of social liberalism and laissez-faire capitalism, as Leo XIII and Abraham Kuyper did. These religious combatants on the social question were both "antiliberal" in their attitudes toward the secular state and its sponsorship of liberal cultural values, but they were also "anticapitalist" in supporting organized challenges to employer domination, such as trade unions, as well as substantial public assistance to insure human welfare and dignity where markets fail. Growing poverty was unmistakable evidence of moral decline and a degenerate political era, a time when small numbers of wealthy men were able "to lay upon the teeming masses of the laboring poor a yoke little better than that of slavery itself," Leo XIII observed in *Rerum novarum* (sec. 3). For Kuyper, confessional pluralism was the basis not of revitalized charity but of an "architectonic critique" of society, a transformative critique of its immoral incentive structures.

The difference between reducing poverty by 20 percent and reducing poverty by 90 percent is theologically significant, Kuyper might point out. He saw poverty not as a question of individual character, but as a characteristic failure of the market system, and as a dangerous enemy of faith. Those who claim to be addressing poverty "do not honor God's word," he declared, if "you ever forget how the Christ (just as his prophets before him and his apostles after him) invariably took sides *against* those who were powerful and living in luxury, and *for* the suffering and oppressed."[132] Both Kuyper and Leo rejected "laissez-faire" economics and, indeed, the whole framework of economic liberalism inherited from Adam Smith. They understood that the economic power accumulating under liberalism was just as serious a threat to society as was the welfare state's overweening secular control and social policies, and so they rejected the idea that the greater good of society (its survival, development, etc.) can be secured merely by unregulated exchange between juridically free individuals. Most critical of all, they understood how liberalism's individualistic, contractual view of freedom masked gross imbalances of power in society—an analysis most fully developed, in fact, by American progressive jurists such as John R. Commons and Robert Hale, but also (to an extent that is significantly under-appreciated) by American Catholic thinkers who were shaped by a Thomistic pluralist framework known as solidarity or "solidarism" (as I discuss further in the next chapter).

One looked in vain for even the faintest echo of such a fundamental critique of liberalism in Bush's faith-based plan, even as the *political* liberalism of the welfare state was challenged as never before, in a pluralistic rethinking of church-state law. The great defenders of religious autonomy more than a century ago did not stop at confronting governments. By contrast, Bush's defense of religious providers seemed merely to superimpose a social critique of liberal statism on top of an unquestioning liberal allegiance to markets, as if the latter were somehow a part of society as religious providers are or as families and churches are. Ignoring this contradiction, the faith-based initiative did not focus our attention on how the U.S. system differs, in critically important ways, precisely from those countries where religious social-service providers are most welcome. On average, American social spending is about 40 percent lower than in Christian Democracies, and the poverty rate is nearly twice as high. Surely the question must be, What is the "ultimate good" of church autonomy in social services if poverty continues to grow and society grows more unequal with each passing day?

Social pluralism is reshaping the basic contours of the American welfare state. This is evident in the acceptance of a new (yet very old) idea of religious freedom, a corporate idea extending constitutional freedom to those aspects of religion that depend on the integrity of the group. As a legal and policy structure, the faith-based initiative gave this idea a startling new coherence in American politics, sending shockwaves through a system bent on individualizing every freedom to the point where there is no separation between the state and the individual or the market and society. It is not something entirely new to our constitutional law, as evidenced in several further Supreme Court cases that I examine in chapter 4.

Stepping back from the philosophical and legal significance of the faith-based initiative, one reasonable conclusion should not go unstated: Bush's application of these rich ideas, viewed as a social policy, is hard to describe as being driven by the goal of reducing poverty. Two obvious points makes this clear: there is simply no evidence that faith-based welfare approaches are significantly more effective than secular approaches, and little evidence of even marginal differences between them. More important, it is also clear that social services (of whatever type) are only one small piece of a much larger problem involving failed education systems, inadequate health care, misguided criminal justice policies, and the collapse of male wages in many communities. In their intensive concern with the pluralistic social rights of religious providers, Bush and his advisors singularly failed to embrace the broader responsibility that is required of government on the Christian Democratic model they emulated in redesigning our social safety net. Even to articulate this as a long-range policy vision would have been a major step forward, as Franklin Roosevelt did in his first Inaugural Address, or as Kuyper did in his speech on the problem of poverty in 1891, the most famous expression of "public justice" in the confessional-pluralist tradition:

> Only one thing is necessary if the social question is to exist for you: you must realize the untenability of the present state of affairs, and you must account for this untenability not by incidental causes but by a fault in the very foundation of our society's organization. If you do not acknowledge this and think that social evil can be exorcised through an increase in piety, or through friendlier treatment or more generous charity, then you may believe we face a religious question or possibly a philanthropic question, but you will not recognize the *social* question. This question does not exist for you until you exercise an architectonic critique of human society, which leads to the desire for a different arrangement of the social order [emphasis in original].[133]

What differentiates Kuyperian and Leonine teaching on the social question from today's faith-based welfare is a simple but fundamental point: "Liberalism" is not only a political threat to religious groups; it is also, fundamentally, an economic threat to families and communities. The Leonine tradition, Pius XI wrote in *Quadragesimo anno*, "completely overthrew" the tenets of economic liberalism, "which had long hampered effective interference by the government."[134] This was the culminating statement in a natural law revival that began as an attack on political liberalism and evolved into an attack on the economic domination at the heart of the liberal order. Christian Democracy followed this, the true path of subsidiarity, by combining confessional pluralism in welfare governance with a social-transfer system capable of protecting families and communities from destructive market forces. In contrast, Bush seems to have taken the political side of this story for the whole meaning of the tradition. This is not surprising for an administration otherwise so given to supply-side policies that benefit the wealthiest Americans, while poverty and inequality grow.[135] But until the social question is properly addressed—that is, pluralistically in regard to the autonomy of religion and other natural roles, but in a comprehensive way confronting both the political and economic dimensions of social decay—until that is clear, the faith-based initiative will falter as an antipoverty vision. It will remain simply an administrative policy for helping religious groups obtain a larger share of social welfare resources. And that, in turn, is likely to spell its doom: divorced from the reality of growing poverty and inequality in the United States, and enfeebled by fiscal retrenchment and failed economic policies, the faith-based initiative will be increasingly isolated from broader public goals and thus more vulnerable to legal and political attacks. In that condition, the culture war will consume it until nothing is left.

FOUR

The Social Law

That same lordship group which, since time immemorial, has been struggling to gain victory over fellowship, is reproduced here in [the form of capital].

—Otto von Gierke (1868)

From Civil Society to Social Sovereignty

The preceding chapters lead to the following fundamental question: If the faith-based model described in this book takes us beyond the liberal welfare state, where does it lead us in the fight against poverty and social deprivation? Many liberal critics fearfully assume the goal is a kind of theocratic devolution that destroys the welfare state by transferring public authority and resources out of conventional welfare programs and into the hands of people who view religious conversion as the only way out of poverty. In this view, religion is being empowered by the government to invade and destroy the welfare state while using public offices and resources to amass new converts. Although certain fragments of the religious right did conceive of faith-based welfare in something like these terms at a certain stage of the policy debate (as we saw in chapter 2), the conservative vision that prevailed— and is now the political baseline for future developments in this area— is quite different. In principle, certainly, it is neither a theocratic empowerment scheme nor a form of government "self-privatization" seeking to replace public assistance with religious charity. Rather, it is a pluralistic reform of social-service administration, with the goal of integrating smaller religious providers into the public welfare system, on the condition of reciprocal protections of religious liberty for both the providers and recipients of aid. Understood in this way and assuming its facial constitutionality under the Supreme Court's evolving neutrality-based approach, now we must explain where the faith-based initiative leads us if we take the confessional ideas that guide it seriously. This will open the door, I hope, to a debate on religion and poverty that neither opponents nor proponents of Bush's efforts were prepared to have when the faith-based initiative was launched in 2001.

In formulating its future promise, it is important to keep in mind the political context in which this vision emerged, some technical parts of which can be fruitfully integrated with the broader ideals I articulate here. As noted in chapter 1, the turn toward faith-based welfare in the late 1990s converged with the broader "civil society" framework that took center stage a decade earlier as the collapse of Communist political systems reenergized welfare-state reforms in the West.[1] The original "devolutionary" thrust of welfare reform in the United States, from the Family Support Act of 1988 to the watershed Personal Responsibility and Work Opportunity Reconciliation Act of 1996, was certainly fueled, in part, by widespread media and academic discussion of civil society "renewal" as filtered through the lens of collapsing Communism. The most penetrating and engaging conservative contributions to this debate were those in the Nisbetian cultural tradition revived by the efforts of the Bradley Foundation.[2] Although in recent years Nisbet's work primarily has been used to challenge government displacement of communal functions, a Nisbetian social critique, with its antirevolutionary roots (shared with the faith-based initiative), is in some ways more capable of grasping the destructive power of market institutions than are many progressive "civil society" critiques. The latter, exemplified by the work of Robert Putnam and Theda Skocpol (notwithstanding their well-known empirical and explanatory differences regarding the health of civil society) focus narrowly on declining civil voluntarism and political participation without really considering how these limited arenas are thoroughly penetrated by market imperatives and ideology and offer little opportunity for the promotion of binding alternative norms that do not conform to market rationality. The very focus on voluntary associations, rather than actual communities with shared cultural and historical roots, betrays a contractual view of social bonds that disturbs nothing in the existing market framework of society and provides no way of thinking about how families and communities might deserve and be granted protections from the market forces that are pulling them apart.[3] In contrast, as noted in chapter 3 and discussed in more detail below, the earlier confessional tradition of communal autonomy (anchored in religious autonomy), aspects of which Nisbet and his followers absorbed through their studies of European anti-revolutionary thought (though without much specific concern for the critical church-state legalities that emerged, particularly around education and social welfare, it must be said), did not accept the contractual model of society that uncritically assimilated market exchange into the framework of liberal political consent, thereby allowing economic power to hide behind the appearance of freedom generated by voluntary exchange. The lack of political coercion in the process of economic exchange satisfied the terms of freedom as set out in the contractual model. Most obviously, to the social-confessional critics of liberalism, the contractual model of freedom, by definition, limits the scope of freedom to the arena of individual exchange, without regard for how such exchange implicates and affects the attachments individuals may have and the natural social structures God has established to help them thrive.

In a more technical vein, the initial political thrust of faith-based welfare after 1996 was also fueled by related ideas of "social capital," which entered public debate with Robert Putnam's famous "bowling alone" thesis about civic decline. Borrowing heavily from neoclassical economics, *social capital* was originally a term used to define how individuals enhance their economic position or value by being connected to other people through various kinds of associations and networks. In this model (developed particularly by sociologist James Coleman and economist Glenn Loury), social capital, like other forms of capital, was something individuals possessed. Putnam somewhat broke free of this economistic framework to consider social capital as an almost qualitative dimension of healthy societies, something closer to a moral culture. Social networks have value in themselves, Putnam argued, because they generate trust, tolerance, and norms of cooperation and reciprocity that benefit individuals while making society as a whole more cohesive and productive.[4] Drawing on data showing dramatic membership declines in traditional civic organizations, Putnam argued that our stock of social capital was being depleted, and, because of this, America's future was threatened.[5] He famously pinned much of the blame for declining social capital on the influence of television. From the beginning, however, critics questioned Putnam's traditional model of civic participation, based primarily on the kinds of social and fraternal membership groups that flourished after World War II. While the data generally does show dramatic membership declines for traditional organizations, other kinds of associations and networks, such as online affinity groups and collective knowledge platforms such as Wikipedia, perhaps reveal a new kind of civic participation that creates community in a different way. It should also be noted that many scholars, especially in the fields of political economy and economic development, have been very critical of the social capital framework for various methodological and ideological reasons.[6]

It is worth considering the role of religious social providers in terms of social capital. John DiIulio and other social scientists have made significant efforts to do so.[7] Putnam himself, in the seminal "Better Together" report of his Saguaro Seminar at Harvard, argued that "nearly half of America's stock of social capital," as measured by membership, philanthropy, and volunteerism, "is religious or religiously affiliated." Or, as John DiIulio terms it, roughly half of our social capital is really "spiritual capital."[8] Yet when Putnam specifies that "houses of worship"* spend $15–20 billion annually on social services, it should also be clear that the scale of spiritual capital (at least by this one measure of involvement) barely touches the magnitude of social needs: $15–20 billion equals approximately $350 annually for every person near or below the poverty line as of 2007. In gross comparative terms, the total spiritual capital of the nation amounts to less than 20 percent of the total "poverty gap" in the United States—the amount by which impoverished people fall below the poverty line, which totaled $107 billion in 2001.[9] This is to say nothing of the tens of millions of people who live near the poverty line on low-wage pay or go through their days only one medical crisis or one corporate merger away from plunging downward to the bottom rungs of the income ladder.

Yet, when one considers the general goal that is implied in most analyses centered on social capital—that is, finding ways to increase the "stock" of social capital just as one can use policy tools (such as tax incentives) to increase the stock of physical or intellectual capital—such an approach seems hardly more scientific than quoting Alexis de Tocqueville (*ad nauseam*, frankly) to prove that that the welfare state is inherently flawed. Even in the narrower frame of existing policy and budgetary formulations of social assistance, it is not really fruitful to focus on the question of whether faith-based services are more "effective" than secular (or government-driven) programs. As noted previously, this has been a leading talking point of faith-based advocates for many years (particularly in conservative think tanks and media). My working assumption, based on the latest social science research and my own experience doing pastoral work in a prison and in other settings, is that faith-based services, *ceteris paribus* (i.e., in terms of funding levels, organizational competence, etc.), can be somewhat more effective than other kinds

---

* This narrow categorization would seem to be a misnomer. An earlier report from the Aspen Institute proposed the same $15–20 billion figure for the much larger category of "religious organizations, national networks, and freestanding organizations."

of services because of the faith factor. For example, there seem to be strong positive correlations between religious involvement (going to church, having a pastor, etc.) and aversion of youth deviancy and criminal behaviors in many poor communities.[10] At a minimum, I think we can stipulate that, in many individual cases and in some communities more broadly, "faith works." We can do so without categorically assuming this (in irresponsible ideological ways) and without, of course, minimizing the serious performance and accountability concerns that arise when money flows to the kind of smaller community groups (faith-based or otherwise) at the center of the faith-based vision anchored in charitable choice.

Yet even if the "faith factor" is definitively proven with further comprehensive research (perhaps leading politicians to prioritize faith-based services beyond current efforts to "level the playing field"), this does nothing to rectify what is obviously a more fundamental problem: the deficient *scale* of faith-based welfare (indeed of all welfare efforts combined) in a country with growing poverty and increasing downward wage pressures affecting tens of millions of households above the poverty line. I posit this question as more fundamental for the simple reason that, however more "effective" a welfare system might become by virtue of elevating faith-based providers, without adequate resources to increase the scale of their restorative work, little can change beyond what might be indicated by the comparative success rates of different types of providers. Certainly such a qualitative change in service-delivery types—assuming that such differences exist—cannot lower the poverty rate or stabilize struggling communities on its own.

Knowing more about what works or does not work within the existing framework of social services is of course an important dimension in any new war on poverty that one might propose for American politics. Increasingly, we can and will know more about what it takes to create an effective social safety net, as far as it goes. But how far the social safety net should extend, and with what level of resources, is another question and a much more difficult one. What social assistance should accomplish and by what means, and how the cost should be borne, assuming that more should be done, is even more difficult. This is obviously a larger question, not just of welfare policy, but of "public purpose," or what Kuyper and his scattered American followers call "public justice." As Kuyper stressed in his famous address on the social question in 1891, the idea that improving social services was an answer to the "social question" of poverty amid plenty is chimerical; like many economic progressives today, he considered it a category error to focus on the "religious" aspects of social needs while ignoring social structures, even as defending the Church remained at the center of his critique of welfare liberalism and socialism.[11]

Of course, no reasonable proponent of faith-based initiatives today argues that the poverty rate or community distress more generally will decline simply if faith-based providers play a larger role in the social safety net. Yet few have seriously considered the inherent limits of a "level playing field" approach—an effort, essentially, to administer constitutional neutrality in the government's welfare procurement regimes. Protecting the Church from the state was one aspect of the struggle against liberalism, indeed the starting point; but protecting "God-willed community" from the "reign of mammon," as Kuyper put it in 1891, was even more fundamental, requiring an "architectonic" critique of social structures. This structural focus reflects a critique of liberalism far more comprehensive than that embraced by George W. Bush, who defended communal autonomy against the state while promoting economic forces that attack families and communities as if they do not even exist. Nevertheless, while that contradiction may be superficially evident (and damning) when you look at George W. Bush's White House record—more social-service grants for faith-based providers side by side with rising poverty and insecurity year after year—this really says little about the viability of faith-based initiatives: first, for the simple reason that their scale all along (as a percentage of total social spending) was extremely small; and second, more broadly, because conventional culture-war politics closed off debate on what the "Republic's faith-based future," as DiIulio terms it, really demands of government and society— and what it could mean if we acknowledge the demands of justice as essential goals of pluralistic freedom and not mere objects of prayer beyond our reach until the end of the world. The deeper transformation of the terms and meaning of welfare reform in our republic's faith-based future is dimly acknowledged in the dramatic first steps of enacting a comprehensive statutory and administrative expression of the Supreme Court's emerging neutrality doctrine as applied to government aid. With that as a spark, now the oxygen of a deeper political understanding can brighten the dimly lit path of a faith-based future in which the churches' level playing field becomes the staging ground for moral challenges that go to the heart of the problem, namely, a liberal market order in which the communities people most need, while pluralistically protected in relation to government (in many ways), are atomistically dissolving in the private sphere.

The challenge of "reengineering" the social safety net along pluralist lines, as Stanley Carlson-Thies has described it,[12] is only part of the struggle to restore impoverished communities across the United States; nevertheless, it is an important and productive part of this struggle because institutional pluralism necessarily upholds the beliefs and values that motivate religious groups within a political order, and these beliefs and values "[lead] to the desire," as Kuyper put it, "for a different arrangement of the social order."[13] Thus, the freedom of the Church from the state leads to the freedom of communities within society. From the perspective of families and communities, and from a religious perspective, restricting the state while ignoring what is happening in society is not genuine pluralism but simply a faith-based alliance with liberal anti-statism. All forces in society that weaken basic social structures, whether they emanate from public programs or from private centers of power, are morally suspect and subject to legal constraint in a genuinely pluralist vision of political order.

It is no great discovery of the faith-based initiative that restoring deprived communities has something to do with a proper coordination of church and state: the long tradition of effective Christian Democratic welfare policy in Europe is founded on this idea. As we have seen, the legal and administrative protections afforded to religious groups by charitable choice law and the faith-based initiative (broadly understood) express a deeper set of concerns about the nature, vitality, and authority of basic social structures within the liberal state. Put simply, the faith-based initiative embodies a pluralist vision of societal restoration, based on legal recognition of the real personality of social groups—most importantly families and their churches and communities—coupled with requisite public provisioning for their security and special needs if this autonomy is infringed or reduced by other centers of power, whether public or private. In its fullness this vision encompasses a mandate of stopping or mitigating the impact of all institutions or organized powers that threaten the "tie-beams and anchors of the social structure," or "God-willed community," as Kuyper put it.[14]

In chapter 3 we looked at pluralism in the legal-historical tradition of Gierke, Figgis, and Laski. This was, essentially, a theory of distributed sovereignty that focused on the legal protection and enablement of group autonomy. In contrast with the later American pluralism associated with Lipset and Dahl, and others, legal pluralism focused less on how different "interest groups" (labor, the various business sectors, racial groups, etc.) competed for power through a neutral political process than on how power *within society* was distributed among groups by the legal architecture of associative rights and by legal and moral understandings of corporate existence. This was primarily an approach oriented to the defense of basic social structures and religious bodies—most prominently, churches and their social agencies and schools—against government programs, statutes, and regulations that threatened to weaken or absorb them in expanding the reach of the state.

Somewhat less clear in this earlier analysis was the similar danger of concentrated *non*governmental power, particularly that of business enterprises and other forms of organized capital. In the United States, institutional economists such as Gardiner Means and legal realists such as Robert Hale described these forms of concentrated nongovernmental power as "private governments," referring to the constitutionally protected sovereignty they enjoy in making "decisions with enormous concentrated consequences for the way of life and opportunities of others, decisions which, in contrast to the ordinary activities of single individuals in a Smithian economy, take on the quality of governance rather than of marginal adjustments to external stimuli, however much the latter are also involved."[15] Although Gierke and certain of the more radical English pluralists, such as G. D. H. Cole, can be described as developing a pluralist economic critique alongside their critique of the state, it was also a contribution of anti-revolutionary, social-confessional thinkers to grasp the destructive essence of liberalism in a way that encompassed both political and economic forms of power as a single continuum (or interlocking system) of antisocial rule. Between the French Revolution and the Great Depression, the confessional-pluralist critique of liberalism grew more comprehensive: in their struggle to remold the state as a cooperative partner in a common mission, confessional parties and movements increasingly saw the major functions of the state— public law and regulation—as a critical toolkit for restoring community systems and social cohesion. The formula of a subsidiary welfare state made it possible for religion, duly protected from political liberalism, to embrace the state as an ally against the excesses of capitalism and market dysfunction. Particularly in Germany, restricting economic power required no concept of property as "private government": liberalism was not so dominant as to force social reformers to conceptualize regulation in such liberal (anti-government) terms. To the contrary, social-Catholic influence and Gierkean legal pluralism helped to shape a modernized Germanic view of property as an inherently social institution bound in part by community needs. In the German Basic Law, property "imposes duties" and "should serve the public weal." Thus, community needs were served by a two-way understanding linking the autonomy secured by a limited state to the social responsibility inherent in the equal worth of all.[16]

In the United States, however, even as charitable choice and the faith-based initiative have established a strong foundation for social pluralism, this is confined within an overarching neoliberal framework that narrowly restricts the claims of communal autonomy to the realm of politics. In a properly subsidiary welfare state, when economic forces weaken families and communities, and they cannot sustain themselves out of their own internal resources, the state is required to compensate natural society for what the market takes away, up to the level of a living family wage. In this respect, faith-based social pluralism as it stands today in the United States remains completely trapped within a debilitating, neoliberal framework. This is not a fully emergent social pluralism, because the question of communal autonomy is limited to one of preventing the state from absorbing natural functions of society. Quite simply, protecting church autonomy from the state, while families and communities grow increasingly powerless in the marketplace, is a still-born pluralism: it cannot achieve the genuine pluralist goal of restoring families, faith, and communities to their proper place of dignity in God's creation.

By the standards of sphere sovereignty and subsidiarity, America's still-born pluralism perhaps originates in our very United States Constitution. Although church autonomy (and in some cases broader communal autonomy, as with the Amish) is constitutionally protected in many ways, by definition the constitutional claims of a given community or religious body are limited to restricting the government. At the same time, constitutional interpretation of one particular communal form, business enterprise or the "communities" of productive property known as "corporate America," gives *this* particular form unique protections attached to their property and their assumed general utility. Thus, while protecting communities from government in many ways, the constitution also insulates economic power from pluralist needs and claims arising *within* society—centrally, the need to prevent families and communities from disintegrating as jobs are sent overseas or public policies drive wages down. Paradoxically, one of the key indicators of our stillborn pluralism is the fact that corporations are considered *persons* for constitutional purposes, a legal status providing high protection for their property. That is, organized economic power functions pluralistically (freely so) within society while also enjoying unique constitutional protection from other social demands. This is, of course, the problem of constitutional "corporate personhood" much debated in American legal history. But this American anomaly takes on new and much more troubling significance, I believe, in light of the pluralistic understanding now emerging to limit state control of religion. Put simply, not all communities are treated equally in the constitutional order that overarches our pluralistic social structure, and there can be no genuine social pluralism until all communities, not just those possessing productive property, are equally or

substantially protected in their nature, supported in their essential purposes, and assisted in at least a compensatory way as material needs arise.

Religious Community and the Constitution

In her important book *Rights Talk*, legal scholar Mary Ann Glendon argues
that "the lack of a well-developed discourse about civil society has made
it easy for Americans to overlook the costs exacted by the modern state
and the market on the family and its surrounding communities of mem-
ory and mutual aid."[17] The neglect of the "social dimension," made up
of "families, neighborhoods, religious associations, and other communities," is a deficiency in the "deep structure" of American law and political
thought, she further argues, noting in a distinctly pluralist (and even older
anti-revolutionary) idiom that "communities are often caught in a pincer
between individual rights on the one hand, and reasons of state on the
other."[18]

As one illustration of how the deep structure of American legal thought
has failed communities, she cites the famous example of the Poletown
neighborhood in Detroit, Michigan. When the City of Detroit, working
with General Motors (and with the support of the United Auto Workers
and much of the news media), sought to exercise eminent domain powers to provide land for a new GM Cadillac plant by razing the entire Poletown neighborhood consisting of 1,500 homes, a school and hospital, 16
churches, 144 local businesses, and numerous community associations, the
residents brought a case against Detroit to prevent the destruction of their
community and their way of life (the name Poletown reflects its founding
by Polish immigrants, although by 1981 it was one of the most integrated
neighborhoods in Detroit). As individual property owners, Poletown residents could not secure any legal recourse against eminent domain. Constructing an important precedent, the Michigan Supreme Court applied a
"public benefit" definition of the "public use" criteria of traditional eminent
domain to permit the transfer from one private owner to another (in this
case General Motors) on the basis of promised general benefits: new jobs,
economic multipliers effects, new tax revenue, and so forth.[19] The plaintiffs
sought refuge in an unsuccessful argument based on environmental protection law. Although the Poletown residents' individual property rights were
at least cognizable in the laws pertaining to this case, the many obvious familial, institutional, and cultural dimensions of their community, and their
shared desire to remain a community, as manifested in extensive organized
resistance, were simply inscrutable to the law. As Glendon summarizes,

judges applying the law in such matters have difficulty "envisioining entities other than individuals, [business] corporations, and the state," exactly
the point that Gierke and other legal pluralists were already arguing in the
late nineteenth century. Yet, importantly, Glendon adds, this lack of solicitude for property rights in what defines and preserves a community "does
not mean that property, more broadly understood, has ceased to command
the respectful attention of the American legal system."[20] Most obviously,
she notes, the rights of incorporated "productive property" receive special
protection in constitutional law, which has fortified such property even as
small residential property and small businesses are increasingly vulnerable
to the will of large corporations and organized capital under many states'
laws of eminent domain.

Although the antisocial, "monistic" impact of government has been
greater than many contemporary liberals understand, as evidenced in the
"school struggles" of the past and now the case of faith-based social services,
in fact our government is constitutionally limited in ways that recognize
communal autonomy in many respects, short of violating a "compelling
state interest" (as in the case of polygamy and other harmful or potentially
harmful practices of certain communities). Indeed, a certain genealogy of
social pluralism can be traced in several important twentieth-century Supreme Court cases, and examining how the law acknowledged communal sovereignty in limited ways in these cases helps us understand the
central argument of this book. One area in which confessional pluralism, in particular, played a distinct but limited role in the formation of
public law as well as church-state law was education policy, particularly
regarding the long-standing struggle over public (particularly federal) aid
to primary and secondary schools. The Protestant denominations and the
Catholic Church both generally opposed the idea of federal aid to education in the early phases of this policy debate before the turn of the twentieth century. But after World War I, federal aid to education increasingly
intersected with anti-immigrant feeling and, closely related, Protestant anti-
Catholic bigotry. Lutherans and especially Catholics opposed federal education proposals more vigorously as these became increasingly intertwined
with cultural politics spurred by the Protestant far-right, led by a resurgent
Ku Klux Klan.

An early constitutional turning point, striking a fatal blow to the Protestant goal of using public education policy to destroy confessional schools,
was *Pierce v. Society of Sisters*, decided in 1925. This startling and seminal
case was brought by two private educational institutions, one Catholic
and the other a military academy, against an Oregon statute that sought to

"Americanize" education by abolishing private schools. This law, the Compulsory Education Act of 1922, required parents to send their children to public schools between the ages of 8 and 16, excepting only for physical disability, excessive distance from any school, completion of eighth grade, or special permission for private tutoring. Failure to comply would bring fines and/or imprisonment. The Ku Klux Klan in Oregon worked through a faction of the Scottish Rite Masons to engineer the ballot initiative, pledging to establish comprehensive public schooling and to protect such "free institutions" with its "white-robed sentinels . . . its blazing torches as signal fires." In this heavily Republican state, Democratic gubernatorial candidate Walter Pierce embraced the education bill and in doing so received heavy Klan support that insured his victory.[21] Although a similar plan had already failed in Michigan, twelve other states were being targeted as the Oregon plan became law by a relatively narrow margin of eleven thousand votes. The conflict over the school bill was described in the *Oregonian* as the "most upsetting factor in the history of Oregon since the agitation over slavery."[22]

Catholics and Lutherans, along with smaller sects such as the Seventh-Day Adventists, immediately organized a legal challenge, which reached the United State Supreme Court in 1925, in the case of *Pierce v. Society of Sisters of the Holy Names of Jesus*. The Court unanimously upheld their challenge (on appeal by the state after the District Court decreed an injunction against the statute) and found the Oregon bill unconstitutional on Fourteenth Amendment due-process grounds. Strikingly, the holding for the plaintiffs centered on the question of property: "By reason of the statute and threat of enforcement, appellee's business is being destroyed and its property depreciated; parents and guardians are refusing to make contracts for the future instruction of their sons, and some are being withdrawn." The deprivation of property by contractual losses and the infringement of the "right to conduct schools," also defined as a form of "property" in the ruling (reaffirming the lower court's declaration of "the right to conduct schools as property"), were the defining issues. Secondarily, Justice McReynolds' opinion offered another rationale of unspecified constitutional derivation but formulated as a right of parental control in executing the family duty of educating children: "The fundamental liberty upon which all governments in this Union repose excludes any general power of the State to standardize its children by forcing them to accept instruction from public teachers only. The child is not the mere creature of the state; those who nurture him and direct his destiny have the right, coupled with the high duty, to recognize and prepare him for additional obligations." The obvious question of religious liberty could not be adjudicated in *Pierce* because the free exercise clause of the First Amendment only applied to the federal government at the time (it was not "incorporated" in the states until the case of *Cantwell v. Connecticut* in 1940, upholding the right of Jehovah's Witnesses to distribute their literature in public).

Celebrating *Pierce* from afar in his renowned encyclical on Christian education, *Divini illius magistri* (1929), Pope Pius XI described the decision as redeeming the "incontestable right of the family," which is "recognized by nations anxious to respect the natural law in their civil enactments":

> Thus, to give one recent example, the Supreme Court of the United States of America, in a decision on an important controversy, declared that it is not in the competence of the State to fix any uniform standard of education by forcing children to receive instruction exclusively in public schools, and it bases its decision on the natural law: "the child is not the mere creature of the State; those who nurture him and direct his destiny have the right coupled with the high duty, to educate him and prepare him for the fulfillment of his obligations."

The immediate context of Pius's concern in citing *Pierce* was of course Mussolini's efforts to limit Catholic influence and control in the education of Italian youth. Generically, both fascist and Klan opposition to confessional education shared a common, essentially liberal belief in the necessity of state-controlled schooling as an instrument of national civic unity. Although the "One Flag, One School, One Language" slogan of the Oregon compulsory schooling movement did not represent an absolutist political vision of the "ethical state," as in fascism, it registered a similar kind of unitary erasure of social pluralism, driven by the fear of dual or separate loyalties that might undermine a presumed national culture and even a racial culture.[23]

Pius XI quoted *Pierce* directly in his formulation stating that "the child is not the mere creature of the state." In contrast to the rather bare assertion of parental rights in *Pierce*, however, the Church's view was embedded in the model of church-state subsidiarity inherited from Leo XIII's "Gelasian" texts (as discussed in chapter 3). In fact, the 1929 encyclical was arguably the most complete and powerful restatement of this theory since *Immortale Dei* was issued in 1877, although it was the more famous *Quadragesimo anno* of 1931 that officially formulated the idea as we know it today (there, of course, Pius called it the "subsidiary function").

As Pius wrote in *Divini illius magistri*, the sole justifiable object of the state, the "common welfare in the temporal order," consists in securing the peace in which families and individual citizens can exercise their natural rights and "enjoy the greatest spiritual and temporal prosperity possible in this life, by the mutual union and co-ordination of the work of all" (sec. 43). In the educational sphere,

> the function therefore of the civil authority residing in the State is twofold, to protect and to foster, but by no means to absorb the family and the individual, or to substitute itself for them. Accordingly in the matter of education, it is the right, or to speak more correctly, it is the duty of the State to protect in its legislation, the prior rights, already described, of the family as regards the Christian education of its offspring, and consequently also to respect the supernatural rights of the Church in this same realm of Christian education. (secs. 43, 44)

Pierce's emphasis on property rights to the exclusion of any other qualities of communal self-determination or autonomy jarringly illustrates the "missing dimension of sociality" described by Glendon as part of a crisis in American law concerning rights: the only thing of any constitutional significance in preventing the state from destroying a religious school system was the property of the school and the future revenues that would be lost. In the logic of the holding, if the schools run by the Society of Sisters of the Holy Names of Jesus had no dependence on tuition revenues (if their services, say, were entirely financed by an endowment provided by the Catholic Church), there would have been no constitutional ground (at the time) for overturning the Oregon compulsory school law. Of course, First Amendment free-exercise rights, applicable in the states after 1940, would have been the primary rationale had it been available at the time, and today the case has been retrofitted as a free-exercise case as well as a privacy case.[24] Indeed, the property angle in *Pierce* was taken over, in the long run, by the secondary theme of parental rights in the original opinion. At the time suggestive of a social-pluralist sensibility, as Pius XI's reaction makes clear, ultimately this element of *Pierce* served as a basis for the radically individualistic construction of procreative "privacy rights" in *Griswold v. Connecticut* and *Roe v. Wade*. What once seemed to suggest the right of families to sustain their religious community by educational means evolved into the right of an individual to be shielded from a community's moral norms.[25] Except as a holder of property, then, the right of a *community* to exist and thrive in its ways (whether in educating its members or otherwise) was constitutionally inscrutable; as *Poletown* showed, moreover, even the right of property would not always prove a barrier to the destruction of communities.

A richer pluralistic understanding of the right of communal autonomy outside the control of the state was formulated in *Kedroff v. Saint Nicholas Cathedral*, decided in 1952. In this case, the Supreme Court overturned a 1935 provision of the Religious Corporations Law of New York State. The provision essentially transferred control of the New York property of the Russian Orthodox Church of North America from Russian to American authorities, effected through American appointment of the archbishop in charge of the cathedral. Appellants in the case, a group of church members, sought to restore the archbishop appointed by the Russian Orthodox Church's supreme authority in Moscow, while defendants justified their action of local ecclesiastical appointment as a legitimate control of property under New York State religious corporation laws. Appealing to the hierarchical polity of Russian Orthodoxy, Justice Stanley Reed's majority opinion rejected the defense on grounds that the statute in question, as applied in the case, violated religious liberty in the form of an "ecclesiastical right, the Church's choice of its hierarchy."

Although largely forgotten today, the case was singled out for special consideration in the *Harvard Law Review's* annual Supreme Court round-up for that year. In that article, Mark DeWolfe Howe noted an important emphasis in Justice Reed's formulation that he deemed unusual in American law: "If the constitutional guarantees of civil liberty were intended to secure the rights of individuals only, and not the rights of groups, the protection thus afforded to religious liberty would seem to find its justification in the security which is given to the rights either of the lay members of the Church who still recognized the authority of the Russian nominee, or of the Archbishop named by Moscow."[26] In contrast, the reasoning in *Kedroff* upheld the Church itself as a proper subject of religious liberty, conferring on a group or body, therefore, what was historically and conventionally thought to be a strictly individual right of belief, worship, and so on.

Perhaps it is not surprising that Howe, the great biographer of Oliver Wendell Holmes, would see in this opinion a rare American legal expression of the "political pluralism" of "Gierke, Maitland, Figgis, and Laski"—the latter, the political theorist Harold Laski, being a longtime intellectual confidant of Holmes. As we discussed in chapter 3, together with the British legal historian F. W. Maitland and the Anglican churchman J. N. Figgis, Laski was one of a small but influential group of Anglo-American interpreters of Otto von Gierke's massive works on the history of German fellowship law. As Howe correctly understood, the school of Gierkean pluralism had a unique importance in the arena of church-state relations, which held a paradigmatic place in the work of Gierke's British interpreters.

The stakes were large, in Howe's view, because a pluralist jurisprudence in America, building on *Kedroff*, would mean that

> the government must recognize that it is not the sole possessor of sovereignty, and that private groups within the community are entitled to lead their own free lives and exercise within the area of their competence an authority so effective as to justify labeling it a sovereign authority. To make this assertion is to suggest that private groups have liberties similar to those of individuals and that those liberties, as such, are to be secured by law from government infringement.[27]

When the courts begin to recognize that "an association of men has liberties different from those of the persons constituting the association," Howe added, "it has taken a step towards pluralism which has significance not only in the history of political theory but may have large consequences in constitutional law."[28]

Howe's prophecy was arguably partly fulfilled in one of the most famous Supreme Court cases of the twentieth century, *Wisconsin v. Yoder*, decided in 1972. In a unanimous decision, the Court overruled the criminal conviction of Old Order Amish parents for violating Wisconsin's compulsory school attendance law by withdrawing their children from all formal schooling after eighth grade. From the pluralistic perspective Howe had formulated regarding *Kedroff*, what is notable about the Court's opinion in *Wisconsin v. Yoder* is its articulation of a communal reality not defined by private property or even (as with *Kedroff*) by an incorporated institutional status. Although held on First Amendment/religious-liberty grounds, the Court's opinion in *Wisconsin v. Yoder* sought to go beyond conventional readings of the free-exercise clause, which account for religious communities only indirectly by upholding the rights of their individual members. In an opinion notably enriched by scholarly research on Amish history and by theological and sociological views of Amish communal life, the Court arguably expanded the basis of First Amendment "subjectivity," according legal recognition and rights not simply to Amish persons, but to the Amish *as* a historical people, an enduring culture, and a self-governing community. By forcing this people and culture to dilute or abandon its religious standards of socialization, the state poses a "very real threat of undermining the Amish community," the Court wrote, implicitly assuming that a community of believers exists in contemplation of the law and has rights as such no less than individual believers do.

The striking pluralist rationale of communal freedom in *Wisconsin v. Yoder* found little intellectual grounding in America's religious-clause canon. Perhaps it was Ernst Troeltsch, in *The Social Teaching of the Christian Churches*, who formulated it best many years earlier. Quoting Gierke, he sought to define community as a legal subject—a source or basis of legal claims—distinct from the legal subjectivity of its individual members:

> Thus from within the Church appears as an organism which is partly an institution for faith, partly a fellowship of believers, while from without she appears to be the rule of a sphere of law which is independent of the State and cannot be touched by the State. It is obvious that here the mutual relationship of Christian individualism and universalism is struggling to find a legal embodiment; Gierke lays stress on the fact that these ideas resemble the Germanic ideas of social unity, which "assert, alongside of the rights of individuals as 'subjects,' distinguished from one another in their peculiarity, the rights which belong to a community, which has arisen out of an association of individuals; in this case the community itself is also regarded as a 'subject' in the eyes of the law."[29]

Broadly, of course, as *Kedroff* illustrated, religious bodies do have rights of autonomy that delineate a "sphere of law which is independent of the State." In a later Supreme Court case testing the "reach" of church autonomy in this essentially medieval sense, Justice Brennan took a more expansive view in a concurring opinion that came to be part of the intellectual arsenal of the faith-based policy movement. In *Corporation of the Presiding Bishop v. Amos*, decided in 1987, an employee of a Mormon nonprofit organization, fired for religious reasons, brought a constitutional challenge against religious hiring rights in the social-service divisions of religious organizations, claiming that such rights were an establishment of religion. Rejecting the claim, the Court upheld the constitutionality of religious hiring rights as provided in the Civil Rights Act of 1964, and it extended the protection afforded by these rights to the nonprofit service agencies of churches and denominations. In an 8–0 decision, Justice Brennan wrote a separate opinion (joined by Justice Thurgood Marshall) that drove to the heart of the question of communal rights, but in a way that must seem more far-reaching now than it did at the time (the Adolescent Family Life Act, arguably the first faith-based initiative, was upheld against an establishment clause challenge the following year in *Bowen v. Kendrick*). The case, Brennan wrote, presents a "confrontation between the rights of religious organizations and those of individuals." But this is deceptive because, for many individuals, he noted (citing the great Reformed theologian Karl Barth), "religious activity derives meaning in large measure from participation in a larger religious community." Such a community "represents an ongoing tradition of shared beliefs, an organic entity not reducible to a mere aggregation of individuals." Regarding the discrimination practiced by religious groups, "we are willing to countenance the imposition of such a condition because we deem it vital that, if certain activities constitute part of a religious community's practice, then a religious organization should be able to require that only members of its community perform those activities." In this line of thinking, the thrust of the faith-based initiative is not to attack individual rights, but to protect collective rights.

Community in the Law

A half-century later, the kind of pluralistic reordering Mark DeWolfe Howe perceived in *Kedroff*, which the Court further invited in *Wisconsin v. Yoder* and *Corporation of the Presiding Bishop v. Amos* (both were decided unanimously) is increasingly well established, and it is no surprise that the arena of Church and state has proved a fruitful laboratory. The argument of this book, put simply, is that the faith-based initiatives of the last eight years reflect just such a pluralist reordering in a key area of social policy. Although it might seem unlikely that American social policy could be informed by such a complex intellectual legacy with European roots, in fact such thinking was a critical influence on the design of European welfare systems, which strongly resemble, in certain basic and important ways, what was proposed and partly implemented in the Faith-Based and Community Initiative of George W. Bush.

Yet we must now confront more directly the heart of the problem I am most concerned with in this book, which appears clearly against the intellectual backdrop of the faith-based initiative, from the anti-revolutionary communalism of the Dutch Calvinists and the social Catholics to the legal pluralism of Gierke and Figgis and the Christian Democratic model of susbsidiary governance in social services, echoed in many ways by the principles of charitable choice. In the legal and political ordering of the new social pluralism in the United States, under charitable choice, the state is required to acknowledge and respect religious groups in their nature as such, determinate within "a sphere of law independent of the state," as Troeltsch put it. At the same time, however, coercive economic power that violates the integrity of communities, arguably much more forcefully than all but the most autocratic governments, is simply not contemplated as a matter of either constitutional law or even the theory of social pluralism in its current faith-based form.

Ironically, however, it is precisely the constitutional recognition of *certain* associative forms—those organized as productive property for commercial purposes—that has facilitated the broader problem of communal inscrutability in American law and political thought, "the missing dimension of sociality," as Glendon terms it. To understand this problem, we need to unravel the complex layering of constitutional empowerment of some communities, those defined by commercial purposes and integrated by the ownership productive property, while others lacking such property or the contractual power that goes along with it remain constitutionally and often politically invisible, enjoying autonomy only in limited ways.

The first step in understanding this problem is unpacking the language and meaning of corporate entities in American law. Although a complete or even partial genealogy of the development of corporation law is far beyond the scope of this book, it is important to note that the roots of modern corporation law lie in the earliest Christian formulations of a believers' union—the Church as "corpus Christi," the body of Christ, as Saint Paul famously described it in his first letter to the Corinthians and his letter to the Galatians ("for you are all one in Christ Jesus"). The spiritual unity of the Church was analogous to the physical integrity of the body, parts working together, interdependently, to form and give life to the whole. Of course, the organic metaphor of the body was not unique to Christianity, but the Christian version had a central place and arguably a unique influence on the development of political theory and law in Europe.

Corporation law and theory, as applied to associations and institutions within the larger Church and in defining the relationship of the Church (and its associations) to civil power, developed as an important subset of canon law, as Harold Berman has shown.[30] Defining the Church as a corporate legal entity was essential for establishing jurisdictions within the Church, from the Papacy to the episcopacy, the monasteries, and the village parish. Beginning in the twelfth century—following in the wake of the Gregorian Reform, the canonists drew on Christian, Roman, and Germanic concepts of association and group identity to develop a new system of corporation law. Before Christianity became the official religion of the Roman Empire, units such as municipalities, cultic associations, and artisanal and trading groups were considered to be corporations under Roman law. While held as a privilege at the discretion of the emperor, corporate status under Roman law entailed a capacity to receive gifts and legacies, as well as certain property and contract rights and the capacity to act through representatives. After Rome embraced Christianity as the state religion, under the Emperor Constantine I, the Church and its associations were simply treated as corporations in this limited sense.

As Berman stresses, many key questions that would later become central to canon law were not considered by the Roman jurists: whether a corporation exists solely through a grant from civil authority, or by the will of its founders or its nature as an association; also, how officers were to be chosen and what kind of recourse members had to control the officers or other representatives of the association.[31] Most fundamentally, Berman stresses, corporation law as developed by the Church (in the twelfth and thirteenth centuries) rejected the Roman view that corporations exist solely through a grant of imperial authority. Under canon law, in contrast, "any group of persons which had the requisite structure and purpose" of a directed entity "constituted a corporation, without special permission of higher authority."[32] Other innovations of canon law, Berman points out, pertained to the internal structure and management of corporate entities: where Roman law gave only public corporations (such as a city) the power to create new law and apply this law through its own judicial authority, the Church determined that any type of corporation, public or private, could have legal jurisdiction and judicial authority over its members. The conciliar view that a corporation could act through the organized will of its members and not only by the authority of its representatives also distinguished canon law from Roman law.[33]

Berman partly agrees with Gierke that Germanic ideas of the corporation as a self-governing fellowship were influential in canon law, although, with Brian Tierney, he is skeptical that the metaphysical question of *Gesammtpersönlichkeit*, or "group personality," shaped the pluralist aspects of medieval canon law, as Gierke argued. According to Tierney, the canonists "were not interested in philosophical problems of a corporation's essence."[34] Of course, in Gierke's view, the communal aspects of canon law ultimately succumbed to the Roman idea of the *Anstalt* (institution), which for Gierke meant an organizational form imposed on a group by an outside authority: in this respect, along with their tendency toward a nominalist view of groups, the canonists, Gierke famously argued, paved the way for political absolutism and the liberal anti-corporatism of the French Revolution.

Modern corporation law in America started with religion as well: religious bodies were the first associations for which general incorporation statutes were established in place of traditional concessionary charters. One of the first general incorporation systems in religion was established in New

York State in 1774. In a series of acts, the state legislature disestablished the Anglican and Dutch Reformed churches by eliminating their tax powers and other privileges, and at the same time established provisions for the general incorporation of religious associations, enabling them "to appoint Trustees who shall be a Body Corporate" able to "take care of temporalities," such as receiving and investing gifts, construction of church facilities, and the power to regulate and adjudicate the renting of pews, and so forth.[35] In 1791, the Commonwealth of Pennsylvania passed an act of general incorporation for literary, charitable, and religious associations, later expanded to beneficial associations and fire-engine companies. As Louis Hartz pointed out long ago, general incorporation laws for economic enterprise would not begin to be legislated until decades later, and it was nearly a century before general incorporation statutes for all types of enterprise came to be. In the meantime, between 1790 and 1860, Pennsylvania granted 2,333 special charters for businesses, nearly 40 percent for transportation projects.[36] It is striking to consider what the expediency of general incorporation in the case of religion (compared to the lag for business) might suggest about early American views of corporate freedom and its objects. How and why a plainly non-economic view gave way to one in which the "corporation" became virtually synonymous with business enterprise is an important question; surely it leads us back, in counterpoint, to concepts of community and corporative responsibility that originate in religion.

Legal scholar Liam Seamus O'Melinn argues that acts for the general incorporation of religious associations in the United States recognized not just their moral purpose, but the moral personality born of their members' will.[37] Summarizing the body of religious general incorporation statutes established in New York and Massachusetts, O'Melinn writes, "There was no suggestion that the corporation was the mere creature of the state in these acts; on the contrary, there was an almost embarrassed admission that the canons of American political and constitutional theory required the recognition of organizations that were in some ways more immediate expressions of the people's will than the government itself."[38] As Figgis and Laski surely would have noted, it is worth considering in this light the battles for church autonomy raging in Germany, France, Italy, and the Netherlands in this same period, in some cases prosecuted under a concession theory of the church (one thinks of Bismarck's comments citing the medieval conflict between priesthood and monarchy as a model for the *Kulturkampf* against the Catholic Church; and of course revolutionary France's literal abolition of all corporations, enacted in 1792). O'Melinn notes further developments in law that set aside the initial trustee model of religious incorporation in favor a membership model, in keeping with the congregational or presbyterian polity of most American churches. Molding religious incorporation to the governance structures of the churches themselves was a further recognition of their moral personality.[39]

General religious incorporation, a mainly statutory undertaking, carried within it an unarticulated communal ontology that found its voice in Chief Justice Marshall's famous opinion in *Trustees of Dartmouth College v. Woodward* (1819), one of the few nonprofit cases to enter the canon of commercial corporation law, which it did with lasting influence. The *Dartmouth College* decision overturned an act of the New Hampshire legislature that altered Dartmouth College's charter in order to reinstate the college's president, who had been deposed by the trustees of the college. The Court based its decision on the Contracts Clause of the Constitution (Article 1, Section 10), prohibiting government "impairment" of contracts (altering, annulling, etc.). As O'Melinn notes, Marshall premises the decision on a seeming concession theory, describing a corporation (such as Dartmouth) as an "artificial being": indeed it was chartered in 1769 by the King of England. Yet the decision was based on the Contracts Clause, to which a Royal Charter granted in 1769 was factually immaterial—and indeed Marshall did not argue that the Dartmouth Charter was simply a contract. What he effectively did (and O'Melinn suggests implicitly meant to do) is use the Contracts Clause to shed Dartmouth's charter of its concessionary status, because, in reality, the college was not artificial (created by the state) but "one immortal being," as were all such corporations. In the very act of overturning the state's supervening of Dartmouth's chartered rights, Marshall effectively decided that corporate existence is not a concession from the state. This was not, however, as Morton Horwitz argues, "one of the earliest efforts to create an oasis of private rights free from state interference."[40] Dartmouth College was a nonprofit entity dedicated to teaching and scholarship, and it was normatively structured, like any successful college, by standards, protocols, and ethical boundaries that could hardly be described as an oasis of private rights. So if the *Dartmouth* decision nullified the concession theory de facto (by setting a precedent for restricting government control over its "artificial creatures," amounting to nullification), it misses the point to deem this a mere release of private power from public responsibility, as Horwitz suggests. The real transformation occurred as commercial corporations assimilated themselves to the result of *Dartmouth* and the moral terms, winning freedom on those terms to pursue their very different ends. "The decision," O'Melinn concludes, "heralded a recognition of the force of the moral personality of the corporate entity, as a consequence of which the corporation went from being the humble servant of the state to being its virtual master."[41]

It is mistake to see this oppressive outcome as inevitable. Writing against the liberal "mythology" of a stateless nineteenth century, exemplified in Louis Hartz's canonical version in *The Liberal Tradition*, historian William Novak argues that, before the Civil War, individuals and enterprise were regulated on a fairly massive scale by state legislatures and democratic jurists such as the great Chief Justice of Massachusetts Lemuel Shaw. This regulatory childhood in America was born of two common law principles viewed as interrelated postulates of consensual government: *sic utere tuo ut alienum non laedas* (literally, "Use what is yours so as not to harm what is others") and *salus populi suprema lex esto* (literally, "Let the welfare of the people be the supreme law"). This "equation of well-regulated governance" was evidenced by aggressive *sic utere* judgments against proprietary nuisance; for example, in a case brought against the Jersey City government by the owner of a condemned fertilizer plant (condemned due to public complaints about the smell), the New Jersey Court of Errors and Appeals, in upholding the action, wrote strikingly that such condemnation (the city actually destroyed the property) is not only constitutional, but it is not even a taking under the Fifth Amendment:

> It is simply the prevention of a noxious and unlawful use, and depends upon principles that every man must use his property so as not to injure his neighbor [*sic utere tuo*], and that the safety of the public is the paramount law [*salus populi*]. These principles are legal maxims or axioms essential to the existence of regulated society. *Written constitutions pre-suppose them, are subordinate to them, and cannot set them aside.* They underlie and justify what is termed the police power of the state [emphasis in original].[42]

Most interesting and important is how communities (in the courts and legislatures) fought back against the *Dartmouth* trend as it pertained to economic corporations. In an 1840 case regarding corporate ownership across state lines, the Supreme Court reaffirmed the concession theory of corporate existence even as it ruled in favor of the corporation: "A corporation can have no legal existence out of the sovereignty by which it is created, as it exists only in contemplation of the law, and by force of the law; and when that law ceases to operate, and is no longer obligatory, the corporation can have no existence. It must dwell in the place of its creation, and cannot migrate to another sovereignty."[43] The Court simply found that the company's state charter placed no restrictions on its ownership of property in other states; in general, there was a tendency to favor commercial activity except where explicitly limited by the chartering statutes in a given case. Yet it was precisely the flexibility of charters, which could be drawn and interpreted to impair commercial interests, that created more and more pressure for general incorporation statutes; and these, of course, vanquished the concession theory for good.

Private corporations hardly flourished after *Dartmouth*, it should be clear. Some struggled to capitalize on *Dartmouth* in particular cases—it was the ever-looming precedent in legal disputes relating to charters. At the same time, efforts to regulate corporations were themselves distinctively shaped by ideas of community and moral purpose. Prior to the rise of national regulatory powers (beginning with the Interstate Commerce Commission in 1877), state courts exhibited varying degrees of judicial deference to legislation resting on "public welfare" or "public interest" criteria, often rejecting private appeals for relief. New England, especially Massachusetts, had the strongest such legal tradition in its "commonwealth" ideal, a derivation of Puritanism. The towering representative figure of the commonwealth tradition in American law, Lemuel Shaw, was a Congregationalist. Serving as chief justice of the Supreme Judicial Court of Massachusetts for three decades, until the eve of the Civil War, he constructed a public welfare jurisprudence of wide scope and singular consistency.[44] The most obvious feature of this jurisprudence was judicial deference to the legislature, particularly in matters of economic legislation: in its thirty years there were only ten cases in which the Shaw Court voided legislative enactments.[45] Doctrinally, Shaw significantly strengthened two key concepts: eminent domain—the power to appropriate private property for public use on a compensatory basis—and, more importantly, the "police power," regulating health and safety and some aspects of economic development. The statutory power "to trench somewhat largely on the profitable use of individual property" for the sake of a more harmonious economic progress was the defining assumption of the Shaw Court.[46] In this Shaw extended the common law principle *sic utere* beyond *ex post facto* application (abating direct, evident harms) to something more like a basis for public codes—general rules to prevent potential harms (i.e., codes of construction, water-use, firearms, waste removal, commercial food preparation, etc.). As Levy describes it, Shaw broke free of common law constraints that limited the function of police power to the abatement of existing nuisances, following Blackstone's narrow maxim that "the public good is in nothing more essentially interested than the protection of every individual's private right." As Levy points out, this narrow principle guided the police-power theory of Joseph

Story and other leading figures of the first generation of American judges.[47] But it became increasingly inadequate for the task of delimiting the rights of property or the function, thereby, of judicial review of statutes and regulations. The common law rights of individuals had to be embedded in a larger framework of public welfare in order to maintain social cohesion while also preserving liberty. This was expressed, not only in expanding police-power functions into a regulatory system, but also in expanding the range of private enterprise that could be categorized as affecting a public interest and so be subject to public controls. Here the medieval "common calling" standards of care ("common calling" literally referred to expectations and duties arising from a person's self-acknowledged professional "calling" in a particular trade, such as brewing) did not match the needs of the public regarding the common resources and infrastructure that all people required for commercial opportunity. This was the age of heavily regulated turnpike and canal companies, which gave way to railroad regulation after the Civil War and eventually to full-fledged public utilities in water supply, electrical power, and public transportation, as well as many large-scale engineering projects with vast commercial effects.

Clearly another critical aspect of American social law was the devising and revision of corporate charters, as we have mentioned. Although the conflict over Dartmouth's charter was an affair among privileged factions, many other such conflicts were driven by popular unrest. The struggle over royal charters was a central issue in English and British-colonial politics reaching back to the English Revolution of the 1640s, and this experience carried over into the American revolutionary spirit. The use of special charters, of course, had become prevalent long before, in the Middle Ages. Many kinds of private associations were incorporated through charters issued by territorial governments—essentially, provisional recognitions of their social existence as entities. Monasteries, guilds, and municipalities commonly operated under royal charters of incorporation, as did merchant enterprises such as the British East India Company, as well as nine of the eleven original colonies of British America.[48] But this legacy of politically constituting corporate existence was inadequate to the rapidly changing commercial forces of the sixteenth and seventeenth centuries, especially those affecting the development of overseas trade and investment. One major reason for the rise of constitutional monarchy and eventually American democracy was the monopoly effect of royal charters, which granted exclusive discovery and trading rights often coupled with delegated government powers (military, monetary, etc.). The English Revolution of the 1640s (sometimes called the Puritan Revolution) was forged, in part, from the struggle of "non-company" overseas merchants (including many operating in the American colonies) to break the grip of royal charters.[49]

The medieval and royal legacy of corporate charters did not disappear with the rise of representative democracy; rather, it evolved in new directions, sometimes with democratic, even populist, implications. In the federal system of the United States, state legislatures devoted much attention to the issue, pressed by public agitation to either abolish state chartering powers (as a dangerous remnant of monarchy) or transform them into a democratic framework for securing public goods. Thus, in the antebellum period, roads, turnpikes, and canals were often built and operated by private companies either formed by public charters or contracted under them.

One pivotal Supreme Court decision relating to charters came in the famous Charles River Bridge case of 1837.[†] The Charles River Bridge was privately constructed and operated under a public charter granted in 1785, stipulating detailed rules of use and reversion of ownership back to the state after forty years. By 1826 it was observed that an original share in the Charles River Bridge corporation costing $333 dollars had returned the principal plus $7,000 in interest and profit. In 1823 the estimated value of the bridge was $300,000.[50] By this time, however, growing congestion on the Charles River Bridge, along with competitive pressures from real estate developers wishing to build a new "free bridge" to increase traffic near their holdings, gave rise to a series of battles in the Massachusetts state legislature. In 1827, rejecting committee recommendations for a compromise offering a phased public buyout of the Charles River Bridge concern, both the House and Senate voted to a grant a charter to another association for the building of a new, free bridge over the river. The first veto ever issued by a Massachusetts governor (Levi Lincoln) quickly followed. Proponents cried out for "public justice" until Lincoln finally gave in, refusing to veto a second bill granting the free-bridge charter in 1828.[51] Six months after the new bridge opened at the end of 1828, toll revenues of the private bridge dropped by 60 percent.[52] Appealed to the Massachusetts Supreme Judicial Court, the case made its way to the United States Supreme Court and was finally decided in 1837, after President Andrew Jackson had the chance to fill three vacancies (including that of Chief Justice John Marshall, who died in 1835), with Democratic appointees. The most momentous of these appointments was that of Roger Brooke Taney for Chief Justice, replacing Marshall. Marshall's 1819 decision in *Dartmouth College* set a high bar for legislative action affecting chartered corporations in the essence or scope of

---

† *Proprietors of the Charles River Bridge v. Proprietors of the Warren Bridge* (1837).

their public grants. Casting them as contracts that create vested property rights, Marshall's "strict construction" view of corporate charters was also read in the other direction, as something to limit corporate immunities only to those specifically expressed in the charter. In the 1830 *Providence Bank v. Billings* case, Marshall himself would embrace this version of the strict construction of charters to deny a bank's shareholders relief from a state bank-tax enacted in 1821 and later increased. The shareholders argued that this impaired the contract created by their charter of incorporation, granted in 1791.[53] However, because the bank's original charter contained no expressed rule granting immunity from future taxation, taxing the bank in no way violated the bank's right of contract, Marhsall argued. The way of thinking about charters expressed in this decision had an important effect on related decisions in that decade, most importantly in Taney's rejection of contractual impairment claims in the Charles River Bridge case. Taking his cue from Marshall's imputation of community prerogative where charters are silent, Taney replicated the same logic, arguing that the plaintiffs must show that the state had provided in their original charter that it would never grant a subsequent charter for a free bridge. Famously, Taney raised the stakes on Marshall's *Providence Bank* precedent to propose a more general defense of taxation as well as other forms of public policy regulating economic development. The "object and end of all government is to promote the happiness and prosperity of the community by which it is established." And it can "never be assumed," he added, referring to the claim that corporate charters imply a broad restriction on subsequent government actions affecting the economic value of the concern, "that the government intended to diminish its power of accomplishing the end for which it was created." Indeed, "while the rights of private property are sacredly guarded, we must not forget that the community also have rights, and that the happiness and well being of every citizen depends on their faithful preservation." This standard pertained against the Charles River Bridge concern, Taney's logic made clear, because the monopoly conditions they wished to preserve for private profit were impairing the community's collective capacity for furthering commerce and sharing in its benefits.

It was in this vexing period of community empowerment over organized capital, with *Dartmouth* still looming on the Marshallian heights, that a movement for general incorporation statutes began to take root, rapidly succeeding after the Civil War, so that by the end of the nineteenth century general incorporation laws for all types of enterprise were enacted in most states, as mentioned earlier. The effect of general incorporation was to remove corporate existence beyond the reach of the state, even as the communal needs that stood in the care of public chartering powers, in the Shaw and Taney mold, had nowhere to stand when those powers declined. Of course, communities began to agitate for regulatory bodies and social policy as a way of reasserting control. The rise of the railroad companies, for example, was challenged as a tyrannical effort to destroy small communities and frontier life. Texas congressman John Reagan led the anti-railroad movement in Congress and spearheaded passage of the Interstate Commerce Act of 1877. This movement was pressed by interior "captive" shippers in the South and Midwest who, producing at a distance from major transportation junctions, paid per-mile "farm-to-market" rates that were much higher than the long-haul through-rates enjoyed by geographically favored producers shipping from market to market.[54] Without regulation to drive down the high short-haul rates on noncompetitive routes, supporters of the Interstate Commerce Act argued, the rail system would "operate to concentrate population and wealth in a handful of great cities—a vision the periphery and midlands found morally as well as economically abhorrent," as historian Elizabeth Sanders summarizes.[55] Reagan explained the problem as one of regulating the power of concentrated wealth over natural communities—essentially, preventing economic concentrations from dictating the life and death of communities. "The railroad companies demand and insist on the right to exercise this vast and dangerous power," he argued, "and under it they are impoverishing some cities, towns and communities, without any fault of their's [sic], and enriching others having no other merit to this favor than the arbitrary power of the transportation companies."[56] In the 1890s, the Supreme Court devastated the Interstate Commerce Commission's rate-review powers.[57] In 1905, Wisconsin Senator Robert LaFollette described the railroads as a threat to the "social economy," reacting to the corporate and judicial assault on the Interstate Commerce Commission. The social economy of "serving a given territory from the center which would serve it best and cheapest, the economy of the multiplication of convenient centers of trade and industry, of the building up of many small cities well distributed over the country, is disregarded," LaFollette argued, by the "schemes of the traffic managers . . . the long haul, the big tonnage, the large revenues, and the dividend. To these considerations all else is sacrificed."[58] West Virginia Senator Stephen B. Elkins, who later passed legislation establishing the Commerce Court to hear appeals against the ICC, considered such thinking nearly atheistic, describing railroad regulation as trying "to reverse the laws of Providence."[59]

Corporation Theory

The organization of capital into extensive market enterprises in the decades before World War I provoked intensive debate about the legal nature of corporations. At the heart of this debate were questions of what night be called corporate "ontology"—namely, what sort of being or existence does a business corporation have, how does this being or existence originate, and what rights or immunities arise directly from its nature?

Scholars generally agree that there were three basic theories of corporate existence in nineteenth-century American law, each of which had certain kinds of real-world implications.[60] The "fiction" theory, with classical and medieval roots, dominated American legal thought until the early nineteenth century. As discussed earlier, the fiction theory holds that the corporation exists solely by grant of the state. Its existence and powers as an entity, apart from the "real" persons comprising it, are brought into being by grant of state authority and only on the terms of the state. The fiction theory arguably culminated in Marshall's eloquent formulations in *Dartmouth College v. Woodward*—although the actual decision in the case implied something closer to a theory of autonomous community. The second prevalent theory was "contractual-association." Here, the corporation is viewed as a partnership of individual members; its existence as an entity is simply the sum of its individual parts, bound by the rights and privileges of every member. The third approach is the "real entity" theory: here, the corporation owes its existence and legitimacy to a distinct purpose and will as a group, set apart from both the individual and state.

The great British legal scholar F. W. Maitland played a singular role in introducing the real entity theory into Anglo-American jurisprudence. His translation of part of Gierke's *Das deutsche Genossenschaftsrecht*, the first in English, was a turning point. The real entity theory, many thought, could augment the power of corporate capital by distinguishing it from other kinds of associations; for example, its real existence (marked by what Gierke termed *Gesammtpersönlichkeit*, or "group personality") could create certain rights in its property or entail certain immunities. While the contractual model gave power to shareholders as members of the corporation, the real entity theory gave power to managers as operators of a larger whole with a will independent of its members. Gierke's emphasis on the distinctive nature of group personality and purpose helped illuminate the growing impact of large aggregates of money and capital and the drastic diminishment of small, independent production. It also echoed in the emerging forms of labor bargaining, as workers obtained more collective power.[61]

Some progressive reformers eagerly embraced real entity theory, seeing it as part of a new politics of cooperative empowerment. The bad social consequences of capitalism, fueled by laissez-faire individualism and inadequate social laws, could be rectified on a new legal basis of cooperation, established by equalizing the power of self-constituting groups.[62] "We begin the reinterpretation of law in terms of our collective needs," the avowed Gierkean Harold Laski wrote.[63] Notably, arguments for corporate personality arose with growing demands for tort and criminal liability reforms. How could a corporation be held liable for torts and crimes if it was nothing but a legal fiction. If that is the case, the *ultra vires* principle (beyond the power) prevents liability by limiting corporate existence to the prescribed purposes of state charters—thus effectively absolving them of anything not prescribed by the state (like torts and crimes).[64] Real entity theory imputed ethical features to the corporation that established collective liability. The wrongful *mens rea* (state of mind) necessary for liability could not exist in a legal fiction or contractual association based on distinct individual wills.

According to Gierke, the fiction theory originated with Pope Innocent IV in the thirteenth century, who declared corporations to be fictions devoid of souls, capable of neither sinning or being punished. This view migrated into English common law, Maitland argued, with the major effect of sheltering corporations from liability for lack of wrongful state of mind.[65] Viewing it as the cornerstone of corporate liability, Gierke pitted the real entity theory against the fiction theory. He believed it was original to German law but undermined by the spread of the Church. In England and the United States, the fiction theory did not obliterate corporate liability, as Gierke believed was the case virtually everywhere, but English jurists recognized the tension. Blackstone, for one, elevated the fiction theory in English common law: "There are also certain privileges and disabilities that attend an aggregate corporation. . . . It can neither maintain, or be made defendant to, an action of battery or such like personal injuries, for a corporation can neither beat nor be beaten, in its body politic. A corporation cannot commit treason, or felony, or other crime in its corporate capacity." In 1840, the German legal historian F. C. Savigny declared that corporations can hold property but cannot be held liable for torts and crimes.[66] "Left-Gierkeans," such as George Deiser, saw the real entity theory as a way of attaching responsibility to corporate acts.

Morton Horwitz is well known for his view that real entity theory facilitated the ascendancy of big business in the early twentieth century. In different ways, he explains, the fiction and contract theories of the past limited business growth or had that potential. The contractual theory created too much risk of liability, while the fiction theory allowed too little autonomy. Some credit the Supreme Court's decision in *Santa Clara County v. Southern Pacific Railroad* (1886) for introducing corporate entity theory. In an infamous headnote attached to the ruling, the Court formally declared that corporations are "persons" under the law. In John Norton Pomeroy's brief for the railroad in *Santa Clara*, he described the nature of the corporation rather vaguely as an extension of the personhood of its individual "corporators"—the owners. Thus the property provisions of the state constitutions and the federal Constitution apply to corporations, even though the language of these provisions, as written, was clearly intended for application to "natural persons," that is, to distinct human individuals. Indeed corporations, he argued, might also be considered "persons" within the legal meaning of the property provisions, because "corporations cannot be separated from the natural persons who compose them." Thus,

> Whatever be the legal nature of a corporation as an artificial, metaphysical being, separate and distinct from the individual members [thus appropriate for limited liability, continuous life, etc.], . . . still in applying the fundamental guaranties of the constitution, and in thus protecting the rights of property, *these metaphysical and technical notions must give way to the reality.* The truth cannot be evaded that, *for the purpose of protecting rights, the property of all business and trading corporations IS the property of the individual corporators.* A State act depriving a business corporation of its property without due process of law, does in fact *deprive the individual corporators of their property.* In this sense, and within the scope of these grand safeguards of private rights, there is no real distinction between artificial persons or corporations, and natural persons[emphases in original].[67]

As Horwtiz asserts, this is not a real entity theory at all; it merely argues that the Constitution is applicable where an individual property interest exists, whether it is individually held or held in some associated form.[68] In fact, the real entity theory emerged only after *Santa Clara*, in part to resolve the philosophical difficulties of corporate personhood that *Santa Clara* did not carefully address or even recognize.

Another corollary to real entity theory in American corporation law was the rise of managerial control of the firm, which was greatly inhibited under a contractual theory—the only remaining rival to the real entity theory by the turn of the twentieth century. However, the more general effects of the real entity theory were also the most profound. The main effect, Horwitz concludes, "was to legitimate large-scale enterprise and to destroy any special basis for state regulation of the corporation that derived from its creation by the state." It facilitated concentration in numerous ways, but most importantly it "obliterated the claim that corporate mergers were different from individual acquisition of property."[69]

Attacks on the idea of corporate personhood traded on the ordinary perception that corporations are obviously not real persons, and they are much more powerful than any one person. Constitutional personhood seemed to give corporate property an undue right or, more simply, more protection than it needs. Where did the propertyless worker, the sickly child, and the poor community stand in the new order of constitutionally shielded economic power? Literally, nowhere. And this could only mean that organized capital would dominate everything else. As O'Melinn describes it,

> The corporation has literally become an outlaw, exempt from the operation of some parts of the law and imbued with a power to impose law on its members. The corporation has not only acquired a power of sovereignty over its membership through a steady delegation of sovereign power from the state, it has also managed to attain real powers of government over the broader public. Now, a broad range of people who are not parties to the "corporate contract," including consumers and employees, are subject to the corporation's sovereignty. . . . The corporation escaped the bounds of the conventional categories of concession and contract, becoming an extraordinary kind of person with legal privileges to rival those of the state.[70]

Corporate Power and Social Pluralism

The business corporation originally had no existence except in being chartered by the state with public responsibilities. It was eventually freed from the state by an evolution in legal thought from fiction theory to real entity theory. Such personification of the business corporation absorbed the communal terms of family, guild, and congregation, but infused them with a proprietary meaning and an economic purpose. The problem of corporate power as it relates to other social structures without constitutional standing (because without property) was never addressed. These relations seriously affect families and communities, but the effects are viewed as a product of individual contractual relations, not competing corporate rights. So, when a worker is laid off, although this action affects him not only as an individual but also as a father and a husband, with all who depend on him, the whole range of negative effects is judged strictly in terms of his individual contractual relations as a worker. There is no legal standing, and therefore no legal remedy, available to families and communities when business decisions threaten to tear them apart.

In a commonplace way and in a legal sense our whole idea of corporate existence has been reduced to a notion of organized productive property dedicated to earning profits in the marketplace. When reference is made to the "corporate environment" or "corporate power" today, few people think of universities, churches, or even small businesses, although many such institutions are chartered as legal "corporations" under state laws. Certainly, no one thinks of families, neighborhoods, or communities, which, from a natural and moral perspective, have a corporate existence more essential and integrated than most other kinds of corporations.

The reason for this should be clear: among the many types of associations or organized social forms, business corporations have obtained an extraordinary degree of power and privilege from having a corporate existence that is recognized and enabled by law in certain distinctive ways. Theirs is a supervening, statelike existence within society, exercising what is effectively a type of governing power over consumers, employees, resources, and living standards. By any noncontractual account of society, certainly by Kuyper's account in the theory of sphere sovereignty, these are not pluralistic associations at all but, as Gierke himself long ago recognized, something closer to *Herrschaft* structures, economic lordship. For Gierke, the community of workers or the "producers' fellowship" was increasingly debilitated by loss of access to productive property or poor terms of access. The "superior strength" of concentrated capital ownership in modern industry and commercial agriculture "robs all these [working] classes of their economic personality," which can only function through the common possession of productive property. Liberal property rights in capital, elevated by the state above other corporate forms and claims, were a public abuse of social law in Gierke's view. Further, the greater the extent and diversity of its structure, the more a capitalist enterprise (legally a *Korporation*) actually functions as *Herrschaft*, a "lordship group." In a striking passage at the end of volume 1 of *Das deustche Genossenschaftsrecht*, Gierke explains why modern capitalism is a lordship system:

> In its inner nature . . . the unitary body (the capitalist corporation) is nothing but a *lordship structure*, in which the representative of capital (the capital body as it were) is the absolute economic master. That same lordship group which, since time immemorial, has been struggling to gain victory over fellowship,

is reproduced here; in a more limited form, on the one hand, because it does not extend beyond the sphere of economics and economic purposes; harsher and less restricted, on the other hand, because the lordship principle, which in former lordship groups was modified at an early age by the emergence of dependent fellowships, is here implemented unconditionally.[71]

In a leap of understanding still relevant today, Gierke explains why "economic lordship organisms" are more effective in establishing domination than any which came before. Although concentrated ownership deprives the worker of economic personality (which requires independent access to capital), so too the Church deprives him of ecclesial personality if he is a layman, because he lacks many rights which others might possess within the body of believers as a whole. Economic lordship is necessarily more comprehensive, however, because the livelihood necessary for all other things is completely within its grasp. For the propertyless wage-earner—already the majority at that time—economic insecurity determines everything else: "Since his whole economic existence is utterly determined and conditioned by an alien power [*eine fremde Macht*], in whose life he is not granted the slightest active participation, he is devoid of economic rights of citizenship not only within the single group but in the entire economy of the nation."[72]

Gierke was an advocate for what he called "producers' fellowship," or what we would call employee ownership. His ideal economy was a system of universal cooperative ownership, which, "in the face of the lordship of dead property . . . conquer[s] the right of citizenship for labour—the right due to it as the manifestation of its living personality."[73] Short of universal cooperative ownership, Gierke's views on social policy conformed rather strikingly to a subsidiary model, echoing the formal Catholic position expressed much later in *Quadragesimo anno* (Gierke himself was Lutheran). "But while *self-help* [such as employee ownership] excludes state initiatives and state structures," he asserted, "it is easily compatible with contributory *state aid*" (emphasis in original).[74] Distinctly conceived as subsidiary aid to enable self-help, nonetheless, it was commanded by right out of both the workers' needs and the state's responsibility for the common good: "A claim on state aid, indeed, is not the working classes' privilege but their right. . . . If the state is a moral being (and not an institution based on reciprocal services), it is its inalienable right and inescapable duty to intercede, in the last resort, for all its members, when individual resources, even when united with others, are not sufficient to achieve the purposes of human personality."[75]

Among the legal pluralists, Gierke came closest to the Progressive understanding of market power as a form of government: it is notable in this respect that many of the Progressive-era institutional economists who originated this view were trained in Germany (most importantly John R. Commons). Undoubtedly the most difficult issue for the social pluralist is the role government must play when the social structures it must not, by right, displace or absorb, are not, in turn, sufficiently protected from coercive power accumulating *within* society. This is especially acute if one recognizes that "those who own economic goods exercise a kind of governmental power."[76] Gierke himself certainly suggested as much in designating capitalism a lordship system. As the American legal theorist Robert Hale likewise explained, "In many matters of everyday life our liberty is restricted by requirements laid down by those who have superior economic power. These stronger persons are not called rulers, or governors, nor are their dictates known as laws or ordinances, however great the pressure which forces obedience. The sway of economic superiors is not thought to be 'government' at all, nor is 'liberty' thought to be curtailed by it."[77] All economic systems, Hale asserted, "are built on legally sanctioned compulsion. Basically, we are compelled to transact in accordance with the governing powers of others."[78]

Except in limited terms, such as race and religion, our Constitution does not contemplate the existence, let alone the rights, of social groups. The protections it provides in terms of race and religion do not apply to the *life* or *integrity* of these groups *as* groups, only to individuals identified as members of a group. As A. S. Miller put it, "The Constitution limits government in favor of individuals, a notion based on the unstated assumption that individuals live and act as autonomous units. No provision was made for the pluralistic social group."[79] Strictly and logically, the subject of constitutional protections is the individual citizen, and the object of its limitations is the federal government (and, as amended in certain limited ways, state governments as well). In its liberal erasure of social groups, it is perhaps the purest expression of what Gierke termed "natural-right constitutionalism." As he wrote in the conclusion to the famous subsection on "Political Theories of the Middle Age" in volume 3 of *Das deutsche Genossenschaftsrecht*:

> The Doctrine of the State that was reared upon a classical ground-work had nothing to say of groups that mediate between the State and the Individual. This being so, the domain of Natural Law was closed to the Corporation, and its very existence was based upon the ground of a Positive Law which the State has made and might at any time alter. And then as the sphere of

the State's Might on the one hand, and the sphere of the Individual's Liberty on the other, became the exclusive and all-sufficing starting-points for a Philosophy of Law, the end was that the Corporation could find a place in the Public Law only as part of the State and a place in Private Law only as an artificial Individual. . . . A combat it was in which the Sovereign State and the Sovereign Individual contended over the delimitation of the provinces assigned to them by Natural Law, and in the course of that struggle all intermediate groups were first degraded into the position of the more or less arbitrarily fashioned creatures of mere Positive Law, and in the end were obliterated.[80]

Of course, Gierke was not arguing that the natural structures of society had been extinguished in reality, only that the legal and moral recognition they need to survive had been eroded by natural-right individualism and its political corollary, the right-giving (and duly universalizing) state. As individual natural rights evolved into socially destructive corporate property rights in the late nineteenth century, and as the welfare state arose to compensate for the resulting dislocations and social problems, family and community seemed doubly imperiled, morally and functionally displaced by external forces. Gierke's legal pluralism focused mainly on the state and civil law, but unlike many advocates of community and family rights today, he took it for granted that, in the modern period, such statism (in the form of national welfare and education systems, etc.) only made inroads where economic forces had overpowered families and communities and undermined their self-sustaining life. Logically, there could be no legitimate pluralist critique of the welfare state that did not also propose to limit or regulate "economic lordship" in the nonstate realm.

Social Protection in Liberal America

Modestly scaled though it was, the faith-based initiative established a social-pluralist policy design and process, anchored in the freedom of the Church. This is something new in American politics: in contrast, the Progressive and New Deal defeat of laissez-faire politics—still the touchstone for contemporary advocates of economic justice—was carried out in terms of "social welfare" and the "common good," not as a pluralist vision of restoring social sovereignty. The "rights" of families and communities under New Deal liberalism did not derive from their sovereignty as social groups, but from a more general principle of social cohesion, resting, ultimately, on the welfare of the individual. Yet, in contrast to Democratic Party liberalism today, much of New Deal social policy was in fact targeted toward protecting and strengthening the traditional family. This tension between liberal and social-pluralist welfare philosophy did not hinder the establishment of key New Deal policies, but it encapsulates the problem of integrating religious ideas about society into a liberal constitutional order and, more importantly, into a polity and public discourse so powerfully shaped by the tenets of economic liberalism.

The story of the Catholic Church and the New Deal is important for understanding this problem and how it persists today. As an electoral phenomenon, the key historical turning point was the dramatic exodus of urban Catholic voters from the Republican Party that began in 1928 behind Al Smith, the first Catholic presidential candidate on a major-party ticket. The trend was enlarged and consolidated by Roosevelt in 1932 and 1936.[81] Another factor, less well known today, was the extraordinary maturation of Catholic thought in this period, beginning with the late nineteenth-century pontificate of Leo XIII. American Catholic thinkers influenced by Leo (and themselves increasingly influential within American Catholic institutions) emerged as a distinctive presence in public life in the decade before World War I. This intellectual trend was part of a broader evolution of Catholic communities along two distinct but related paths: gaining acceptance within a majority Protestant culture, and embracing government action on the basis of Catholic social teachings.

The most important single figure in this transformation was the Catholic theologian and social reformer John A. Ryan. In his first magazine article, published in *Catholic World* in 1900, Ryan reviewed Henry Demarest Lloyd's *A Country without Strikes*, a study of New Zealand's 1894 compulsory labor arbitration law. Here Ryan formulates a defense of "state interference with freedom of contract," anticipating the arguments of progressive legal theory that would culminate in the Supreme Court's turnabout on state minimum wage laws in 1937 (in *West Coast Hotel Co. v. Parrish*).

At the time there was a more fundamental labor critique that rejected not only unequal bargaining power but the wage system itself (which "commodified" labor and thereby stole the worker's humanity just as slaveholders once did). Sometimes this view drew on radical interpretations of John Locke's labor theory of property. But Catholic social teaching, beginning with *Rerum novarum*, did not view the wage contract as intrinsically evil. In the Leonine approach developed by Ryan, what was important was the natural right of the worker. This was not defined by his labor but understood as the "moral means or opportunities by which the individual attains the end appointed him by nature." God-given ends and purposes define the realm of "natural right" in contrast with other kinds of claims or demands. What God ordains for the worker, Ryan argued in his first book, *A Living Wage* (1906), is a "right and reasonable life," meaning a life consistent with the moral worth of the person as measured by his intrinsic and equally given (God-given) faculties of reason, self-improvement, and love of God. It was not seriously debated whether material sustenance was the foundation of this. Establishing a "living wage" was arguably the conservative position on a spectrum that also included redistributing productive assets to give everyone a share of ownership in the real wealth of society.[82]

In his major ethical work *Distributive Justice* (1916), Ryan argued that when a worker "accepts a wage insufficient for his needs under the compulsion of avoiding the worse evil of starvation," his contract is "no more free than the contract by which the helpless wayfarer gives up his purse to escape the pistol of the robber. . . . Like the wayfarer, he merely submits to superior force. The fact that the force imposed on him is economic does not affect the morality of the transaction."[83]

Ryan's growing influence reflected a broader shift in Catholic teaching, reaching from Leo XIII to the more radical views of Pius XI. At the heart of this shift was an evolution in Catholic natural law thinking, a tradition revived in the wake of the French Revolution. At base, Catholic natural law thinking in this period moved beyond the essentially political problems of revolutionary liberalism (with its strong governmental encroachments on religious institutions and authority, as typified in France) toward a more communitarian critique of the *economic* domination at the core of the liberal state. Drawing on this deeper intellectual transformation, Ryan constructed a consistent moral defense of state intervention in the economy, as well as a specific legislative framework in support of workers and their families—one that, in many respects, would ultimately be ratified under the New Deal.

At the center of the natural law revival that fueled Ryan's thinking stood the great thirteenth-century moral theologian Thomas Aquinas. Thomas had defined natural law as "the rational creature's participation in the eternal law," the eternal law being God's law as it directs the whole universe to its appointed end. As applied to political order, Thomistic natural law is the grounding or set of principles that orient human laws to what is right and good in God's eyes. Thomas said that the fundamental objective of natural law is that the good be done, and evil avoided. Thus, the law of a people is "nothing else than an ordinance of reason for the common good, made by him who has care of the community."[84] The fundamental orientation of natural law in ordering political society is the preservation of life, out of love for God's creation and out of the unique responsibility God gave humanity regarding its care.

In its economic dimensions, this approach is guided by the biblical understanding that God gave the earth to all human beings in common. The law codes of the Hebrew Bible, defended by the prophets, established a comprehensive system of economic security and restoration based on the principle of the earth being a common gift. This included provisions for the control and remission of debt, the release of slaves, and the periodic return of alienated lands in order to restore family stability and prevent concentrated wealth.[85] Thomas viewed the latter policy of the "Old Law" as especially significant and compared it favorably with Aristotle's views of property. For Thomas, private property is notably an integral feature of the common good and useful for human society, but it is a conventional institution fully subordinate to the directives of God's law, which is oriented to the common welfare. Thus, property is defined as having a twofold nature of private possession and common use. "Man may fully possess [material goods] as his own," Thomas wrote. But "as regards their use . . . a man ought not to look upon them as his own, but as common, so that he may readily minister to the needs of others."[86]

In Catholic tradition, these mandates are encapsulated by a principle termed "the universal destination of goods," which is deemed "primordial" in the Church's Catechism. Leo XIII established the modern template for Catholic teaching from this principle in *Rerum novarum*, cautiously recognizing the need for state intervention to secure it. Although seemingly a bold departure from the dominant, laissez-faire ethos of the period, the interventionist thrust of *Rerum novarum* was in fact deeply rooted in Catholic thought. In his great work *De Legibus*, the sixteenth-century Jesuit philosopher Francisco Suárez argued plainly, for example, that "the object of civil legislation is the natural welfare of the community and of its individual members, in order that they may live in peace and justice, with a sufficiency of those goods that are necessary for physical conservation and comfort, and with those moral conditions which are required for private well-being and public prosperity."[87]

While Leo vigorously condemned political liberalism for its philosophical individualism and its vesting of sovereignty in the people or its representatives rather than God, it is important to understand how Catholic thought in this period, as I have already discussed, became increasingly concerned with economic liberalism (much more directly so than today's "communitarian" critics of liberalism). As Ryan's work illustrates, in the wake of *Rerum novarum*, with its defense of "isolated and helpless" workers against the "hardheartedness of employers and the greed of unchecked competition" (sec. 3), the dangers of economic liberalism, anchored in the unencumbered reign of "freedom of contract," became much more pronounced in Catholic teaching.

Jesuit Solidarism and American Social Welfare

One of the most influential concepts to emerge from the mainly Jesuit circles behind the rise of Leonine social Catholicism in late nineteenth-century Europe was termed *solidarity*.[88] This concept also had a distinctive if limited influence in the United States, playing an important role in John Ryan's efforts, among others', to integrate Catholic social teaching into the legal and policy framework of American liberalism.

The idea of solidarity has a rich European heritage reaching back to early socialist thinkers such as Charles Fourier, who described his concept of public assistance as *la garantie familiale solidaire*.[89] But by the turn of the twentieth century, the Church had thoroughly assimilated the idea, rechristening it in the fulcrum of Leonine neo-Thomistic social teaching, a distinctly Jesuit enterprise. A secular, social-democratic variant also emerged in response to the "social question" of the late nineteenth century, particularly in Catholic-dominant republics. Léon Bourgeois's formulation of "solidarism" in the 1890s became something like the national creed of the French Third Republic (Bourgeois was the sixty-fourth prime minister of France); in France, the theory of solidarity was closely identified with social legislation efforts, particularly the idea of funding social insurance programs with revenues generated by progressive taxation. Strongly resonating with the Catholic doctrine of the universal destination of goods (with its roots in the creation-debt theology of the Hebrew Bible), French solidarism achieved public renown in Bourgeois's 1896 book *Solidarité*, where he wrote:

> Man does not only become the debtor of his contemporaries in the course of his life; from the very day of his birth, he is a debtor. Man is born a debtor of human association. On entering such an association, he takes his share of an inheritance built up by his own ancestors and those of all others; at birth, he begins to benefit from an immense capital which previous generations have accumulated.[90]

Although rarely studied today in American social policy, Bourgeois's writings and ideas were very influential among American Progressive-era economists, most importantly John R. Commons and the Commons-led "Wisconsin School" of social research; the Wisconsin School, in turn, was a major intellectual source for the development of Social Security and other social insurance ideas developed during the New Deal and after.[91]

The chief Catholic theorist of solidarity (*Solidarismus* in German) was the Jesuit scholar Heinrich Pesch, born in Cologne in 1854. Forced to study abroad in England during the *Kulturkampf*, Pesch was profoundly influenced, like his more radical countryman Friedrich Engels, by the industrial conditions he witnessed in northwest England. This inspired him to seek permission from the Society of Jesus to become an economist when he returned to Germany. Notably, Pesch was the teacher of Oswald von Nell-Breuning, the primary author of *Quadragesimo anno*, and his influence on subsequent papal teaching, particularly that of John Paul II, is undoubted as well (John Paul's native Poland, of course, saw the rise of the Solidarity trade-union movement in the 1980s, which was supported by the Catholic Church).

Pesch's five-volume *Lehrbuch der Nationalökonomie* (reputedly the longest economics textbook ever published) was organized around a Catholic understanding of the idea of solidarity.[92] Early on in the *Lehrbuch* Pesch inserted a programmatic essay on "Solidarismus," which begins by distinguishing Catholic solidarism from the Social Democratic (and largely French) version. Pesch argued that French solidarism was, at its philosophical core, still a liberal social-contract theory, one rooted in the idea of harmonizing individual self-interest with common benefits. If it was justified by a concept of inherited or common assets that the Church might trace back to the original gift of Creation, nevertheless, as a theory of society and social policy, "the introduction of state intervention is approached here in a totally individualistic manner."[93] In Pesch's view, what was needed to build a truly solidaristic social order was, first and foremost, a recognition (and understanding) of the non-individualistic dimensions of human nature and psychology. The German public finance economist Adolph Wagner was one of Pesch's sources on this issue. As Wagner put it, "The particular error of the older [liberal] theory, of British economics especially, was the fact that it segregated man's economic nature too much from his integral human nature."[94]

From the false anthropology of liberal economics derives the reactionary political idea that state intervention in the economy—taxation, social programs, and so forth—are inhumanly coercive if not criminal. A more socially integrated view of human nature, in contrast, casts many forms of public action in a positive moral light, one that reveals a rebalancing of individual rights with the right of all human beings to a level of resources and security that befits their God-given potential for productive work, domestic happiness, and spiritual growth. Solidarity is thus both descriptive of the social instincts and social dependency of every individual, and at the same time normative for law and policy according to a principle of common human fulfillment. As Pesch wrote in "Solidarismus":

> But critical laws here are first and foremost, by their very nature, social demands on the individual and on the community as a whole, with reference to the purposes of life in society. Each individual and the community, along with those in authority, have to comport themselves in such a way, and establish economic conditions in such a manner . . .that the ultimate goal of life in the political order and in society—the genuine welfare of all and the free development of the personalities along with all of the wealth of their particular talents and capacities—can achieve their full realization for every member of society according to the full extent that this is possible.[95]

In both Europe and the United States, Pesch's influence was felt in the emergence of two important policy ideas—industrial corporatism and the just wage. On the first, Peschian solidarism was premised on a kind of power analysis of modern capitalism, seeking ways to give workers sufficient collective power to compete with organized capital. The basic idea was to establish a framework of mandatory, equal-power negotiation between business representatives and occupational groups (fellowships, syndicates, unions), harmonizing the major bodies of labor and capital in each industrial sector and by that route "making whole" a production and wage structure sufficient to the needs of all. The New Deal's National Industrial Recovery Act of 1933, arriving shortly in the wake of the Pesch-influenced *Quadragesimo anno*, was interpreted by some as an attempt to implement a corporative industrial policy along Catholic-solidarist lines. As Thomas Kolhler argues, however, American labor law in its own right, as developed in the 1930s, has a distinctly "un-American" character that could be attributed to solidarist influences. The cornerstone of American labor law, the National Labor Relations Act of 1935, had a primary goal of establishing "a legal structure through which employees can gain a voice in managerial decision making," normally (in conventional liberalism) a pure prerogative of legal ownership of the enterprise.[96] The organizing principle of this regime of collective bargaining power is the right of a group of workers, by majority decision, to impose its representative will on individual members of the group, and through the resulting group cohesion to exert power in setting the terms of contractual relations with the employer. The legal assimilation of such power in America's liberal constitutional order was no small achievement, Kohler believes, one that, more than anything, reflects Catholicism's prevalence in the leadership and membership of the trade union movement and also in New Deal congressional strongholds. Senator Robert Wagner, the author of the National Labor Relations Act (a.k.a. the Wagner Act), for example, was a product of German Catholic heritage and carried on extensive correspondence with John Ryan and other Catholic ethicists involved in social policy. *Quadragesimo anno* was clearly a major influence on Wagner as well; among his legislative papers are two heavily annotated copies of the encyclical.[97]

If a corporatist tendency in solidarist thought was expressed in the Wagner Act, the neo-Scholastic idea of the just wage was perhaps more broadly salient for social reformers. As Thomas Storck explains well, Pesch did not reject the conventional wage-setting factors of consumer demand and marginal productivity; rather, he argued that employers are responsible for providing sufficiently productive work, and sufficiently desirable products, to generate good wages:

> [If] the only way in which an employer can afford to sell his product is to set his prices so low that he cannot afford to pay his workers a living wage, then clearly his product lacks sufficient consumer demand. It is as if he had to bribe the public to buy his product by charging less than its genuine production cost. Today we are inundated with cheap goods produced abroad, sometimes, as with those produced in China, in conditions little better than slavery. This is a distortion of the economic process. If the item is worth buying, it is worth paying a price that fully compensates all who are involved in its production. If someone revived chattel slavery today and boasted that he could undersell his competitors, who would doubt but that his entire enterprise was an economic as well as a moral evil, no matter how cheaply he could produce? The same logic must be applied to any enterprise that cannot afford to pay its workers a just wage. This kind of analysis, which respects both real economic facts as well as ethical principles, is characteristic of Pesch and of the Catholic tradition at its best.[98]

Solidarism influenced institutional movements no less than legislative reformers. Though little studied today, the development of social-Catholic cooperatives and advocacy networks in the German Midwest was deeply influenced by Pesch's ideas. The organizational vehicle of this was the German-Catholic Central-Verein, founded in 1855 as a national federation of Catholic mutual-aid societies.[99] In 1901, the Central-Verein publicly embraced the teachings of *Rerum novarum* and pledged to work for social reform on Leonine principles, and by the end of the decade it was publishing a bilingual periodical, *Central-Blatt and Social Justice*, the first German-American Catholic publication devoted exclusively to the "social question." In 1909 the group instituted a Central Bureau for organizing educational and reform activities through a network of statewide leagues. A major focus of their advocacy was workplace safety legislation and workmen's compensation.

The guiding force of the modern Central-Verein was Frederick Kenkel, who embraced Peschian solidarism as the basis for a corporatist "middle path" between state collectivism and free-market individualism—one mandating cooperation between social groups and providing compensatory relief where private organizations fail in their social responsibilities. In the German-American version promoted by the Central-Verein, the Leonine principle of subsidiarity, requiring public protection of and assistance for the natural structures of society, was paramount. "As a result," one Central-Verein leader stated in 1915 , "the solidaric state is strong enough to overthrow the absolutism of liberty for the protection of the fettered and the afflicted without becoming a menace itself."[100] Although the Central-Verein grew increasingly influential in this period, with a peak membership of 125,000 and a notable presence in various reform coalitions (particularly with the American Federal of Labor), its influence and membership declined after the U.S. entry into World War I, which considerably altered the political climate for German-American social reformers. Nonetheless, the group's solidarist influence (sharply refined by Kenkel's ongoing editorship of *Central-Blatt and Social Justice*) remained an important part of the progressive Catholic story. Among other things, Kenkel helped launch the National Catholic Rural Life Conference in 1923, which introduced English "Distributist" ideas of cooperative agriculture, public credit, and worker ownership. The radical antimarket tenor of these ideas, felt in many parts of the Church, culminated in Pius XI's 1931 encyclical *Quadragesimo anno*, with its Peschian solidarist roots. *Quadragesimo anno* had a major impact on John Ryan and, in Catholic eyes at least, helped to define the early stages of New Deal economic policy.

New Deal Catholicism

In his memoir, Ryan recounted his "great comfort" when, on May 15, 1931, he listened to a radio transmission of Pope Pius XI's encyclical *Quadrages-*

imo anno in the offices of the *New York Times*. His long effort to integrate Leonine natural law teaching with concrete social policy had been "vindicated," as one colleague put it.[101] That summer he published a commentary on *Quadragesimo anno* in the *American Ecclesiastical Review*, highlighting its important contributions. Among the most important was the idea that the distribution of income and wealth "must be brought into conformity with the demands of the common good and social justice"; that the worker has a right to a wage of "ample sufficiency" for himself and his family (what was called a "family wage" in social policy of the 1920s, something widely debated in Europe); and that the worker has a right to accumulate a "modest fortune" by sharing ownership of capital with employers.[102]

Quadragesimo anno (issued in the "fortieth year" after *Rerum novarum*) was subtitled *On Reconstruction of the Social Order*. It was arguably the most radical and controversial Church-wide statement in all of Catholic history to that point, and the political culmination of the natural law revival in Catholic thought that began under Leo XIII. As noted earlier, Pius XI declared that *Rerum novarum* "completely overthrew" the tenets of economic liberalism, "which had long hampered effective interference by the government," and this had a galvanizing effect on Catholic social reform:

> *Rerum novarum* . . . prevailed upon the peoples themselves to develop their social policy more intensely and on truer lines, and encouraged the elite among Catholics to give such efficacious help and assistance to rulers of the state that in legislative assemblies they were not infrequently the foremost advocates of the new policy. Furthermore, not a few recent laws dealing with social questions were originally proposed to the suffrages of the people's representatives by ecclesiastics thoroughly imbued with Leo's teaching, who afterwards with watchful care promoted and fostered their execution. . . . As a result of these steady and tireless efforts, there has arisen a new branch of jurisprudence unknown to earlier times, whose aim is the energetic defense of those sacred rights of the workingman which proceed from his dignity as a man and as a Christian. (secs. 27, 28)

Most controversially, *Quadragesimo anno* proposed (in a section specifically designated "Reconstruction of the Social Order") the establishment of a corporatist industrial order built around occupational councils comprising industry, labor, and government representatives. Charged with negotiating fair wages, hours, prices, and business practices, the councils would replace pure market forces with mandatory bargaining. This was to "bind men together not according to the position which they occupy in the labor market but according to the diverse functions which they exercise in society." As noted in chapter 3, authoritarian regimes in Austria, Spain, and Portugal took *Quadragesimo Anno* as a model for corporatist experiments, despite specific criticism of fascist corporatism in the encyclical.

Quadragesimo Anno thus had a broad influence that tended to be shaped by the political culture in which it was interpreted. In the United States, challenging business power amassed under economic liberalism and supporting social policy for the protection of wage-earning families were the main interpretive focal points. For example, in a 1932 speech titled "The Philosophy of Social Justice through Social Action," Franklin Roosevelt happily ignored politics, focusing instead on the "fundamentals that antedate parties, and antedate republics and empires." In the culmination of the speech, Roosevelt called for "social justice, through social action," and quoted at length from the source of this idea, *Quadragesimo anno*:

> It is patent in our days that not alone is wealth accumulated, but immense power and despotic economic domination are concentrated in the hands of a few, and that those few are frequently not the owners but only the trustees and directors of invested funds which they administer at their good pleasure. . . . This accumulation of power, the characteristic note of the modern economic order, is a natural result of limitless free competition, which permits the survival of those only who are the strongest, which often means those who fight most relentlessly, who pay least heed to the dictates of conscience. . . . This concentration of power has led to a three-fold struggle for domination: First, there is the struggle for dictatorship in the economic sphere itself; then the fierce battle to acquire control of the Government, so that its resources and authority may be abused in the economic struggle; and, finally, the clash between the Governments themselves. (secs. 106, 107, 108)

Ryan translated these ideas for an American Catholic audience whose leaders sere increasingly radicalized against laissez-faire ideology in the 1920s. The Leonine interpretation of the rights of labor, "as demanding a living wage regardless of free contract, or the law of supply and demand, or any other false philosophy has proved the most revolutionary idea that has been injected into modern economic life," he declared.[103] Inspired by such thinking, Catholic institutions mobilized what the *New York Times* called a "crusade for social justice" after Roosevelt was elected president in 1932. The National Catholic Alumni Federation held regional conferences to promote a radical transformation of the capitalist system, based on the tenets of Leo XIII and Pius XI. "The immediate goal of the crusade," said the *Times*, "is the education of industrialists and workmen to the realization that capitalism, in its present form, has failed and must continue to fail." Ryan, who was a prominent speaker at one of the regional conferences (held at Fordham University), argued at the time that an "occupational group system,"[104] creating a new balance of power between capital and labor, could spur a recovery from the Great Depression in some sectors of the economy.

In Roosevelt's first major New Deal program, under the National Industrial Recovery Act, Ryan saw a partial embodiment of the corporatist vision put forward by Pius XI. Title I of the act created government powers to establish and enforce sectoral business codes for setting wages, hours, bargaining rules, and fair business practices (the act was thrown out by the Supreme Court in 1935). Ryan was appointed to a three-person advisory panel of the National Recovery Administration, the agency that implemented the law, and he was subsequently a fixture in other counsels of the New Deal, serving on numerous committees and also publicly defending Roosevelt on many fronts.

Less well-known than these "corporatist" tendencies in the early New Deal are the "familist" tendencies of the later New Deal. In fact, the primary objective listed in the Democratic platform of 1936 was "The Protection of the Family and the Home," in defense of which, it specified, "We shall continue to use the powers of government to end the activities of the malefactors of great wealth who defraud and exploit the people." As the historian Allan Carlson stresses, New Deal social-assistance programs such as Aid to Dependent Children were designed to "reconstruct" the home or, as the Roosevelt appointee Grace Abbott testified, "to give some security in the home." The Home Owners Loan Act of 1933 provided more than one million long-term, low-interest loans to prevent foreclosures. The 1939 amendments to the Social Security Act, which created dependent and survivor benefits, were particularly emblematic of this philosophy, extending the policy focus from the individual worker to "the economic security of the family unit." Arthur Altmeyer, the chief architect of Social Security, it should be noted, came from a German-Catholic family and was educated at the University of Wisconsin, an important meeting place for progressive economics and Christian thought in the decades prior to the New Deal.[105]

The landmark 1937 Supreme Court decision, *West Coast Hotel v. Parrish*, which overturned a long-standing precedent in support of a state minimum wage law, bore unmistakable marks of a Catholic vision of the common good, going beyond the progressive legal critique of unequal power toward a broader mandate of communal responsibility. Concluding the Court's decision, Chief Justice Charles Evans Hughes stressed "an additional and compelling consideration which recent economic experience has brought into a strong light":

> The exploitation of a class of workers who are in an unequal position with respect to bargaining power and are thus relatively defenseless against the denial of a living wage is not only detrimental to their health and well being, but casts a direct burden for their support upon the community. What these workers lose in wages the taxpayers are called upon to pay. The bare cost of living must be met. . . . The community is not bound to provide what is in effect a subsidy for unconscionable employers. The community may direct its law-making power to correct the abuse which springs from their selfish disregard of the public interest.

If it is disheartening to read these bold words in light of the wage structure today and the pitiful state of the minimum wage, the common good ideal at the heart of this policy statement is still recognizable and offers hope of a better future. Should the community begin to direct "its law-making power" in this way again, it will be part of Ryan's legacy of integrating Catholic social teaching into American public policy and, more broadly, redefining market liberalism by the social destruction it caused, the result of releasing economic power from the moral law which binds it to God's purposes for humanity.

Market Monism and Family Justice

Although the family orientation of some New Deal legislation is comparatively striking today, the lack of a corresponding social-pluralist approach in church-state relations in the New Deal period foreshadows the eventual dissolution of family and community protections in our welfare system in subsequent decades. One reason for this, I would argue, was that Catholic solidarism, so influential in the 1920s and 1930s, was insufficiently pluralist, focusing too much on finding a harmonious "middle way" between free-market individualism and state collectivism and not enough on protecting the social structures naturally suited to creating community and securing communal goods. Pesch himself certainly understood the capitalist threat to family and community life and direly warned against it, but this did not hold his attention as a matter of social and legal theory (and legal power) as with Gierke and the anti-revolutionaries. One could fairly easily reinscribe Pesch's concern for the family in a liberal social-welfare framework, and in the United States especially, where liberalism was the overpowering Constitutional and philosophical tendency, solidarism therefore proved totally inadequate to the task of establishing the kind of communitarian legal framework we would have needed (and still need) to prevent the massive depletion of average wages, benefits, security, and well-being that began in the Reagan years.

Beginning in the 1960s, corporations were subjected to antidiscrimination laws on behalf of minority groups, and this is sometimes considered to be an achievement of social pluralism. Although based on shared biological traits, such as race, these laws protect *individual members* of the race. No such protections exist for groups defined by their biologically based moral character—most obviously, the traditional family as an integrated living unit ordained to very specific and essential purposes. So too, families bound together in communities benefit from no legal contemplation of their needs and purposes in so binding together. Thus, in America, we have ended up with a stillborn pluralism, affording business corporations extraordinary protection from the state while leaving all other associations unprotected from the statelike powers amassed by big business. It is a simple matter of realistic logic to recognize how such imbalances of legal status and economic power lead to distress and diminishment of the weaker, less protected, social structures.

No account of social pluralism that seeks to tame the government out of protective concern for the integrity and durability of local communities can ignore what is happening economically to these very same communities (at least many of them) and to the large groups of wage-earning households that form the backbone of strong communities across the regional, racial, and cultural divides that otherwise define our national politics. The fact is, wage-earning families across much of America are in distress today, and public policy in recent years has done little to relieve that stress and arguably much to create it. The most important trends relate to income, debt, and job security. By the simplest measure of middle-class living standards—median family income—something like a large middle class appeared to be holding its own, but not exactly thriving, in recent decades. In 1981, the median family income was about $49,000, and by 2006 it had risen (in inflation-adjusted terms) to nearly $58,000, a 15.5 percent gain. However, this gain was not nearly as substantial as that of the previous two decades, which saw the real median family income rise from approximately $30,000 in 1960 to nearly $50,000 in 1981, for a gain of approximately 40 percent. More importantly, the historically smaller middle-class gains of the Reagan, Bush Sr., and Clinton years were not generated by higher wages. The median male hourly wage was $15.76 in 1973. Adjusted for inflation, it was $15.64 in 2005. For those with only a high school diploma, there was a sharp real decline over roughly the same period, from annual pay of $42,358 in 1979 to only $37,550 in 2005.[106] The wages of those without a high school diploma have fallen nearly 30 percent since the late 1970s. So how did median family income hold its own against the riptide of falling wages? The answer is *more work*—approximately five hundred more work hours per household annually, mostly in the form of wives and mothers entering paid employment. And, contrary to the common belief that today's wealthy families work harder than everyone else, it was families in the lowest quintile of society that increased their work hours the most in recent decades, by nearly 18 percent, as compared to 17 percent for the middle quintile and only 12 percent for the top quintile.[107]

The mounting distress in families and communities is measured not only in wages but in rising costs and economic insecurity. Over the past two decades, the cost of living has risen 90 percent—driven up mainly by rising health care, housing, and child-care costs—while average wages for the bottom 60 percent of households rose only 5–15 percent.[108] The collapse in buying power one might have expected with costs so dramatically outstripping wages was averted in two basic ways: first, as mentioned above, more hours of work per household; and second—and even more problematic— the assumption of record levels of consumer debt.

In the wake of the George W. Bush years, more than two-thirds of middle-class households, twenty-three million families, qualified as either insecure or highly insecure as defined by levels of assets, income, education, and health care coverage.[109] And next to declining security in the middle, nearly fifty million people are living below the poverty line or less than 25 percent above it. Asset disparities, always the norm, have created two different economies in America, one economy of wealth and another of wages. The bottom 50 percent of the population is almost completely dependent on wages, holding less than 3 percent of the total financial wealth, while the top 5 percent of households hold nearly 58 percent of financial wealth.[110]

The erosion of family security was invited, in part, by the rise of individualistic social liberalism in the 1960s and 1970s. Legally and culturally, this development contributed to the weakening of familial and communal norms in public life, the very heart of New Deal social policy. The protection of the family and the home from economic insecurity and dislocation was no longer a certain or even desirable policy objective in an era of individual liberation marshaled *against* the traditional culture of family and community. Consider even the direct example of abortion: while *Roe v. Wade* gave women a constitutional right to choose abortion in the case of an unwanted pregnancy, many women are routinely *denied* the same choice when poverty or other circumstances compel them to get an abortion. It is reasonable to assume that compelled abortion is more common than forced childbirth in America today. Yet the libertarian ethic of abortion rights has influenced our political culture to such an extent that we do not even notice the moral contradiction of constitutionally protecting a woman's right to choose abortion while doing little or nothing to remove powerful constraints on her "right to choose life" or, more broadly, on many childbearing decisions.

As big business, feeding on social liberalism, reestablished its dominance in American politics, families and communities received no new protection from the government even as older protections came under attack. The family living wage paid by a substantial majority of U.S. businesses had literally vanished from the country by the late 1970s. Although many mothers initially went into the work force willingly and happily, in search of more variety and accomplishment in their lives, today a majority of working mothers do not view employment positively. According to survey data reported by Public Agenda in 2000, 80 percent of mothers would prefer to stay at home with their children if they could. Of course, the profound lack of employer and government support for working mothers in the United States contributes to this attitude—how much so is a central point of contention between conservatives and feminists. Clearly, however, many working mothers take jobs out of necessity, not choice, and to ignore this compulsion, as both conservatives and feminists generally do, is morally incoherent at best in a country boasting high regard for "family values." The resulting extraordinary changes in family life have gone almost completely unaccounted for in American economic policy. The only policy one might cite in this regard is the Family and Medical Leave Act of 1993, which entitles workers to three months' unpaid leave for certain purposes, such as dealing with family medical problems or staying home with a newborn.

This faint echo of European family policy surely has had some positive effects, but more than that it reveals precisely how far we are, morally and politically, from seriously addressing family needs in public policy.[111] If anything, the opposite has been true. Instead of helping families, government power helped big business extort more labor for less pay and less security, and it did so without interference from anyone's "rights."[112]

Conclusion: A New Hope

The faith-based initiative was (and is) a new policy design for helping poor and distressed communities. The magnitude of the problems entails a significant government role, the benefits of which, and the dangers, are addressed in the legal and philosophical framework I have examined in this book and believe will continue to be viable as we go forward beyond the Bush years. But this very point leads me to emphasize again that sphere sovereignty and subsidiarity do not only protect religion from the state. Restricting the state is part of a larger mission of protecting the natural structures of society—families, churches, communities—from coercive, "monistic" powers, *whether public or private*. This begins with a critique of the state, but that is not where it ends: other kinds of power, particularly the state-like powers of large corporations, high finance, and concentrated wealth, also pose a significant threat to the diverse, God-given purposes of families, churches, and communities. Kuyper openly said so, as did his Catholic counterparts in the struggle against liberalism, Pope Leo XIII and Pope Pius XI. Gierke, the father of modern social pluralism, directly and unequivocally argued that organized capital, no less than the state, is a threat to the natural structures of society. In this he bore out the prediction of none other than Alexis de Tocqueville, who is much more famous today for his fearful prophecy of the "tutelary" welfare state. But as he wrote in volume 2 of *Democracy in America*, "The manufacturing aristocracy which is growing up under our eyes, is one of the harshest which ever existed in the world." And therefore, he warned, the "friends of Democracy should keep their eyes anxiously fixed in this direction; for if ever a permanent inequality of conditions and aristocracy again penetrate into the world, it may be predicted that this is the channel by which they will enter."[113]

The confessionals and social pluralists, great traditionalists, saw that liberalism is not just a political and cultural assault, but also an economic assault. Liberalism shields this economic assault behind individual contractual rights that exclude the moral claims of families and communities. But sphere sovereignty reinstates these collective moral claims as a foundation of political order. On this account, the religious critique of liberalism increasingly will be forced to confront the destructive economic power that is hidden by the liberal social contract. European Christian Democracy did this by establishing a family-wage system to protect the natural structures of society from market damages—an approach that was predicated on the theories of confessional freedom developed by Pope Leo XIII and Abraham Kuyper. The Dutch and German welfare systems successfully implemented these ideas, and these systems are important models for today's faith-based initiatives.

These ideas can be usefully compared with the better-known "communitarian" critique of liberalism formulated by Michael Sandel and other American philosophers. Yet in mandating social protection and economic stability as a basis for human fulfillment under God, the Christian Democratic critique of liberalism goes much further than the liberal-communitarian debate in the United States. Unlike Germany and the Netherlands, America does not have a rich tradition of corporate or communal freedom to draw on in justifying and creating social protections. This is due to liberalism's sweeping exclusion of family and community from the domain of legal subjectivity and public rights, a deprivation that partly accounts, Antony Black suggests, "for the weakness of the communitarian dimension in Anglophone thought generally."[114] Yet in this new era of faith-based initiatives, we find a type of communal freedom flourishing in the design of American social policy. And by this example, a new light dawns on American liberalism's exclusion of family and community from legal subjectivity and the domain of rights. It shows the way to a better future.

As I have stressed in these pages, there is in fact one powerful legacy of communal legal protection in the United States, and it is a profoundly ironic one: American business corporations assumed their dominant political and social position in the early twentieth century partly with the aid of legal theories influenced by Gierkean and English pluralist thought on the nature and rights of associations. This once-heated theoretical debate is surprising today, as the legal status of business corporations is no longer in question. Ultimately, the work of Horwitz, O'Melinn, and other legal historians in this area helps us to unearth the devastating paradox of an American liberalism that empowered business corporations with a protective legal status partly constructed from ideas of associative moral personhood, while at the same time excluding families, churches, and communities—self-evidently much more legitimate bearers of collective rights—from any such legal protection. Bringing this paradox to light sets the stage for a revitalized communitarian challenge to the liberal economic order. We have had a beginning: by enabling religious self-governance in the social safety net, the faith-based initiative established a new moral template for conceptualizing and codifying the natural rights of families and communities in our liberal economic order. More than anything else, this points to the end of destabilizing, coercive, unaccountable economic powers that demean so many lives.

The fundamental core of charitable choice law and the faith-based initiative (broadly understood) is a vision of societal restoration. As we saw in chapter 3, this vision arises out of a conservative diagnosis of liberalism that originated in the struggles of confessional churches to preserve their autonomy, their beliefs, and their cultural influence against the twin forces of market individualism and state-centered welfare in nineteenth-century Europe. Although the former brought forth substantial religious critiques in the United States in the same period—culminating in the Catholic Bishops' Program of Reconstruction after World War I—the latter problem was not as sharply defined in the United States as it was in Europe.[115] This was the case for two simple reasons: (1) the kind of welfare state that concerned Kupyer and Leo and the confessional parties of Europe did not begin to emerge in the United States until the 1930s; and (2) the constitutional disestablishment and great diversity of faiths in America left them without the kind of legal and political leverage enjoyed by the large confessional churches of Europe, which in many countries (particularly Germany, the Netherlands, and Italy) waged protracted political struggles against the "principles of 1789."

Although "liberalism" in America has been under attack from religious forces for several decades, this has mainly focused on the role of the courts in disestablishing moral standards (on abortion, marriage, etc.) while at the same time placing strict limits on religious speech and activities in public institutions or in connection with public funding. As the latter legal barriers have been lowered over the last twenty-five years (beginning with the "equal access" decisions of the mid-1980s), the church-state struggle has increasingly become a matter of statutory initiative and administrative design. The watershed for this new stage of church-state relations was George W. Bush's faith-based initiative, and it is no coincidence that this effort brought us full circle with the original church-state conflict in public services, waged in Catholic and Calvinist Europe: constitutionally, we have moved in this direction, and so too, now, politically. In doing so, we have reconnected American policy, and our hope for society, with a rich philosophical tradition concerning the fate of natural social structures caught in the vice grips of market liberalism and liberal statism. This represents a new starting point for legal and political understanding in the United States.

The severe economic crisis that swept across America in 2008 and 2009 is a sad vindication of the kind of "architectonic critique" Abraham Kuyper long ago urged, which "leads to the desire," he explained, "for a different arrangement of the social order." By the winter of 2009, 4.4 million jobs were lost, with more job losses certain to follow. By March 2009, an estimated 10 percent of homeowners faced foreclosure or were delinquent on their mortgage payments, and 20 percent of homes with a mortgage were "underwater"—worth less than the cost of the loan. Some blue chip stocks were trading at one or two dollars a share.

Skyrocketing demand at food banks, even in wealthy suburban enclaves, was the clearest sign of grave distress. "I've been here for over twenty years. . . . I've never seen such a dramatic increase in need," reported one food bank worker in Orange County, California, last spring. In some poorer states, such as Ohio, welfare enrollment began rising after steadily declining over the previous ten years, with one-third entering the welfare system for the first time. And yet most of the states suffering the severest job losses in 2008 either reduced or kept constant the number of people receiving welfare payments, their systems increasingly trapped—"re-missioned"—by the shallow political logic of welfare reform.

In untangling the philosophical roots of America's faith-based turn in social policy, my goal was to start a new conversation about public responsibility for social needs and how and why this is narrowing the church-state divide in a particular (social-pluralist) way. For all of that, however, the crisis at hand provides no better proof of the ultimate need I diagnose—the need for a new moral standardization of policy goals around the ideal of family and community protection, with a new legal framework to enforce those goals and secure that ideal. What that new structure will look like is the subject of serious new efforts among a group of younger, like-minded thinkers and advocates from the right and the left, working together, in some cases, to develop new policy models and modes of control. This work in progress (even as I write) may represent a genuinely new political alignment in our future.

The policy structure we need to replace, however, should be clear: over the last two decades, our political leaders made an unstated but fundamental decision from which all (or most) domestic policies flowed. Put simply, they decided to let good jobs disappear in America, following a cost-reduction model of competitiveness rather than one based on innovation and social investment; then, to replace the buying power lost with the decline of good jobs, they flooded the economy with easy credit. This pattern was doomed from the beginning: job- and wage-killing trade policy, deunionization, immigration, and workfare, along with all manner of rewriting wage-and-hour rules (such as on overtime), declining labor-rights enforcement, and outright wage theft—all this, coupled with sweeping deregulation at virtually every financial entry point across the entire economy, had an unmistakably destructive logic.* In short, credit-based consumption replaced wage-based consumption until too much debt became unpayable against the real buying power in our economy, and the whole system came crashing down.

The faith-based initiative may seem irrelevant amid all the boldface headlines about America's decline. It is mainly directed, of course, at urban poverty, a problem more or less unchanged since the 1960s, with only a limited set of means-tested programs at issue. Yet I would suggest that the faith-based initiative's pluralistic reordering of our social safety net is foundational for broader change, and this will become clearer as the importance of family and community—and faith—is crystallized amid the rubble of the economic crash.

The bottom half of the U.S. population, one-third of whom already lived near or below the poverty line before the crash, will not quietly give up on their dreams or their children's future. The policies and leadership (of both parties) that have left them with less than 3 percent of the total net worth of the country and without adequate protection against global capi-

---

* The under-reported problem of wage theft is finally getting widespread attention thanks to Kim Bobo's recent book *Wage Theft in America* (New York: New Press, 2009). It is a widespread problem for construction, garment, nursing home, farm, and restaurant workers. In a report released on March 25, 2009 (GA0-09-0458T), the Government Accountability Office, based on an undercover investigation, found severe inadequacies in the Department of Labor's treatment of wage-theft complaints.

talism simply cannot continue. Virtually all of the economic growth of the last thirty years was captured by the top 20 percent of households, if not the top 5 percent, while the average household worked more hours for lower wages, fewer benefits, and less security. We will begin to fight back against such a politics of upward redistribution, fighting not for "welfare" as a social right, as in the 1960s, but for comprehensive family security—for protection and support of the family unit in its threefold structure of children, working parents, and elders.

Security for the life cycle of the family is the fundamental moral purpose of political order and the proper social objective of a caring state. By the 1970s, we seemed to have achieved that goal in large measure by crushing the power if not the desire of aristocracy—rule by the wealthy; we did this by the accumulating force of democratic government, born out of violent revolution, civil war, and social movements; but then we lost control of that power as general affluence for many (and real hope for many more) began to weaken our grip.

Confessional intransigents all, our nineteenth-century pluralist predecessors clearly understood what we, too, might begin to recognize in the crisis at hand—put simply, a failure of politics to protect society by establishing legal and moral control of the economic domination at the core of the liberal state. Reestablishing the place of community, families, and faith in our political order should be a paramount goal of all who recognize the crisis at hand for what it is. In the pluralist heritage, church autonomy was the Archimedean point of just such a comprehensive social vision. It could be so again if the freedom of the church transforms our politics as prophetic tradition demands.

On the presidential campaign trail in 2008, Barack Obama promised to revive the faith-based initiative, and in his first days as president he set up a White House office and advisory council to oversee this effort, "the foundation," he said, "for a new project of American renewal." The surprising resurrection of George W. Bush's most maligned and misunderstood domestic policy strengthened Obama's claim to a new kind of politics, even as he sharply contrasted his own faith-based vision with Bush's "photo-op" version. Notably, Obama has said that social advocacy is just as important as direct social aid, following more closely than Bush the Bible's thematic structure linking compassion and charitable works with the prophets' critique of power and social injustice.

Embracing the faith-based initiative came naturally to this former community organizer who, like any community organizer, knows that churches and faith-based coalitions have long been the most vital components of renewal efforts in urban America. Many who commented on the matter seemed to have forgotten his previous (and, among presidential candidates, unprecedented) experience in this arena, focusing instead on the political calculations involved. But Obama's surge into faith-based territory was not simply a raw political calculation to attract religious voters: the simple fact is, given the extraordinary economic problems that emerged in 2008, Obama could have left the faith-based initiative to die along with most of the rest of Bush's policies without affecting his chances in 2008 or, for that matter, going forward to 2012. Yet he chose to revive the idea and with it the sprawling legal and political controversy surrounding religious involvement in public welfare. From his speeches on the presidential campaign trail, it is clear that he did so not only because he believes that faith-based providers in struggling communities should be supported by the government, but because supporting them will help "set our national agenda"—by placing the churches' prophetic encounter with society at the center of a new understanding of public responsibility. No other president since Franklin Roosevelt has so much potential, and so much need, to reignite the prophetic witness of our major faith traditions.

The nearly complete political breakdown on this issue during Bush's presidency offers many lessons for the current administration. With a favorable legal environment and significant statutory groundwork to stand on (most importantly, the charitable choice provisions included in several major bills, beginning with welfare reform in 1996), Bush did not need broad political support or congressional help to implement his faith-based initiative. The original goal, as I discussed in chapter 1, was to "level the playing field" for smaller faith-based providers—that is, to remove regulatory and administrative barriers that prevent or limit the involvement of faith-based organizations in our social safety net. It bears repeating that there was already a long history of government contracting with larger faith-based agencies such as Catholic Charities and Lutheran Social Services, but in leveling the playing field for smaller religious agencies, Bush's main goal was to do so in a way that did not suppress their religious character and motivation. He used executive orders and legal interpretation to extend the protections provided in charitable choice to programs not already covered by those laws.

The political failure of Bush's original plan was largely due to the entrenched influence of two powerful blocs in national politics—the cultural left of the Democratic Party and the antigovernment right within the Republican Party (dominant in the Republican leadership during the Bush years). Most important, the latter's majority control through 2006 basically insured that the faith-based initiative would not be able to deliver on its promise of bringing new help to distressed communities. Bush shares the blame for this because he added little new social spending and carelessly stood by as key White House agencies were gutted from within by cronies and ideologues bent on proving the Reaganite maxim that government is not the solution but part of the problem, a strategy of willful neglect brought into sharp relief by Hurricane Katrina. All of this made it much easier for the cultural left to attack the faith-based initiative as a dangerous religious assault on public programs. And so poverty, the central issue, ended up as little more than a stage prop in the continuing culture war between religion and secularism in public life.

Then as now, the most controversial issue in the debate about faith-based initiatives is religious employment. The question still looms: Does federal funding disqualify faith-based groups from using religious criteria in employment decisions and policies—an allowance they enjoy under civil rights law as well as under Supreme Court rulings in cases not involving federal funding? When Obama entered the White House promising to revive the faith-based initiative, the culture-war faithful readied their battle-plans on the newly redrawn political map. With the Democrats in power, some on the cultural left were particularly emboldened and threatened a legal trench-war to the bitter end if President Obama did not repeal existing protections for religious employment. This should not deter the president— and seems not to have deterred him thus far—from seeing what is really at stake and acting accordingly, a moral decision that ultimately rests on whether strong communities are important in his political vision. To that end, Bush's many other failings should not prevent us from considering the significant political ideas about community that shaped his controversial "redesign" of church-state relations in social welfare. These ideas, the focus of this book, bear directly on the continuing controversy over religious employment in the faith-based initiative, and they are vital to so much more if we can resolve that controversy.

President Obama's stated views on the constitutionality of faith-based initiatives, expressed on the presidential campaign trail and reiterated in his campaign's initial paper on the matter, suggested that religious-employment protections hold an uncertain place in his policy vision and may be rolled back. But the executive order he issued on February 5, 2000, authorizing the new White House Office and Advisory Council for Faith-Based and Neighborhood Partnerships, did not directly address the issue. The reprieve was good news for many allies of the faith-based initiative.

President Obama says he wants to defend families and communities from destabilizing forces like foreclosure and job loss. Putting a high secular price on public resources—insisting that no public support is available unless helping your community bears no real trace of your religious identity—does not serve that objective and in some ways contradicts it. Leave aside the fact that existing civil-rights law and Supreme Court rulings support religious hiring rights, and that only one federal court, a district court in Mississippi, has ruled that religious-employment discretion is forfeited with the acceptance of government funds. Leave aside a more recent federal court decision upholding the constitutionality of faith-based employment in a federally funded social agency (*Lown v. Salvation Army*, 2005). The more important reason these protections should not be repealed is a moral reason. Put simply, restricting religious hiring rights in the faith-based initiative attacks the very thing it claims to be supporting. That is, it attacks communities.

As I discussed in chapter 1, the Supreme Court's greatest advocate for the poor, Justice William Brennan, deciphered these issues carefully in his separate opinion in *Corporation of the Presiding Bishop v. Amos* (1987), the key constitutional case on religious hiring rights. It is worth repeating what he wrote: "For many individuals, religious activity derives meaning in large measure from participation in a larger religious community. Such a community represents an ongoing tradition of shared beliefs, an organic entity not reducible to a mere aggregation of individuals." He concluded that faith-based hiring rights as protected under civil rights law do not represent an unconstitutional "establishment" of religion but merely a recognition that communities of believers lie at the heart of all (or most) religious traditions, and these have a right to maintain their identity as communities. For government to restrict the criteria and discretion by which religious communities define and maintain their identity threatens the very existence of religion as Justice Brennan understood it.

Ultimately, then, repealing religious hiring rights in the faith-based initiative is not only constitutionally unnecessary; it is morally incoherent according to the president's own stated ideal of serving and protecting communities. The political abandonment for three decades of poor communities and working families, the effects of which are becoming ever more visible, can only be compounded by a new wave of unreflective liberal orthodoxy on the role of religious communities in our welfare system. To save America from social ruin, it is precisely the moral and legal standing of families and communities that we need to discern, express, and codify—first in our government, but ultimately in the marketplace. On this path forward, society is publicly protected, not ruled by the government or abandoned to private destruction. Public support for the life-saving work of faith-based providers is protective in this sense; suppressing their religious identities as a condition of public support is not.

Let me also be clear about the political implications. Nine years on in this important national debate about religious involvement in government social programs, the Democratic Party holds all the power in Washington, and yet some in the party still seemed determined to squander its stake in our republic's faith-based future. Put simply, the theory and ideal of strict separation of government and religion, particularly as applied in the realm of public welfare, is more than just legally moribund; it is politically blind. If the Democrats want government to do more to help struggling communities, there is no better strategy to build support for such aid than enlisting smaller faith-based providers in the delivery of social services, because this will create a new class of stakeholders in the welfare state and a new source of legitimacy for social spending. After thirty years of calculated destruction of the public sector—and misguided secularism within it—that would indeed be a new kind of politics.

NOTES

INTRODUCTION

1. George W. Bush, "Duty of Hope," speech delivered in Indianapolis, Indiana, 22 July 1999.
2. John DiIulio provides a good summary of the research on faith-based effectiveness in *Godly Republic: A Centrist Blueprint for America's Faith-Based Future* (Berkeley and Los Angeles: University of California Press, 2007), chap. 5.
3. A policy based on evidence showing how religious providers can be more effective with the support of government is undoubtedly the goal of many of the social scientists who are sympathetic to the faith-based initiative. Yet if you were to construct an equation measuring even dramatically enhanced faith-based inputs against the value and opportunities being taken out of America's most troubled communities— by job-loss, home foreclosures, budget cuts, and so forth—surely it would show a net loss. We will return to this fundamental point in chapter 4.
4. In *McDaniel v. Paty* (1978), the Supreme Court overturned a Tennessee constitutional provision prohibiting ministers from holding public office. The lower court's rationale that such a law is necessary to "prevent those most intensely involved in religion from injecting sectarian goals and politics into the lawmaking process" was rejected as factually uncompelling and at the same time an undue constraint on religious liberty. Justice Brennan's majority opinion was notable for its warning against using the establishment clause "as a sword to justify repression of religion or its adherents from any aspect of public life." On the broader question of why religious conviction cannot be constitutionally proscribed from policymaking, see Michael J. Perry, "Why Political Reliance on Religiously Grounded Morality Does Not Violate the Establishment Clause," *William and Mary Law Review* 42 (March 2001): 663–83.
5. Letter quoted in Michel Mollat, *The Poor in the Middle Ages* (New Haven, CT: Yale University Press, 1986), 108.
6. Ibid., 38
7. The Central European and English Reformations cannot be separated from the rise of capitalism, particularly in the case of the latter. In the English case, spurred by the capital windfall of confiscated monastic lands in the 1530s, commons' enclosure and the erosion of customary land tenure marked the emergence of agrarian capitalism based on large estates, commercial tenancy, and proletarianized wage labor. (These tendencies were vividly depicted in 1516 by Thomas More in his *Utopia*; More

was beatified by Pope Leo XIII in 1886 and canonized in 1935 by Pope Pius XI—these two leaders being the most important Catholic architects of modern welfare conservatism as exemplified in Christian Democratic Europe). Harold Berman's study of legal transformation under the Protestant Reformations in *Law and Revolution II* (Cambridge, MA: Belknap Press of Harvard University Press, 2003) devotes less than four pages out of nearly four hundred to the question of land tenure and enclosure (in England), with no consideration of the relevant historical literature on agrarian capitalism, most importantly the work of Robert Brenner and the continuing debate spawned by his work; see T. H. Aston and C. H. E. Philpin, eds., *The Brenner Debate: Agrarian Class Structure and Economic Development in Pre-Industrial Europe* (Cambridge: Cambridge University Press, 1985), and, more recently, Ellen Meiksins Wood, *The Pristine Culture of Capitalism* (New York: Verso Books, 1991). Berman is correct (as R. H. Tawney had long ago emphasized in his Holland Lectures, published as *Religion and the Rise of Capitalism* in 1926), that the magisterial Reformers, from Luther himself to the great Elizabethan Anglican divines, introduced no doctrinal innovations on usury, just price, and so on, that could be characterized as a "Protestant capitalist ethic."

The problem with taking Reformed theologians' assessment of commercial practices as a yardstick for measuring the "Protestant ethic" (Berman is almost entirely dismissive of Max Weber's famous study) is that capitalism, at least in England, originated not in commercial and financial London but in the countryside, with the aristocracy's destruction (legal and extralegal) of customary tenure and commons' rights starting at the end of the fifteenth century. This is what set in motion the separation of producers from the means of production, which is, by any definition, a central feature of capitalist systems. By retaining a conventional definition of capitalism linked to a rising commercial bourgeoisie, Berman misses entirely the capitalist transformation of the landlord aristocracy that emerged in the sixteenth century, culminated politically in the overthrow of the Stuart monarchy, led particularly by American-oriented overseas traders allied with commercially oriented landowners in Parliament (as Brenner demonstrated with vast scholarship in *Merchants and Revolution* [New York: Verso Books, 1993]), and resulting, by the mid-eighteenth century, in a monopolization of 70–75 percent of the arable land in England by large commercial estates parceled into capitalist tenancies employing landless laborers. One theological aspect that this erasure of agrarian capitalism prevents Berman from considering is the close linkage of Puritanism (Presbyterian and Congregational) with the burgeoning literature on agrarian improvement in the seventeenth century—in turn a major influence on Locke's famous "labor-entitlement" theory of property, the philosophical cornerstone of contemporary anti–welfare state politics. Berman's focus on legal institutions also necessarily prevents a closer analysis of Protestant influence in political philosophy. Whereas Berman (dismissing Weber) argues that Calvinism exerted a "communitarian" influence through the idea of covenant (as exemplified in the formation of joint-stock companies, he argues), a comparative of view of early modern French and English political theory reveals very distinctive social-contract tendencies in the latter, emerging rather plainly out of the shadows of Catholic communalism. Certainly the great Elizabethan (and Calvinist) political theorist Sir Thomas Smith was strikingly innovative in his famous description of the "commonwealth" as a "multitude of free men collected together," a view which can be distinguished as "individualistic" compared to, say, Jean Bodin's definition of the state as a "harmony" of "families, colleges, or corporate bodies." Berman's interpretation of the Bank of England as a "communitarian" enterprise obviously divorces the concept from any definition one could derive from Thomistic thought or the guild and village structures of Germanic communal law.

8. Luther was much better on the Eighth Commandment, favorably comparing the wood thief to the "swivel-chair robbers" of law and commerce. On the Eighth Commandment as applied to wealthy exploiters, see Robert Gnuse, *You Shall Not Steal: Community and Property in the Biblical Tradition* (Maryknoll, NY: Orbis Books, 1985). In this important book, Gnuse analyzes biblical teachings on poverty and property through the lens of the Eighth Commandment. The force of his argument comes with his explication of the commandment itself, which he argues did not primarily refer to personal theft in a narrow, individual sense but to dispossession of the poor—any denial of rightful access to land and resources given by God. "The command not to steal spoke against those who sought to appropriate communal possessions for their own private use," Gnuse asserts (6).

9. On Protestant approaches to the "house poor," see Katharine A. Lynch, *Individuals, Families and Communities in Europe, 1200–1800* (Cambridge: Cambridge University Press, 2003), 119–35.

10. In *The Development of the Family and Marriage in Europe* (Cambridge: Cambridge University Press, 1983), British anthropologist Jack Goody argues from vast scholarship that Catholic Church doctrine and teaching on celibacy, marriage, birth legitimacy, and inheritance were instrumental for expanding and protecting ecclesial property. At its height the Church owned as much as one-third of the land of Europe.

11. "Pitilessly torn asunder" is the phrase Marx and Engels used in *The Communist Manifesto* to describe the destruction of traditional institutions by the bourgeoisie.

12. Peter H. Lindert, *Growing Public: Social Spending and Economic Growth Since the Eighteenth Century* (Cambridge: Cambridge University Press, 2004), Table 1.1.

13. Isabel V. Sawhill, "Poverty in the United States," in *The Concise Encyclopedia of Economics,* online edition at http://www.econlib.org/Library/Enc/PovertyintheUnited States.html (accessed 6 February 2008).

14. Richard A. Easterlin, "How Beneficent Is the Market? A Look at the Modern History of Mortality," in *The Reluctant Economist: Perspectives on Economics, Economic History, and Demography* (Cambridge: Cambridge University Press, 2004), chap. 7. Easterlin concludes, "[The] assumption that the market, in solving the problem of economic growth, will also solve that of health and life expectancy is belied by the lessons of experience. Rather than a story of the success of free market institutions, the history of mortality is testimony to the critical need for collective action" (138).

15. Milton Friedman, *Capitalism and Freedom* (Chicago: University of Chicago Press, 1962). Essentially a data-free book, *Capitalism and Freedom* concludes by surveying the advances in living standards after World War II and assessing the role of government programs and the tax system, which he argued make a "dismal" record. Instead of government, "All this," Friedman wrote, "has been the product of the initiative and drive of individuals co-operating through the free market. Government measures have hampered not helped this development. We have been able to afford and surmount these measures only because of the extraordinary fecundity of the market. The invisible hand has been more potent for progress than the visible hand for retrogression" (200). Contrast Friedman to Lindert's *Growing Public,* which marshals empirical evidence demonstrating the positive role of public investment. Using sophisticated statistical models and comparative historical evidence, Lindert shows that social spending did not slow economic growth and probably contributed

in key ways to economic growth. Comparing the low-spending, free-market model of the United States to the high-budget welfare states of Europe, Lindert concludes that "there are good reasons why statistical tests keep coming up with near-zero estimates of the net damage from social programs on economic growth. It's not just that the tales of deadweight losses describe particularly bad policies. It's also that the real-world welfare states benefit from a style of taxing and spending that is in many ways more pro-growth than the policies of most free-market countries" (*Growing Public*, 227).

16. Arthur M. Okun, *Equality and Efficiency: The Big Tradeoff* (Washington DC: Brookings Institution, 1975). See also Jonas Pontusson, "Whither Social Europe?" *Challenge* 49 (November–December 2006): 35–54. Comparing Anglo-American performance to that of the Nordic economies, Pontusson writes, "[Cross-national] comparison provides no support whatsoever for the proposition that more egalitarian countries have grown more slowly than less egalitarian countries, nor does it confirm the proposition that social spending is bad for economic growth" (36).

17. Hans Urs von Balthasar, *The Glory of the Lord*, vol. 6, *Theology: The Old Covenant* (San Francisco: Ignatius Press, 1991), 316–17.

18. The best general study of the theme of biblical justice is Enrique Nardoni's *Los que buscan la justicia: Un studio de la justicia en el mundo biblico* (Estella, Spain: Verbo Divino, 1997). An English translation has been published: *Rise Up, O Judge: A Study of Justice in the Biblical World*, trans. Seán Charles Martin (Peabody, MA: Hendrickson, 2004).

19. Pope Pius XI, *Divini redemptoris* (1937).

20. DiIulio, *Godly Republic*, chap. 3.

21. Mary Ann Glendon, *Rights Talk: The Impoverishment of Political Discourse* (New York: Free Press, 1991), 112–15.

22. My rather loose definition of a new or emerging policy field is one that has gained dedicated support from foundations; is a major focus of research organizations or of research programs within larger organizations; has become a common focus of multiple academic disciplines that are increasingly in dialogue concerning policy development; and has an identifiable set of stakeholder groups or networks involved in routine political advocacy on the subject. Although not on the level of, say, global warming, faith-based social policy certainly fits these criteria, some aspects of which will emerge in due course below. A simple Lexis-Nexis search finds more than a thousand references to the "faith-based initiative" in its database of major U.S. newspapers over the last decade.

23. The much-noted turn toward progressive activism among evangelicals in recent years is described in eyewitness terms by Jim Wallis in *The Great Awakening: Reviving Faith and Politics in a Post-Religious Right America* (New York: Harper Collins, 2008). E. J. Dionne looks deeply at the rich heritage of Catholic social justice and the challenges now faced by America's largest church in *Souled Out: Reclaiming Faith and Politics After the Religious Right* (Princeton, NJ: Princeton University Press, 2008).

24. As Al From of the Democratic Leadership Council put it in 2000, "Who's running against welfare now? . . . Who's running against poor people? Crime and welfare were surrogates for race. By taking both of them away as political issues, we did a lot of good for minorities and low-income communities. We also changed the tone of the political debate to where it is more tolerant and inclusive" (quoted in Jason DeParle and Steven A. Holmes, "A War on Poverty Subtly Linked to Race," *New York Times*, 26 December 2000).

25. David Kuo, *Tempting Faith: An Inside Story of Political Seduction* (New York: Free Press,

2007). More than a year after he left the White House, John DiIulio went on record, in an *Esquire* story by Ron Suskind, with a scathing critique that he immediately tried to recant. The 22 October 2002 letter to Suskind from which DiIulio's critical comments were drawn for the story (most famously, describing White House policymaking as the "reign of the Mayberry Machiavellis") was made public and is available on the *Esquire* Web site at www.esquire.com/features/dilulio.

26. DiIulio, *Godly Republic*, chap. 6.

27. Al Gore's major presidential campaign speech on faith-based organizations was delivered in Atlanta, Georgia, on 24 May 1999.

28. Peter L. Berger and Richard John Neuhaus, *To Empower People: The Role of Mediating Structures in Public Policy* (Washington, DC: AEI Press, 1977).

CHAPTER ONE

1. George W. Bush, "Duty of Hope," speech delivered in Indianapolis, IN, 22 July 1999.

2. Alexis de Tocqueville, *Democracy in America*, vol. 1, chap. 7 (New York: Schocken Books, 1961), 369–70.

3. Michael B. Katz, *The Price of Citizenship: Redefining the American Welfare State* (New York: Metropolitan Books, 2001), 137–42.

4. Ibid., 141.

5. More recent data suggests an added value of at least 30 percent from voluntary labor time. For example, in 1997–98, total revenues of the nonprofit sector equaled approximately $665 billion, while total voluntary labor time added the equivalent of $226 billion. See *The New Nonprofit Almanac IN BRIEF*, Independent Sector (2001), 3.

6. Quoted in Robert E. Rodes Jr., "The Last Day of Erastianism: Forms in the American Church-State Nexus," *Harvard Theological Review* 62 (July 1969): 302–3.

7. Quoted in John A. Ryan, *Social Doctrine in Action* (New York: Harper & Brothers, 1941), 25. Archbishop Ireland inspired (and ordained) John A. Ryan, for one, who became the chief intellectual architect of Catholic support for labor laws, public poor relief, and social insurance over the next four decades, culminating in his significant involvement in the New Deal.

8. Peter H. Lindert, *Growing Public: Social Spending and Economic Growth Since the Eighteenth Century* (Cambridge: Cambridge University Press, 2004), 61, fig. 3.5.

9. Ibid..

10. Thomas W. Pickrell and Mitchell A. Horwich, "Religion as an Engine of Social Policy: A Comment on the First Amendment Limitations on the Church-State Partnership in the Social Welfare Field," *Law and Contemporary Social Problems* 44 (Spring 1981): 114.

11. Monroe Billington, "Catholic Clergymen, Franklin D. Roosevelt, and the New Deal," *Catholic Historical Review* 79 (January 1993): 65–83. The most famous clerical critic of the New Deal was the radio priest Charles Coughlin. Though an early supporter of Roosevelt ("the New Deal is Christ's Deal" was one of his slogans), Coughlin's combination of conservative social Catholicism and radical populist economic theory led him to reject the New Deal (particularly its refusal to implement public currency controls) and embrace anti-Semitic conspiracy theory and pro-Nazi sentiment in the late 1930s. Coughlin's effort to mount a third-party challenge to Roosevelt in 1936 was thwarted in part by Father John Ryan, who broadcast a national radio speech defending Roosevelt late in the campaign.

12. Ambrose A. Clegg Jr., "Church Groups and Federal Aid to Education, 1933–1939," *History of Education Quarterly* 3 (September 1964): 141–42. The details that follow are also drawn from Clegg's interesting article.

13. Quoted in ibid., 148.
14. *Churches and Social Welfare* (Cleveland, OH: National Council of Churches of Christ in the USA, 1956), 152.
15. Ibid., 158.
16. Ibid., 161.
17. Religiously affiliated hospitals (or other medical facilities) are also reimbursed by the Medicare and Medicaid programs.
18. Bernard J. Coughlin, *Church and State in Social Welfare* (New York: Columbia University Press, 1965), 160, table A6.
19. Ibid., appendix 2, 153.
20. Ibid, appendix 5, 165. In a 2001 survey the Pew Research Center found that 45 percent did not think government funding of faith-based social services would "interfere with church-state separation," while 68 percent did fear that such efforts would get "government too involved with organizations." By this rough measure, at least, the level of concern regarding church-state separation is about the same as it was fifty years ago, but there is more concern today about interaction with government. See, "Faith-Based Funding Backed, but Church-State Doubts Abound," Pew Research Center, available online at http://people-press.org/reports/display .php3?PageID=112.
21. Pickrell and Horwich, "Religion as an Engine of Social Policy," 113–14.
22. Robert R. Sullivan, "The Politics of Altruism: The American Church-State Conflict in the Food-for-Peace Program," *Journal of Church and State* 11, no. 47 (1969): 48.
23. Ibid., 50–51.
24. In particular, Humphrey supported expanded faith-based contracting under President Kennedy's Latin American economic development initiative, the Alliance for Progress. He offered support in his Senate Report on the Alliance for Progress (1963); see Robert R. Sullivan, "The Role of the Presidency in Shaping Lower Level Policy-Making Processes," *Polity* 3 (Winter 1970): 211–15.
25. Sullivan, "Politics of Altruism," 57–58.
26. There is surprisingly little scholarship on this aspect of Johnson's War on Poverty. But see the interesting oral history put together from Johnson's White House tapes by Guian Mckee of the Miller Center for Public Affairs at the University of Virginia: available online at http://tapes.millercenter.virginia.edu/exhibits/faith/. As Mckee emphasizes, church-state partnerships in Johnson's framework of public intervention were conceived quite differently from Bush's comparable efforts. My limited knowledge of the earlier debates suggests that strict secular requirements were broadly imputed and, except for Catholic advocates, there was little concern for balancing secular requirements with protections for religious providers.
27. A snapshot from 1997 shows that, across the nonprofit sector as a whole, government funding comprised 31 percent of revenues, compared to private revenues at 20 percent. This trend toward public funding is most prominent in the health field (correlated with new streams of Medicare and Medicaid funding in particular).
28. See Donald F. Kettl, *Government by Proxy* (Washington, DC: Congressional Quarterly Press, 1988). Steven Rathgeb Smith and Michael Lipsky broke important ground with their balanced critical assessment of the "turn to nonprofits" in federal social policy, focusing particularly on issues of privatization ("One critical issue is the legitimacy of giving over state power to private providers"). See *Nonprofits for Hire: The Welfare State in the Age of Contracting* (Cambridge, MA: Harvard University Press, 1993). Interestingly, they do not discuss the church-state issues that had already

emerged in two major government-by-proxy social-welfare bills of the 1980s, the Adolescent Family Life Act and the Child Care Development Block Grant. See further discussion of this legislation below.

29. Stephen V. Monsma, *When Sacred and Secular Mix: Religious Nonprofit Organizations and Public Money* (Lanham, MD: Rowman & Littlefield, 1996), 1. In 1996, Catholic Charities received $1.3 billion from the government, amounting to 64 percent of its income. See Amy E. Black, Douglas L. Koopman, and David K. Ryden, *Of Little Faith: The Politics of George W. Bush's Faith-Based Initiatives* (Washington, DC: Georgetown University Press, 2004), 21. This pattern of dominant public funding was detectable much earlier in the area of orphan care.

30. Helen Rose Ebaugh, Janet S. Chafetz, and Paula Pipes, "Funding Good Works: Funding Sources of Faith-Based Social Service Coalitions," *Nonprofit and Voluntary Sector Quarterly* 34 (December 2005): 456, table 1.

31. George F. Will, "Keeping Faith behind Initiatives," *Washington Post*, 4 February 2001, B7.

32. Peter L. Berger and Richard John Neuhaus, *To Empower People: The Role of Mediating Structures in Public Policy* (Washington, DC: American Enterprise Institute, 1977), 28.

33. E. Theodore Bachmann, quoted in Coughlin, *Church and State in Social Welfare*, 27. Bachmann was a leading Lutheran church historian who died in 1995.

34. Brian M. Riedl, "The Myth of Spending Cuts for the Poor, Tax Cuts for the Rich," Heritage Foundation, Backgrounder #1912, 14 February 2006, available online at http://www.heritage.org/Research/Budget/bg1912.cfm. Riedl does not discuss Reagan's social budget cuts, which flattened social spending as a share of total federal spending across the 1980s and did so, more importantly, in the face of increasing social need.

35. Daniel M. Hungerman, "Are Church and State Substitutes? Evidence from the 1996 Welfare Reform," *Journal of Public Economics* 89, nos. 11–12 (2005): 2259.

36. Government spending explains virtually all of the measured decline in religious giving during the 1930s, the authors further argue. Nevertheless, as a share of total New Deal spending, they also note, this crowd-out effect was actually very small due to a low overall baseline of church spending. Thus in pointing to crowd-out, one could also ask "crowd-out of what?" See Jonathan Gruber and Daniel M. Hungerman, "Faith-Based Charity and Crowd Out During the Great Depression," NBER Working Paper Series 1132 (May 2005), 25; available online at http://www.nber .org/papers/w11332.pdf.

37. As Carl Esbeck has written, "With the advent of the welfare/regulatory state in the middle third of this century, continuing to enforce a strict rule of no aid has the effect of confining religious social ministries to ever smaller enclaves of private life. If the charities of faith-based groups are to participate along with secular organizations in meaningfully serving civil society, they are put to a cruel choice. No-aid separationism demands that religious ministries either secularize and thereby qualify for government aid, or close their doors for lack of funding. Thus, in its present-day impact, no-aid separationism is hostile toward faith-based charities. The changed circumstances work such unfairness that denial of all aid is no longer a plausible ordering of church/state relations. The absence of evenhandedness not only suffocates social and religious pluralism by creating a monolithic, secular-dominated structure for the delivery of welfare services, but the no-aid view eliminates a fuller range of provider choices for the poor and needy." See Carl H. Esbeck, "Myths, Miscues, and Misconceptions: No-Aid Separationism and

the Establishment Clause," *Notre Dame Journal of Law, Ethics and Public Policy* 13, no. 2 (1999): 290.

38. John J. DiIulio Jr., "Government by Proxy: A Faithful Overview," *Harvard Law Review* 116 (March 2003): 1227–28.

39. Ibid., 1227.

40. Monsma, *When Sacred and Secular Mix*, 105.

41. The speaker was Dr. Daisy Alford-Smith, director of the Summit County Department of Job and Family Services in Akron, Ohio. The April 24, 2002, event was a press briefing entitled "The Growing Impact of Government Partnerships with Faith-Based Organizations," focused on survey research presented by Amy Sherman of the Hudson Institute. It was co-sponsored by the Center for Public Justice.

42. Stephen V. Monsma, *Working Faith: How Religious Organizations Provide Welfare-to-Work Services* (Philadelphia, PA: Center for Research on Religion and Urban Civil Society, 2002), 17. This view is consistent with what Monsma generally found in his earlier book synthesizing available data, *When Sacred and Secular Mix* (cited above).

43. As the report states (GAO-06-616, 7), "While officials in all 26 FBOs that we visited told us that they understood that federal funds could not be used for inherently religious activities, 4 of the 13 FBOs that offered voluntary religious activities—such as prayer or worship—did not appear to understand the requirement to separate these activities in time or location from their program services funded with federal funds. For example, one FBO official told us that she discusses religious issues while providing federally funded services if requested by a participant and no other participants object, and a few told us that they pray with beneficiaries during program time if requested by the beneficiary."

44. Brian L. Anderson's widely discussed essay, "How Catholic Charities Lost its Soul," published in the Manhattan Institute's *City Journal* (Winter 2000), is perhaps the benchmark piece in this vein; available online at www.city-journal.org/html/10_1_how_catholic_charities.html.), n.p.

45. Ibid.

46. Charles L. Glenn, *The Ambiguous Embrace: Government and Faith-Based Schools and Social Agencies* (Princeton, NJ: Princeton University Press, 2000), chaps. 6–8. I discuss Glenn's views in more detail below.

47. Glenn, *Ambiguous Embrace*, 255.

48. Robert Rector, "Implementing Welfare Reform and Restoring Marriage," Priorities for the President (Washington, DC: Heritage Foundation, 2001), 74.

49. In the *Bradfield* case, the District of Columbia gave $30,000 to the Providence Hospital of the Sisters of Charity for the construction of two new wards (for contagious diseases), as well a contract paying $250 annually for each patient treated in the wards.

50. Laurence H. Tribe, *American Constitutional Law*, 2nd ed. (Mineola, NY: Foundation Press, 1988), 1215–16. Stephen Monsma brought Tribe's interesting point to my attention in his book *Positive Neutrality: Letting Religious Freedom Ring* (Grand Rapids, MI: Baker Books, 1993), 26.

51. "Developments in the Law: Religion and the State," *Harvard Law Review* 100 (1987): 1632. Following the precedent of an earlier free-exercise decision, *Cantwell v Connecticut* (1940), *Everson* "incorporated" the establishment clause into the Fourteenth Amendment, thereby making it applicable to the states, many of which had aid programs for which private and parochial schools (or, more often, private and parochial

school students/parents) were eligible: thus, it was the fountainhead of decades of controversy.

52. Black's interpretation showed a streak of moderation on the facts that appalled the *Everson* dissenters. Justice Wiley Rutledge's dissent, for example, dismissed any solicitous nuance in the facts of the case (this was "not just a little case over bus fares," he wrote) to argue that the purpose of the religion clauses "was broader than separating church and state in a narrow sense. It was to create a complete and permanent separation of the spheres of religious activity and civil authority by comprehensively forbidding every form of public aid or support for religion."

53. In the year after *Everson*, the Supreme Court ruled against a release-time program providing religious instruction for public school students on school premises. Black again wrote the majority opinion in the case, *McCollum v. Board of Education*, illustrating his readiness to bar any public policy perceived to advance religion and reflecting how close to the "verge" *Everson* had actually been.

54. Black's dissent in *Board of Education v. Allen* (a 1968 decision upholding a New York State textbook loan program for which religious schools were eligible) gave extreme expression to this type of "religion creep" theory, whereby any kind of assistance was considered aid to religion. No other opinion of the no-aid era matched Black's dissent in *Board of Education v. Allen* for sheer conspiratorial (and anti-Catholic) vitriol: "It is true, of course, that the New York law does not, as yet, formally adopt or establish a state religion. But it takes a great stride in that direction, and coming events cast their shadows before them. The same powerful sectarian religious propagandists who have succeeded in securing passage of the present law to help religious schools carry on their sectarian religious purposes can, and doubtless will, continue their propaganda, looking toward complete domination and supremacy of their particular brand of religion. And it nearly always is by insidious approaches that the citadels of liberty are most successfully attacked."

55. Carl H. Esbeck, "Equal Treatment: Its Constitutional Status," in Stephen V. Monsma and J. Christopher Soper, eds., *Equal Treatment of Religion in a Pluralistic Society* (Grand Rapids, MI: William. B. Eerdmans, 1998), 14–15. See also Derek H. Davis, "Equal Treatment: A Christian Separationist Perspective," in Monsma and Soper, *Equal Treatment of Religion*, chap. 6. The distinction between public access and institutional endorsement or establishment, however, is still in play. Official prayer activities in public schools remain blocked because of this (cf. *Santa Fe Independent School District v. Doe*, 2000, in which the Supreme Court ruled that official "opening prayers" at public school athletic events violate the establishment clause). The Christian Legal Society's litigation and advocacy arm, the Center for Law and Religious Freedom, helped draft the Equal Access Act. See its informative *Guide to the Equal Access Act* (Annandale, VA: Christian Legal Society, rev. ed., 1993).

56. Rebekah Saul, "Whatever Happened to the Adolescent Family Life Act," *The Guttmacher Report on Public Policy*, 1, no. 2 (April 1998), available online at http://www.guttmacher.org/pubs/tgr/01/2/gr010205.html (2/3/08), n.p.

57. Ibid.

58. U.S. House of Representatives, Subcommittee on the Constitution, Committee on the Judiciary, "Prepared Statement of Professor Ira C. Lupu," entitled *The Constitutional Role of Faith-Based Organizations in Competitions for Federal Social Service Funds*, 107th Cong., 1st sess., June 7, 2001.

59. Carl Esbeck, "A Constitutional Case for Governmental Cooperation with Faith-Based Social Service Providers," *Emory Law Journal* 46 (Winter 1997): 4–5.

60. S 1885, 100th Cong., 1st sess. (Nov. 19, 1987). A House version (HR 3660) was introduced at the same time by Representative Dale Kildee of Michigan.

61. See Rob Boston, "To Raise Up a Child," *Church and State* 41 (March 1988): 52–54.

62. Recent survey data shows that a large majority of parents believe that government should focus more attention on helping families provide stay-at-home parent care to young children [Public Agenda Survey, June 2000, available online at http://www.publicagenda.org/issues/red_flags_detail.cfm?issue_type=childcare&list=2&area=1].

63. Linda Greenhouse, "Church-State Debate Blocks Day Care Bill," *New York Times*, 8 September 1988.

64. Ibid.

65. On liberal church-state concerns, see Abbie Gordon Klein, *The Debate Over Child Care, 1969–1990* (Albany, NY: SUNY Press, 1992), 103–26; Susan Mandel, "Suffer the Little Children," *National Review*, 1 September 1989.

66. Klein, *Child Care*, 116–18.

67. See the presentation by Mary Bogle, "Sacred Places, Civic Purposes: Child Care Conference," Pew Forum on Religion and Public Life, March 14, 2001), available on line at http://pewforum.org/events/?EventID=6.

68. Stanley Carlson-Thies and James W. Skillen, eds., *Welfare in America: Christian Perspectives on a Policy in Crisis* (Grand Rapids, MI: William B. Eerdmans, 1996), 560.

69. See Title 42 of the *U.S. Code*, Section 12584.

70. Esbeck, quoted in Terry Mattingly, "Is the Faith-Based Experiment Hazardous to Faith?" *Crisis Magazine*, June 2001, n.p.

71. Carl H. Esbeck, "Institutional Independence—Religious Social Sector: General Language for Placement in Legislation" (March 25, 1995), memorandum on file with author.

72. Carl H. Esbeck, "The Regulation of Religious Organizations as Recipients of Government Financial Assistance," 4 April 1995, unpublished briefing paper on file with author.

73. Ibid., 3.

74. Ibid.

75. In a phone interview with me, Professor Esbeck agreed that *devolution* or *de-centralization* rather than *privatization* was the better term here.

76. Carl H. Esbeck, "Nondiscrimination and Institutional Independence" (draft legislation), 11April 1995, on file with author.

77. Ibid., 2.

78. See *Congressional Record* 141, August 11, 1995 (S12428–S12513), available online at http://frwebgate1.access.gpo.gov/cgi-bin/waisgate.cgi?WAISdocID=511308434540+0+0+0&WAISaction=retrieve.

79. The following summary of the enacted provisions draws upon the Charitable Choice Guide of the Center for Public Justice, available online at http://www.cpjustice.org/charitablechoice/guide/analysis.

80. Douglas Laycock, prepared statement, United States House of Representatives, Subcommittee on the Constitution, Committee on the Judiciary, *Constitutional Role of Faith-Based Organizations in Competitions for Federal Social Service Funds*, 107th Cong., 1st sess., 7 June 2001.

81. Although this position effectively killed any federal legislation expanding charitable choice during the Bush presidency, it was upheld in federal District Court in 2005 and seems likely to survive further legal challenge. From a neutrality standpoint, the logic of faith-based hiring rights is quite clear. A secular federal contrac-

tor like Planned Parenthood, which receives more than $100 million annually from the federal government, certainly does its own version of "faith-based hiring," as do virtually all groups with vested positions on issues (particularly controversial issues like abortion and family planning). Planned Parenthood operates (and advocates) on strong principles of reproductive choice. Yet they are not obligated to hire people who reject those principles in programs receiving federal funds. Religious institutions should not be singled out for mandated loss of hiring rights when other contractors with similarly distinct philosophies are not. The best legal analysis of this issue I have seen is a Justice Department memorandum pertaining to grants allocated by Substance Abuse and Mental Health Services program, written by Assistant Attorney General Randolph Moss and dated October 12, 2000 (on file with author).

82. President George W. Bush, *Rallying the Armies of Compassion*, January 2001, 15 (paper issued by the Bush administration; copy on file with author).

83. Ibid., 15–16.

84. Laurie Goodstein, "Bush's Charity Plan Worries Some on the Religious Right," *New York Times*, 3 March 2001, A1; Laurie Goodstein, "Bush's Call to Church Groups to Get Untraditional Replies," *New York Times*, 20 February 2001, A1.

85. The speech was delivered on March 7, 2001. DiIulio was attacked as an anti-evangelical bigot after the speech, particularly with reference to these lines:

> [C]ompared to predominantly ex-urban white evangelical churches, urban African-American and Latino faith communities have benevolent traditions and histories that make them generally more dedicated to community-serving missions, and generally more confident about engaging public and secular partners in achieving those missions without enervating their spiritual identities or religious characters. There are, to be sure, many urban clergy who want nothing whatsoever to do with government as well. But the "hijacked faith" fears expressed by some are less pointed and less prevalent in metropolitan America. As Professor Cnaan learned, when Charitable Choice is explained to them, large fractions of urban community-serving ministers say "amen." . . .
>
> There are some old wounds within the churches that have yet to heal, wounds that require greater efforts at racial reconciliation and would benefit from less talk and more wholehearted "truth and action," as in 1 John 3:17 (NRSV): "Little children, let us love, not in word or speech, but in truth and action."
>
> In all truth and grace, and speaking now only for myself and as a fellow Christian, I would call upon the National Association of Evangelicals to (as we say on the inner-city streets) get real—and get affiliated church leaders and their congregations to get real—about helping the poor, the sick, the imprisoned, and others among "the least of these."
>
> We all have to have ears to hear and a heart to listen—and act. It's fine to fret about "hijacked faith," but to many brothers and sisters who are desperately ministering to the needs of those whom the rest of us in this prosperous society have left behind, such frets would persuade more and rankle less if they were backed by real human and financial help.

86. HR 7, 107th Cong., 1st sess., (29 March 2001), sec. 1994A(e)(1).

87. President Bush created several small experimental voucher programs, including

the Access to Recovery program, which initially allocated $300 million over three years to fourteen states and one Indian tribe for the purpose of operating individual voucher programs for addiction-recovery services. In 2007, the program was renewed and expanded with a further appropriation of nearly $300 million over three years. Some among the White House faith-based leadership, however, were generally skeptical of efforts to "voucherize" existing programs because of the major difficulties involved in reformulating large programs in this way, as well as inherent problems of under-utilization in voucher programs due to information deficits and other limitations. On this, see Stanley Carlson-Thies, "Keeping Faith in the Faith-Based Initiative: From Formal Neutrality to Full Pluralism in Government Partnerships with Faith-Based Social Services," 2005 Kuyper Lecture, 17–19, available online at http://cpjustice.org/files/2005KuyperLecture_1.pdf.

88. On the legislative history of the CARE Act, see Black, Koopman, and Ryden,, Of Little Faith, 146–83.

89. Robert Tuttle, "The State of the Law: Opening Remarks," Roundtable on Religion and Social Welfare Policy (Albany, NY: Rockefeller Institute of Government, 2007), 32, available on line at http://www.religionandsocialpolicy.org/events/2007_annual_conference/2007_Opening-SOL_transcript.pdf.

90. Anne Farris, Richard P. Nathan, and David J. Wright, "The Expanding Administrative Presidency: George W. Bush and the Faith-Based Initiative," Roundtable on Religion and Social Welfare Policy ((Albany, NY: Rockefeller Institute of Government, August 2004), ii.

91. Ibid., 2.

92. Ibid., i.

93. Data reported in "The Quiet Revolution," a White House progress report on the FBCI issued in February 2008 (copy on file with the author).

94. Mark Ragan and David J. Wright, "The Policy Environment for Faith-Based Social Services in the United States: What has Changed Since 2002?" Roundtable on Religion and Social Welfare Policy (Albany, NY: Rockefeller Institute of Government, 2005).

95. "Quiet Revolution," chap. 5.

96. Ragan and Wright, "Policy Environment for Faith-Based Social Services" 14–20.

97. Carl H. Esbeck, "Church-State Relations in America: What's at Stake and What's Not," Liberty Magazine, 25 May; available online at http://www.libertymagazine.org/article/articleview/495/1/82/?PrintableVersion=enabled.

98. Mark E. Chopko, "Constitutional Protection for Church Autonomy: A Practitioner's View," in Gerhard Robbers, ed., Church Autonomy (Frankfurt am Main: Peter Lang, 2001), 96.

99. On ministry exception and the limits of clergy tort and contract claims against religious bodies, see ibid., 5–6.

100. Edward McGlynn Gaffney Jr., "Religious Autonomy and the Exemption of Religious Organizations from Federal Taxation in the United States," in Robbers, Church Autonomy, 220–24. The Federal Insurance Contribution Act (FICA) originally exempted religious employers from paying FICA taxes, and the Federal Unemployment Tax Act (which imposes an excise tax on employers to finance federal unemployment benefits) also originally exempted religious employers. In 1983, Congress repealed the FICA exemption for religious employers, and this survived a constitutional challenge in Bethel Baptist Church v. United States (1988). Congress later restored the exemption by allowing churches, denominations, and religiously affiliated schools, to peti-

tion for a FICA waiver on religious grounds. Church employees, however, must pay the self-employment tax if their employers secure a FICA exemption.

101. From *Ons Program* ("Our Program"), reprinted in James W. Skillen and Rockne M. McCarthy, eds., *Political Order and the Plural Structure of Society* (Atlanta, GA: Scholars Press, 1991), 252.

102. According to Monsma and Soper, there is evidence that government funding of social services in the Netherlands has been accompanied by increasing government control in an effort to restructure the allocation of resources more efficiently, but this has not entailed aggression against distinctive religious identities or religion in general. See Stephen V. Monsma and J. Christopher Soper, *The Challenge of Pluralism: Church and State in Five Democracies* (Lanham, MD: Rowman & Littlefield, 1997), 78–79.

103. Axel Freiherr von Campenhausen, "Church Autonomy in Germany," in Robbers, *Church Autonom*, 79–80.

104. Carl H. Esbeck, "What the *Hein* Decision Can Tell Us about the Roberts Court and the Establishment Clause," Legal Research Paper Series No. 2008-07, Columbia, MO, University of Missouri School of Law (2008).

105. Ira Lupu and Robert Tuttle, "The State of the Law, 2005," Roundtable on Religion and Social Welfare Policy (Albany, NY: Rockefeller Institute of Government, December 2005), 35–48.

106. Joe Loconte, *Seducing the Samaritan: How Government Contracts Are Reshaping Social Services* (Boston: Pioneer Institute, 1997), 210.

107. Glenn, *Ambiguous Embrace*, 226. On her death in 2004, Joan Kroc (the widow of the founder of McDonald's restaurants) bequeathed the Salvation Army a gift worth more than $1.5 billion to finance new community centers.

108. Many observers probably do not even know that the Salvation Army is, in fact, a practicing Christian church with ordained ministers and a body of semi-ordained "soldiers" (members fourteen years or older who commit to the church). With its vast extension into social services, today the Salvation Army has nearly half as many employees as it does actual members (a ratio unheard of in any other church). On this subject, see Glenn, *Ambiguous Embrace*, 226.

109. One notable case in liberal San Francisco is perhaps an exception that proves the rule. In 1998, the Salvation Army walked away from $3.5 million in government contracts after the city refused to exempt them from a new law requiring employers with city contracts to include "domestic partners" in employee benefit programs.

110. Glenn, *Ambiguous Embrace*, 227.

111. Ibid., 234–40.

112. Carl H. Esbeck, "Equal Treatment: Its Constitutional Status," in Monsma and Soper, *Equal Treatment of Religion*, 29.

113. Methodist Church, *Research Consultation on the Church and State*, Fourth Assembly (1960), Part 3 (4, 24–25), quoted in Coughlin, *Church and State in Social Welfare*, 119.

114. Paul Kauper, *Religion and the Constitution* (Baton Rouge, LA: Louisiana State University Press, 1964), 108.

115. Monsma, *Positive Neutrality*, 192.

116. Noah Feldman, *Divided by God: America's Church-State Problem—And What We Should Do about It* (New York: Farrar, Strauss, and Giroux, 2005).

117. Ira C. Lupu drew attention to this emerging duality in "Government Messages and Government Money: *Santa Fe*, *Mitchell v. Helms*, and the Arc of the Establishment Clause," *William and Mary Law Review* 42 (March 2001): 771–822. I would place

much greater emphasis on the changing structure of the welfare state in precipitating the new level of constitutional accommodation.

CHAPTER TWO

1. Barbara Ehrenreich, "The Faith Factor," *Nation*, 11 November 2004. Barbara Ehrenreich (with whom I agree on many other things) has been outspoken in this kind of analysis, recently describing the "dream" of "the faith-based approach coming from the Bush administration" as "Let's turn all social welfare functions over to churches" (quoted in an interview published online at www.tomdispatch .com/post/88568/tomdispatch_interview_ehrenreich_the_prey_and_the_predators (June 4, 2006). As someone who has worked in "liberal" nonprofit settings (focusing on economic justice) for the last six years, I can attest that this view is quite common among critics of the faith-based initiative. The title of a three-part series on charitable choice in the *San Francisco Chronicle*, "Waging Holy War on Welfare," captures the viewpoint of many on the left (Don Lattin, "Waging Holy War on Welfare, *San Francisco Chronicle*, 14 September 1998). That many simply assume this view is reflected in the sarcastic title of another article, "Social Security Privatization: A Faith-Based Initiative" (by the progressive economist Dean Baker).

2. Steven Rathgeb Smith and Michael Lipsky, *Nonprofits for Hire: The Welfare State in the Age of Contracting* (Cambridge, MA: Harvard University Press, 1993), 11.

3. Stanley Carlson-Thies, "Charitable Choice: Bringing Religion Back into American Welfare," *Journal of Policy History* 13, no. 1: 109–32.

4. Michael Horowitz and Marvin Olasky, "Statement of Principles," 31 January 2001, available online at www.hudson.org/index.cfm?useaction=publication_details&id=780. See also Michael Horowitz, "Subsidies May Cost Churches their Souls," *Wall Street Journal*, 4 January 2000.

5. Marvin Olasky, "How Much Risk: Conservative Reaction to President Bush's Faith-Based Initiative," *Compassion and Culture*, April 2001.

6. Joe Loconte, "President Bush's Faith-Based Initiative," *All Things Considered*, aired 18 July 2001.

7. E. J. Dionne, "Religion's Third Renegotiation with the Public Square," in *Religion and the Public Square in the Twenty-first Century*, edited by Ryan Streeter (Indianapolis, IN: The Hudson Institute, 2001), 29.

8. On "faith factor" research, see Luis Lugo, "Religion and Social Welfare Policy Strategy Paper" (The Pew Charitable Trusts, Religion Program, March 2001). A leading researcher in this growing field is Byron R. Johnson, now at Baylor University and formerly at the University of Pennsylvania and the Manhattan Institute in New York City. He published the first comprehensive survey of the literature assessing the effectiveness of faith-based social-service organizations, through his Center for Research on Religion and Urban Civil Society at Penn, which was launched with funding from the Pew Charitable Trusts' Religion Program under the direction of Luis Lugo. See the report *Objective Hope: Assessing the Effectiveness of Faith-Based Organizations: A Review of the Literature* (2002), available online at http://www.manhattan-institute .org/html/crrucs-obj_hope.htm. In the farther reaches of faith factor research, there is a growing movement for the scientific study of spiritual transformation. The major research program in this emerging field, based at the Metanexus Institute on Religion and Science, was launched by the John Templeton Fund in 2002, with initial funding of $3.3 million. See the prospectus at www.metanexus.net/spiritual _transformation/news/STRP%20Prospectus%202004_high.pdf.

9. The benchmark volume on intelligent design bills the movement as a challenge to the "reigning ideology of materialistic naturalism." Its primary target is the Darwinian theory of natural selection. Some critics call it "soft creationism." See William A. Dembski, ed., *Mere Creation: Science, Faith and Intelligent Design* (Downers Grove, IL: InterVarsity Press, 1998).

10. On the "religious turn in professional ethics," see Martha Minow, "On Being a Religious Professional," *University of Pennsylvania Law Review* 150 (December 2001): 661–88.

11. Edward J. Feulner, "Looking Ahead: Conservative Prospects for 2002," *Insider*, January 2002, available online at www.policyexperts.org/insider/2002/jan02.

12. Paul Krugman, *The Conscience of a Liberal* (New York: W. W. Norton, 2007) 174–76.

13. Princeton sociologist Robert Wuthnow has taken the lead in examining the decline of mainline Protestant influence in public life, overseeing a three-year project called "The Public Role of Mainline Protestantism," the results of which were published in Robert Wuthnow and John H. Evans, eds., *The Quiet Hand of God: Faith-Based Activism and the Public Role of Mainline Protestantism* (Berkeley and Los Angeles: University of California Press, 2002). Wuthnow believes that a revitalized public role for mainline Protestantism is possible, despite significant membership loss and financial deterioration. I think he underestimates how social liberalism among mainline Protestant leaders (on abortion, gay rights, bioethics, and charitable choice) has eroded the religious authority of the mainline churches and thereby weakened the moral force of their economic advocacy. For a summary of the findings of Wuthnow's project, see "Moral Minority: Liberal Protestant Denominations Are Still a Force for Social Justice," *American Prospect*, 22 May 2000, 31–33.

14. The thesis of mainline membership decline as an antiliberal exodus is carefully debunked in Andrew Greeley and Michael Hout, *The Truth about Conservative Christians* (Chicago: University of Chicago Press, 2006), chap. 7.

15. Stephen L. Carter, The Culture of Disbelief (New York: Anchor, 1994). These intellectuals include University of Chicago professor Jean Bethke Elshtain, who co-chaired the Pew Forum on Religion and Public Life for several years after it was launched in 2001; Alan Wolfe, director of the Boisi Center for Religion and American Public Life at Boston College, whose watershed *Atlantic Monthly* piece, "The Opening of the Evangelical Mind" (October 2000), marked the end of Protestant evangelicalism's second-class intellectual status and its new and subtler power in public affairs; James Davison Hunter, director of the Pew-funded Center for Religion and Democracy at the University of Virginia, and a major influence on the religious right's concept of "culture war"; Princeton professor Robert P. George, the driving force behind a revival of Catholic natural law thinking in American public life; and Peter Berger (really an elder statesman of this academic movement), who directs the Institute for the Study of Economic Culture at Boston University and is a leading sociologist of religion. These public intellectuals, to name just a few, are not matched by a similarly prominent group of liberal religious intellectuals, although someone like E. J. Dionne shows how progressive Christians can hold their own in a fairly hostile, right-leaning climate.

16. Robert William Fogel, *The Fourth Great Awakening and the Future of Egalitarianism* (Chicago: University of Chicago Press, 2000), 27.

17. From a biblical point of view, see Obery M. Hendricks Jr., *The Politics of Jesus: Rediscovering the True Revolutionary Nature of Jesus' Teachings and How They Have Been Corrupted* (New York: Doubleday, 2006). From a social Catholic perspective, see E. J.

Dionne, *Souled Out: Reclaiming Faith and Politics After the Religious Right* (Princeton, NJ: Princeton University Press, 2008).

18. Ralph Reed's *Active Faith* (New York: Free Press, 1996) claimed that the contemporary pro-family movement is an extension of nineteenth-century abolitionism and the civil rights movement (67). Fogel explicitly defends the religious right in *The Fourth Great Awakening*, in fact, claiming that the "reform agenda spelled out by the religious Right, with its focus on the restoration of the traditional family and its emphasis on equality of opportunity, more fully addresses the new issues of egalitarianism than does the agenda of the Third Great Awakening" (180). Fogel's term "Third Great Awakening" refers to the interventionist public reformism that shaped the New Deal and the Great Society. The best study of Reagan's assault on the poor and working class remains Thomas Byrne Edsall, *The New Politics of Inequality* (New York: W. W. Norton, 1984).

19. Fogel, *Fourth Great Awakening*, 26, 176.

20. In a characteristic passage, Fogel writes "Now, at the dawn of the new millennium, it is necessary to address such postmodern concerns as the struggle for self-realization, the desire to find a deeper meaning in life than the endless accumulation of consumer durables and the pursuit of pleasure, access to the miracles of modern medicine, education not only for careers but for spiritual values, methods of financing an early, fruitful, and long-lasting retirement, and increasing the amount of quality time available for family activities. Unlike the reform agenda of the Third Great Awakening , that of the Fourth emphasizes the spiritual needs of life in a country where even the poor are materially rich by the standards prevailing a century ago and where many of those who are materially rich are spiritually deprived" (ibid., 176–77).

21. Huntingon's article, "The Clash of Civilizations," was published in *Foreign Affairs* 72 (Summer 1993). Kurth, a former student of Huntington now at Swarthmore, responded with "The Real Clash," *National Interest* 37 (Fall 1994): 3–15.

22. Robert P. George, *The Clash of Orthodoxies: Law, Religion, and Morality in Crisis* (Wilmington, DE: ISI Books, 2001).

23. This unfortunate rhetorical strategy, based on extremely superficial assumptions about Nazism's antagonism toward Christianity and official church structures in the 1930s, is increasingly common in public debate. In the mainline Presbyterian Church (USA), for example, conservative evangelicals have assumed the mantle of the anti-Nazi Barmen Declaration and Confessing Church, claiming that the official leadership of the Presbyterian church has accommodated today's prevailing culture in ways that are analogous to the "German Christians" accommodation of Nazism. See James R. Edwards, "At the Crossroads: The Battle for a Denomination's Soul," *Christianity Today*, 11 August 1997, 21–25.

24. Greg Easterbrook, "Religion in America: The New Ecumenicalism," *Brookings Review* (Winter 2002): 48.

25. "Majority Whip DeLay Floor Statement in Support of Faith-Based Assistance," 19 July 2001, copy on file with author.

26. Delay, quoted in Steve Benen, "Bush-Whacked," *Church and State* (September 2001). Available online at http://www.au.org/site/News2?abbr=cs_&page=NewsArticle&id=5641&news_iv_ctrl=1068.

27. Philadelphia seemed to be a hotbed of such corruption and received a lot of media attention. One example was Reverend Herbert Lusk of North Philadelphia's Greater Exodus Baptist Church. Lusk endorsed Bush during the Republican Party conven-

tion in 2000, via satellite hookup from his church, and in 2002 the social-service arm of his church received a $1 million grant from the U.S. Administration for Children and Families. Another Philadelphia pastor, Luis Cortes, told the *New York Times* that his endorsement of Bush in 2004 was essentially bought with government grant money. Although he had previously endorsed Ralph Nader in 2000, Cortes's Nueva Esperanza, a community development corporation, received more than $7 million from the faith-based initiative during Bush's first term. If the faith-based initiative was simply a political patronage scheme, as some thought, it was not very effective even where it did generate big endorsements for Bush. In 2004, John Kerry received 81 percent of the Philadelphia city vote and two-thirds of the suburban vote, surpassing Gore's margin of victory there in 2000.

28. The House Democrats' leaders against charitable choice were Bobby Scott of Virginia, Chet Edwards of Texas, Jerrold Nadler of New York, and Barney Frank of Massachusetts (see their "Memorandum: to Senators," 12 April 2002, on file with author). Scott is a strong civil rights advocate and strict separationist on church-state issues. In 2002, he was one of five House members to vote against a congressional resolution condemning the decision of the Ninth Circuit Court of Appeals in *Elk Grove Unified School District v. Newdow*, which found that the words "under God" in the Pledge of Allegiance, and school policies promoting student recitation of the Pledge, violate the establishment clause. This decision, leading to the aforementioned resolution (passed nearly unanimously in both the Senate and House) was later overturned by the Supreme Court on other grounds.

29. Larry Witham, "One-Hundred-Year-Old Idea Inspires Proposals to Revamp Welfare," *Washington Times*, 3 January 1996, A2.

30. Dan Coats, *Mending Fences: Renewing Justice Between Government and Civil Society* (Grand Rapids, MI: Baker Publishing Group, 1998), 41.

31. Amy E. Black, Douglas L. Koopman, and David K. Ryden, *Of Little Faith: The Politics of George W. Bush's Faith-Based Initiatives* (Washington, DC: Georgetown University Press, 2004) 46–48.

32. Stanley Carlson-Thies, "Transatlantic Perspectives on Welfare Reform," Public Justice Report, January–February 1997. Available online at www.scjustice.org/stories/storyReader$757.

33. Stanley Carlson-Thies, "Abraham Kuyper in the White House," Convocation Address, Dordt College (Sioux Center, IA), 2006.

34. Monsma's more recent survey-based work on faith-based social contracting is required reading for policymakers and practitioners involved in this issue. See in particular *When Sacred and Secular Mix: Religious Nonprofit Organizations and Public Money* (Lanham, MD: Rowman & Littlefield, 1996). Monsma's most important work on the subject, however, is *Positive Neutrality: Letting Religious Freedom Ring* (Grand Rapids: Baker Books, 1993). This remarkable work of the legal and political theory of pluralism and particularly confessional pluralism, published well ahead of the faith-based political curve, introduced me to the subject ten years ago and is still the best starting point in the debate on faith-based initiatives.

35. In a debate challenging Cal Thomas's book *Blinded by Might*, which urged conservative retreat from politics, Christian right legal strategist Jay Sekulow cited Kuyper as "one of my favorite theologians," quoting Kuyper's famous proclamation that "there is not one square inch of the entire creation about which Jesus Christ does not cry out, 'This is mine, this belongs to me'" (the Thomas-Sekulow debate transcript was partially reprinted in AEI's *American Enterprise*, 1 April 2000, 14). Sekulow was a

staunch supporter of the faith-based initiative. Among other efforts, the American Center for Law and Justice, which Sekulow leads, submitted a brief in defense of the White House in *Hein v. Freedom from Religion Foundation*. Sekulow also successfully argued two "equal access" cases, *Board of Education of Westside Community Schools v. Mergens* (1990) and *Lamb's Chapel v. Center Moriches School District* (1993), before the Supreme Court in the 1980s. Another avowed Kuyperian and high-ranking evangelical advocate of the faith-based initiative is Charles Colson. Colson's Inner-Change prison rehabilitation ministry program was the subject of a federal lawsuit in 2006. A federal district court judge ruled that the State of Iowa must cease its contractual funding of an InnerChange program in one of its state prisons, and the decision was upheld with modifications on appeal. The state had provided more than $1.5 million to that point.

36. "Religious Organizations and Social Service Agencies Call on Congress to Remember the Poor in Making Decisions on Welfare Reform," *Congressional Record*, 11 August 1995, S12360–S12361.

37. George F. Will, "Keeping Faith Behind Initiatives," *Washington Post*, 4 February 2001, B7.

38. John J. DiIulio Jr., "The Political Theory of Compassionate Conservatism," *Weekly Standard*, 23 August 1999.

39. The bishops' justly celebrated pastoral letter "Economic Justice for All," issued in 1986, devoted only one paragraph to restating the principle of subsidiarity as a general rule of welfare provision. It does not address any issues regarding church-state conflict in the welfare domain or the problem of government funding and the secularization of faith-based providers. "A Decade after Economic Justice for All," a statement revisiting the pastoral letter in 1995, is also silent on these issues. Of course, the Catholic bishops were far from silent on church-state issues before the Supreme Court in this period, and they lobbied in support of the Equal Access Act as well as the Child Care Development Block Grant. Nevertheless, the concerns later encapsulated in charitable choice were not really a central focus of Catholic advocacy prior to the launching of the faith-based initiative. However, some Catholic advocates outside the national structures of the Church did in fact propose reforms quite similar to charitable choice in the late 1980s, as we will see below.

40. Jo Renee Formicola and Mary Segers, "The Bush Faith-Based Initiative: the Catholic Response," *Journal of Church and State* 44 (September 2002): 693–716.

41. Michael Novak et al., *The New Consensus on Family and Welfare* (Washington, DC: American Enterprise Institute, 1987), 109.

42. The report was issued in 1987. The working group on federalism was announced by Ed Meese at the American Enterprise Institute on September 6, 1985.

43. "Gary Bauer Profile," *National Journal* 31, no. 45: 3214.

44. As the report put it, "A general and system-wide waiver authority is required so that state demonstrations may differ in whole or in large part from established rules and procedures" (*Up from Dependency*, 57–58).

45. Novak et al., *New Consensus*, 109, 107–19.

46. Stanley Carlson-Thies, letter to Michael Gerson, 12 September 1995 (on file in the Coats Archive, Project for American Renewal, Archives of the Billy Graham Center, Wheaton College, Wheaton, IL).

47. Carlson-Thies and his associate James Skillen were both doing historical work on the Dutch pluralist model at the time, and both also wrote doctoral dissertations on the subject. See James W. Skillen and Stanley Carlson-Thies, "Religion and Political Development in Nineteenth-Century Holland," *Publius* 12 (Summer 1982): 43–64.

48. Kuyper's influence was in fact broadening by this point due to the extensive personal influence of Francis Schaeffer and his L'Abri Fellowship, where Kuyper's "Christian worldview" approach was very influential.

49. See James W. Skillen and Rockne M. McCarthy, eds., *Political Order and the Plural Structure of Society* (Atlanta, GA: Scholars Press, 1991) 315–32.

50. George Grant, *Bringing in the Sheaves: Transforming Poverty into Productivity* (Brentwood, TN: Wolgemuth & Hyatt, 1988).

51. Ibid, xvii.

52. George Grant, *The Changing of the Guard: Biblical Principles for Political Action* (Fort Worth, TX: Dominion Press, 1987), 126.

53. George Grant, *In the Shadow of Plenty* (Arlington Heights, IL: Christian Liberty Press, 1998), 120–21.

54. Marvin Olasky, *The Tragedy of American Compassion* (Washington, DC: Regnery, 1992). For those who are interested in tracing the limited but not negligible dominionist influences within the conservative movement, one notable feature of Olasky's development is the Villars Committee on Relief and Development, which is singled out in the acknowledgements to *The Tragedy of American Compassion* (and later Olasky books as well) as a major influence. The Villars Committee, named after the city in Switzerland where its first meeting was held, was set up in 1987 by California savings-and-loan heir Howard Ahmanson (himself an evangelical Episcopalian) as a forum for developing dominionist approaches to poverty in the developing world. Among the members of the committee Olasky cites in the acknowledgements to *Tragedy* are George Grant, Herbert Schlossberg, and Howard and Robert Ahmanson. Schlossberg, now a fellow of the Ethics and Public Policy Center, has remained in the mainline Presbyterian Church, USA, where he was active for many years in that church's formidable conservative renewal movement. His book *Idols for Destruction: The Conflict of Christian Faith and American Culture* (Wheaton, IL: Crossway Books, 1993). is considered a classic work of dominionist cultural criticism.

55. William S. Lind and William H. Marshner, *Cultural Conservatism: Toward a New National Agenda* (Washington, DC: Free Congress Research and Education Foundation, 1988).

56. Lind and Marshner, *Cultural Conservatism*, 84.

57. Ibid., 85.

58. Ibid., 86–87.

59. Ibid., 23–24.

60. Some might consider the Bush policy of spending TANF funds on marriage programs just such an effort to legislate morality and a disturbing indication of where the framework of faith-based initiatives is heading. In 2006, Congress appropriated $750 million over five years for marriage promotion and fatherhood initiatives. However, these programs are explicitly voluntary and must follow the same charitable choice rules as any other form of TANF spending.

61. Charles Murray, *Losing Ground: American Social Policy, 1950–1980* (New York: Basic Books, 1984). When he was head of the Olin Foundation, Joyce provided funds to the Manhattan Institute in support of *Losing Ground*. The book project grew out of an article Murray had previously submitted to Irving Kristol at the *Public Interest*. See Eric Alterman, "The 'Right' Books and Big Ideas," *Nation*, 22 November 1999.

62. The *New Consensus* was sponsored by the Institute for Family Values at Marquette University, the establishment of which was financed by the Bradley Foundation with a $700,000 grant to Marquette earmarked for the Institute (along with two other

projects) in 1986. From 1986 to 1988, Bradley gave Marquette $1.9 million for the institute and related projects. For this data, see the Lynde and Harry Bradley Foundation, IRS Form 990s, 1985–1987.

63. David Ellwood, *Poor Support: Poverty in the American Family* (New York: Basic Books, 1988). As R. Kent Weaver puts it "[*Poor Support*] helped legitimate the idea of putting time limits on cash welfare benefits, albeit with a job or community service guarantee at the end. This distinction between 'soft' and 'hard' time limits would often become blurred in the welfare reform debates during the years that followed." See R. Kent Weaver, *Ending Welfare as We Know It* (Washington, DC: Brookings Institution Press, 2000) 125–26. See also Glenn Loury's comments on Ellwood's *Poor Support* in his response to Robert Solow's 1997 Tanner Lectures, published in Amy Gutmann, ed., *Work and Welfare* (Princeton, NJ: Princeton University Press, 1998), 48.

64. Lee Edwards, *The Power of Ideas: The Heritage Foundation at Twenty-five Years* (Ottowa, IL: Jameson Books, 1997), 120–22.

65. William J. Bennett, *Index of Leading Cultural Indicators* (New York: Touchstone, 1994) and *The Book of Virtues* (New York: Simon and Schuster, 1996).

66. Edwards, *Power of Ideas*, 92–93. Edwards mentions Olasky's "Christmas meditation on compassion" to a full house in Heritage's Lehrman Auditorium as one highlight of his residency.

67. "Foundations—Banker with a Cause," *National Journal*, 6 March 1993.

68. "Kristol Ball: William Kristol Looks at the Future," *Policy Review* (Winter 1994), 14.

69. Michael S. Joyce, "On Self-Government," *Policy Review*, no. 90 (July–August 1998), 41–48.

70. The Contract with America, of course, was the main policy platform of the self-proclaimed "Republican Revolution" in Congress ushered in in 1994. One key player linking the new citizenship movement to the later development of the faith-based initiative was Don Eberly. Beginning in the mid-1990s, Eberly wrote or edited a series of publications that laid important groundwork for later development in faith-based social policy. Among the most important of these are *America's Promise: Civil Society and the Renewal of Culture* (Lanham, MD: Rowman and Littlefield, 1998), and *Building a Healthy Culture: Strategies for an American Renaissance* (Grand Rapids, MI: William B. Eerdmans, 2001). The latter is a collection of essays examining historical models and strategies for cultural renewal as well as the cultural reform of "professions and elite fields." It is introduced by Senator Sam Brownback, who uses Italian revolutionary Antonio Gramsci's motif of "marching through the institutions" to describe the project. *America's Promise*, an attempt to recover the philosophical and historical foundations of civil society from the clutches of the liberal welfare state, was characterized as "masterful," the work of "one of our few true intellectual and moral statesmen," by John DiIulio upon its publication in 1998. Eberly was part of the transition team that helped set up the White House Office of Faith-Based and Community Initiatives early in 2001, and he later served as liaison for faith-based initiatives in the United States Agency for International Development (USAID).

71. Schambra played an important role in injecting communitarian ideas into the welfare reform debate, first as a senior program officer and then as vice president for general programs at the Bradley Foundation. Although he had worked in the White House in several capacities in the 1980s, he got his start on these ideas at the American Enterprise Institute in the 1970s, where he worked on federalist theory and was greatly influenced by Berger and Neuhaus's *To Empower People*. Schambra later organized a Bradley-financed second edition of the essay, including a new set

of commentaries designed to update the "mediating structures" analysis in light of new policy developments. This was published by the American Enterprise Institute in 1995 under the title *To Empower People: From State to Civil Society*.

72. William A. Schambra, "By the People: The Old Values of the New Citizenship," *Policy Review* (Summer 1994): 32.

73. Michael Joyce, "On Self-Government," 42.

74. April Lassiter, *Congress and Civil Society: How Legislators Can Champion Civic Renewal in Their Districts* (Washington, DC: Heritage Foundation, 1998).

75. Christopher Beem, *The Necessity of Politics: Reclaiming American Public Life* (Chicago: University of Chicago Press, 1999), 77.

76. Nicholas Lemann, "Paradigm Lost: The Shortcomings of the Small-Town Solution," *Washington Monthly* 23 (April 1991): 46.

77. Michael S. Joyce, "Citizenship in the Twenty-first Century: Individual Self-Government," in Don E. Eberly, ed., *Building a Community of Citizens: Civil Society in the Twenty-first Century* (Lanham, MD: University Press of America, 1994), 6.

78. William A. Schambra, "By the People" (copy on file with author). Despite the fact that the Office of the Public Liaison has long been an important avenue for the conservative movement in Washington, Schambra, with characteristic antigovernment alacrity, notes that "[almost] instantly, of course, the office became a mere retail outlet for selling presidential initiatives to special interest groups."

79. James Pinkerton, "Mediating Structures, 1977–1995," in *To Empower People: From State to Civil Society*, ed. Michael Novak (Washington, DC: American Enterprise Institute Press, 1995), 51–57.

80. Novak, ed., *To Empower People*, 8.

81. On the fundamental limits of Tocquevillian democracy and its contemporary renaissance today, see Rogers M. Smith, *Civic Ideals: Conflicting Visions of Citizenship in U.S. History* (New Haven, CT: Yale University Press, 1997) 15–30. In his feminist rejoinder, Mill did not limit his criticism to the question of enfranchisement, but went to the "social question" as well: there is no "greater abuse of social arrangements," he says, "than that of regularly educating an entire half of the species for a position of systematic dependence and compulsory inferiority." Cf. Alexis de Tocqueville, *Democracy In America*, vol. 1 (New York: Schocken Books, 1961), xii.

82. In his *Recollections* of the French revolution of 1848, Tocqueville recalls how, in the wake of the June revolt, the National Assembly established a "parliamentary dictatorship," with measures suspending political clubs and clamping down on the press, along with other measures to "regularize the state of siege." By conservative estimates 1,400 people died in the June revolt, and thousands more were transported to Algeria. One of the main planks of the workers' platform in 1848 was the "right to work," which encompassed a range of entitlements from public employment to income assistance to public education. This was among the first political platforms for the modern welfare state, the Enlightenment lineage of which ultimately goes back to Thomas Paine's vision of public welfare in the *Rights of Man* (1791). As a member of the National Assembly's constitutional drafting committee in 1848, Tocqueville strongly opposed the "right to work," seeing in it a dangerous "socialization" of labor and accusing its supporters of trying to create a socialist system. See August H. Nimtz Jr., *Marx and Engels: Their Contribution to the Democratic Breakthrough* (Albany: State University of New York Press, 2000), 131, 127; and chap. 5.

83. Alexis de Tocqueville, *Democracy In America*, vol. 2 (New York: Schocken Books, 1961), 193–94.

84. Robert Nisbet, *The Quest for Community* (San Francisco: Institute for Contemporary Studies, 1990), xii.

85. Paul M. Weyrich, "Bush Understands Catholic Principle of Subsidiarity," *Free Congress Commentary*, 13 March 2001, available online at www.freecongress.org/press/off-press/010313PWfcc.htm.

86. A stimulating presentation of this view is given in Novak's book *Freedom with Justice: Catholic Social Thought and Liberal Institutions* (New York: Harper & Row, 1984).

87. Marjorie Hyer, "Group Plans to Counter Catholic Bishops' Letter," *Washington Post*, 19 May 1984, B8. This so-called "lay" movement was led almost entirely by Republican elites and businessmen. It was literally run out of the offices of the John M. Olin Foundation, and the original source of their rebellion was not "Economic Justice for All" but an earlier Bishops' letter urging nuclear disarmament, which was seen as an attack on Reagan's military buildup against the evil empire. The story is told in John J. Miller, *The Gift of Freedom: How the John M. Olin Foundation Changed America* (San Francisco: Encounter Books, 2006), 117–22.

88. Lay Commission on Catholic Social Teaching and the U.S. Economy, *Toward the Future: Catholic Social Thought and the U.S. Economy* (New York: American Catholic Committee, 1984), 78–79. The complete absence of any discussion of the common good in *Toward the Future* predicts certain errors in its market-centered analysis of society, and this is indeed the case. In contrast with traditional teaching on the protection of "intermediate bodies" for the human values they sustain, the important point for the Lay Commission was to understand how the free market benefits the intermediary structures, even allowing "such bodies to *affect* the market or originate new markets" (78; emphasis in original). The scope they give to market rationality as an organizing principle of society renders their vision of human sociality essentially barren of uncommodified value. In the Lay Commission's "free and open" society, sociality means all people working together to create a healthy "market environment." This includes recognizing the "dependence of one people on another, simple dependencies in such mundane matters as imports and exports, scarce capital and abundant labor, social ideas and such dazzling new industries as electronics, computers, and robotics" (79). And "social justice," they further argue (again, quite erroneously), is simply the guarantee of legal and social norms that give everyone the opportunity to participate in the market.

89. Michael S. Joyce, "Bad Economics," *Crisis*, November 1996, available online at www.ewtn.com/library/BUSINESS/BADECONO.HTM.

90. In the spring of 2001, Michael Joyce announced his retirement as president of the Lynde and Harry Bradley Foundation, a position he had held for more than fifteen years. He then moved to Washington to lobby for charitable choice legislation, reportedly at the urging of Karl Rove himself. In early June, Americans for Community and Faith-Centered Enterprise, a 501(c)(4) organization and registered federal lobby, opened its doors on Pennsylvania Avenue with Joyce as president and CEO. Collaterally, a 501(c)(3) Foundation for Community and Faith-Centered Enterprise was established to develop private-sector, faith-based initiatives directly. These efforts stalled with the collapse of legislative progress on the faith-based initiative in the summer of 2001. In 2003, Joyce issued a report called "Nurturing the Roots of Charity: A Review of the President's Initiatives for Faith-Centered and Community Organizations" (posted online, but no longer available there), but little was heard of the new foundation after that, and then Joyce died in 2006.

91. Olasky, *Tragedy of American Compassion*, 105. Bush's "Duty of Hope" speech is re-

printed as an appendix to Olasky's *Compassionate Conservatism* (New York: Free Press, 2000).

92. See Rogers Smith's fine critique of "Tocquevillian" democracy's exclusion of African Americans and women in *Civic Ideals*, chap. 1.

93. My own experience working with inmates in a federal prison certainly does not confirm Olasky's views on stigma-based help. The men I worked with were much more responsive to the message that God still loves them even in their darkest hour. In accepting God's love, angry, violent men can learn to emulate that love in their own relationships. Accepting God's love is the divine source of the ability to love your neighbor as your self, and so I mainly counseled the need to recognize that God is always waiting for us to accept his love.

94. Charles Murray, testimony before the Senate Finance Committee, April 27, 1995, cited in Judith Havemann, "'Bell Curve' Author Addresses Welfare," *Washington Post*, 28 April 1995, A4.

95. Richard J. Herrnstein and Charles Murray, *The Bell Curve: Intelligence and Class Structure in American Life* (New York: Free Press, 1996). *The Bell Curve* was significantly indebted to an older body of work in the tradition of scientific racism. See Jack Fischel, "Strange 'Bell' Fellows," *Commonweal*, 10 February 1995, 16, for a brief overview of this lineage. The unlikely survival of scientific racism and far-right hereditarian social theory in America is largely due to an organization called the Pioneer Fund. See Jean Stefancic and Richard Delgado, *No Mercy: How Conservative Think Tanks and Foundations Changed America's Social Agenda* (Philadelphia, PA: Temple University Press, 1996), 33–44, for a review of the racialist/neofascist history and politics of the Pioneer Fund. Murray and Herrnstein drew on a significant cross-section of Pioneer-funded research in *The Bell Curve*, but did not themselves receive any funding from Pioneer. Notably, however, Pioneer Fund president Harry Weyher claims that he would have funded Murray and Herrnstein if they had asked (43). For more on the Pioneer Fund, see Stefan Kuhl, *The Nazi Connection: Eugenics, American Racism, and German National Socialism* (New York: Oxford University Press, 1994).

96. Cf. Olasky's remarkable thirty-page *Vita*, available online at www.utexas.edu/coc/journalism/SOURCE/faculty/facul/olasky_vita.html.

97. Ibid.

98. Marvin N. Olasky, "Testimony," 13 January 1995, Subcommittee on Human Resources of the Committee on Ways and Means, U.S. House of Representatives.

99. Other members included, in the Senate, Spencer Abraham, John Ashcroft, Sam Brownback, Paul Coverdell, Mike DeWine, Rod Grams, Charles Grassley, Chuck Hagel, Tim Hutchinson, Jon Kyl, John McCain, and Rick Santorum; and in the House, Phil English, Kay Granger, Kenny Hulshof, John Kasich, Joseph Knollenberg, Jim Kolbe, David McIntosh, Ron Packard, Charles Pickering, Joe Pitts, Frank Riggs, James Rogan, Mark Souder, James Talent, Zach Wamp, and J. C. Watts.

100. Dan Coats, et. al., "Can Congress Revive Civil Society," *Policy Review* no. 75 (January–February 1996): 28.

101. Ibid., 26.

102. "Charity Tax Credits: Federal Policy and Three Leading States," Pew Forum on Religion and Public Life, 9 May 2001, available online at www.pewforum.org/events/0509 (Horowitz made these remarks during the discussion period of forum, which was recorded and transcribed).

103. Marvin Olasky's *World* magazine columns throughout the spring of 2001 dealt extensively with the Office of Faith-Based and Community Initiatives and its brokering

with conservatives and liberals. See the issue of 7April 2001, for his coverage of the Free Congress intervention.

104. Don E. Eberly, "Charity and the Next Presidency, Part 2," *Alternatives in Philanthropy*, July 2000, 4–5.

105. John C. Goodman, Gerald W. Reed, and Peter S. Ferrara, "Why Not Abolish the Welfare State?" (Dallas, TX: National Center for Policy Analysis, 1994).

106. "Charity Tax Credits—And Debits," *Policy Review* no. 87 (January–February 1998). Notably, Carlson-Thies stressed the need for government guidance of the charitable giving funded by tax credits in order to avoid misallocation to organizations that are not focused on the areas of greatest social need. This is consonant with the Center for Public Justice's communitarian focus on government as a tool of social restoration. Rector took a harder line in this vein, focusing on the entrenched liberalism of the very charities that were likely to benefit from tax credits.

107. "Coats Continues to Build Case for 'Real Life' Legislative Package," Congressional Press Release, 18 May 1998; copy on file with author.

108. As explained in Renewal Alliance strategy paper on file with author.

109. The *Cato Handbook for Congress* is available online for the 105th through the 108th Congress at http://www.cato.org/pubs/handbook/handbooks.html (as of 4 February 2008).

110. Amy L. Sherman, *The Growing Impact of Charitable Choice: A Catalogue of New Collaborations Between Government and Faith-Based Organizations in Nine States* (Washington, DC: Center for Public Justice, 2000). Joseph Loconte, "The Anxious Samaritan: Charitable Choice and the Mission of the Catholic Charities" (Annapolis, MD: Center for Public Justice, May 2000).

111. "Center for Public Justice Applauds New White House Office," Center for Public Justice, press release, 31 January 2001; copy on file with author.

112. Stanley W. Carlson-Thies, "Church-State Cooperation in Welfare Reform: The Charitable Choice Provision," *Religious Liberties News* (Federalist Society Religious Liberties Practice Group), 2 (Winter 1998): 7.

113. James W. Skillen, Memo to Associates and Friends of the Center for Public Justice, January 31, 2001.

114. See the Institute for Justice's profile, "Challenging the Welfare State," available online at www.ij.org/profile/HF_broch_folder/HF_WelfState.html.

115. Marvin Olasky, "Addicted to Bureaucracy," *Wall Street Journal*, 15 August 1995, A16.

116. William Mellor, "Teen Challenge: Overcoming Substance Abuse by Spiritual Renewal," *Philanthropy, Culture and Society* (Capital Research Center), October 1996, 1–8.

117. This report is available online at www.twc.state.tx.us/scvs/charchoice/faithful.pdf.

118. State of Texas, Office of the Governor, Executive Order GWB 96-10, December 17, 1996.

119. See the Texas Freedom Network's detailed chronology online at www.tfn.org/site/PageServer?pagename=txtimeline (accessed 1 April 2002). InnerChange is a twenty-four-hour voluntary "Christian prison," with the state providing food, clothing, shelter, and security while IFI staff provides the program for inmates. Among IFI's evangelistic principles: "Criminal behavior is a manifestation of an alienation between the self and God"; "Transformation happens through an instantaneous miracle; it then builds the prisoner up with familiarity of the Bible." As noted in chapter 1, in 2006 a federal district court ordered the state of Iowa to desist its funding of an InnerChange ministry in one of its prisons, and the decision was upheld on appeal.

120. Pamela Colloff, "Remember the Christian Alamo," *Texas Monthly*, December 2001, available online at www.tfn.org/issues/charitablechoice/txmonthly.htm (accessed 1 December 2001). For those who are interested, here is the basic story. The Roloff Homes, a three-pronged operation for troubled adults, boys, and girls, was founded by legendary Texas revivalist Lester Roloff in the 1960s. According to Colloff, Roloff's youth homes were fundamentalist "reformatories," long shadowed by complaints and lawsuits alleging physical and psychological abuse. They came under state scrutiny in the 1970s but survived until 1985, when the homes were finally forced to shut down by the state courts for operating without a license. Roloff had a strong ally in William B. Clements, who, in 1978 became the first Republican governor of Texas since Reconstruction, defeating John Hill by eighteen thousand votes—a margin of victory for which Roloff took credit. Despite Clements's support, in 1979 the Texas Supreme Court ordered the Roloff homes to obtain licenses or be forced to close. With supporters massed to barricade the flagship Rebekah Home, a three-day standoff with state authorities ensued, ending when Roloff finally agreed to move operations out-of-state. Instead, he refashioned the corporate structure of his homes and reopened them in Texas several months later. Pressure from the state continued, however, until Wiley Cameron, who succeeded Roloff after he died in 1983, moved operations to Missouri in 1985, where no license was required. According to Colloff, this legislation was drafted by Don Willett, who had earlier brought Cameron before the advisory task force to explain why state licensure violated religious freedom. Roloff Homes' attorney David Gibbs, a member of the National Center for Neighborhood Enterprise's faith-based roundtable formed in 1997, was the lead witness during hearings on the legislation before the Texas House Human Services Committee. His affiliation with the Roloff Homes, however, was never revealed. Shortly after the legislation passed, the Texas Association of Christian Child Care Agencies (TACCA) was formed, essentially to allow religious child-care providers to regulate themselves. It was headed by Roloff Homes' advocate David Blaser, and Wiley Cameron himself served on its board of directors. At the invitation of Governor Bush, the Roloff Homes returned to Texas and became the first accredited child-care provider under the TACCA. On April 10, 2000, Texas authorities arrested five men in connection with allegations of abuse at one of the Roloff Homes. Two teenagers complained of being tied together and forced to dig in a sewage pit through the night. The TACCA re-accredited the Roloff Homes two weeks after the arrests, but in the summer of 2001 a sunset clause on the licensure legislation forced the law back onto the floor of the state legislature, where it was not renewed, in part because of publicity surrounding the Roloff Homes but also because only eight providers had sought out the alternative accreditation. Following this, Cameron closed the Roloff Homes in Texas for good.

121. The report, "Texas Faith-Based Initiative at Five Years," is available at www.tfn.org/site/PageServer?pagename=faithbased.

122. David Kuo, interview, 26 February 2003, Roundtable on Religion and Social Welfare Policy, available online at www.religionandsocialpolicy.org/interviews/interview.cfm?id=28.

123. Carlson-Thies, quoted in Coats, *Mending Fences*, 71.

124. Ibid., 41.

125. Stanley Carlson-Thies, Address at the Dordt College Spring Convocation, 12 January 2006.

CHAPTER THREE

1.   Charles Glenn, *Ambiguous Embrace*, 24.

2.   Virgil Nemoianu, "Compassionate Conservatism and Christian Democracy," *Intercollegiate Review* 38, no. 1 (2002): 44.

3.   Remarkably, a Lexis-Nexis U.S. major news search returns only 19 usages of the term *subsidiarity* between 1981, the first year it appears, and 1985. Between 1985 and 1990, the term was used 349 times, and between 1991 and 2001, it was used more than a thousand times. Much of the increased focus on subsidiary in the late 1980s was in the context of European Community debates, in particular about the proposed Social Charter sought primarily by the French government. Spearheaded by Margaret Thatcher's opposition to the Social Charter, subsidiarity was (and remains) the primary intellectual construct for opposition to universal social-welfare and labor standards in the European Community (now of course called the European Union). The idea entered American public discourse through columns by George Will and other commentators on the European situation. Will later championed the Bush administration's faith-based initiative for its basis in Catholic subsidiarity as well [see his TownHall column (4 Februrary 2001), available online at www.townhall.com/columnists/georgewill/gw200010204.shtml.

4.   For a brief but lucid general discussion of Murray's "brilliant critical analysis" of the Leonine corpus on church-state theory, examined further below, see Thomas T. Love, *John Courtney Murray: Contemporary Church-State Theory* (Garden City, NY: Doubleday, 1965), 178–90.

5.   Williams, quoted in John Witte Jr., "The American Constitutional Experiment in Religious Human Rights: The Perennial Search for Principles," in *Religious Human Rights in Global Perspective: Legal Perspectives*, ed. Johan D. van der Vyver and John Witte Jr. (The Hague: Martinus Nijhoff Publishers, 1996), 516.

6.   Richard W. Garnett, "The Freedom of the Church," Notre Dame Law School Legal Studies Research Paper No. 06-12 (2006), 5. Regarding the corporative assumptions of the "freedom of church," as compared with American "religious liberty," it is worth pointing out that "liberty" and "freedom" are, linguistically and culturally, quite distinctive words and in some ways opposed in meaning. The historian David Hackett Fischer looks at our political heritage through this semantic lens in his book *Liberty and Freedom* (Oxford University Press, 2005). As he points out, *liberty* is a Greco-Roman word deriving from the Latin *libertas* and the Greek *eleutheria*. The meaning here is "release from restraint," or, more generally, being separate and distinct from others. *Freedom*, on the other hand, is an Anglo-Saxon word that derives from the Indo-European root *friya* or *priya*, which, strikingly, means "dear" or "beloved." The Norse, German, Dutch, Flemish, Celtic, Welsh, and English words for *freedom* all share this root in the concept of endearment or belovedness. We see this in the English word "friend," sharing the same root as "free," as with *Freund* and *frei* in German. The oldest known word associated with these concepts is a Sumerian word that is very close in meaning to Anglo-Saxon *freedom*. It literally means "going home to mother," and was used to describe the slave's return to his family and his transformation from a condition of bondage to one of belonging.

From the New Testament communalism of the German Peasants' War, to Gierke's *Genossenschaftstheorie* and the Germanic social justice embraced by Pius XI, it is notable and richly suggestive that *freedom*, given its linguistic roots in a concept of belonging rather than individual autonomy, is a central idea in this long development of social thought. From Anglo-Saxon culture no less than its linguistic roots, we can say that *freedom* means "being joined to a free people," joined by rights of belonging and by reciprocal duties of membership in that people. Freedom is a condition of belonging, and the belonging that frees us is sustained by an equality of rights and duties within the group, independent of other authorities. It is implicitly a concept attached to groups if not groups of families, that is, communities. *Liberty*, in contrast, means emancipation *from* other people—individual separation and independence from others' control. It is, implicitly, a concept attached to individuals rather than groups. In its common use in the Roman Empire, *liberty* was the opposite of *slavery*: in the classical world of liberty, there was only the imperial state stratified into nobility, commons, freedmen, and slaves. Liberty meant release from slavery into the status of freedmen, nothing more. There is no concept of community or of social rights derived from membership in a community, the very point a young Karl Marx (an unmistakably German thinker) made when he argued that "individuals achieve their freedom at one and the same time in and through their association."

There being no Latin word for freedom in a corporate sense (although Latin does have the language of "corporation" itself, of course), *libertas ecclesiae* is a Roman designation for an essentially Christian idea far removed from classical liberty, a difference brought out in the Anglo-Saxon designation "*freedom* of the church." Our Bill of Rights is the world's greatest monument to negative liberty in a classical sense, contrasting starkly, of course, with freedom as described in the Gospel, which is defined in terms of connectedness and self-sacrifice. Fischer points to Martin Luther, who describes the "freedom of a Christian" as a seemingly paradoxical combination of two principles. As Luther wrote in his famous tract "On Christian Freedom," "A Christian man is the most free lord of all, and subject to none"; at the same time, "A Christian man is the most dutiful servant of all, and subject to every one." Through Christ the person is made free, subject to no other person, and yet, the person is also bound in Christ to serve others. Many of us grew up in churches where something like this was taught. The famous aphorism of Hillel strikes the same chord: "If I am not for myself, who will be? But if I am only for myself, what am I?" It is an obvious point that the United States Constitution is not a Christian document; nevertheless, a Christian perspective helps us understand the more interesting point that it does not contemplate communal freedom either, except perhaps by faint echo in invoking promotion of the "general welfare" in the Preamble.

7. John Courtney Murray, "Leo XIII: Separation of Church and State," *Theological Studies* 14, no. 2 (1953), 145–214, available online at http://woodstock.georgetown.edu/library/Murray/1953c.htm, n.p.

8. Harold J. Laski, *Studies in the Problem of Sovereignty* (New York: Howard Fertig, 1968), 253–54.

9. Ibid., 257.

10. Murray, "Leo XIII: Separation of Church and State," n.p.

11. In 1302, Pope Boniface VIII issued the most extreme statement of monistic Papal regalism in *Unam Sanctum*, an attack on Philip IV of France. "Certainly anyone who denies that the temporal sword is in the power of Peter has not paid heed to the words of the Lord when he said, 'Put up thy sword into its sheath,' (Matthew 26:52). Both then are in the power of the church, the material sword and the spiritual. But the one is exercised for the church, the other by the church, the one by the hand of the priest, the other by the hand of kings and soldiers, though at the will and sufferance of the priest. One sword ought to be under the other and the temporal authority

subject to the spiritual power" (quoted in Brian Tierney, *The Crisis of Church and State 1050–1300* [Toronto: University of Toronto Press, 1988], 188–89).

12. Tierney, *Crisis of Church and State*, 9.

13. Ibid., 13.

14. Ibid., 14–15.

15. Murray, quoted in Garnett, "Freedom of the Church," 8.

16. Robert Louis Wilken, "Gregory VII and the Politics of the Spirit," *First Things* 89 (January 1999), available online at www.firstthings.com/ftissues/ft9901/wilken.html, n.p. The classic legal-historical treatment of the Gregorian Reform is Harold Berman, *Law and Revolution: The Formation of the Western Legal Tradition* (Cambridge, MA: Harvard University Press, 1983), chap. 2. See in particular 88–94 for fascinating detail on the civil domination of church affairs in the period before the "Papal Revolution" of the later eleventh century. Berman sees an important precedent in the Cluniac Reform movement that began in the previous century.

17. Wilken, "Gregory VII and the Politics of the Spirit," n.p.

18. Ibid.

19. Ibid.

20. Berman, *Law and Revolution*, 23, quoting Joseph R. Strayer.

21. George Weigel, *The Cube and the Cathedral: Europe, America, and Politics without God* (New York: Basic Books, 2005), 101.

22. John Courtney Murray, "On the Structure of the Church-State Problem," in *The Catholic Church in World Affairs*, ed. Waldemar Gurian and M.A. Fitzsimmons (Notre Dame, IN: University of Notre Dame Press, 1954), 145–214, available online at http://woodstock.georgetown.edu/library/Murray/1953c.htm (n.p.).

23. Ibid.

24. Ibid.

25. Compare Gierke's description of what he called the theory of the two coordinate powers: "In general throughout the Middle Age the doctrine of the State's partisans remained content with the older teaching of the Church: namely, that Church and State were two Co-ordinate Powers, that the Two Swords were *potestates distinctae*, that *Sacerdotium* and *Imperium* were two independent spheres instituted by God himself. This doctrine therefore claimed for the Temporal Power an inherent authority not derived from the ecclesiastical canons. . . . Still it conceded a like sovereignty and independence to the Spiritual Sword, and merely demanded that the Ecclesiastical Power should confine itself within the limit of genuinely spiritual affairs, the Church having been instituted and ordained by God as a purely spiritual realm" (Gierke, *Political Theories of the Middle Age*, 16–17].

26. Quoted in Murray, "Leo XIII: Separation of Church and State," n.p.

27. *Arcanum*, quoted in ibid.

28. Frank J. Coppa, "From Liberalism to Fascism: The Church-State Conflict over Italy's Schools," *History Teacher* 28 (February 1995): 138–39.

29. The famous *Old Catholic Encyclopedia* (1914; available online at www.newadvent .org/cathen/) described Cavour's ideal as a "Qualified Liberalism." It states, "While claiming to admit that the Church is more or less a perfect society with foundations in the Divine Positive Law of Christian Revelation, it contends that the Church and State are disparate in such fashion as to prosecute their respective ends independently in behalf of the individual, having no subordination whatever one to the other. Consequently, in all public affairs the State must prescind from every religious

society, and deal with such either as private associations existing within the State or as foreign corporations to be treated with accordingly." A concluding point reflects the experience of the Church, particularly in Germany under the *Kulturkampf*: "The axiom of this newer Liberalism is 'A free Church in a free State,' which in point of fact means an emasculated Church with no more freedom than the shifting politics, internal and external, of a State chose to give, which in the event, as was to be foreseen, amounted to servitude." See the article "State and Church," available online at www.newadvent.org/cathen/14250c.htm.

30. The Coppino Law sparked a retreat from official *Non Expedit* policy, as Catholics were encouraged to participate in local politics, which were pivotal in applying the law. As Coppa stresses, not stipulating religious requirements was not the same thing as stipulating their exclusion: many if not most schools continued to include religious instruction if families wanted it. On all these developments, see Coppa, "From Liberalism to Fascism," 137–41.

31. Ibid., 142.

32. Ibid., 144.

33. The official English translation of *Rerum novarum* incorrectly uses "spoliation" (withholding evidence) where the meaning clearly is "spoilation" (plunder).

34. Taparelli has received fairly little scholarly attention in European Catholic studies and, until recently, virtually no attention in Anglophone scholarship. But in his recent dissertation on Taparelli, which I rely on here, Thomas Behr argues that Taparelli was misread as a reactionary conservative and was unduly marginalized from the intellectual history of Catholic social teaching, particularly so regarding the influences on *Quadragesimo anno*. See Thomas Chauncey Behr, "Luigi Taparelli and the Nineteenth-Century Neo-Thomistic 'Revolution' in Natural Law and Catholic Social Sciences," PhD diss. (Buffalo, NY: State University of New York at Buffalo, 2000), 12–26; ch. 6, passim.

35. For an excellent overview on this subject, see Russell Hittinger, "Introduction," in *The Teachings of Modern Roman Catholicism*, eds. John Witte Jr. and Frank Alexander (New York: Columbia University Press, 2007), 3–18. But also see Owen Bradley, *A Modern Maistre* (Lincoln: University of Nebraska Press, 1999), for a sympathetic reading of Maistre as prophet (not exponent) of modern authoritarianism and organized state violence.

36. Hittinger, "Introduction," 14. See also Heinrich A. Rommen, *The Natural Law: A Study in Legal and Social History and Philosophy*, trans. Thomas R. Hanley (Indianapolis, IN: Liberty Fund, 1998 [orig. pub. 1936]), 212–18. The important later contributions of Jacques Maritain to the development of Catholic "social ontology" are lucidly assessed in Patrick McKinley Brennan, "Differentiating Church and State (Without Losing the Church)," Working Paper 12 (Philadelphia, PA: Villanova University School of Law, 2008).

37. Behr, "Luigi Taparelli," 223–32.

38. Quoted in Brennan, "Differentiating Church and State," 23.

39. Maritain's own thinking on this issue evolved from a moderate establishmentarian perspective to one of full confessional pluralism. See Brennan, "Differentiating Church and State," 28–29.

40. Skillen and McCarthy, *Political Order*, 142.

41. Ibid.

42. Behr, "Taparelli," 223.

43. See Nell-Breuning's "Subsidiarity" in the article "Social Movements," in *Sacramentum Mundi*, vol. 6, ed. Karl Rahner, Cornelius Ernst, and Kevin Smyth (New York: Herder and Herder), 114–15.

44. Johannes Messner, "Freedom as a Principle of Social Order," *The Modern Schoolman* 28 (January 1951): 103–4.

45. John Courtney Murray, "Leo XIII: Two Concepts of Government, *Theological Studies* 14 (December 1953): 556–57.

46. Nisbet, *Quest for Community*, 21.

47. Quoted from a selection of Groen's *Unbelief and Revolution* (trans. Harry Van Dyke), reprinted in Skillen and McCarthy, *Political Order*, 58.

48. Friedrich Julius Stahl, *Principles of Law*, ed. and trans. Ruben Alvarado (Aalten, the Netherlands: Wordbridge), 78.

49. Skillen and McCarthy, *Political Order*, 69.

50. Hans Daalder, "Parties and Politics in the Netherlands," *Political Studies* 3 (February 1955): 6.

51. Harry van Dyke, ed., *Groen van Prinsterer's Lectures on Unbelief and Revolution* (Jordan Station, Ontario: Wedge Publishing Foundation, 1989), Lecture 10, 242.

52. Ibid., 249.

53. Ibid., 64. Tocqueville's famous passage (from vol. 2 of *Democracy in America*, bk. 4, chap. 6) is worth quoting in full to clarify the contrast I am making here:

> I seek to trace the novel features under which despotism may appear in the world. The first thing that strikes the observation is an innumerable multitude of men, all equal and alike, incessantly endeavoring to procure the petty and paltry pleasures with which they glut their lives. Each of them, living apart, is as a stranger to the fate of all the rest; his children and his private friends constitute to him the whole of mankind. As for the rest of his fellow citizens, he is close to them, but he does not see them; he touches them, but he does not feel them; he exists only in himself and for himself alone; and if his kindred still remain to him, he may be said at any rate to have lost his country.
>
> Above this race of men stands an immense and tutelary power, which takes upon itself alone to secure their gratifications and to watch over their fate. That power is absolute, minute, regular, provident, and mild. It would be like the authority of a parent if, like that authority, its object was to prepare men for manhood; but it seeks, on the contrary, to keep them in perpetual childhood: it is well content that the people should rejoice, provided they think of nothing but rejoicing. For their happiness such a government willingly labors, but it chooses to be the sole agent and the only arbiter of that happiness; it provides for their security, foresees and supplies their necessities, facilitates their pleasures, manages their principal concerns, directs their industry, regulates the descent of property, and subdivides their inheritances: what remains, but to spare them all the care of thinking and all the trouble of living?
>
> Thus it every day renders the exercise of the free agency of man less useful and less frequent; it circumscribes the will within a narrower range and gradually robs a man of all the uses of himself. The principle of equality has prepared men for these things; it has predisposed men to endure them and often to look on them as benefits.

> After having thus successively taken each member of the community in its powerful grasp and fashioned him at will, the supreme power then extends its arm over the whole community. It covers the surface of society with a network of small complicated rules, minute and uniform, through which the most original minds and the most energetic characters cannot penetrate, to rise above the crowd. The will of man is not shattered, but softened, bent, and guided; men are seldom forced by it to act, but they are constantly restrained from acting. Such a power does not destroy, but it prevents existence; it does not tyrannize, but it compresses, enervates, extinguishes, and stupefies a people, till each nation is reduced to nothing better than a flock of timid and industrious animals, of which the government is the shepherd. (1961 Schocken edition, 380–81)

54. Van Dyke, ed., *Lectures on Unbelief and Revolution*, 70.

55. The Dutch *Réveil* also fomented two major secessions from the national Reformed Church, and in later phases some *Réveil* circles embraced social activism in contrast with Bilderdijk's highly eschatological posture of social withdrawal. See Gerrit J. tenZythoff, *Sources of Secession: The Netherlands Hervormde Kerk on the Eve of the Dutch Immigration to the Midwest* (Grand Rapids, MI: William. B. Eerdmans, 1987), esp. chap. 4.

56. Ibid. Rejecting historical criticism of the Bible, leaders of the *Réveil* declared that "the Holy Spirit was their only professor" (99).

57. Stathis N. Kalyvas *The Rise of Christian Democracy in Europe* (Ithaca, NY: Cornell University Press, 1996), 194; McKendree R. Langley, *Emancipation and Apologetics: The Formation of Abraham Kuyper's Anti-Revolutionary Party in the Netherlands, 1872–1880* (PhD diss., Westminster Theological Seminary, 1985), 125.

58. Langley, *Emancipation and Apologetics*, 131.

59. Herman Bakvis, *Catholic Power in the Netherlands* (Montreal: McGill-Queen's University Press, 1981), 61. Groen had long advocated such a confessional alliance. In his *Ongeloof en Revolutie*, he approvingly cited Stahl's declaration that "if the power of our time, unbelief and hatred of God, should triumph, believing Catholics and believing Protestants will mount the scaffold hand in hand." See Van Dyke, ed., *Lectures on Unbelief and Revolution*, 407.

60. As quoted in McKendree R. Langley, "Abraham Kuyper: A Christian Worldview," *New Horizons*, January 1999, n.p.

61. Kalyvas *Rise of Christian Democracy*, 194.

62. Johannes Althusius, *Politica*, ed. and trans. Frederick S. Carney (Indianapolis, IN: Liberty Fund, 1995), 17.

63. Herman Dooyeweerd, *A New Critique of Theoretical Thought*, vol. 3, trans. David H. Freeman and H. de Jongste (Presbyterian and Reformed Publishing, 1969), 633. Notably, Althusius was also an important influence on Robert Nisbet. See especially Robert Nisbet, *The Social Philosophers* (New York: Washington Square Press, 1983), 179–87.

64. Johann van der Vyver, *Leuven Lectures on Religious Institutions, Religious Communities, and Rights* (Leuven, Belgium: Uitgeverij Peeters, 2004), 38.

65. Althusius, *Politica*, 28.

66. Ibid., 32–33. Althusius and other theorists of association (such as Bodin) had a much richer moral and psychological understanding of the family as a collective economic unit than that provided by economic theory today. As William Lazonick

points out, "Neoclassical economists generally recognize that the relevant unit of analysis is the household rather than the individual. But they offer no theory of the family as a collectivity"; see "The Breaking of the American Working Class," *Reviews in American History* 17 (June 1989): 335, n. 83. Compare the rational-choice model of the family as a unit of individual utility maximization (for example, in Gary Becker's *Treatise on the Family*) to the early modern view of the family as an association of mutual rights and obligations, consisting "partly in advantages, partly in responsibilities, and in the bringing together and sustaining these advantages mutually among the kinsmen. . . . Such advantages are, first, the affection, love, and goodwill of the blood relative and kinsman. From this affection arises the solicitude by which the individual is concerned for the welfare and advantages of his kinsman, and labors for them no less than for his own" (Althusius, *Politica*, 30).

67. Kuyper, quoted in Skillen and McCarthy, *Political Order*, 258.
68. Abraham Kuyper, "Calvinism and Politics," Stone Lectures (1898), available online at http://www.lgmarshall.org/Reformed/kuyper_lecturescalvinism.html#lecture1, n.p.
69. Skillen and McCarthy, *Political Order*, 260.
70. Kuyper, quoted in Skillen and McCarthy, 258.
71. Ibid., 259.
72. Ibid., 260.
73. Quoted in Johan D. van der Vyver, "Sphere Sovereignty of Religious Institutions," in *Church Autonomy*, by Gerhard Robbers (Frankfurt am Main: Peter Lang, 2001), 653.
74. Kuyper, "Calvinism and Politics," n.p.
75. Skillen and McCarthy, *Political Order*, 260–61.
76. Liam Séamus O'Melinn, "The Sanctity of Association: The Corporation and Individualism in American Law," *San Diego Law Review* 37, no. 101 (2000), 111–12.
77. Quite fluent in Catholic controversies, Groen cited an interesting passage in one of Tocqueville's letters in which he describes the Church as "enslaved" when the Pope unrestrainedly overrules local religious authorities, but decries as far worse the church's enslavement as an office of the state. "I must admit," Tocqueville concluded, "that I still regard the enslavement of the Church to its spiritual head, and thus an exaggerated separation of the spiritual and temporal powers, as preferable to the union of both in the hands of a lay dynasty"; see Van Dyke, *Lectures on Unbelief and Revolution*, 407.
78. Quoted in O'Melinn, "Sanctity of Association," 115. Thouret, elected president of the National Assembly four times, was later executed during the Reign of Terror.
79. Kuyper, *Problem of Poverty*, 43–44.
80. Regarding the Kuyper's "creation theology" of social order, liberal critics of sphere sovereignty sometimes point to the fact that Kuyper's thought influenced Afrikaner racial nationalism and, more particularly, South African apartheid through the South African Dutch Reformed Church's theology of racial separation. Recent scholarship has shown that Afrikaner theology selectively appropriated and distorted Kuyper's themes, and a movement of Black Reformed Christians in South Africa has worked since the early 1980s to critically reclaim the liberative aspects Dutch Calvinism and the Kuyperian tradition. For a good overview of this debate, see H. Russel Botman, "Is Blood Thicker Than Justice," in *Religion, Pluralism, and Public Life: Abraham Kuyper's Legacy for the Twenty-First Century*, ed. Luis E. Lugo (Grand Rapids, MI: William B. Eerdmans, 2000), 342–59. Kuyper undoubtedly shared the general racial attitudes common to leading men of the era of African colonization, and he gave speeches in support of the Boers that were cul-

turally if not racially chauvinistic. More important, the importance of "creation ordering" in Kuyperian neo-Calvinism must be carefully considered as it pertains to the "visible pluriformity" of different races. A progressive Barthian movement in the Dutch Reformed Church attempted this kind of analysis, developing a Christocentric critique of racial-separatist creation theology during the last two decades of apartheid (unsuccessfully, according to J. J. F. Durand in "Church and State in South Africa: Karl Barth vs. Abraham Kuyper," in *On Reading Karl Barth in South Africa*, ed. Charles Villa-Vicencio (Grand Rapids, MI: William B. Eerdmans, 1988), 122.

81. James W. Skillen, "American Statecraft: A New Art for the Twenty-first Century," The 2000 Kuyper Lecture (Washington, DC: The Center for Public Justice, 2000), n.p.

82. Kuyper memo, quoted in Harry Van Dyke, "Abraham Kuyper: Heir of an Anti-Revolutionary Tradition," 20, available online at http://alpha.redeemer.ca/~tplant// rr/hvd-02.pdf.

83. Ibid.

84. Göran Therborn, "Pillarization and Popular Movements: Two Variants of Welfare State Capitalism: The Netherlands and Sweden," in *The Comparative History of Public Policy*, ed. Francis G. Castles (Cambridge: Polity Press, 1989), 202–3.

85. Otto von Gierke, *Das Deutsche Genossenschaftsrecht*, 4 vols. (Berlin: Weidmann, 1868–1913). For a good introduction to their thought and a selection of their writings, see Paul Q. Hirst, *The Pluralist Theory of the State: Selected Writings of G. D. H. Cole, J. N. Figgis, and H. J. Laski* (London: Routledge, 1989).

86. Skillen and McCarthy, *Political Order*, 97–98.

87. J. N. Figgis, *Churches in the Modern State* (Bristol, England: Thoemmes Press, 1997), 56.

88. Figgis analyzes the case in the first of the four lectures comprising *Churches in the Modern State*, 18–22; 32–41.

89. Ibid., 39–40.

90. Ibid., 40.

91. David Runciman, *Pluralism and the Personality of the State* (Cambridge: Cambridge University Press, 1997), 136.

92. Figgis, *Churches in the Modern State*, 50–51.

93. Ibid., 51.

94. Otto Gierke, *Natural Law and the Theory of Society 1500–1800*, trans. Ernest Barker (Boston: Beacon Press, 1957), 114. (This volume is an edition of several sections of vol. 4 of *Das deutsche Genossenschaftsrecht*.)

95. Gierke, *Political Theories of the Middle Age*, 87. Gierke's seminal work on Althusius was *Johannes Althusius und die Entwicklung der naturrechtlichen Staatstheorien* (Breslau: M. & H. Marcus, 1913 [1880]).

96. From the earliest historical stages of the German peoples, Gierke stated in the introduction to volume 1 of *Das deutsche Genossenschaftsrecht*, "the basic form of all society" was "the free fellowship of the old law," the law of the clans "for upholding peace and law based on *natural* affinity, [transferring] all right to the collectivity." But from the beginning, "it is confronted by the opposite form of human community, in which one individual is the bond of all—the *lordship group*." See the selection from volume 1 edited by Antony Black, *Community in Historical Perspective* (Cambridge: Cambridge University Press, 1990), 10.

97. Michael Stolleis, *Public Law in Germany, 1800–1914* (New York: Berghan Books, 2001), 339. In addition to his teacher Georg Beseler, an important influence on Gierke's concept of social law was the great eighteenth-century legal scholar Daniel

Nettelbladt. Gierke viewed Nettelbladt as a pioneer in the revival of German *Genossenschaftstheorie*. See particularly Gierke's exposition in *Natural Law and the Theory of Society*, 175–95.

98. Otto von Gierke, *Der Entwurf Eines Bürgerlichen Gesetzbuches und das Deutsche Recht* (Leipzig: Dunker and Humblot, 1889). See also generally the discussion of Gierke's concept of social law in Stolleis, *Public Law in Germany*, 337–40.

99. Michael John, *Politics and the Law in Late Nineteenth-Century Germany: The Origins of the Civil Code* (Oxford: Clarendon Press, 1989), 89.

100. Ibid., 136, 132-38.

101. Ibid., 91–92.

102. Ibid., 97–98.

103. This is a view that Harold Berman and others have found to be overdrawn. More generally, contemporary scholars such as Antony Black find that Gierke overestimated the extent of the fiction theory (and corresponding weakness of nonstate associations) in medieval law and legal thought; see Black's introduction to *Community in Historical Perspective*, xxviii–xxix.

104. Gierke, *Political Theories of the Middle Age*, 94.

105. Friedrich Julius Stahl, *Principles of Law*, 26–27. Objective law, meaning moral law, was termed *objective* in the sense that it is not humanly created but exists as an order of values outside of positive law and as the ultimate guidance of such law. As Edward Eberle has explained, a corresponding idea of "objective rights" gave German constitutional tradition a unique concern for moral harms arising from the exercise of private power, in striking contrast to American constitutional law, which pertains only to the actions of the state. We return to this issue in chapter 4. See Edward J. Eberle, *Dignity and Liberty: Constitutional Visions in Germany and the United States* (Westport, CT: Praeger, 2002), 25–32.

106. Stahl, *Principles of Law*, 27.

107. Ibid., 27; emphasis in original.

108. Lisa Sowle Cahill, "The Catholic Tradition: Religion, Morality, and the Common Good," *Journal of Law and Religion* 5, no. 1 (1987): 79–80.

109. James D. Bratt, "Passionate about the Poor: The Social Attitudes of Abraham Kuyper," *Journal of Markets and Morality* 5 (Spring 2002): 35–44; the Kuyper material that follows in the text is quoted in Bratt.

110. According to Harry Van Dyke, it was also organized to relieve growing pressure within the Anti-Revolutionary Party for more action on labor issues, including comments about forming a new Christian Labour Party by the leader of Patrimonium, then the largest Christian workingmen's society in the Netherlands and closely aligned with the ARP. See Van Dyke, "Abraham Kuyper: Heir of an Anti-Revolutionary Tradition," 16–17.

111. Groen, quoted in ibid., 16.

112. Nisbet, *Quest for Community*, 246–47.

113. George Metlake, *Ketteler's Social Reform* (Philadelphia, PA: Dolphin Press, 1912), 210–11.

114. On the general "crisis of pauperism" in Vormärz Germany, see Hermann Beck, *The Origins of the Authoritarian Welfare State in Prussia* (Ann Arbor: University of Michigan Press, 1995), introduction. On industrial liberalization and the role of artisanal radicalization in the revolution of 1848, see Theodore S. Hamerow, *Restoration, Revolution, Reaction* (Princeton, NJ: Princeton University Press, 1958), chaps. 1–2.

115. An early essay by Peter Drucker, recently translated into the English, examines the conservative state theory of the Lutheran legal philosopher Friedrich Juilus Stahl (a

major influence on Groen and Kuyper, as noted earlier). Drucker's conclusion captures the theological orientation of German conservative state theory, spurred by liberal anti-clericalism and the rationalist ascendancy against revealed ethics and traditional natural law. Drucker writes, "The Conservative theory of the state must affirm the state because and insofar as it represents an obligation. It must also, however, prevent the state from becoming the only obligation, from becoming the 'total state,' for the state is an order of this world, an institution arisen out of the dissolution of a supreme, timeless order, a kingdom with a human goal and meaning. And this meaning and goal, that is to say, power, is evil and demoralising, destructive, if it is not bound to a divine, immutable order, if it is not bound to God's plan for the world." The essay, published in 1933, is available online at www.peterdrucker .at/en/texts/stahl_02.html.

116. Radowitz, quoted in Hermann Beck, *The Origins of the Authoritarian Welfare State in Germany* (Ann Arbor: University of Michigan Press, 1997), 68.

117. Ibid., 198.

118. Kees van Kersbergen, *Social Capitalism: A Study of Christian Democracy and the Welfare State* (London: Routledge, 1995).

119. My understanding of the Weimar church-state struggle relies on Young-Sun Hong, *Welfare, Modernity, and the Weimar State, 1919–1933* (Princeton, NJ: Princeton University Press, 1998).

120. Quoted in ibid., 188.

121. Ibid., 185.

122. Ibid., 273.

123. Ibid., 271.

124. Helmut K. Anheier and Wolfgang Seibel, "Defining the Nonprofit Sector: Germany," Working Papers of the Johns Hopkins Comparative Nonprofit Sector Project, No. 6 (Baltimore, MD: Johns Hopkins Institute for Policy Studies, 1993), 7.

125. Oliver Lepsius, "The Problem of Perceptions of National Socialist Law; or, Was There a Constitutional Theory of National Socialism?" in *Darker Legacies of Law in Europe: The Shadow of National Socialism and Fascism over Europe and its Legal Traditions*, ed. Christian Joerges and Navraj Singh Ghaleigh (Portland, OR: Hart, 2003), 22.

126. Lester M. Salamon and Helmut K. Anheier, "The Third Route: Government-Nonprofit Collaboration in Germany and the United States," in *Private Action and the Public Good*, ed. Walter W. Powell and Elisabeth S. Clemens (New Haven, CT: Yale University Press, 1998), 158.

127. Kersbergen, *Social Capitalism*, 177–91.

128. Ibid., 180–81.

129. Ibid., 188, 189.

130. Robert E. Goodin, Bruce Headey, Ruud Muffels, and Henk-Jan Dirven, *The Real Worlds of Welfare Capitalism* (Cambridge: Cambridge University Press, 1999), 166–67.

131. Alberto Alesina and Edward L. Glaeser, *Fighting Poverty in the US and Europe: A World of Difference* (New York: Oxford University Press, 2005), 31–32.

132. Kuyper, *Problem of Poverty*, 62.

133. Ibid., 50–51.

134. *Quadragesimo anno*, sec. 27, as cited in Oswald Von Nell-Breuning, *Reorganization of Social Economy*, ed. Bernard W. Dempsey (New York: Bruce Publishing, 1936), 32.

135. Daniel Altman, *Neoconomy: George W. Bush's Revolutionary Gamble with America's Future* (New York: Public Affairs, 2004), 71–99.

CHAPTER FOUR

1. The role of religion in the East European civil-society movements of the 1980s is not well documented. American interpretations in particular have not emphasized religion, with the exception of conservatives such as George Weigel; see his important book *The Final Revolution: The Resistance Church and the Collapse of Communism* (New York: Oxford University Press, 1992); see also Christopher Beem's sophisticated theoretical discussion of the Polish Solidarity movement in *The Necessity of Politics: Reclaiming American Public Life* (Chicago: University of Chicago Press, 1999). It is notable that one of the most militant factions of Poland's Solidarity movement in the 1980s, Solidarność Walcząca (Fighting Solidarity), was also among the most explicitly Catholic movements in the anticommunist fight and was specifically inspired by Leonine solidarist ideas of a social economy. Unfortunately, there is little research in English on the role of Catholic social thought in the reform programs of Solidarity and the more radical social movements of this pivotal decade in Poland. This has contributed to the tendency of English and American scholars to model Solidarity and related social movements on the Reagan-Thatcher type of neoliberal anti-statism, seriously downplaying antiliberal economic ideas (mainly corporatist and social Catholic) in the Polish democracy movement and its diverse reform programs. A brief discussion of Fighting Solidarity appears in Sabrina Petra Ramet, *Social Currents in Eastern Europe: The Sources and Consequences of the Great Transformation* (Durham, NC: Duke University Press, 1991), 97–99.

2. The programmatic statement of this effort was presented in William A. Schambra, "By the People," *Policy Review* (Summer 1994): 32–38.

3. Amitai Etzioni puts it bluntly concerning the civil society approach exemplified by Robert Putnam's classic work *Bowling Alone* (see further discussion below): "People who bowl together, watch birds together, play chess or bridge—key examples to which Putnam returns again and again—do not weave strong social bonds, and weave a rather minimal moral culture that mainly consists of a few norms concerning their playing conduct, more matters of manner and etiquette than morality. . . . People who bowl together do not come to new shared understandings as to how far we should let globalism intrude on our lives, how much we should allow inequality to rise, what parents owe to their children and children to their parents, and how to deal with the tough issues related to new developments in biotech, when to interfere in the internal affairs of other countries, and so on" (Etzioni, "Survey Article: On Social and Moral Revival," *Journal of Political Philosophy* 9, no. 3 [2001]: 362–63). The key point in my view is that while voluntary associations create certain kinds of interpersonal bonds that encourage cooperation in limited but important ways, these activities in themselves are not generative of (or revitalizing of) the kind of normative concern, the feelings of moral endangerment or hope, that compel people into activities of social change and sometimes conflict with institutions, such as broadcast media, school systems, or employers. While these social-change activities are often carried out through voluntary associations in a technical sense, they are compelled by a very different sense of involvement, often with personal consequences that ordinary social activities would never produce.

4. The "Social Capital Primer" from Putnam's Saguaro Seminar provides a good overview of this version of the concept: available online at http://www.ksg.harvard .edu/saguaro/primer.htm. Perhaps the most useful of Putnam's ideas was his distinction between "bonding" social capital, which occurs between members of so-

cially and culturally homogeneous groups, and "bridging" social capital, which occurs as groups from different backgrounds interact.

5. Putnam published "Bowling Alone: America's Declining Social Capital" in the *Journal of Democracy* (6, no. 1 [1995]: 65–78), and in 2000 he published the book by the same name, in which he added new evidence and engaged with critics of the original article. See Robert D. Putnam, *Bowling Alone: The Collapse and Revival of American Community* (New York: Simon and Schuster, 2000).

6. Ben Fine delivers a powerful political critique of social capital as a form of economic "colonization" of the social sciences in *Social Capital versus Social Theory: Political Economy and Social Science at the Turn of the Millennium* (London: Routledge, 2001). For a defense of economistic approaches to social capital (against "exogenous" approaches that place too much emphasis on political culture, exemplified by Putnam), see Robert W. Jackman and Ross A. Miller, "Social Capital and Politics," *Annual Review of Political Science* 1 (June 1998): 47–73. Putnam's approach has sometimes been termed "neo-Tocquevillian"—referring to Alexis de Tocqueville's cultural and psychological emphases in his great study of Jacksonian America, *Democracy in America*. Some critics argue that injecting moral and psychological "value" into social capital renders it empirically useless; they urge a return to the more traditional economic models employed by earlier social-capital theorists such as James Coleman and Pierre Bourdieu. On this question, see Bob Edwards and Michael A. Foley, "Civil Society and Social Capital Beyond Putnam," *American Behavioral Scientist* 42 (September 1998): 124–39.

7. The latest findings are described in DiIulio's *Godly Republic* (Berkeley and Los Angeles: University of California Press, 2007), chap. 5.

8. In *Godly Republic* (155), DiIulio claims to have coined the term "spiritual capital" in the mid-1990s.

9. For data on the poverty gap, see James P. Ziliak, "Filling the Poverty Gap, Then and Now," Working Paper Series no. 03-8 (Ann Arbor: University of Michigan National Poverty Center, 2003), table 2. A recent study by the Center on Philanthropy at the University of Indiana ("Patterns of Household Charitable Giving by Income Group 2005") estimates that only 20 percent of charitable giving to religious organizations goes toward helping the poor. Overall, out of a total of $250 billion in charitable donations in 2005, only $78 billion targeted people in need.

10. Faith factor research is in its relative infancy as social science, but in a series of articles and his new book *Godly Republic*, John DiIulio has established careful parameters for resolving the most difficult problem at the heart of such research: how to define and measure "faith" analytically as it relates to social outcomes. For a good summary of the problem, see DiIulio's article "The Three Faith Factors," *Public Interest* 149 (Fall 2002): 50–64. For an argument that faith factor research has no scientific validity (by Karl Popper's epistemological standard of falsifiability), see Paul Knepper, "Faith, Public Policy, and the Limits of Social Science," *Criminology and Public Policy* 2 (March 2003): 331–52.

11. Kuyper, *Problem of Poverty*. As Kuyper explained in an endnote to the 1891 speech, "We do not say here that the religious and philanthropic aspects of the problem are not important, but only that one who sees no further and senses no more than this is not even in contact with the social question."

12. Roundtable on Religion and Social Policy, "Interview with Stanley Carlson-Thies," 2002, available online at www.religionandsocialpolicy.org.

13. Kuyper, *Problem of Poverty*, 51.

14. Ibid., 51–52.

15. Warren J. Samuels and Steven G. Medema, *Gardiner C. Means: Institutionalist and Post-Keynesian* (Armonk, NY: M. E. Sharpe, 1990), 51. A leading economist in the New Deal circle, Means was coauthor with Adolph Berle of *The Modern Corporation and Private Property* (New York: Macmillan, 1932), second only to Keynes's *General Theory* in its impact on New Deal–era public policy. Robert Hale's profound work in the area of property rights and economic coercion, developed in many law review articles primarily between the two World Wars, is brilliantly excavated by Barbara H. Fried, *The Progressive Assault on Laissez Faire: Robert Hale and the First Law and Economics Movement* (Cambridge, MA: Harvard University Press, 1998). In the so-called Lochner Era (following *Lochner v. New York State* in 1905), the Supreme Court attacked social reform legislation and labor rights as a form of unconstitutional coercion against individual liberty (in the form of property rights). As Fried explains, "Hale's response was to reformulate the problem of coercion, to show that under any coherent definition of coercion, the sphere of private, 'voluntary' market relations was indistinguishable from direct exercises of public power." As Hale wrote, "We live, then, under two governments, 'economic' and 'political'" (quoted in Fried, *Progressive Assault*, 36). Thus, "when government intervened in private market relations to curb the use of certain private bargaining power," Fried summarizes, "it did not inject coercion for the first time into those relations. Rather, it merely changed the relative distribution of coercive power" (36).

16. On social obligation in German property rights, see Gregory S. Alexander, *The Global Debate over Constitutional Property* (Chicago: University of Chicago Press, 2006), chap. 3.

17. Mary Ann Glendon, *Rights Talk: The Impoverishment of Social Discourse* (New York: Free Press, 1991), 136.

18. Ibid., 110–11.

19. In 2005, the United States Supreme Court upheld the exercise of eminent domain powers for private economic development in the controversial *Kelo v. City of New London* case, which brought new attention to the issue and a public outcry, leading twenty-one states to pass reform legislation limiting eminent domain. Ironically, in 2004 the Michigan Supreme Court overruled its own *Poletown* decision in prohibiting Wayne County from seizing private land for the development of an industrial park.

20. Glendon, *Rights Talk*, 30.

21. The Oregon Klan's first choice for governor was state senator Charles Hall, whom it supported in the Republican primary, but he lost narrowly to incumbent Republican governor Ben Olcott, a strong opponent of the Klan. This illustrates an important fact about the "second Klan" of the post–World War I period as distinct from the first Klan of the Reconstruction era: its party alignment varied across regions and even from state to state, with the one unifying thread being Anglo-Protestant religion. In terms of policy, the two most common planks in Klan politics were enforcing Prohibition and strengthening public education.

22. David B. Tyack, "The Perils of Pluralism: The Background of the Pierce Case," *American Historical Review* 74 (October 1968): 74–76, 91.

23. On the second Ku Klux Klan and church-state relations, see Philip Hamburger, *Separation of Church and State* (Cambridge, MA: Harvard University Press, 2002), 399–434; on *Pierce*, see 415–19. See also Robert D. Johnston, *The Radical Middle*

Class: Populist Democracy and the Question of Capitalism in Progressive Era Portland, Oregon (Princeton, NJ: Princeton University Press, 2003), chap. 18, for an alternative social interpretation of the Oregon compulsory school bill, focusing on democratic-egalitarian support and arguing that the Klan's role is generally overemphasized.

24. See, for example, the interpretation of *Pierce* in Justice Scalia's majority opinion in *Employment Division v. Smith* (1990).

25. For a concise summary of the evolution of privacy rights stemming from *Pierce*, see "Development of the Right of Privacy" available online at http://supreme.justia .com/constitution/amendment-14/30-right-of-privacy.html.

26. Mark DeWolfe Howe, "The Supreme Court, 1952 Term," *Harvard Law Review* 67 (November 1953): 92.

27. Ibid., 91.

28. Ibid., 92.

29. Ernst Troeltsch, *The Social Teaching of the Christian Churches* (Louisville, KY: Westminster John Knox Press, 1992), 1:98.

30. Harold J. Berman, *Law and Revolution: The Formation of the Western Legal Tradition* (Cambridge, MA: Harvard University Press, 1983), 215–21.

31. Ibid., 216.

32. Ibid., 219.

33. Ibid.

34. Brian Tierney, *Foundations of the Conciliar Theory: The Contribution of the Medieval Canonists from Gratian to the Great Schism* (Leiden: Brill, 1998), 94.

35. William G. McLoughlin, "The Role of Religion in the Revolution," in *Essays on the American Revolution*, ed. Stephen G. Kurtz and James H. Hutson (Chapel Hill: University of North Carolina Press, 1973), 234–35.

36. Louis Hartz, *Economic Policy and Democratic Thought: Pennsylvania 1776–1860* (Chicago: Quadrangle Books, 1948), 38–39.

37. Liam Seamus O'Melinn, "Neither Contract nor Concession: The Public Personality of the Corporation," *George Washington Law Review* 74 (February 2006): 225.

38. Ibid.

39. Ibid., 225–26. Ironically, the recognition of church autonomy was even further reinforced when New York State (and other states) altered its religious incorporation statutes to accommodate the hierarchical polity of the Catholic Church, where all local power is vested in individual bishops. Essentially, the form of a *corporation sole* was created in the law to accommodate the Catholic Church; see McLoughlin, "Role of Religion in the Revolution," 246–47.

40. Morton J. Horwitz, *The Transformation of American Law, 1879–1960* (New York: Oxford University Press, 1992), 11.

41. O'Melinn, "Neither Contract nor Concession," 205.

42. William J. Novak, *The People's Welfare: Law and Regulation in Nineteenth-Century America* (Chapel Hill: University of North Carolina Press, 1996), 227.

43. The case was *Runyan v. Lessee of Coster* (1840).

44. In literary history, Shaw is more famous for being the father-in-law and generous patron of Herman Melville.

45. Leonard W. Levy, "The Law of the Commonwealth and Chief Justice Shaw," in *American Law and the Constitutional Order*, ed. Lawrence M. Friedman and Harry N. Scheiber (Cambridge, MA: Harvard University Press, 1988), 156.

46. Ibid., 154.

47. Ibid., 155.
48. For example, the Charter of Massachusetts Bay (1629) was issued to its "Governor and Company."
49. For those who followed the fall of the Marxist interpretation of the English Revolution in the 1970s, it has risen again with Robert Brenner's masterwork *Merchants and Revolution* (New York: Verso, 2003). In tracing the development of the parliamentary coalition that overthrew the Caroline monarchy in the 1640s, Brenner assembles massive evidence of a sociopolitical conflict pitting royal-mercantile commerce and property forms against emerging capitalist enterprise rooted in nonpolitical property rights, free trade, and a commercially oriented foreign policy.
50. Stanley I. Kutler, *Privilege and Creative Destruction: The Charles River Bridge Case* (New York: W. W. Norton, 1971), 9–12, 18.
51. Ibid., 29.
52. Ibid., 35.
53. Ibid., 64.
54. Elizabeth Sanders, *Roots of Reform: Farmers, Workers, and the American State, 1877–1917* (Chicago: University of Chicago Press, 1999), 185–87.
55. Ibid., 195.
56. Gerald Berk, *Alternative Tracks: The Constitution of American Industrial Order, 1865–1917* (Baltimore, MD: Johns Hopkins University Press, 1997), 94.
57. The key Supreme Court case was *Interstate Commerce Commission v. Alabama Midland Ry. Co.* (1897), ruling in favor of competitive exemptions from long- and short-haul rate discrimination.
58. Berk, *Alternative Tracks*, 113.
59. Ibid., 113.
60. Here I rely on the extensive law review literature on corporate theory, especially Mark M. Hager, "Bodies Politic: The Progressive History of Organizational Real Entity Theory," *University of Pittsburgh Law Review* 50 (1988–89): 575–654; and Gregory A. Mark, "The Personification of the Business Corporation in American Law," *University of Chicago Law Review* 54 (Fall 1987): 1441–82.
61. Hager, "Bodies Politic," 583.
62. Ibid., 585.
63. Laski, quoted in ibid., 584.
64. Ibid., 586.
65. Ibid.
66. Ibid., 588.
67. Pomeroy, quoted in Horwitz, *Transformation of American Law*, 70.
68. Ibid., 69–70. This argument tracked closely with Justice Field's circuit court opinion in *San Mateo v. Southern Pacific Railroad*, a companion case to *Santa Clara*. Later, in his concurring opinion in *Pollock v. Farmers' Loan and Trust Co.* (1895 [throwing out the federal income tax of 1894]), Field clarified the reasoning behind his jurisprudence: "The present assault on capital is but the beginning . . . It will be but the stepping-stone to others, larger and more sweeping, till our political contests will become a war of the poor against the rich; a war constantly growing in intensity and bitterness."
69. Ibid., 104.
70. O'Melinn, "Neither Contract nor Concession," 3.
71. Otto von Gierke, *Community in Historical Perspective* (Cambridge, MA: Cambridge University Press, 1990), 212.

72. Ibid., 213.

73. Ibid., 220.

74. Ibid., 216.

75. Ibid.

76. Edmond Cahn, Review of Robert L. Hale, *Freedom through Law*, *New York Times*, 18 January 1953, 14.

77. Hale, quoted in Neil Duxbury, "Robert Hale and the Economy of Legal Force," *Modern Law Review* 53 (July 1990): 435.

78. Hale, quoted in ibid., 438.

79. Arthur Selwyn Miller, *The Supreme Court and American Capitalism* (New York: Free Press, 1968), 14.

80. Otto Gierke, *Political Theories of the Middle Age* (Boston: Beacon Press, 1958), 99–100.

81. Democratic gains in the four most heavily Catholic Northeastern states (Massachusetts, Connecticut, Rhode Island, and Maryland) indicate the growing magnitude of the Catholic-Democratic trend by 1932. In 1924, Democratic presidential candidate John W. Davis won on average only 33 percent of the vote in these states (note that the Ku Klux Klan placed hundreds of delegates at the Democratic convention that year, forcing Al Smith off the ballot and preventing a party resolution condemning the Klan). From this low point (Democrats got the lowest number of votes in their history that year), Smith and Roosevelt engineered a profound shift that would define their party for the next four decades. In 1932, Roosevelt won a solid majority of 54 percent of the vote in the most Catholic northeastern states, a 21-point swing from 1924. In 1936, Roosevelt received 61 percent of the national vote, and an estimated 75–81 percent of Catholic votes. For these figures and other key episodes in the history of Catholic voting, see George Marlin's essential guide, *The American Catholic Voter* (South Bend, IN: St. Augustine's Press, 2006).

82. On the latter, see especially G. K. Chesterton, "The Outline of Sanity," in *Collected Works*, vol. 5 (Ft. Collins, CO: Ignatius Press, 1987).

83. Quoted in John A. Ryan, *Economic Justice: Selections from "Distributive Justice" and "A Living Wage,"* ed. Harlan R. Beckley (Louisville, KY: Westminster John Knox Press, 1996), 103.

84. Thomas, quoted in *Catechism of the Catholic Church*, 2nd ed. (New York: Doubleday, 1995), 534, item no. 1976.

85. See Albino Barrera, *Economic Compulsion and Christian Ethics* (Cambridge: Cambridge University Press, 2005), part 2. See also the excellent brief discussion in the introduction to Helen Alford et al., *Rediscovering Abundance: Interdisciplinary Essays on Wealth, Income, and Their Distribution in the Catholic Social Tradition* (Notre Dame, IN: University of Notre Dame Press, 2006), 11–14, contrasting Catholic views of property as an instrument of the common good with the Anglo-American liberal tradition of property entitlement reaching back to John Locke. A key distinction is well-formulated as follows: "In the Catholic tradition, individual ownership is seen as a means of implementing the common human right to be sustained by, and to flourish from, God's gift of natural goods: 'ownership' means private *possession* of goods for the sake of making goods' *use* common to all. Far from *withdrawing* goods from the purview of the common right, private possession *implements* the common right" (13).

86. Quoted in Ryan, *Economic Justice*, 89.

87. Quoted in John A. Ryan and Moorhouse F. X. Millar, *The State and the Church* (New York: Macmillan, 1922), 233.

88. In his introduction to *The Teachings of Modern Roman Catholicism*, ed. John Witte Jr.

and Frank S. Alexander (New York: Columbia University Press, 2007), Russell Hittinger provides a good, brief overview of the Jesuit-led neo-Thomistic revival, the fulcrum of Catholic social teaching as introduced to the world in *Rerum novarum* (3–15). The most important figure was Leo XIII's boyhood teacher Luigi Taparelli, who co-founded the periodical *Civiltà Cattolica* in 1850 as a platform not only for mounting a neo-Thomist attack on liberal philosophy and politics, but for applying Thomistic thought to the escalating social and political conflicts of the time. Taparelli is considered to have coined the term *social justice*, and, as Thomas Behr stresses, he was a much harsher critic of capitalism than one might think, given his influence on *Rerum novarum*, the somewhat conciliatory tone of which on capitalism and private property bears the imprint, Behr argues, of Taparelli's more moderate younger colleague Matteo Liberatore. See Thomas Chauncey Behr, "Luigi Taparelli and the Nineteenth-Century Neo-Thomistic 'Revolution' in Natural Law and Catholic Social Sciences," PhD diss., State University of New York at Buffalo, August 2000, 255–64. Behr also argues convincingly for Taparelli's origination of the idea of subsidiarity in its modern Catholic form (225–40).

89. Steinar Stjernø, *Solidarity in Europe: The History of an Idea* (Cambridge: Cambridge University Press, 2005), 28.

90. Bourgeois, quoted in J. E. S. Hayward, "The Official Social Philosophy of the French Third Republic: Léon Bourgeois and Solidarism," *International Review of Social History* 6 (1961): 29.

91. See Arthur J. Altmeyer, "The Development and Status of Social Security in America," in *Labor, Management, and Social Policy: Essays in the John R. Commons Tradition*, ed. Gerald G. Somers (Madison: University of Wisconsin Press, 1993); available online at www.ssa.gov/history/aja1963.html. Altmeyer himself served as commissioner of the Social Security Administration.

92. The first volume of the *Lehrbuch* was published by Herder in Germany in 1905. A complete English translation prepared by Pesch scholar Rupert J. Ederer and titled *Teaching Guide to Economics* was published in series in the early 2000s by the Edwin Mellen Press in Lewiston, New York.

93. Heinrich Pesch, *Heinrich Pesch on Solidarist Economics: Excerpts from the "Lehrbuch der Nationalökonomie,"* trans. Rupert J. Ederer (Lanham, MD: University Press of America, 1998), 40–41.

94. Wagner, quoted in ibid., 49.

95. Ibid., 60.

96. As Thomas Kolhler argues, however, American labor law in its own right, as developed in the 1930s, has a distinctly "un-American" character that could be attributed to solidarist influences. The cornerstone of American labor law, the National Labor Relations Act of 1935, had a primary goal of establishing "a legal structure through which employees can gain a voice in managerial decision making," normally (in conventional liberalism) a pure prerogative of legal ownership of the enterprise.

97. Ibid., 922–33.

98. Thomas Storck, "A Giant among Catholic Economists," *New Oxford Review*, February 2005, available online at www.newoxfordreview.org/reviews.jsp?did=0205-storck.

99. The essential study, which I draw on here, is Philip Gleason, *The Conservative Reformers: German-American Catholics and the Social Order* (Notre Dame, IN: University of Notre Dame Press, 1968).

100. Ibid., 133.

101. John A. Ryan, *Social Doctrine in Action* (New York: Harper & Brothers, 1941), 242.

102. Ryan, *Social Doctrine in Action*, 242–43.
103. John A. Ryan, *Declining Liberty and Other Papers* (Freeport, NY: Ayer Co., 1977), 198. (Orig. pub. 1927.)
104. "Catholic Crusade for Social Justice," *New York Times*, 9 November 1932, 19.
105. Allan H. Carlson, *The "American Way": Family and Community in the Shaping of the American Identity* (Wilmington, DE: ISI Books, 2003), chap. 3.
106. Jeff Madrick and Nikolaos Papanikolauo, "The Stagnation of Male Wages" (New York: Schwartz Center for Economic Policy Analysis, The New School, n.d.), 6, table 1.1.
107. Monica Lesmerises, *The Middle Class at Risk* (New York: The Century Foundation, 2007), 24, fig. 11.
108. Jose Garcia, James Lardner, and Cindy Zeldin, *Up to Our Eyeballs: How Shady Lenders and Failed Economic Policies Are Drowning Americans in Debt* (New York: New Press, 2008), 10.
109. Jennifer Wheary, Thomas M. Shapiro, Tamara Draut, and Tatjana Meschede, *From Middle Ground to Shaky Ground* (New York: Demos, 2008).
110. Figures for 2004, in Arthur B. Kennickell, "Currents and Undercurrents: Changes in the Distribution of Wealth, 1989–2004," Federal Reserve Board, 30 January, 2006, 29, table 11a.
111. As Kimberly Morgan summarizes, "Policies for working parents in the United States have hardly changed since the mid-1970s." See her *Working Mothers and the Welfare State: Religion and the Politics of Work-Family Policies in Western Europe and the United States* (Stanford, CA: Stanford University Press, 2006), 135.
112. On the failed politics and policies of persistent poverty since the late 1960s, see Frances Fox Piven and Richard A. Cloward, *The Breaking of the American Social Compact* (New York: New Press, 1997). On the policy failures surrounding low-wage employment, see Beth Shulman, *The Betrayal of Work* (New York: New Press, 2003). For the best analysis of the political economy of Reaganomics compared to the New Deal order, see Robert Kuttner, *The Squandering of America: How the Failure of Our Politics Undermines Our Prosperity* (New York: Alfred A. Knopf, 2007). Robert H. Frank's *Falling Behind: How Rising Inequality Harms the Middle Class* (Berkeley and Los Angeles: University of California Press, 2007) examines the destabilizing social effects of having too much wealth and income concentrated at the top.
113. Tocqueville, *Democracy in America*, 2:194.
114. Antony Black, "Communal Democracy and Its History," *Political Studies* 45, no. 1 (1997): 5.
115. On the Catholic Bishops' Program for Social Reconstruction, issued in 1919, see Joseph M. McShane, *"Sufficiently Radical": Catholicism, Progressivism, and the Bishops' Program of 1919* (Washington, DC: Catholic University of America Press, 1986), as well as my assessment in "In Search of the Common Good: The Catholic Roots of American Liberalism," in *Religion and Culture*, Web Forum, September 2007, available online at http://divinity.uchicago.edu/martycenter/publications/webforum/092007/).

SELECTED BIBLIOGRAPHY

The following list is limited to selected books in English. All other sources are cited in the endnotes.

Alesina, Alberto, and Edward L. Glaeser. *Fighting Poverty in the US and Europe: A World of Difference*. New York: Oxford University Press, 2005.

Alexander, Gregory S. *The Global Debate over Constitutional Property*. Chicago: University of Chicago Press, 2006.

Alford, Helen, Charles M. A. Clark, S. A. Cortright, and Michael J. Naughton, eds. *Rediscovering Abundance: Interdisciplinary Essays on Wealth, Income, and Their Distribution in the Catholic Social Tradition*. Notre Dame, IN: University of Notre Dame Press, 2006.

Altman, Daniel. *Neoconomy: George W. Bush's Revolutionary Gamble with America's Future*. New York: Public Affairs, 2004.

Althusius, Johannes. *Politica*. Edited and translated by Frederick S. Carney. Indianapolis, IN: Liberty Fund, 1995.

Bakvis, Herman. *Catholic Power in the Netherlands*. Montreal: McGill-Queen's University Press, 1981.

Balthasar, Hans Urs von. *The Glory of the Lord*. Vol. 6 *Theology: The Old Covenant*. San Francisco: Ignatius Press, 1991.

Barrera, Albino. *Economic Compulsion and Christian Ethics*. Cambridge: Cambridge University Press, 2005.

Beck, Hermann. *The Origins of the Authoritarian Welfare State in Prussia*. Ann Arbor: University of Michigan Press, 1995.

Beem, Christopher. *The Necessity of Politics: Reclaiming American Public Life*. Chicago: University of Chicago Press, 1999.

Berger, Peter L., and Richard John Neuhaus. *To Empower People: The Role of Mediating Structures in Public Policy*. Washington, DC: American Enterprise Institute, 1977.

Berman, Harold J. *Law and Revolution: The Formation of the Western Legal Tradition*. Cambridge, MA: Harvard University Press, 1983.

———. *Law and Revolution II: The Impact of the Protestant Reformations on the Western Legal Tradition*. Cambridge, MA: Belknap Press of Harvard University Press, 2003.

Black, Amy E., Douglas L. Koopman, and David. K. Ryden. *Of Little Faith: The Politics of George W. Bush's Faith-Based Initiatives*. Washington, DC: Georgetown University Press, 2004.

Brose, Eric Dorn. *Christian Labor and the Politics of Frustration in Imperial Germany.* Washington, DC: Catholic University of America Press, 1985.

Carlson, Allan H. *The "American Way": Family and Community in the Shaping of the American Identity.* Wilmington, DE: ISI Books, 2003.

Castles, Francis G., ed. *The Comparative History of Public Policy.* Cambridge: Polity Press, 1989.

Coats, Daniel R. *Mending Fences: Renewing Justice between Government and Civil Society.* Grand Rapids, MI: Baker Publishing Group, 1998.

Coughlin, Bernard J. *Church and State in Social Welfare.* New York: Columbia University Press, 1965.

DiIulio, John J. *Godly Republic: A Centrist Blueprint for America's Faith-Based Future.* Berkeley and Los Angeles: University of California Press, 2007.

Dionne, E. J. *Souled Out: Reclaiming Faith and Politics after the Religious Right.* Princeton, NJ: Princeton University Press, 2008.

Dooyeweerd, Herman. *A New Critique of Theoretical Thought.* Vol. 3. Translated by David H. Freeman and H. de Jongste. Philipsburg, NJ: Presbyterian and Reformed Publishing, 1969.

Eberle, Edward J. *Dignity and Liberty: Constitutional Visions in Germany and the United States.* Westport, CT: Praeger, 2002.

Feldman, Noah. *Divided by God: America's Church-State Problem—and What We Should Do About It* (New York: Farrar, Strauss, Giroux, 2005).

Figgis, John Neville. *Churches in the Modern State.* Bristol, England: Thoemmes Press, 1997. (Orig. pub. 1914.)

Fine, Ben. *Social Capital versus Social Theory: Political Economy and Social Science at the Turn of the Millennium.* London: Routledge, 2001.

Fogel, Robert William. *The Fourth Great Awakening and the Future of Egalitarianism.* Chicago: University of Chicago Press, 2000.

Frank, Robert H. *Falling Behind: How Rising Inequality Harms the Middle Class.* Berkeley and Los Angeles: University of California Press, 2007.

Fried, Barbara H. *The Progressive Assault on Laissez Faire: Robert Hale and the First Law and Economics Movement.* Cambridge, MA: Harvard University Press, 1998.

Friedman, Lawrence M., and Harry N. Scheiber, eds. *American Law and the Constitutional Order: Historical Perspectives.* Cambridge, MA: Harvard University Press, 1988.

Garcia, Jose, James Lardner, and Cindy Zeldin. *Up to Our Eyeballs: How Shady Lenders and Failed Economic Policies Are Drowning Americans in Debt.* New York: New Press, 2008.

George, Robert P. *The Clash of Orthodoxies: Law, Religion, and Morality in Crisis.* Wilmington, DE: ISI Books, 2001.

Gierke, Otto von. *Community in Historical Perspective: A translation of selections from "Das deutsche Genossenschaftsrecht."* Translated by Mary Fischer. Selected and edited by Antony Black. Cambridge, MA: Cambridge University Press, 1990.

——. *Natural Law and the Theory of Society 1500–1800.* Translated by Ernest Barker. Boston: Beacon Press, 1957.

——. *Political Theories of the Middle Age.* Translated by Frederic William Maitland. Boston: Beacon Press, 1958.

Gilbert, Neil. *A Mother's Work: How Feminism, the Market, and Policy Shape Family Life.* New Haven, CT: Yale University Press, 2008.

Gleason, Philip. *The Conservative Reformers: German-American Catholics and the Social Order.* Notre Dame, IN: University of Notre Dame Press, 1968.

Glendon, Mary Ann. *Rights Talk: The Impoverishment of Social Discourse.* New York: Free Press, 1991.

Glenn, Charles L. *The Ambiguous Embrace: Government and Faith-Based Schools and Social Agencies.* Princeton, NJ: Princeton University Press, 2000.

Gnuse, Robert. *You Shall Not Steal: Community and Property in the Biblical Tradition.* Maryknoll, NY: Orbis Books, 1985.

Goodin, Robert E., Bruce Headey, Ruud Muffels, and Henk-Jan Dirven. *The Real Worlds of Welfare Capitalism.* Cambridge: Cambridge University Press, 1999.

Goody, Jack. *The Development of the Family and Marriage in Europe.* Cambridge: Cambridge University Press, 1983.

Grant, George. *Bringing in the Sheaves: Transforming Poverty into Productivity.* Brentwood, TN: Wolgemuth & Hyatt, 1988.

———. *The Changing of the Guard: Biblical Principles for Political Action.* Fort Worth, TX: Dominion Press, 1987.

———. *In the Shadow of Plenty.* Arlington Heights, IL: Christian Liberty Press, 1998. (Orig. pub. 1986.)

Greeley, Andrew, and Michael Hout. *The Truth about Conservative Christians.* Chicago: University of Chicago Press, 2006.

Gurvitch, Georges. *Sociology of Law.* New Brunswick, NJ: Transaction Publishers, 2001.

Hamburger, Philip. *Separation of Church and State.* Cambridge, MA: Harvard University Press, 2002.

Hamerow, Theodore S. *Restoration, Revolution, Reaction.* Princeton, NJ: Princeton University Press, 1958.

Hartz, Louis. *Economic Policy and Democratic Thought: Pennsylvania, 1776–1860.* Chicago: Quadrangle Books, 1948.

Hirst, Paul Q. *The Pluralist Theory of the State: Selected Writings of G. D. H. Cole, J. N. Figgis, and H. J. Laski.* London: Routledge, 1989.

Hong, Young-Sun. *Welfare, Modernity, and the Weimar State, 1919–1933.* Princeton, NJ: Princeton University Press, 1998.

Horwitz, Morton J. *The Transformation of American Law, 1879–1960.* New York: Oxford University Press, 1992.

Joerges, Christian, and Navraj Singh Ghaleigh, eds. *Darker Legacies of Law in Europe: The Shadow of National Socialism and Fascism over Europe and Its Legal Traditions.* Portland, OR: Hart, 2003.

John, Michael. *Politics and the Law in Late Nineteenth-Century Germany: The Origins of the Civil Code.* Oxford: Clarendon Press, 1989.

Johnston, Robert D. *The Radical Middle Class: Populist Democracy and the Question of Capitalism in Progressive Era Portland, Oregon.* Princeton, NJ: Princeton University Press, 2003.

Kalyvas, Stathis N. *The Rise of Christian Democracy in Europe.* Ithaca, NY: Cornell University Press, 1996.

Katz, Michael B. *The Price of Citizenship: Redefining the American Welfare State.* New York: Metropolitan Books, 2001.

Kersbergen, Kees van. *Social Capitalism: A Study of Christian Democracy and the Welfare State.* New York: Routledge, 1995.

Kommers, Donald P. *The Constitutional Jurisprudence of the Federal Republic of Germany.* Durham, NC: Duke University Press, 1989.

Kutler, Stanley I. *Privilege and Creative Destruction: The Charles River Bridge Case.* New York: W. W. Norton, 1971.

Kuyper, Abraham. *The Problem of Poverty.* Edited by James W. Skillen. Grand Rapids, MI: Baker Book House, 1991.

Langley, McKendree R. *Emancipation and Apologetics: The Formation of Abraham Kuyper's Anti-Revolutionary Party in the Netherlands, 1872–1880.* PhD diss., Westminster Theological Seminary, 1985.

Lassiter, April. *Congress and Civil Society: How Legislators Can Champion Civic Renewal in Their Districts.* Washington, DC: Heritage Foundation, 1998.

Laski, Harold J. *Studies in the Problem of Sovereignty.* New York: Howard Fertig, 1968.

Lindert, Peter H. *Growing Public: Social Spending and Economic Growth Since the Eighteenth Century.* Cambridge: Cambridge University Press, 2004.

Love, Thomas T. *John Courtney Murray: Contemporary Church-State Theory.* New York: Doubleday, 1965.

Lugo, Luis E., ed. *Religion, Pluralism, and Public Life: Abraham Kuyper's Legacy for the Twenty-First Century.* Grand Rapids, MI: William B. Eerdmans, 2000.

Lynch, Katharine A. *Individuals, Families and Communities in Europe, 1200–1800.* Cambridge: Cambridge University Press, 2003.

Maier, Hans. *Revolution and Church: The Early History of Christian Democracy, 1789–1901.* Translated by Emily M. Schossberger. Notre Dame, IN: University of Notre Dame Press, 1969.

Marlin, George. *The American Catholic Voter: Two Hundred Years of Political Impact.* South Bend, IN: St. Augustine's Press, 2006.

McCarthy, Rockne, Donald Oppewal, Walfred Peterson, and Gordon Spykman. *Society, State, and Schools: A Case for Structural and Confessional Pluralism.* Grand Rapids, MI: William B. Eerdmans, 1981.

McHugh, Francis P., and Samuel M. Natale. *Things Old and New: Catholic Social Teaching Revised.* Lanham, MD: University Press of America, 1993.

McShane, Joseph M. *"Sufficiently Radical" Catholicism, Progressivism, and the Bishops' Program of 1919.* Washington, DC: Catholic University of America Press, 1986.

Metlake, George. *Ketteler's Social Reform.* Philadelphia, PA: Dolphin Press, 1912.

Miller, Arthur Selwyn. *The Supreme Court and American Capitalism.* New York: Free Press, 1968.

Minow, Martha. *Partners, Not Rivals: Privatization and the Public Good.* Boston: Beacon Press, 2002.

Mollat, Michel. *The Poor in the Middle Ages.* New Haven, CT: Yale University Press, 1986.

Monsma, Stephen V. *Positive Neutrality: Letting Religious Freedom Ring.* Grand Rapids, MI: Baker Book House, 1993.

Monsma, Stephen V. *When Sacred and Secular Mix: Religious Nonprofit Organizations and Public Money.* Lanham, MD: Rowman & Littlefield, 1996.

Monsma, Stephen V., and J. Christopher Soper. *The Challenge of Pluralism: Church and State in Five Democracies.* Lanham, MD: Rowman & Littlefield, 1997.

———, eds. *Equal Treatment of Religion in a Pluralistic Society.* Grand Rapids, MI: William B. Eerdmans, 1998.

Morgan, Kimberly. *Working Mothers and the Welfare State: Religion and the Politics of Work-Family Policies in Western Europe and the United States.* Stanford, CA: Stanford University Press, 2006.

Mueller, Franz H. *The Church and the Social Question.* Washington, DC: American Enterprise Institute for Public Policy Research, 1984.

Nardoni, Enrique. *Rise Up, O Judge: A Study of Justice in the Biblical World.* Translated by Seán Charles Martin. Peabody, MA: Hendrickson, 2004.

National Council of Churches of Christ in the USA. *Churches and Social Welfare.* Cleveland, OH: National Council of Churches of Christ in the USA, 1956.

Nell-Breuning, Oswald von. *Reorganization of the Social Economy.* New York: Bruce, 1936.

Nisbet, Robert. *The Quest for Community: A Study in the Ethics and Order of Freedom.* San Francisco: Institute for Contemporary Studies, 1990. (Orig. pub. 1953.)

——. *The Social Philosophers: Community and Conflict in Western Thought.* New York: Washington Square Press, 1973.

——. *Tradition and Revolt.* New Brunswick, NJ: Transaction Publishers, 1999. (Orig. pub. 1968).

Novak, Michael. *Freedom with Justice: Catholic Social Thought and Liberal Institutions* New York: Harper & Row, 1984.

Novak, Michael, ed. *To Empower People: From State to Civil Society.* By Peter L. Berger and Richard John Neuhaus. Washington, DC: American Enterprise Institute Press, 1995.

Novak, Michael, et al. *The New Consensus on Family and Welfare.* Washington, DC: American Enterprise Institute, 1987.

Novak, William J. *The People's Welfare: Law and Regulation in Nineteenth-Century America.* Chapel Hill: University of North Carolina Press, 1996.

Okun, Arthur M. *Equality and Efficiency: The Big Tradeoff.* Washington, DC: Brookings Institution, 1975.

Olasky, Marvin. *The Tragedy of American Compassion.* Washington, DC: Regnery, 1992.

Pesch, Heinrich. *Heinrich Pesch on Solidarist Economics: Excerpts from the "Lehrbuch der Nationalökonomie."* Translated by Rupert J. Ederer. Lanham, MD: University Press of America, 1998.

Powell, Walter W., and Elisabeth S. Clemens, eds. *Private Action and the Public Good.* New Haven, CT: Yale University Press, 1998.

Robbers, Gerhard, ed. *Church Autonomy.* Frankfurt am Main: Peter Lang, 2001.

Rommen, Heinrich A. *The Natural Law: A Study in Legal and Social History and Philosophy.* Translated by Thomas R. Hanley. Indianapolis, IN: Liberty Fund, 1998. (Orig. pub. 1936.)

Runciman, David. *Pluralism and the Personality of the State.* Cambridge: Cambridge University Press, 1997.

Ryan, John A. *Economic Justice: Selections from "Distributive Justice" and "A Living Wage."* Edited by Harlan R. Beckley. Louisville, KY: Westminster John Knox Press, 1996.

——. *A Living Wage.* New York: Macmillan, 1920. (Orig. pub. 1906.)

——. *Social Doctrine in Action.* New York: Harper & Brothers, 1941.

Sanders, Elizabeth. *Roots of Reform: Farmers, Workers, and the American State, 1877–1917.* Chicago: University of Chicago Press, 1999.

Skillen, James W., and Rockne M. McCarthy. *Political Order and the Plural Structure of Society.* Atlanta, GA: Scholars Press, 1991.

Smith, Steven Rathgeb, and Michael Lipsky. *Nonprofits for Hire: The Welfare State in the Age of Contracting.* Cambridge, MA: Harvard University Press, 1993.

Stahl, Friedrich Julius. *Principles of Law.* Translated and edited by Ruben Alvarado. Aalten, the Netherlands: Wordbridge, 2007.

Stolleis, Michael. *Public Law in Germany, 1800–1914.* New York: Berghan Books, 2001.

tenZythoff, Gerrit J. *Sources of Secession: The Netherlands Hervormde Kerk on the Eve of the Dutch Immigration to the Midwest.* Grand Rapids, MI: William B. Eerdmans, 1987.

Tierney, Brian. *The Crisis of Church and State, 1050–1300.* Toronto: University of Toronto Press, 1988. (Orig. pub. 1964.)

——. *Foundations of the Conciliar Theory: The Contribution of the Medieval Canonists from Gratian to the Great Schism.* Leiden: Brill, 1998. (Orig. pub. 1955.)

Troeltsch, Ernst. *The Social Teaching of the Christian Churches.* Louisville, KY: Westminster John Knox Press, 1992.

Van der Vyver, Johan D. *Leuven Lectures on Religious Institutions, Religious Communities, and Rights.* Leuven, Belgium: Uitgeverij Peeters, 2004.

Van der Vyver, Johan D., and John Witte Jr., eds. *Religious Human Rights in Global Perspective: Legal Perspectives.* The Hague: Martinus Nijhoff, 1996.

Van Dyke, Harry, ed. *Groen van Prinsterer's Lectures on Unbelief and Revolution.* Jordan Station, Ontario: Wedge Publishing Foundation, 1989.

Warren, Elizabeth, and Amelia Warren Tyagi. *The Two-Income Trap: Why Middle-Class Parents Are Going Broke.* New York: Basic Books, 2003.

Weaver, R. Kent. *Ending Welfare as We Know It.* Washington, DC: Brookings Institution Press, 2000.

Weigel, George. *The Cube and the Cathedral: Europe, America, and Politics without God.* New York: Basic Books, 2005.

————. *The Final Revolution: The Resistance Church and the Collapse of Communism.* New York: Oxford University Press, 1992.

Witte Jr., John, and Frank Alexander, eds. *The Teachings of Modern Roman Catholicism.* New York: Columbia University Press, 2007.

Wuthnow, Robert. *Saving America: Faith-Based Services and the Future of Civil Society.* Princeton, NJ: Princeton University Press, 2004.

Wuthnow, Robert, and John H. Evans, eds. *The Quiet Hand of God: Faith-Based Activism and the Public Role of Mainline Protestantism.* Berkeley and Los Angeles: University of California Press, 2002.